Teaching Strategies, Inc.

CONSTRUCTING Curriculum

F O R T H E

Primary Grades

Diane Trister Dodge
Judy R. Jablon
Toni S. Bickart

Contributing Authors
Elizabeth Servidio
Wickes MacColl
Laura Thorp Katz
Charlotte Stetson

Illustrator
Jody Eastman

TEACHING STRATEGIES INC.

Washington, DC

Graphic Design
Winge and Associates, Inc.

Copyright © 1994 by
Teaching Strategies, Inc.

Published by
Teaching Strategies, Inc.
P.O. Box 42243
Washington, DC 20015

Distributed by
Gryphon House
P.O. Box 207
Beltsville, MD 20704-0207

Printings: 1994, 1995

ISBN: 1-879537-12-5

Library of Congress Catalog
Card Number: 94-060859

Acknowledgments

Many people deserve our appreciation and acknowledgement for the role they played in helping us shape and refine this book. First and foremost, we want to thank three individuals whose expertise was invaluable in preparing the content chapters: Elizabeth Servidio, who drafted Language and Literacy and extensively reviewed and critiqued all chapters of the book; Wickes MacColl, who prepared the chapter on Mathematical Thinking; and Laura Thorpe Katz, who drafted the chapter on Scientific Thinking.

Charlotte Stetson and Pamela Becker reviewed and commented on all chapters. Their thoughtful critiques and often extensive suggestions greatly enriched the content and approach of our book. The chapter on Arts and Technology grew out of original work on Art drafted for us by Lila Hochberg. Denise Gershowitz and Martha Hansen were very helpful in conceptualizing Part One of the book.

We are most grateful to Thérèse Keegan for her contributions to the entire book; to Linda Espinosa who critiqued our first draft and prepared written recommendations for the chapter on Developing a Partnership with Families; to Debra Foulks, M. Parker Anderson, and Sue Korenbaum for their assistance on the topic of cultural diversity; and to Bill Sparks for input and direction on the inclusion of children with disabilities. Insightful reviews and comments were also provided by Jenni Klein, Charlotte Kowitch, Rebecca Severeide, Yvette Meltzer Ramsier, Sybil Wolin, Joan Cenedella, Jennifer Swanson Voorhees, Julie Mikuta, and primary grade teachers in the Department of Defense Schools in Mannheim, Germany.

We want to acknowledge the close ties between *Constructing Curriculum* and *The Work Sampling System*™ of assessment developed by Samuel Meisels, Judy Jablon, Dorothea Marsden, Margo Dichtelmiller, and Aviva Dorfman at the University of Michigan. Because of Judy Jablon's authorship on both projects, The *Work Sampling System's*™ performance indicators for each domain of development informed our thinking about skills and knowledge in the content chapters of *Constructing Curriculum* and about the role of assessment in curriculum planning and implementation.

Development of this book was funded in part by a Discretionary Grant from the U.S. Department of Health and Human Services, Administration for Children and Families, Head Start Bureau. This collaborative effort involved Teaching Strategies, the National Child Day Care Association, the District of Columbia Public Schools (DCPS) Head Start Program and Early Learning Years working together to enhance children's Head Start experience by extending developmentally appropriate practice into the early grades. We are indebted to Austine Fowler, the project liaison, for her steadfast support. The project

Constructing

Curriculum

for the

Primary Grades

also benefitted from the expertise and guidance of Michele Plutro, our Program Officer, and was guided by a Steering Committee that included the following individuals:

Helen H. Taylor, Executive Director, National Child Day Care Association, Inc.

Maurice R. Sykes, Deputy Superintendent, Center for Systematic Educational Change, DCPS

Beverly Langford Thomas, Executive Director, Head Start Program, DCPS

Austine Fowler, Early Childhood Specialist, DCPS

John Sparrow, Principal, Marie Reed Elementary School, DCPS

Joyce Thompson, Principal, Katie C. Lewis Elementary School, DCPS

Diane Trister Dodge, Project Director

In the last year of the project, a team of primary grade teachers at two elementary schools served on a Curriculum Review Team and provided us with their impressions and reactions to each chapter. We want to particularly thank the following teachers at K.C. Lewis Elementary School: Rick Brown, Brian Kaigler, Marsha Harris, Creighton Rice, and Gwendolyn Williams; at Marie Reed Elementary School: Carolyn Unkovic and Ursula Sherard.

During the development of *Constructing Curriculum*, Teaching Strategies and National Child Day Care Association collaborated again to sponsor a Follow Through Project in Brattleboro, Vermont. We are grateful to the following teachers who reviewed the curriculum and gave us specific recommendations: Jean Allbee, Pamela Becker, Patricia Berger, Deborah Hall, Janis Kiehle, Polly Kurty, Donna Natowich, and Charlotte Stetson. We also appreciate the support of Judie Jerald, project director for the Brattleboro Follow Through Project, and Mark Taft and Robert Neubauer, principals of the two Follow Through elementary schools.

Several individuals provided editorial assistance during the development of this book. Cynthia Scherr and Sue Korenbaum were of great help in conceptualizing and editing early drafts. The final draft was edited and proofed with the assistance of Thérèse Keegan, Emily Kohn, and Matt Gross. Graphic design was coordinated by Cynthia Scherr and John Fay, and production by Debra Foulks. We want to thank the many teachers who allowed us to take pictures in their classrooms which were used as the basis for the illustrations drawn by Jody Eastman. We would also like to thank Robin Winge of Winge & Associates for the design and layout of the book.

And finally, we want to acknowledge the real life stories of many teachers (including our own) that are reflected in the examples provided throughout this book. To all of these people, we extend our deep gratitude and thanks.

Introduction

During the early elementary school years, children are "sizing up" the world. They are deciding whether it is a fair and interesting place, and just what they have to gain from and offer to it. They are deciding whether learning is worthwhile for them. Teachers can shape children's attitudes about school and learning—attitudes that can influence children's success in life. When children feel confident, competent, and accepted as learners, teachers know that they have made a difference.

Being responsible for shaping children's attitudes about school and learning is a tall order, and good teaching is hard work. Too often, teachers are alone in their classrooms. Their children may or may not respond to instructional approaches learned in teacher education courses or staff development workshops. Consequently, teachers must make many decisions every day based on their knowledge of child development and their own intuitive beliefs and daily observations in the classroom about what is effective. These decisions are more confidently made when teachers have the confidence and support of administrators and peers.

The energy for teachers' important work also comes from the classroom itself. Teaching is satisfying when the classroom atmosphere instills a sense of community in which teachers and children collaborate in their learning. And there is vitality and freshness in the fact that each year is different as the community (and therefore interests and characteristics) change with each new group of children. Being open to what curriculum will look like for each child and each group of children is central to good teaching. Helping teachers to develop a vision for their curriculum is the task of this book.

Who Should Use This Book

Constructing Curriculum for the Primary Grades is for elementary school teachers who work with children in grades one through three. Its purpose is to provide a practical framework for making curriculum effective and meaningful for children in the primary grades. Although the book addresses classroom teachers, it also offers administrators and parents insight into effective classrooms.

We strongly believe that teachers should be the ultimate decision-makers in their classrooms. Curriculum guidelines and textbooks provided by a school system offer direction about what to teach, but it is the classroom teacher, with the input and involvement of families, who knows the children well enough to make informed decisions about what children need to become competent learners.

The teaching strategies described here build on approaches that teachers have found most effective for helping children develop social competence and become confident learners. Because teachers bring personal experiences, beliefs, and goals to the task of planning curriculum, our framework allows teachers to construct and clarify their own ideas and beliefs about the teaching practices that work best for them and for the children they teach. We offer a clear and practical approach to organizing and implementing curriculum in grades one through three.

How Teachers Construct Curriculum

Teachers make good decisions about curriculum and assessment when they have a clear philosophy about teaching and learning. The philosophical framework suggested here is based on:

- a knowledge of child development: how children grow and develop emotionally, socially, cognitively, and physically;
- a respect for the unique qualities of each child in the context of family and culture; and
- an understanding of how children think and learn.

This philosophical framework is now called "developmentally appropriate practice," but it is not new. It reflects what many primary grade teachers have intuitively known and believed but have not always been able to put into practice. It is based on the same philosophy John Dewey described at the beginning of this century, and that guided the work of Lucy Sprague Mitchell and Carolyn Pratt. Constructivist philosophers, including Jerome Bruner and Lev Vygotsky have extended the understanding of early childhood education and therefore their ability to define appropriate practice.

Developmentally appropriate practice has two dimensions: age appropriateness and individual appropriateness (Bredekamp 1987). Curriculum that is *age appropriate* guides teachers in planning a learning environment and experiences that address the normal sequences of growth for children at their particular stage of development. Curriculum that is *individually appropriate* gives teachers flexible instructional approaches for addressing the learning needs of each child by recognizing the individual patterns of growth, and unique interests, experiences, and strengths that all children bring to the learning process.

Why We Need a New Look at Curriculum in the Primary Grades

There is a growing consensus among educators today that a major reason why traditional curriculum approaches that emphasize drills, worksheets, and the teaching of skills in isolation have failed is that they are not based on a knowledge of what is age appropriate or what is individually appropriate for each child. In order for children to achieve grade level expectations and become competent learners, professional practice must reflect what we know about how learning takes place. Teachers increasingly express concerns about the numbers of children who exhibit behavior problems that interfere with classroom life and successful learning. Too many teachers are discouraged, and too many children are failing.

The debate about curriculum practices in the primary grades may have already touched you personally. Regardless of your level of experience, you have probably read, heard, or even written about innovative approaches to education. You may have personal concerns about the tremendous needs many children bring to school and about the failure of traditional approaches to address these needs successfully. You are not alone in your concerns. Leading professional organizations dedicated to improving the quality of education for young children, including the National Association for the Education of Young Children (NAEYC), the National Association of Elementary School Principals, (NAESP) and the National Association of State Boards of Education (NASBE), have been directing and supporting efforts to identify more effective curriculum, teaching strategies, and assessment tools. These organizations and others are now advocating an approach to curriculum and assessment based on developmentally appropriate practice. The goals, principles, and instructional approaches that emerge from a developmentally appropriate philosophy give us a clear framework to help children acquire the skills and understandings they will need to function productively as we move into the twenty-first century.

What Children Should Learn in the Primary Grades

Curriculum planning should be guided by long-term goals for children. We believe that the fundamental goals of education are to enable children to:

- gain an increasing understanding of themselves and the world around them.
- develop the dispositions to be a learner—curiosity, independence, responsibility, initiative, creativity, willingness to take risks, to ask questions, and to persevere (Katz and Chard 1989, 30).
- acquire the skills they need to be successful learners—language and literacy, mathematical thinking, scientific thinking, social inquiry, and the ability to express their ideas through the arts and technology.
- function as contributing members of a community by developing social skills and by making choices that are good for their own welfare and helpful to society at large.

Curriculum is a plan for achieving these fundamental goals of education. It provides an overview of what children can be expected to learn and suggests an approach and specific strategies to promote the development of skills and content in each subject area.

The goals that underlie a developmentally appropriate approach to curriculum are designed to answer the question: "What do we want children to learn during the primary grades that will help them to become successful learners, lead fulfilling lives, and contribute to society?" This important question is at the heart of our approach and offers a fresh way of thinking about curriculum.

To answer this question we outline goals for children's emotional, social, cognitive, and physical development. Subject areas, which have traditionally provided the goals and objectives for children's learning in the primary grades, provide the content through which these fundamental goals are achieved. Together, they address all aspects of learning and daily classroom life in the primary grades.

Goals for Emotional Development

- To acquire a sense of confidence about one's abilities.
- To take pride in one's heritage and family background.
- To experience a sense of belonging and learn to trust others.
- To be flexible and willing to take appropriate risks.

Goals for Social Development

- To develop positive relationships with peers and adults.
- To work cooperatively with others to achieve shared goals.
- To recognize and respect people's differences.
- To contribute to establishing and maintaining rules for group living.
- To solve problems in nonviolent ways.

Goals for Cognitive Development

- To demonstrate curiosity and initiative in seeking out an increasing understanding about the world.
- To make increasing sense of the physical and social world through direct experiences and explorations.
- To express and communicate ideas and feelings.
- To read and write with understanding and increasing accuracy.
- To use mathematical thinking skills.
- To use the skills of scientific and social inquiry.
- To identify, reason through, and solve real-life problems.
- To develop critical thinking skills.
- To question stereotypes based on various aspects of diversity (ethnicity, gender, age, ability, physical characteristics).

Goals for Physical Development

- To build and expand gross and fine motor skills.
- To show confidence in what their bodies can do.
- To value and promote personal health, safety, and fitness.

How to Use This Book

Constructing Curriculum for the Primary Grades is organized into two parts, one that presents the teaching strategies for making curriculum meaningful and effective, and the second which describes subject areas addressed in grades one through three.

Part One–Six Strategies for Implementing Curriculum provides teachers with a practical framework for making decisions about curriculum.

- **Knowing the Children You Teach** means understanding developmental stages, individual characteristics, and the influence of culture. Because every group is unique, constructing curriculum is a dynamic process ultimately shaped by the attributes and interests of each group of children.

- **Building a Classroom Community** involves having daily class meetings, helping children learn to work collaboratively, and teaching children to resolve conflicts peacefully. When a classroom functions as a community, children experience a sense of belonging and a sense of empowerment that are essential to their well-being and their academic success.

- **Establishing a Structure for the Classroom** involves organizing the classroom environment, establishing consistent routines and schedules, and conveying specific expectations for behavior. An explicit structure enables teachers to facilitate children's learning and helps children to become self-directed learners.

- **Guiding Children's Learning** describes how teachers create opportunities for children to acquire skills and content as children actively investigate, represent, and reflect on their increasing understanding of the world around them. Teachers organize the curriculum using an integrated approach that allows children to apply skills they are learning across the curriculum in reading, writing, math, science, social studies, and the arts and technology.

- **Assessing Children's Learning** occurs every day as teachers observe children and collect samples of their work. A comprehensive approach to assessment enables teachers to make informed decisions about curriculum, plan instruction, monitor, and share children's progress with families in a meaningful way.

- **Building a Partnership with Families** means taking time to learn about each child's family, involving families in the school community, establishing a structure for ongoing communication, sharing the curriculum, and involving families in the assessment process. When families are involved, children's achievement is enhanced, teachers obtain support, and schools become better places for learning.

Part Two–Curriculum Content describes the five subject areas that teachers address in the primary grades.

- **Language and Literacy:** As children develop their language and literacy skills, they learn how to communicate effectively through listening, speaking, reading, and writing. Teachers expose children to a wide range of literature and print materials, give children opportunities to write, and make conversations and discussions integral parts of classroom life.

- **Mathematical Thinking:** Math is defined as a way to organize information and represent relationships. Children learn about number concepts and operations, patterns and relationships, estimation, geometry and spatial relationships, measurement, probability, and statistics. Through hands-on experiences, children develop problem-solving strategies and critical thinking skills.

- **Social Studies:** In social studies, children learn about people and places. As they pose questions, conduct research, engage in discussions, and present their findings about themselves, their families, and their communities, children begin to make connections between what they are learning and their own daily lives. Social studies experiences promote children's understanding of geography, culture, and heritage.

- **Scientific Thinking:** Children wonder about and search for ways to explain the natural and physical world. By nurturing their excitement and curiosity about the world around them, teachers can guide children in the methods of scientific investigation—questioning, predicting, observing, experimenting, explaining, and communicating—and help them acquire knowledge and understanding of natural and physical phenomena.

- **The Arts and Technology:** Exploring the varied media of the arts and technology expands children's opportunities to become active learners. Teachers incorporate art, drama, music, dance, blocks, and the use of tools including rulers, hammers, calculators, and computers to support children's varied learning styles. Teachers build on children's natural inclination to explore, invent, and make things, using those tendencies to promote an appreciation for the arts and technology.

In each chapter we present an overview of the subject areas based on current research. We outline the skills and content children are expected to learn, and offer practical teaching strategies for guiding children's learning. The content chapters show how the six strategies provide a practical and focused approach to constructing curriculum.

We hope that this book will validate what teachers already know, help them construct a clear philosophy for themselves, and give them the confidence to follow their own beliefs.

References

Bredekamp, Sue, Ed. 1987. *Developmentally Appropriate Practice in Early Childhood Programs Serving Children from Birth Through Age 8.* Washington, DC: National Association for the Education of Young Children.

Katz, Lilian and Sylvia Chard. 1989. *Engaging Children's Minds: The Project Approach.* Norwood, NJ: Ablex Publishing Co.

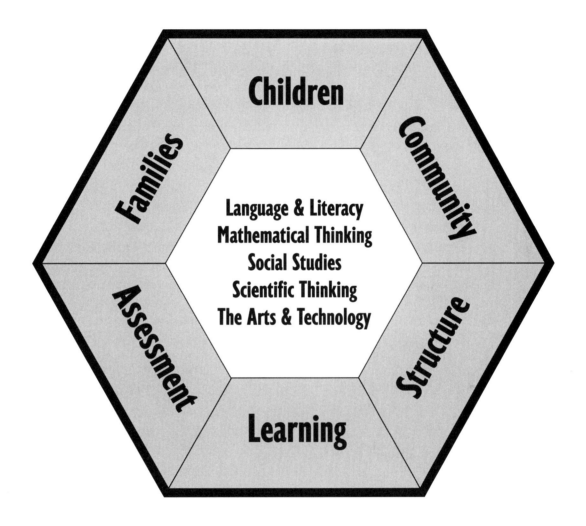

Children

Community

Families

Language & Literacy
Mathematical Thinking
Social Studies
Scientific Thinking
The Arts & Technology

Structure

Assessment

Learning

PART ONE

1

KNOWING
THE CHILDREN
YOU TEACH

The foundation for constructing curriculum is knowing about children—developmentally and individually. To construct curriculum effectively, teachers rely on their prior knowledge and experience and also consider what they learn about every new group of children they teach—the knowledge, interests and experiences each child brings into the classroom. Because every group of children is unique, the curriculum will vary somewhat each year.

There are two reasons why knowing the children you teach is the first strategy for constructing curriculum. First, the developmental and individual characteristics of children influence the kinds of learning experiences you plan. Second, knowing children well makes it possible to build positive relationships with them, which is often the key to their success in school.

No matter how similar the children in your classroom may appear, every group is made up of individuals who bring their own set of experiences, interests, learning styles, and expectations into the classroom. This chapter describes how you can learn about the children you teach by understanding:

- ***developmental characteristics of children***—emotional, social, cognitive, and physical;

- ***individual characteristics of children***—temperament, interests, talents, learning styles, life experiences, and special needs;

- the ***cultural context*** in which children have been raised and its influence upon their communication and interaction styles and other expectations about their behavior.

We conclude this chapter with some specific suggestions for going beyond first impressions and initial expectations to learn about the children in your classroom.

Knowing About Child Development

Understanding child development helps teachers know how and why children behave as they do and what to expect of children within each age group. Child development refers to the generally predictable patterns of change that occur as children grow. An abundance of literature provides guidelines for the normal sequence of growth in all areas of development. The theories of psychologists Erik Erikson, Jean Piaget, and Lev Vygotsky have contributed to our understanding of children's emotional, social and cognitive growth.

Curriculum is considered "age appropriate" or "developmentally appropriate" if it is based on knowledge of how most children grow and what they can do—socially, emotionally, cognitively, and physically—at a particular stage of development. This knowledge enables teachers to plan classroom activities that will be appropriate to children's developmental abilities. It helps teachers to anticipate children's behavior and have reasonable expectations about how children will respond to classroom activities.

Social development addresses how the child relates to others and the child's ability to make friends. Emotional development relates to feelings about self and others. Cognitive development refers to how the child thinks, processes information, solves problems, and uses language to communicate. Physical development includes growth in size, strength, motor skills, and coordination. Although we can look at each aspect of development separately, all areas of development are interrelated. By knowing the developmental characteristics of primary grade children, teachers can determine the kinds of experiences children are ready to undertake and how to support each child's growth and learning.

Differences in the Rate of Development Are Normal

While there are predictable patterns of development, children do not grow and develop at the same rate. Within any group of children the same age, a two-and-a-half-year span of development is perfectly normal. In addition, an individual child's development does not follow an even course across all domains: a six year old may have the fine motor skills of some seven year olds but the language skills of some five year olds. It is also important to remember that in September, a typical class of first graders will include some children who have not yet turned six and others who are approaching seven.

Describing Middle Childhood

Children in the primary grades are in a developmental period often called "middle childhood." During this period children grow in size, strength, and coordination. Their sense of personal identity develops and they begin to define themselves in terms of attributes and achievements:

"I wear glasses."   "I'm good at soccer."

"My skin is brown."   "I can read long books with chapters."

Middle childhood is characterized by a decrease in egocentricity and an increasing interest in others, especially peers. Children often express interest and awareness of social issues as they read stories, observe local happenings, and hear about current events. Establishing friendships takes on importance although children sometimes lack the skills necessary to do so. Many children this age think about how they look in the eyes of others and become increasingly self-conscious. A noticeable characteristic of children in the middle years is the emergence of a sense of humor. Less dependent on adults and more dependent on peers, children are likely to question authority and test limits.

Theories of Erikson

Erik Erikson (1963) describes eight "psychosocial" stages; during each, a psychosocial strength is developed. As children move from one stage to the next, the strengths of prior stages remain and are related to the others.

Each stage is characterized in terms of a positive and negative attribute. According to Erikson, children between six and eight are in the fourth psychosocial stage, that of "Industry vs. Inferiority." Industry means that children become increasingly product oriented, want to do a job well, and want to feel competent. When children do not achieve a positive sense of industry they feel inferior ("I can't do it."). Erikson's theories explain how important it is for teachers to provide children with appropriate challenges so they can feel successful.

Theories of Piaget

Jean Piaget (1952) describes how children's thinking changes as they progress through four stages. During each stage, children construct an understanding of their experiences with people and objects in the environment. Until about the age of twelve, children's constructions of reality are often distortions or approximations of how things actually are.

Between the ages of six and eight, children progress from what Piaget calls "pre-operational thinking" to "concrete operational thinking." Children at the pre-operational stage rely primarily on sensory experience for thinking and learning. They base their understanding of the world on what they learn from first-hand experience. The new set of mental abilities (concrete operations) that they acquire enables them to manipulate lsymbols in their minds, while a younger child can only manipulate concrete objects. This change in thinking affects many aspects of children's learning. Some examples of how their thinking changes include the following:

- They can classify things in terms of hierarchical relationships (e.g., cats and dogs are all animals).
- They can explore something visually rather than only manually (e.g., looking at a set of Tangrams and mentally deciding on how they will fit into a pre-drawn shape, rather than having to push them around until they form the shape).
- They can follow a set of rules when playing a game.

Theories of Vygotsky

Lev Vygotsky (1978) developed the theory of "scaffolding." In this model, children's learning is compared to a new building, temporarily supported by an outside structure as the construction progresses. Vygotsky stresses the importance of adults and "competent peers" to support children's learning, pointing out that emerging abilities appear first in a context of support from others. It is through social interaction that children encounter new knowledge.

Teachers strive to strike the right balance between engaging children at their existing level of competence and extending their range of capability. Vygotsky's theories remind teachers of the need to set up new challenges for children. They highlight the relationship between social interaction and learning. Building on this theory, the teacher's role is a facilitator and guide.

Recognizing Developmental Characteristics of Primary Grade Children

In this section we describe some typical characteristics of children in first through third grades. Most children in these grades are between the ages of six and eight. However, many enter first grade having not quite turned six, and by the middle of third grade, some children have turned nine. In addition, more and more primary classrooms have mixed-age groups, including those that combine five and six year olds. For these reasons, we begin this section with a brief overview of five year olds and end by describing nine year olds.

Leaving Age Five

Five year olds revel in their newly acquired skills. Often emotionally solid and good tempered, they tend to be energetic and friendly. They can be overly confident about their abilities, having gained sufficient physical strength and control to have a sense of competence and power.

The egocentricity of five year olds is evident in the way they learn and relate to peers. Because they rely on their senses to take in new information, their questions about the natural and social world relate to what they see. They learn through their own direct involvement. Watching someone else have a turn doing something, or listening to a story about how something is done, does not help them learn as much as doing it themselves. Five year olds begin to make generalizations from repeated experiences, and their thinking depends on their actions. They frequently confuse fantasy and reality.

Five year olds are usually eager to please and to receive affection. It may be hard for them to share because they are so focused on themselves and have trouble understanding another point of view. However, while sharing may be frustrating one minute, the next minute a five year old may give up a turn or a toy to someone else as a way to please and make a friend. Although eager for friendships, five year olds may not have the skills to make and keep a friend. They often use language with ease and sometimes sound like adults, but they do not act or think like we do. Adult guidance and support is needed to help fives figure out what is fair when it comes to sharing materials, standing up for themselves, and negotiating friendships. As children turn six, they often move into a less stable phase.

Six Year Olds

Emotionally

The moods of six year olds can change abruptly from one extreme to another. One minute they are friendly and enthusiastic and the next, they can be rebellious and irritable. Within a matter of seconds they can be best friends or worst enemies with the same person. The same six year old who acts silly and delights in a newly developing sense of humor may be prone to frequent tears and tantrums. Sixes generally enjoy routines. It is best to let them make transitions slowly, as they may be easily overwhelmed by excitement. It may be hard for them to make choices or decisions because they often want to weigh alternatives carefully and assess all of their options. Invested in doing things their own way, they may respond negatively to adult demands.

Socially

Eager to feel connected to their peers, six year olds work hard at making friends. However, because many have not yet developed the skills needed to do this successfully, social struggles are frequent. Sixes may be bossy in play activities and, like five year olds, demand their own way. Threesomes can be difficult for them. They need guidance on rules, cooperative play, and sharing. To make a situation come out the way they want, it is not uncommon for them to resort to changing the rules (cheating), or changing the story (lying). They can be very competitive and insist on being first (or last). Although slowly moving away from dependence on adults, sixes still want adult approval and praise. When they tattle, it is usually to show adults they really know the rules. Six year olds benefit tremendously fromsocial coaching.

A supportive adult can provide the right words or a suggestion for a solution to a problem. Extensive social coaching and modeling teaches six year olds the skills they need to relate positively to peers. Easily discouraged and frustrated, sixes cope poorly with failure and do not take criticism well.

Cognitively

Six year olds are likely to be curious learners who are interested in both process and product. They learn best through their active involvement with people and materials. They are more like fives than sevens, however, in that process holds greater pleasure and importance than product. It isn't unusual for a six year old to rush through work, eager to move on to something new. Six year olds are beginning to think logically, and to organize concepts symbolically. For example, many understand that the number "three" can represent someone who is three years old, something that weighs three pounds, or three cookies. Unlike five year olds whose thinking is based on what they see, six year olds are moving towards what Piaget calls "conservation." For example, many can recognize that two sets of ten cubes are equivalent even when one is spread apart and the other is clustered together.

Physically

Six year olds seem to be in perpetual motion; they squirm as they sit, or gesture with their bodies as they talk. Although quite energetic, they can tire easily and benefit from activities such as listening to a story or quietly looking at books after recess. In the classroom, they need to be able to move around and have a variety of active and quiet activities. By six, most children are excelling at gross motor skills such as running and jumping, beginning to use a bat, throwing and catching with increasing skill, and doing somersaults. They are gradually gaining control of fine motor activities and can use tools such as scissors, pencils, markers, paintbrushes, saws, and hammers with increasing ease. Like five year olds, they gain confidence with their increasing physical competence.

Seven Year Olds

Emotionally

Emotional changes between six and seven are gradual and depend on the individual child and his or her own environment. Most seven year olds are eager to master new skills and begin to demand perfection of themselves. Thus, they are likely to draw the same picture or write stories about the very same theme over and over, striving to achieve perfection. They can be highly self-critical, and more inhibited and worried about making mistakes than they were a year earlier. Seven year olds tend to take life seriously and often feel that things are unjust. Schedules and routines are important to them and they expect that these will be followed exactly. Like sixes, they often find transitions uncomfortable and benefit from having time to prepare for them.

Socially

At seven, children are evolving into more capable social beings. They are eager for approval from peers and adults. They establish strong friendships and want to feel that they are part of the group. In group discussions and projects, they can listen to and appreciate the contributions of others. In their effort to feel a sense of security and belonging, they often imitate the actions of their friends. They will more easily join in playground games and work with others in the classroom. Despite their interest in being with others, it is not unusual for seven year olds to want to work by themselves in a quiet space. They often begin to develop special interests such as collecting baseball cards, doing gymnastics, tap dancing, playing the violin, or playing soccer. Their tendency toward repetitive actions can be seen in their desire to play the same game over and over. While four to six year olds have a developing awareness of differences (e.g., gender, race, physical abilities), seven year olds can verbalize them and may even use them as a basis for exclusion.

Cognitively

Like six year olds, sevens continue to learn most readily through concrete experiences and active participation. They enjoy experimenting and have the intellectual capacity to organize their experiences mentally. Seven year olds are willing to take time to think and plan before they set out to work, and they are gaining the ability to reflect on what they have done. While sevens show an increasing ability to distinguish between reality and fantasy, they enjoy imaginative play and like to put on puppet shows and dramatize stories.

Physically

Seven is typically a period of slow but steady growth. Children this age have increased stamina, control, and balance, and a greater interest in team sports. Like the six year old, sevens are active and energetic and sometimes are unable to control their energy. Although their small muscles are still developing, their increased and improved eye-hand coordination enable them to draw and write more easily.

Eight Year Olds

Emotionally

At eight, children gradually view themselves as individuals in the context of the larger world. They are keenly aware of the difference between the adult world and the world of children. Eager to be a part of the adult world, they are often frustrated by their limitations. As they begin to assert themselves, they can act rude and unreasonable or be easily disappointed when things do not go their way. Many will readily argue their point of view. At the same time, their increased ability to evaluate themselves and others makes them even more self-critical than they were at seven. Although they still want praise from adults, they are very sensitive about being told what to do by adults. They respond better to hints and cues than to direct orders. Reasonably consistent standards and demands from adults help them to successfully move out on their own. Because they can become overwhelmed and frustrated easily, they often need adults to help them come up with strategies for accomplishing tasks.

Socially

Eight year olds crave acceptance from their peers, and group membership grows in importance. They establish close friendships but are likely to struggle with endless disagreements. Some eights can be very moody about friends—close one day and fighting the next. Unlike many sevens, eights generally do not like to work or play alone. Eight year olds are very likely to form clubs and spend time planning who will be included and who will be excluded. They like team games and group projects and discussions. Trading and collecting is often a major social activity for eight year olds. They enjoy table games and are likely to invent their own. They look forward to roles, responsibilities, and even school traditions associated with being this age. For example, in some schools third graders are cafeteria monitors or perform in plays. Typically, third graders take pride in these special traditions and view themselves as especially important. While they can manage transitions more easily than at earlier ages, these times are liable to be busy and noisy because of the eight year old's desire to socialize.

Cognitively

Eight year olds have the capacity for more abstract thinking as long as what they are thinking about relates to something they have experienced directly. As they begin to learn about what life was like long ago, they make comparisons to their own experiences. Maps capture their interest and they gain understanding of them by making maps of their own surroundings. Their work is more and more detailed. Although they continue to learn best through active, concrete experiences, they can use books as a source of information as well. By age eight, children have a longer attention span. Increasingly able to think and reason logically, they enjoy collecting, organizing and classifying objects and information. Eight year olds like action. Their drawings often contain people and objects in motion. Imaginative play continues to be an important learning tool for them and they can become very involved in skits, role plays, and puppet shows.

Physically

The increased agility and high energy of eight year olds can make them seem restless and fidgety. Many enjoy rough and tumble play such as tackling games, as well as games that call for exactness, such as team sports (e.g., soccer or softball). Children this age take pleasure in the physical skills they have acquired and may be physically daring. They are also eager to learn new techniques for sports and other physical activities. They have increased speed and smoothness in fine muscle work as well as greater interest and control in skills that call for eye-hand coordination. Typically, the artwork of eight year olds becomes smaller and more detailed.

Becoming Nine

As children turn nine, they want to be independent and are strongly aligned with their peer group. They respond well to appreciation of their efforts. At this age, sex role identification becomes stronger. Like many eights, nines are easily embarrassed and can be very sensitive to teasing. They also tend to form clubs especially designed to include some peers and exclude others. Whereas eight year olds are still prone to tattling on peers, by nine, children are becoming more loyal to their peers and are less likely to do so. Supportive adults who are present but not demanding are very helpful to nine year olds. Nines often want and need the "ear" of an adult to talk over ideas and feelings. Adults can provide a cooperative setting in which children can share thoughts and feelings with peers and feel confident that they will not be "put down."

Nine year olds are intellectually competent in many ways. They can puzzle over problems mentally, whereas when they were younger they required actual objects to reach the same conclusions. Nines begin to see things from a variety of perspectives. Their attention span is expanding and they tend to enjoy projects that extend over a period of time. Even as they gradually move towards abstract thinking, they are still likely to rely on familiar experiences as a frame of reference.

Nines are becoming more and more competent physically. Most have good eye-hand coordination and enjoy detail work such as crafts, woodworking, drawing, and painting. They are becoming progressively more skillful in tasks that require motor skills.

Responding to Developmental Characteristics of Children

From these brief developmental descriptions, it is evident that many characteristics recur throughout this age span. The following chart summarizes those characteristics common to most children in the primary grades and suggests how an awareness of these developmental characteristics can help teachers plan an environment and activities that will enable all children to experience success.

Emotional Characteristics	How Teachers Can Respond
Sensitive to teasing, insults and put-downs	• Plan group discussions about personal feelings and those of others. • Take children's concerns seriously by asking questions and offering guidance. • Help children express feelings verbally. • Read stories aloud related to personal feelings and empathy towards others. • Be aware of your own comments and reactions and how they may be interpreted.
Act self-assured, but can still have many self-doubts (e.g., may overestimate abilities, don't want to fail, eager to do things perfectly)	• Allow children to take reasonable risks by providing clear boundaries and creating a classroom atmosphere where mistakes are accepted. • Provide reassurance and encouragement and convey confidence in children's abilities by being specific with praise. • Provide experiences in which children can be competent and then gradually increase the difficulty of tasks.
Beginning to see that rules are important and developing a strong sense of fair play	• Use meetings for discussions on necessary rules, problem solving, and conflict resolution. • Use role play, puppet plays, and stories to practice problem solving, and conflict resolution. • Involve children in establishing classroom rules and consequences.
Able to assume some responsibility for self	• Establish clear methods for storing belongings and bringing homework back and forth (e.g., a folder, a binder, a manila envelope). • With the children, generate a list of jobs for maintaining the classroom and discuss together how these jobs will be accomplished. • Provide time for discussions to establish guidelines and strategies for completing assignments on time.

Social Characteristics	How Teachers Can Respond
Display strong likes and opinions	• Provide opportunities for children to talk about and dramatize their feelings and express their ideas (e.g., debates) and reassure them that differences are okay. • If you see a child exhibit prejudice toward another person, intervene immediately by helping the child, and the class as a whole, understand why such behavior is hurtful. • Set up activities in which children can conduct surveys and make graphs regarding personal interests and opinions. • Read and discuss stories about issues and feelings that are typical of children this age. (See suggestions in the resources section of this chapter.)
Eager to be independent of adults and may challenge authority	• Provide choices for children each day so that they feel a sense of power and control. • Plan activities that children can do independently or with peers. • Let children select research topics within the context of a study. • Involve children in deciding on rules and consequences, and in resolving conflicts that arise. • Give children positive feedback when you notice they are working well. • Set reasonable limits and adhere to the pre-established consequences.
Eager to make friends and be with peers but not always successful at doing so	• Plan a variety of small group activities and provide opportunities for children to pick their own work partners, from time to time. • Provide a "free choice time" several times each week, if not daily, so that children have opportunities to engage in social experiences with some guidance and supervision. • Plan time for children to discuss what does and does not work when two or more people work or play together. • Provide children with supportive "social coaching" (e.g., "Why don't you try saying it this way…?").
Enjoy working/playing with others as well as alone	• Provide collaborative work activities as well as time for children to work alone. • Set up the room so children can work collaboratively on tasks or on their own (e.g., different sized tables, moveable carrels, dividers).

Social Characteristics	How Teachers Can Respond
Developing a strong group identity	• Plan integrated, long-term studies as a way to foster a sense of community. • Organize cooperative games that help bond a group. • Encourage class spirit (e.g., doing group activities, projects, celebrations). • Establish some classroom routines (e.g., signals, greetings, goodbyes). • Display children's work in the classroom and in school hallways.
Like affection from adults though often embarrassed or uncomfortable	• Show children you care about them by offering personal greetings and by taking time to have individual conversations. • Use a sense of humor to convey certain messages and engage in casual joking. • Compliment children for their efforts and behaviors (e.g., "It was really thoughtful of you to include room for more people in your skit.").
Enjoy cooperative games and games with rules but may have difficulty coping with winning and losing	• Plan indoor and outdoor cooperative group games. • Have board and card games available in the classroom and allocate time in the schedule for children to play. • Use meetings for discussions and role plays about winning and losing.

Cognitive Characteristics	How Teachers Can Respond
Increasingly skilled and interested in reading and expressing themselves verbally and in writing	• Offer times for children to select and read their own books. • Give children opportunities to choose their own writing topics. • Expose children to a variety of writing and reading experiences (e.g., fiction, non-fiction, poetry, humor, mystery). • Engage children in discussions about reading and writing by asking extensive questions, encouraging personal responses, and letting them critique work. • Create opportunities for sharing jokes, riddles, puns, and imaginative language.
Able to work on long-term projects	• Provide opportunities for children to select, design, and carry out projects using a variety of media (e.g., puzzles, model making, cooking, weaving, planting). • Allow time for children to explore a topic in depth.
Developing the ability to hold more than one idea in their minds at a time	• Give multi-step directions and take time to go over them. • Use charts to list directions, choices, what to do when you're finished.
Ask questions that are fact oriented—How, Why, and When	• Begin long-term studies by having children generate a list of questions that are of interest to them ("What do you want to know about…?"). • Provide opportunities for research (e.g., interviewing, collecting data, going through books, studying maps and charts).

Cognitive Characteristics	How Teachers Can Respond
Acquiring the ability to see another person's point of view	• Provide opportunities to dramatize situations (related to literature, social studies topics, etc.) in which children experience different roles. • Have discussions in which children express their ideas and hear opposing views about stories, current events, beliefs, interests. • Read books aloud and discuss how the characters have different points of view, relating the content to children's personal experiences. • Supervise opportunities for children to explore devices or equipment used by people with disabilities (e.g., wheelchairs, crutches, eyeglasses, braille books). • Introduce topics for study in which children learn about how others live, encouraging children to observe similarities and differences.
Like to use their imagination	• Provide opportunities for children to make up stories, skits, dances, plays, and puppet shows and then share them with others. • Offer opportunities for children to write and perform stories, poetry, and songs and to create artwork and music. • Set up opportunities for children to create inventions.

Physical Characteristics	How Teachers Can Respond
Very active and energetic (although they may suddenly get tired)	• Provide opportunities for movement throughout the day (e.g., variety in schedule, short indoor and outdoor breaks during the day). • Allow children to move about the room within reasonable limits during work times. • Have reasonable expectations for how long children can sit still.
Likely to become hungry in mid-morning and have low energy	• Provide time for mid-morning snack (either brought from home or prepared in the classroom). • Incorporate cooking experiences into projects.
Increasingly able to control and coordinate their actions	• Plan times for children to use large muscle skills (e.g., group games, moving furniture). • Provide activities that use fine motor skills (e.g., beadwork, construction, sewing, weaving, and building with a variety of manipulative materials). • Have reasonable expectations about quantity and quality of paper and pencil work.
Refining eye-hand coordination	• Provide opportunities for using these skills (e.g., woodworking, constructing models, cutting and pasting, mapping). • Provide alternatives to copying information from a blackboard.

Recognizing a Child's Individuality

I n the previous section, we described the developmental characteristics of children between five and nine years old and offered some practical suggestions for responding to the developing skills and interests of children in the primary grades. Knowing these characteristics helps you to have reasonable expectations for children. However, each child is also an individual who brings a unique set of characteristics and experiences to the classroom. These characteristics and experiences affect how that child learns and relates to others. Careful observation will help you become more aware of the many influences that make each child unique.

There is no such thing as a homogeneous group of children. Even when all the children "look the same," every classroom contains a diverse group of individuals. The term "diversity" refers to the many factors that make people different, including gender, ethnicity, culture, religion, family structure, age, ability, physical characteristics, learning style, language, economic position, and more.

For children to thrive as successful learners, the classroom has to be a place where each child feels comfortable and valued as an individual. This section will describe how temperament, interests and talents, learning styles, resiliency, life experiences, and the presence of a diagnosed disability all contribute to a child's individuality, and how these factors affect each child's approach and response to learning experiences.

Temperament

Temperament refers to a person's mental outlook—the mood or spirit with which an individual approaches life: active, reserved, quiet, outgoing, tenacious, slow. A few minutes in a classroom of busy children reveals how different children can be in terms of their temperament. Some may be shy, while others are outgoing. Some may be flexible, willing to go along with daily happenings, while others are more rigid, needing to stick to a tried and true approach or a personal opinion.

Often, children behave differently in different settings. A child who is reserved at school may be outgoing at home. A child may act one way around peers and entirely differently around adults. As you observe and engage with children in an effort to learn about their temperaments, it is important to notice how they behave in a range of settings and to confer with parents about what the child is like at home. This information can be very useful in understanding how a child goes about making friends, solving problems, and learning new skills.

Interests and Talents

Children bring their special interests into your classroom. Some children gravitate toward physical activities, others toward art. Some love the natural world and will delight in bringing all sorts of creatures and plant life into school. When you assess children to find out what they especially like to do, it enables you to tap into these interests.

Children also have special talents, some learned and others innate. You may have a child who is a fine artist, an author, a gifted poet, a skilled soccer player, or a computer wiz. Sometimes a child's particular talent is obvious and other times it is not. For example, a child who studies violin or the drums after school and has become skilled at playing may not have an opportunity to exhibit this strength in the course of daily classroom life.

You can learn about children's interests and special talents by observing them and by talking with them and with members of their families. Encouraging children to interview one another will also help you get to know them. When teachers know children's special interests and what they are good at, they can more effectively support their growth and self-confidence.

Learning Styles

We all have our own preferred ways of taking in new information. Think about how you approach learning. Are you aurally, or visually oriented? Would you rather watch a demonstration, or study a chart or a diagram? Do you remember what a lecturer said by simply listening, or do you have to take notes?

Traditionally, schools have emphasized oral and written communication as the primary means of learning and demonstrating knowledge. As important as these communication skills are, they are not the only ways of acquiring information and skills. Research has expanded our views of how people approach learning and how important it is to recognize and use the various ways children learn in the classroom.

Howard Gardner (1993) has expanded our concept of intelligence and therefore our ability to recognize each child's unique strengths. According to Gardner, there are seven different kinds of intelligence:

- *Logical-Mathematical Intelligence*—the ability to solve problems rapidly, often in one's head. Children who have strong potential in this area might solve difficult brain teasers, or easily calculate the solution to a math problem.

- *Linguistic Intelligence*—the ability to use words creatively and with ease. Children who have strong potential in this area might write poems and plays, include lots of detail in writing a story, report on an event with accuracy, use descriptive language, and acquire a large vocabulary.

- *Musical Intelligence*—the ability to produce and appreciate different forms of music. Children who have strong potential in this area might easily recognize the instruments playing a piece of music, sing in harmony with others, and enjoy many kinds of music, from classical to popular.

- *Spatial Intelligence*—the ability to form a mental model of the spatial world. Children who have strong potential in this area might be outstanding chess players, plan and create three-dimensional structures, or create and read maps with ease.

- ***Bodily Kinesthetic Intelligence***—the ability to use one's body with great skill. Children who have strong potential in this area might excel in dance or gymnastics, take apart and rebuild a radio or clock, or invent a squirrel-proof birdfeeder.
- ***Interpersonal Intelligence***—the ability to understand and work effectively with other people. Children who have strong potential in this area might be very aware of group dynamics, mediate conflicts between other children, or organize the group to perform a talent show.
- ***Intrapersonal Intelligence***—the ability to recognize one's own strengths, weaknesses, desires, and intelligences and operate effectively. Children who have strong potential in this area might write an autobiography, set and pursue long-term goals, or give advice to a friend on how to handle a difficult personal problem.

Children who have strong potential in the first two areas—logical and linguistic thinking—tend to do well on standardized tests and are considered "smart." Too often, children gifted in other areas are not recognized for their strengths and are even made to feel incompetent. Gardner points out that while all of us partake of each intelligence to some degree, certain individuals are highly endowed with the core abilities and skills of a particular type of intelligence.

How often have we judged children as not being very "smart" because they did not excel in linguistic or logical intelligence? Perhaps these children excelled in another way, but we failed to provide opportunities for them to practice and use their areas of strength. Peter Jennings (1992) suggests that rather than looking at each child and asking, "How smart is this child?", we rephrase the question and ask "How is this child smart?" In so doing, we will discover new ways of appreciating each child's unique abilities and strengths.

Nancy Curry and Carl Johnson, in their book *Beyond Self-Esteem,* remind us that "middle childhood is an important period for developing a sense of industry or competence. Children need to experience themselves as growing, learning, and developing in valued ways" (1990, 130). By providing a wide range of classroom experiences that enables all children to do well and learn in comfortable ways, we are more likely to help every child achieve a feeling of confidence and competence.

Resiliency

You may have children in your classroom who come from families with severe problems. They may be struggling with drug or alcohol abuse, violence, poverty, or health problems. Children from multistressed families are often labeled "at risk," "disadvantaged," or "crack babies." These labels are neither useful nor accurate. They often lower our expectations of what children can accomplish. While children growing up in hardship conditions will experience problems, many still develop normally, learn to cope successfully, and lead fulfilling lives. These children are said to have resiliency.

Researchers have begun to focus their attention on the characteristics of children who seem to be resilient even in the face of impossible life circumstances. They have identified four attributes that appear to help children cope and succeed (Benard 1991).

- *Social competence*—Children with resiliency have social skills that enable them to establish positive relationships with others. They are active, adaptable, and exhibit a sense of humor about life.

- *Problem-solving skills*—From the time they are very young, children who are resilient demonstrate an ability to think about and come up with solutions for both social and cognitive problems. When faced with a frustrating situation, they can find alternative ways to handle the problem, thus giving them a sense of control over their environment.

- *Autonomy*—Children with resiliency have a sense of their own identity and a strong sense of independence. Their ability to see themselves as separate from their problems enables them to retain a sense of self-esteem.

- *Sense of purpose/future*—In spite of very depressing life circumstances, children who demonstrate resiliency believe that the future will be brighter and things will work out for them. They are goal directed, have a sense of anticipation about life, and high expectations for themselves.

The research on this subject helps educators to focus on children's strengths instead of the damage that hardship conditions have caused. In the next chapter on community, we show how teachers can create a classroom environment that promotes these characteristics of resiliency.

Life Experiences

Children bring into the classroom a range of life experiences which affect who they are and how they engage with other children, adults, materials and activities. These experiences contribute significantly to each child's individuality and ability to relate to others. Some factors that may influence the child's outlook include:

- the child's position in the family—where the child fits in the line of siblings, or being an only child;

- the child's family structure (e.g., single-parent family, two parents, adoptive parents, foster care, two same sex parents, extended family, etc.);

- where the child has lived (e.g., in the same neighborhood since birth, having moved from another country or having moved within the same city);

- whether the child's home language is English or another language;

- the living situation (e.g., urban, rural, house, apartment, shelter);

- the type of community in which the child lives;

- the kind of work family members do;

- the family's interests and activities;
- the economic situation and stability of the child's family (e.g., poverty, frequent family unemployment, middle or upper-middle class);
- whether the child has been exposed to violence or abuse;
- the existence of chronic health problems or drug abuse in the child's family;
- whether the child has a physical disability (or a sibling or parent with a disability).

When teachers take time to learn about the life experiences of the children in their classroom, they can more effectively meet children's emotional and learning needs. Knowing, for example, that John has lived in numerous foster homes, helps his teacher understand why he acts out when everyone is making Mother's Day cards. When Jamal refuses to eat during snack and lunch, it is important to know that his family is observing Ramadan. If Cindy comes to school with suspicious bruises, teachers are required by law to report this to the school counselor or principal.

How Children Feel About Their Circumstances

Many children have to deal with difficult family and life situations that affect their sense of well-being and emotional stability. You may learn about the problem from the parents, or note a change in a child's behavior that leads you to ask questions. Children are usually willing to talk about their feelings if they trust that an adult will be open, caring, and accepting.

In a study of primary grade children dealing with separation and divorce, researchers found that "children believe that they will do better work in school if their teachers understand what is going on in their lives. Children hope that teachers, knowing about the pressures the children are experiencing, will be more tolerant of occasional lapses in their school performance" (Frieman 1993, 59). This doesn't mean that teachers will excuse any behavior, only that they show they care and are flexible about adapting the curriculum to meet a child's needs. For example, a child who cannot concentrate on a reading task might prefer to write in his journal about something that is on his mind.

Special Needs

You may find that you have children in your classroom with special needs, including diagnosed disabilities. It is important to recognize that any individual teacher is not expected to possess indepth knowledge about every type of disability. As a teacher, each year you meet new children and discover new challenges. Teaching children with special needs, like all teaching, builds upon the knowledge and experience you continually acquire. One person cannot become an expert on all disabilities, but it is possible to focus upon and learn a great deal about the particular special needs of individual children in your classroom.

Too often, children are labeled as having disabilities before a formal diagnosis has been made. A complete diagnosis involves thorough evaluation by specialists in the appropriate field, as well as consultation with the child's family. When the classroom encourages many different approaches to solving problems and completing tasks, children can work at their own pace and mislabeling is less likely to occur.

Diagnosed disabilities of children in your classroom may range from language impairment to physical disabilities. It is important to gather information about the way the disability manifests itself in a particular child. It is also important to know that a child may have more than one disability. A child with a physical disability, may also have perceptual difficulties. Another child may have a medical diagnosis requiring treatment (e.g., diabetes) but may not be eligible for special education services.

Laws and Regulations About Inclusion

The past several decades have seen a succession of federal, state, and local laws and regulations which require that children with disabilities be included in regular education settings. The landmark Education for All Handicapped Children Act of 1975 (P.L. 94-142), more recently amended and reauthorized as the Individuals with Disabilities Education Act (IDEA), calls for a "free, appropriate public education" in the "least restrictive environment" for children with disabilities. And the Americans with Disabilities Act (ADA) of 1990 extends the principle of non-discrimination to a wide variety of other settings with respect to people with disabilities.

It is not enough just to mainstream children with disabilities and hope for the best. These legal provisions reflect the importance of "supplementary aids and services" (e.g., classroom aides, consultations, or resource services) to achieve the inclusion of children with disabilities in regular classes. The laws require state and local regulations to ensure that teachers "are provided with the technical assistance and training necessary to assist them in this effort" (Individuals with Disabilities Education Act 1991). The advice of specialists should always be sought when addressing needs that may be beyond your experience or expertise. Ask for support without guilt or self-blame. Even special education teachers are not always prepared for every kind of disability or every expression of a disability.

When successfully executed, the inclusion of children with disabilities in the classroom (or mainstreaming) can be a very rewarding experience for everyone involved. Inclusion provides an educational environment in which all children can succeed. It helps children with disabilities to gain independence and autonomy; enables all children to develop comfortable, fair relationships with others; and teaches all children to resist stereotypes, name calling, and overcoming other barriers when they appear (Derman-Sparks 1990). Children with disabilities are children first. They thrive in an environment that accepts differences and where adults strive to meet each child's individual needs.

Where to Start

Getting to know a child with disabilities and that child's family is the first step toward meeting the child's needs. Planning for children with disabilities requires careful thought and often the assistance of specialists.

We have already stated that an individual child's development may vary greatly across domains, revealing greater or lesser degrees of skill in different areas. Within every category of disability, individual children will develop differently and the span of development will be even wider than in children who are not disabled. A nine-year-old child with Down's Syndrome may be very verbal, social, and able to read on a first grade level, or the child may be rarely verbal, or social, and unable to match picture cards.

It is very important to know the child's learning styles, likes, and dislikes, and how the specific disability may or may not affect the child's learning and activities. The following steps will help you to formulate the best plans for a child with a diagnosed disability.

- *Consult with the child.* Find out whether the child would rather talk with you alone, or with a family member present. Ask what has helped in the past and how you can best support the child now.

- *Consult with the family.* While this is important for all children, families of children with special needs may have extra information to communicate as well as specific suggestions to share.

- *Consult with a specialist.* Although the strategies for working with different disabilities may overlap, it is essential for teachers to have specific guidance on each type of disability. Advice should be sought from specialists (including the school nurse, school psychologist, or other resource personnel) to learn the most up-to-date instructional approaches.

- *Gather resources.* You can find or create the resources you need to mainstream and include all children. Resources range from the hiring of a special education assistant to aid you and the child all day, to finding articles about special strategies to support the child's learning. Attending a workshop or asking your principal to provide an inservice event might help you to acquire new skills to meet a child's special needs. You are not expected to address every child's needs without support and resources.

The strategies presented in Part One of *Constructing Curriculum* work to the advantage of all children, including those with special needs. Knowing the child means working with the family and specialists to gain a full understanding of the disability as one aspect of a child's identity. The classroom community creates a sense of belonging through which a child with special needs may contribute and flourish. A clear structure in the classroom helps a child with disabilities to feel safe and to focus. When teachers guide learning through investigations and representation experiences, individual needs can be accommodated. Assessment that is ongoing in the context of classroom learning informs teachers about a child's strengths by showing what a child with special needs can do.

Understanding the Influence of Culture

Ward Goodenough defines culture as "the set of standards or rules for perceiving, believing, acting, and evaluating others" (1971, 62). A person's culture is the product of many elements that have to be viewed and understood collectively. Too often, we give people cultural labels that only serve to perpetuate stereotypes. It is a misconception to think that all people from a particular group think or act in the same way. For example, a Latino child living in rural Mexico has a different cultural context from a Latino child living in inner city Los Angeles. Each of us is the product of many cultural influences. Race, ethnicity, social class, region, gender, religion, physical abilities and sexual orientation are some of the dimensions of the human experience that define each person's culture.

Why is it essential to consider the culture of the child? Culture affects how we communicate and interact with others and the kinds of expectations we have. We are all influenced by the various cultures to which we belong. The greater the cultural differences between a teacher and the children, the more effort the teacher must make to get to know children to support their learning most effectively. A deeper understanding of children in the context of culture can have a significant impact on whether or not they succeed in school.

Each of us has a set of beliefs about ourselves as well as attitudes, assumptions, and expectations about people and events around us. This grows out of the culture in which we have been raised. An essential part of building relationships with children is being aware of and open to the beliefs, attitudes, assumptions, and expectations that children may have that are different from our own. Teachers cannot possibly learn about all of the cultural factors influencing the children they teach. But they can be open to the many ways in which children are influenced by culture.

Culture and Communication

Culture gives us our "communication framework"—our words, actions, postures, gestures, tones of voice, facial expressions, the way we handle time, space, and materials, and the way we work and play (Hall 1976, 42). Each culture has norms and rules for communicating and interacting with others. The meaning of each of these behaviors and actions may be different from one culture to another. What does silence mean? How are questions asked? What does it mean to interrupt? All children learn to understand these actions and behaviors from the beginning of their lives. By the time children enter school, they have achieved what researchers commonly term "communicative competence" within their own culture. And every culture has its own definition of communicative competence.

Each of us interprets what we see and experience through our own "cultural lens." In other words, we interpret what we see or hear from the perspective of our own beliefs, values, and experiences. Therefore, it is always possible to misunderstand or misinterpret the communication style of someone from a different culture.

Consider how this may affect life in the classroom. If children come from a culture different from that of the teacher, the teacher may have difficulty interpreting the children's ways of communicating. The reverse is also likely; some children may not understand the teacher's ways of communicating and interacting. When we fail to take into account the culture of each child we teach, we are in danger of reaching only those children who share our own ways of communicating and interacting. When communication between teachers and children fails, learning also fails.

It is easy to misinterpret the actions and behaviors of others. Was I being interrupted? Whose turn is it to speak now? Is my authority being challenged? What is happening now—aggression or enthusiasm? As educators, it is our responsibility to look for ways to understand the child's actions and perceptions of situations or tasks. The following examples illustrate how culture can influence children's responses to questions, their participation in group experiences, and their participation in sharing times.

Responses to Questions

Shirley Brice Heath (1982) examined the role of questioning in language and socialization to discover why a group of African-American children, from a working class community in a moderate-sized city in the Southeast, seemed unresponsive to questions posed by white teachers. Through her ethnographic study, Heath learned that the predominant characteristic of teacher questioning was the use of closed questions calling for a single answer. For example, (pointing to a picture of an apple) "What is this?" or "What is the name of the person who puts out fires?" In the children's community, questioning took a very different form. Here, people asked questions about whole events or about objects and their uses, causes and effects. Examples of such questions might be: "What did you see at the firehouse?" or "What was happening at the firehouse while you were there?" or "What did you like about the trip?" Community members accepted many answers and ways of answering and their answers almost always involved telling a story, describing a situation, or making comparisons between the event or object described and another known to the audience.

Children were unfamiliar with the kinds of questions teachers were asking. They perceived such questions as silly because the teachers already knew the answer, and therefore they did not respond. Because the children didn't respond, the teachers thought that they did not know the answers. Heath's five-year study documents how differently questions were used within the home and school communities, and identifies additional cultural factors that influenced how children were taught to communicate, or not, with others.

Heath also describes how the teachers in the study, determined to find ways of supporting children's success in school, made accommodations in their practice. First, they began using more open-ended questions such as those listed above. Second, in an effort to build children's repertoire of questioning strategies, they used tape recordings to accompany picture books of "closed questions," which children could use at a listening center.

Group Participation

Susan Philips (1972) studied ways people participate in groups, both in the classroom and in the community, on the Warm Springs Indian Reservation in Central Oregon. By observing Indian children in classrooms with non-Indian teachers, she noted that the children were reluctant to talk during group lessons controlled by the teacher. However, the same children were extremely verbal when interacting with their peers.

Philips suggests that in the classrooms, a basic rule was established right from the start: the teacher controls the activity of the classroom and the student is expected to accept her authority. This includes controlling who will talk and when. However, within the community there is no context in which one person arbitrarily controls another person's actions, and certainly not their talk. Unfamiliar with the unspoken code of the classroom, the children withdrew. Their behavior was misinterpreted by teachers. It was assumed that they were unable to participate in the classroom activities. Misperceptions such as these lead to school failure and low self-esteem in children.

Participation in Group Sharing Time

Sara Michaels and Jenny Cook-Gumperz (1979) observed children's responses to sharing time in a first grade classroom where half the children were white and half African-American. A sharing time was planned by the teacher to offer practice in oral discourse, but the researchers observed significant differences in how children participated.

White children used a style termed "topic-centered" in which the stories were organized and centered on a single topic. African-American children used a "topic-chaining style," moving easily from topic to topic and focusing mainly on personal relations. It appeared to the teacher that these children were simply rambling on because she saw no clear beginning, middle, and end to their stories.

The teacher, who was white, was more familiar with a "topic-centered" style. When African-American children shared their stories, the teacher had difficulty understanding the topic and where the story line was going. Her questions often threw children off balance and stopped them in the middle of a thought. Because of the cultural mismatch between the teacher and the African-American children, white children were given more opportunities to share, got more practice, and received more positive feedback from the teacher. If the teacher had a better understanding of why children shared stories differently, she might have been more sensitive in her responses so that all the children felt comfortable sharing.

Culture and Expectations

What is acceptable behavior in certain situations? Should boys and girls engage in the same kinds of activities? What is appropriate dress for school? What kinds of activities should children be doing in school? What does it mean to work independently? Is it important to work independently? When you complete a project, how do you feel and how are these feelings expressed? Is waving a hand to get attention an indication of disruptive behavior or an expression of enthusiasm? It is natural to assume that our responses to these questions would be the same for all people. However, this is a misperception that often leads to misunderstandings.

Expectations for appropriate behavior, goals for personal achievement, and measures of success are developed within the context of culture and community. Therefore, an important aspect of knowing the children you teach is learning about what expectations the child and the child's family have. When the cultural background of the teacher, or that of the school community is not shared by the child and the child's family, it can result in misunderstandings of what is expected in terms of school behavior and success.

In a research study of classrooms of Hawaiian children, teachers were frustrated because they felt that children were not "doing their own work" (Gallimore, Boggs, Jordan 1974). Teachers perceived children as cheating when they answered one another's questions or sought one another's assistance. In their home culture, this behavior was highly valued. Children were accustomed to helping one another and being helped by siblings and peers more than by adults. When the teachers changed the classroom structure so that collaborative work was encouraged, the children were more successful in their school work.

The following is an example of conflicting expectations between a third grade teacher and the parents of a child in her class:

> *Naoko, a Japanese-American child, is a very competent student, especially excelling in story writing. She has friends in the class and works quietly with them during cooperative activities. During class discussions, Naoko is an active listener, but rarely, if ever, speaks up. In the teacher's culture, verbal interactions are a dominant mode of expression. Her expectations for her students are that they, too, will use oral expression in group discussions as a means of sharing ideas and information. During the first parent conference, the teacher talks enthusiastically about Naoko's work in third grade, but notes her concern about Naoko's lack of oral participation in group discussions. The teacher explains to the parents that she hopes their daughter will become more outgoing in the classroom. The parents leave the conference very upset and*

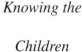
seek the ear of the principal. The principal helps the teacher understand how her personal expectations of what is appropriate and valued behavior are culturally biased. The principal suggests that in their next meeting the teacher should describe the child's classroom activities and ask the parents to talk about their expectations and goals for Naoko.

In situations where the school culture is not shared by the child and the child's family and community, teachers have to work with the family and community to develop shared expectations and views of what it means to be successful in school.

The examples offered above are *not* intended to provide specific insights about particular cultural groups. As discussed earlier in the chapter, when we assign cultural labels to any group we risk promoting stereotypes. Rather, our purpose is to highlight how easy it is to misinterpret a situation because of one's own cultural lens. An essential first step in constructing curriculum that helps all children to succeed is to recognize that each child comes to school with a unique set of cultural and experiential influences that shape how the child learns.

Going Beyond First Impressions and Expectations

First impressions based on physical appearance and initial behavior affect how people relate to each other. Often first impressions are linked to expectations which are rooted in people's culture and experience. When we meet someone for the first time, many thoughts are likely to run through our minds as we react to physical appearance, ethnic/racial identity, or manner of dressing. Expectations and cultural biases, both positive and negative, are likely to determine whether and how we establish a relationship with that person. Of course this applies to teaching children. First impressions can have a significant impact on how teachers get to know and develop a relationship with each child.

Teachers, however, must make a commitment to go beyond first impressions in order to help *all* children learn and to assess them fairly. Appreciating each child's individuality means recognizing differences and setting aside biases. Only when we acknowledge and accept differences and appreciate the ways they add richness to the classroom, can we develop a positive and supportive relationship with each child.

When you take the time to go beyond first impressions by learning about child development, the individual strengths of children, and the influences of culture, you have gone a long way toward getting to know the children you teach. Here are some things you might do at the beginning of the year to acquaint you with the children in your class.

- Begin by taking a walk in the neighborhood near your school with other teachers, and perhaps a parent or family member who lives in the area who can point out interesting things or introduce you to people.
- Gather information by talking to family members about their children so that you will have more information about the particular children in your class.
- Talk to the teachers who had your children last year. Try to find out about the special interests of children.

In the classroom, taking the time to observe and listen to children is both a way to get to know them better, and the beginning of the assessment process. Here are some suggestions:

- Make time during the day for informal conversations with children—at arrival, at snack or lunch time, during reading or writing conferences, or at choice times.
- When you talk informally with children, ask about what they do after school; discuss the weekend; find out who they plan to play with outside of school; find out about particular things they like to do.
- Spend time observing children at work and at play and make some notes about your observations.
- Be an active listener. Concentrate on listening and give children the time they need to construct answers.

If the content of the curriculum is culturally sensitive and diverse, children's self-image and confidence will be protected while they learn new skills and knowledge. There are also specific things you can do to help children feel comfortable no matter what their learning or interactive styles:

- If there are children who do not speak English, try to learn some phrases in the children's primary languages and use them in some classroom experiences.

- Vary the structure of classroom activities. For example, if very few children speak up during class discussions, suggest that children turn and talk with the person next to them to respond to the question. Then, after everyone has had a chance to say something, have a few children volunteer to share with the entire group.

- Vary the type of classroom activities. Some children are more comfortable working and sharing as part of a small group rather than responding to direct questions in front of the whole class. Provide different choices about ways to demonstrate what children have learned through writing, drama, art, music, or building.

Finally, even in situations where there is not much obvious diversity but, perhaps one child who is hearing impaired, Jewish, or Chinese-American, making too much of that child's particular differences may cause discomfort, depending on how the child's family expresses its identity. Children in all classrooms can be exposed to diversity by using books, posters, and videos, inviting visitors to the classroom, and discussing similarities and differences in an atmosphere that conveys acceptance and caring.

Closing Thoughts

Constructing curriculum is a dynamic process, ultimately shaped by the attributes and interests of the children you teach. You learn about the children by understanding child development, recognizing each child's individual characteristics, and appreciating the influence of a child's cultural background. The strategies that follow will help you to build from this base to develop a positive relationship with each of the children in your classroom and ensure their success.

Resources for Knowing the Children You Teach

The Child from Five to Ten. Gesell, Arnold and Francis Ilg. New York: Harper and Row Publishers, 1946.

Childhood and Society. Erikson, Erik. New York: W.W. Norton & Co., 1963.

The Growth and Development of Children, 4th edition. Lee, Catherine. New York: Longman Press, 1990.

The Learning Child: Guidelines for Parents and Teachers. Cohen, Dorothy. New York: Pantheon Press, 1972.

The Middle Years of Childhood. Minuchin, Patricia. Monterey, CA: Brooks Cole Publishing Co., 1977.

Multicultural Education: Issues and Perspectives. Banks, James. Boston: Allyn and Bacon, 1989.

A Notebook for Teachers: Making Changes in the Elementary Curriculum. Greenfield, MA: The Northeast Foundation for Children, 1991.

Observing and Recording the Behavior of Young Children. Cohen, Dorothy, Virginia Stern, and Nancy Balaban. New York: Teachers College Press, 1983.

Open Minds to Equality: A Sourcebook of Learning Activities to Promote Race, Sex, Class and Age Equity. Schniedewind, Nancy and Ellen Davidson. Englewood Cliffs, NJ: Prentice Hall, 1983.

Playground Politics: Understanding the Emotional Life of Your School-Age Child. Greenspan, Stanley I. New York: Addison-Wesley Publishing Co., 1993.

Reaching Potentials: Appropriate Curriculum and Assessment for Young Children, Volume I. Bredekamp, Sue and Teresa Rosegrant. Washington, DC: NAEYC, 1993.

Teaching and Learning in a Diverse World: Multicultural Education for Young Children. New York: Teacher's College Press, 1987.

Valuing Diversity: The Primary Years. McCracken, Janet Brown. Washington, DC: National Association for the Education of Young Children, 1993.

Yardsticks: Children in the Classroom Ages 4-12. Wood, Chip. Greenfield, MA: Northeast Foundation for Children, 1994.

References

Americans with Disabilities Act. 1990. *U.S. Code, Vol. 42,* secs. 12101-12213.

Benard, Bonnie. 1991. *Fostering Resiliency in Kids: Protective Factors in the Family, School, and Community.* Portland: Western Regional Center, Drug Free Schools and Communities, 3-6.

Curry, Nancy and Carl Johnson. 1990. *Beyond Self-Esteem: Developing a Genuine Sense of Human Value.* Washington, DC: NAEYC.

Derman-Sparks, Louise, and The ABC Task Force. 1989. *Anti-Bias Curriculum: Tools for Empowering Young Children.* Washington, DC: NAEYC.

Erikson, Erik. 1963. *Childhood and Society.* New York: W.W. Norton & Co.

Frieman, Barry B. 1993. Separation and Divorce—Children Want Their Teachers to Know: Meeting the Emotional Needs of Preschool and Primary School Children. *Young Children,* (September): 59.

Gallimore, Ronald, Joan Whitehorn Boggs, and Cathie Jordan. 1974. Culture, Behavior and Education: A Study of Hawaiian-Americans. *Volume 11, Sage Library of Social Research.* Beverly Hills, CA: SAGE Publications, Inc.

Gardner, Howard. 1993. *Multiple Intelligences: The Theory in Practice.* New York: Basic Books.

Goodenough, Ward. 1981. *Culture, Language, and Society*. Menlo Park, CA: Benjamin Cummings Publishing.

Hall, Edward. 1976. *Beyond Culture.* New York: Doubleday.

Heath, Shirley Brice. 1982. Questioning at Home and at School: A Comparative Study, Doing the Ethnography of Schooling. In *Educational Anthropology in Action.* Edited by George Spindler. New York: Holt, Rinehart, Winston.

Individuals with Disabilities Education Act. 1991. *U.S. Code, Vol. 20,* secs. 1412 (1), 1412 (5) (B).

Jennings, Peter. January 23, 1992. *Common Miracles: The New Revolution in Learning.* New York: ABC-TV.

Maslow, Abraham H. 1956. Defense and Growth, *Merrill-Palmer Quarterly, III.*

Michaels, Sara and Jenny Cook-Gumperz. 1979. A Study of Sharing Times with First-Grade Students: Discourse Narratives in the Classroom. Paper presented at the Education Research Forum at the University of Pennsylvania.

Philips, Susan. 1972. Participant Structures and Communicative Competence: Warm Springs Children in Community and Classroom. In *Functions of Language in the Classroom.* Edited by Courtney Cazden et al. New York: Teachers College Press.

Piaget, Jean. 1952. *The Origins of Intelligence.* New York: International Universities Press.

Vygotsky, Lev S. 1978. Mind in Society: *The Development of Higher Psychological Functions.* Cambridge, MA: Harvard University Press.

2 BUILDING A CLASSROOM COMMUNITY

Every classroom, like every community, has its own distinct culture, values, and rules. Children belong to many different communities. By building a community in the classroom, teachers create a common and predictable cultural experience that helps children feel connected to others.

A community is a place where individuals share common values, goals, and activities. It is a place where each member takes on roles to provide sufficient services so that the community's goals are reached. In communities, everyone does not do the same thing at the same time, but groups work together to achieve common goals. A community is a place where social bonds are established and individuals can flourish (Bredekamp and Rosegrant 1992, 81).

Because a community is built around the shared interests, values, and goals of its members, the culture of your classroom community changes each year to the next as children change and as you change. One year, you have a group that loves singing, and you make singing an important part of classroom life. Another year, the children become concerned about the welfare of a homeless person who has set up a tent on the street near the school, and the issue of homelessness becomes the focus of a long-term study. You can't tell from one year to the next what dominant interests or events will emerge and how they will define your classroom community and the content for studies.

Building a classroom community is the second strategy for constructing curriculum. This chapter explains how creating a sense of community in the classroom enables teachers to address children's social, emotional, and cognitive development. It describes how teachers build community by making meetings a central part of classroom life, helping children relate positively to others, and teaching children to resolve conflicts peacefully.

The Value of a Classroom Community

The loss of community is a serious problem in today's society, as fewer children and families experience its benefits. Many of us grew up during a time when neighborhoods were communities that nurtured children and families. Families knew their neighbors and shared a common sense of responsibility for everyone who lived in the neighborhood. When children played outdoors, they were under the watchful eye of an adult who would not hesitate to keep them in line if their parents were not present. These caring communities helped children feel safe and gave them a sense of belonging.

Today, families from all socio-economic backgrounds are under varying degrees of stress. Children are the largest percentage of the poor in the United States today. An increasing number of children live in single parent households, or in families in which both parents work. Many parents juggle hectic schedules that allow them little time or energy to be with their children. Television has become a babysitter for many children who come home to empty houses. Parents do not feel it is safe to let their children play outdoors. As a result, many children grow up lacking the social experiences that would help them develop the skills needed for cooperative living.

The opportunity to participate as a contributing member of a community is essential for children's well-being and academic success. A classroom community enables teachers to address children's basic needs, promote their resilience to hardship conditions, teach the values of respect and responsibility, and foster their social and academic competence.

Addressing Children's Basic Needs

For children to participate in a classroom community—to relate positively to others and become successful learners—their basic needs for sustenance, safety, and belonging must be met. Abraham Maslow's "Hierarchy of Needs" (1955) illustrates that having one's basic needs met is the foundation for building "higher levels" of knowing and understanding.

Physiological needs are the most basic needs of all living creatures. Children who are hungry think about their bellies instead of learning. Efforts to teach a hungry child are destined to fail. This is why many schools provide breakfast, snacks, and lunch for children who otherwise might not receive a balanced meal, or any meal, before coming to school.

Safety is the feeling of security, comfort, and being out of danger. For many children today, danger has replaced the sense of safety they need in order to thrive. These children may live in communities where violent acts happen every day, and they have had experiences that threaten their feelings of safety. Children need to feel that they will be safe in school and that no harm will come to them. When teachers create a safe classroom community, children are able to relate positively to others, explore their environment, and engage in learning.

Belongingness—feeling accepted and loved—is the third level of need. Children who do not experience a sense of belonging deem themselves unworthy of being loved or accepted. In an effort to seek acceptance and love from adults, these children often exhibit behavior that tests acceptance—acting out and attacking others because they are angry or hurt. They expect to be rejected and therefore behave in ways that prove to everyone around them that they are worthy of rejection. These children need adults who can create a classroom environment where everyone feels accepted and valued.

Self-esteem—a sense of one's own worth—is the fourth basic need. Children acquire self-esteem when they do things every day that make them feel competent. If the important adults in their lives regularly shame and belittle them in an effort to make them conform and behave, children hear the following messages:

> "You are a failure."

> "You can't do it right."

> "You will never be able to do it."

Young children are especially vulnerable to the messages they receive from others. It takes many positive experiences to build a child's self-esteem, but very few to undermine a child's confidence. Children who feel good about themselves are more open to new experiences, better able to empathize with others, and more willing to persevere in learning tasks than are children with low self-esteem.

Maslow's Hierarchy of Needs

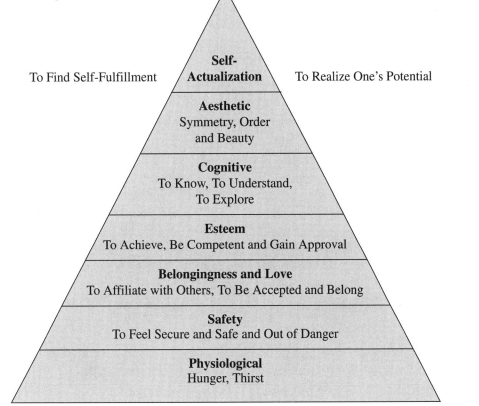

To Find Self-Fulfillment — To Realize One's Potential

Self-Actualization

Aesthetic
Symmetry, Order and Beauty

Cognitive
To Know, To Understand, To Explore

Esteem
To Achieve, Be Competent and Gain Approval

Belongingness and Love
To Affiliate with Others, To Be Accepted and Belong

Safety
To Feel Secure and Safe and Out of Danger

Physiological
Hunger, Thirst

Applying Maslow's Theory to the Classroom

Learning the first four basic needs in Maslow's Hierarchy will shed light on why some children may be unresponsive, aggressive, or self-destructive in the classroom. When children's basic needs have not been met, it has a profound affect on their ability to learn and to relate positively to others. Creating a caring community in the classroom is one of the most effective strategies for addressing children's basic needs for physical and emotional comfort so that they can be open to learning and feel hopeful about the future.

Promoting Resiliency

You may have children in your classroom whose sense of security and safety is threatened. These children may live in chaotic and disruptive circumstances that jeopardize their emotional well-being. Some have had first-hand experience with violence in their neighborhoods or in their own homes. They may be neglected or abused. These children often have fears and anger that they cannot express or describe in words. Unable to control their anger, they may act out, become withdrawn, or be unresponsive in class.

While teachers cannot completely counter the effects of hardship conditions on a child, a caring and effective teacher can do much to promote a child's resilience. If you take time to learn about the life circumstances and experiences of the children in your class, you can more effectively address their fears and concerns and help them to develop coping skills. By creating a safe and caring environment in the classroom, children will be able to experience a positive and productive sense of their own power, a feeling that many children do not have in other life settings.

Environmental Factors That Support Resiliency

In the previous chapter we discussed four characteristics that are commonly found in children who show resiliency in the face of difficult life circumstances. These characteristics include social competence, problem-solving skills, a strong sense of independence, and a sense of purpose and hope for a better future. New research points to three factors in the child's environment that can support resiliency (Benard 1991). In the classroom, these environmental factors include *caring and support*, *high expectations*, and opportunities for *participation*.

Caring and Support. Children who are able to succeed in school and in life in spite of overwhelming difficulties get a great deal of emotional support either from a family member or someone outside their immediate family. Many children mention a favorite teacher who had become a role model, friend, and confidant, and who was particularly supportive when their own family was unable to cope with overwhelming problems (Clark 1990; Werner 1990).

Teachers can provide a great deal of emotional support, thus offering children a refuge from troubled family life. Children also benefit enormously from positive relationships with their peers. Creating a community in the classroom where children learn how to relate positively to others can promote their resiliency as well as their learning.

High Expectations. Teachers who hold high expectations for all their students, and offer them the support they need to achieve, can promote positive outcomes for children from even the most stressful backgrounds. Classroom experiences that allow children to use their individual talents (e.g., in music, art, and sports, as well as language and logical thinking) enable every child to experience success in the classroom.

When children receive daily messages that others see them as capable and caring people, they come to believe in themselves and strive to live up to these expectations. Their self-esteem grows, they achieve socially and academically, and schools report fewer emotional and behavioral disturbances (Rutter 1979).

Participation. Children need opportunities to participate actively, to belong, and to exercise some control over their lives. They are empowered in a classroom where they are able to make choices during the day, to establish goals for themselves, to make decisions about their community, and to undertake work that is meaningful and engaging.

Participating in a classroom community provides children with countless opportunities to be part of a dynamic group, letting them see how the behavior of one person affects others. They feel competent when they help a peer understand a math problem and feel comfortable when they ask for help. All children benefit from the experience of working together to create a safe, comfortable environment for all.

Teaching Respect and Responsibility

Schools of the past taught values and morals as part of the curriculum. The McGuffey Readers, for example, conveyed the values that underlie a democratic society: respect, responsibility, justice, and equality.

In the 1970s and '80s, there was a debate about whether it was appropriate for schools to teach values. If schools teach values, it was argued, whose values should be taught? Many educators became uneasy about teaching morals and therefore schools tended to avoid the issue entirely. This failure to agree on the importance of teaching basic values that underlie a democratic society is cited by some teachers as contributing to the poor behavior of children: their lack of discipline, inability to empathize with the suffering of others, disrespect towards their elders, cruelty towards peers, acceptance of violence as a way to resolve conflicts, and materialism.

Thomas Lickona, in his book *Educating for Character*, discusses the need for schools to return to teaching morals. He states:

> Children learn morality by living it. They need to be in a community—to interact, form relationships, work out problems, grow as a group, and learn directly, from their first-hand experience, lessons about fair play, cooperation, forgiveness, and respect for the worth and dignity of every individual (Lickona 1992, 90).

Participating in a classroom community can teach children two very important values: *respect* for self and for others, and a sense of *responsibility* for self, the community, and the environment. These values are central to a democratic society.

In a classroom community, children can learn to recognize and accept differences. They have countless opportunities to hear other points of view and to express their own ideas. They experience first-hand how a diverse group of people can work and play together harmoniously. The classroom community is a place to confront bias, teach respect, and demonstrate how differences can be resolved without resorting to verbal or physical abuse.

For children to understand, believe, and live by the values of respect and responsibility, those values should guide all interactions with children, instructional approaches, and the content teachers address in the curriculum.

Promoting Children's Social and Academic Competence

A central concern for children six to eight years old is their relationships with peers. Children want to know that their peers find them competent and worthy of respect. Out of peer acceptance grows self-acceptance. Therefore, the children you teach are likely to be preoccupied with answering the following questions:

- Do I fit in with the group?
- Am I accepted by others?
- Do I have friends?
- How do I measure up to others?
- Am I competent?

To achieve acceptance, children must acquire social competence—the ability to relate positively to others and to make friends. Research points to the connection between social competence and academic success (Clark 1992; Pellegrini and Glickman 1991). Children who are able to work cooperatively with their peers, to use adults and classmates as resources, and who have friends themselves are more likely to succeed academically and lead fulfilling lives.

This connection between social competence and academic success is of critical importance to teachers who are held accountable for meeting curriculum goals established by the school system, and who find that they have to teach social skills first. Social skills directly tied to academic success include the abilities to:

- share ideas with others;
- listen when others are speaking;
- take turns and share;
- compromise;
- accept different points of view;
- negotiate in order to build consensus;
- take appropriate risks without fear of failure;
- respect another person's belongings and physical space.

Social competence can be taught and nurtured most effectively when children are young, before negative behavior patterns become entrenched. Children who do not develop social skills in the early years are more likely to act out in serious ways that interfere with their learning: becoming disruptive in the classroom, attacking their peers, failing to do their work, and dropping out of school.

Supporting Inclusion of All Children

Building a classroom community is one of the most effective ways to fully integrate children with disabilities in the classroom. Membership in a classroom community has proven to be a leading factor in successful mainstreaming (Jorgenson 1992). It involves inclusion in all aspects of the classroom—in responsibilities, jobs, projects with partners, special events, and in the use of the same equipment and materials. The teacher can make sure that every child feels involved in the life of the classroom.

Children with disabilities may have been treated differently in other settings and may even have come to expect rejection from a group. Barriers, exclusion, and teasing have a devastating effect on the child who is left out, and also harm the children who are excluding. The teaching of respect and inclusion is a central part of the curriculum. In a classroom community where meetings take place throughout the day, children have opportunities to learn about one another, to express feelings, to talk about differences, and to ask questions in a safe environment.

It is hard work for teachers to model respectful interactions and to demonstrate through their actions and words that all members are accepted and appreciated for their contributions. This kind of modeling first requires an examination of your own feelings about including a child with special needs in your classroom. It may be new to you and you may be unsure of how to deal with a child's particular disability. Often, another child in the class becomes an unexpected resource and demonstrates how to relate to and support a child with disabilities. And, as stated in the previous chapter, the child with a disability can often suggest ways he or she wants to be supported and included.

The approaches to building a classroom community that are described in the remainder of this chapter will help you to address the social and emotional needs of all children, including those with special needs, and to promote every child's academic success. Teachers build a classroom community by:

- welcoming children to the classroom community;
- holding daily class meetings to share ideas and discuss issues of importance to group living;
- helping children relate positively to others;
- teaching children to solve problems and resolve conflicts peacefully.

Welcoming Children to the Classroom Community

Teachers start building a classroom community before school begins. Preparing for the children's arrival can give children consistent messages about what a teacher expects and values and can prevent many problems. Many teachers lament halfway into the school year, "I wish I could start over with my group and achieve a better sense of order in my classroom." Prevention is always the best cure.

Try to put yourself in the place of the children who will be entering your classroom for the first time. What are they likely to worry about before school starts? Typically, young children want to know:

- Will I have friends?
- Is the teacher going to like me?
- How will I know what to do?
- Can I do the work?
- How will I find the bathrooms?
- When is lunch?
- Will I be comfortable and safe in school?
- Is the teacher going to take care of me?
- Will I lose the things I bring to school?

Try to anticipate children's concerns from the first day. If you do this successfully, children will learn that the classroom is a safe place, that they belong, and that you are a person they can trust.

Planning for the First Days

In the days and weeks before school opens, you can take steps to build a classroom community. Contacting children and families, arranging the classroom and displays, learning children's names, and planning initial activities will help you feel prepared.

Contacts with Children and Families

You can begin to build a relationship with children and their families by sending a postcard or letter introducing yourself and welcoming them to your classroom. You can also call each family or arrange a home visit, as discussed in the chapter on Families. If feasible, extend an invitation to visit the classroom when you know you will be there setting up so children and family members can meet you and see the classroom.

Some teachers give children an opening week assignment that fosters community building such as bringing an object to school in a paper bag that shows a particular interest they have. During class meetings they play 20 Questions to figure out what each child has brought. This builds a sense of community by enabling everyone to learn something significant about each member of the class.

Classroom Displays

How you set up the room will convey powerful messages to the children. There's no need to spend a lot of money or time on lavish bulletin board displays. A sparsely decorated room with lots of space for children's work conveys the message: "This is your space and your work will be displayed here." You might display objects or pictures related to what children will be studying at the beginning of the year. In another place, display photographs of all the children in the class. Include your own picture and those of any other significant adults who will be involved in children's lives at school.

If you are not able to obtain pictures of all the children before school, you might take pictures of children as they arrive, or have them draw self-portraits.

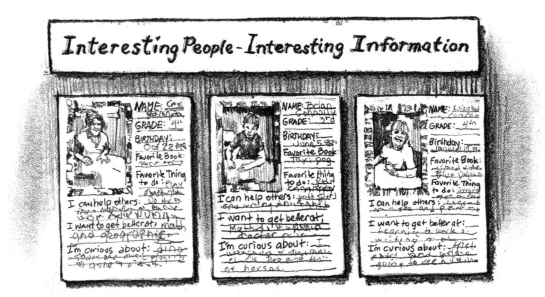

Children's Names

All of us are connected to our names; they are part of our identity and are often related to family history. Children with unusual names are often teased by their peers. They may become confused when teachers fail to pronounce their names properly. The importance of properly pronouncing children's names cannot be overstated. Before school begins, look over the class list and identify names that are unfamiliar and challenging to pronounce. The child's last teacher or school guidance counselor may be able to help you. Or, make a phone call to the child's family before school begins. Taking the time to learn the proper pronunciation of a child's name conveys to the child and family a positive message of respect.

Many teachers plan activities during the first weeks of school that help everyone learn names. Some activities include the following:

- Singing songs and playing games during meetings that use children's names, such as "My Name Is" and "Cookie Jar."
- Having children create and decorate labels for their cubbies, journals, and message boxes.
- Having discussions on ways we are all the same and ways we are different. Charts generated from these discussions can be displayed in the classroom near the photographs.
- Assigning each child to a partner and having them interview one another. The children make graphs of the data collected on topics such as favorite foods, colors, pets, TV programs. This activity encourages social interaction among classmates.
- Hanging up the alphabet in the classroom and displaying the children's names next to the corresponding letter.

Initial Activities

The activities you offer children when they first arrive should be carefully selected. As much as possible, choose activities that the children can do independently or with one or more children, such as drawing pictures of themselves, exploring with manipulative materials, or playing a board game. This will engage children so that you can respond easily to individuals or small groups.

Orienting Children to the Environment

To help children feel they belong, plan time to introduce children to the classroom environment, to teach them the systems for routines, and to show them around the school.

Talking About the Classroom Organization

In setting up your classroom, begin with basic materials that you know the children can handle successfully—art materials such as paper, markers, pencils, and glue, two or three kinds of manipulatives, puzzles, a few board games, and a selection of books. Children can easily become overwhelmed by a classroom that appears cluttered and offers too many choices.

At the very first meeting you might ask the children, "What do you notice about our classroom?" The responses will tell you what attracts the children's attention and what they focus on. The question itself conveys that you care about their perceptions. As children become more familiar with the classroom environment, you can reinforce the principle that everything has a place by asking questions such as the following:

> *"Suppose I wanted to read a book. Where would I find one? Where could I go to read it?"*
>
> *"What if I wanted to write a story or draw a picture? Who can show us where to find the materials I would need?"*

Do not assume that children know how to use basic materials. Everything in the classroom should, therefore, be introduced to the children. In the beginning, this may be done during class meetings and involve the whole group. You will want to take children's previous experiences with materials into account and might begin by asking what they already know about using a particular object. Later on, you can introduce a new game or set of materials to a small group of children and ask them to teach the other children. (Room arrangement and introducing materials to children are explained in detail in the next chapter on Establishing a Structure for the Classroom.)

Systems for Using the Bathroom

The location of the bathrooms and procedure for using them is likely to be a concern of the children. Like adults, children don't all have to go to the bathroom at the same time and they prefer to have privacy. If the bathrooms are not connected to your room, set up a procedure to keep track of who is out of the room and when.

One system for using the bathroom might be to have children go with a buddy and place their name tags in an envelope by the door indicating that they are out the room using the bathroom. Teachers of older children find it's best to allow one child at a time to use the bathroom; otherwise there is a tendency for two friends to stay out together for long periods. Another idea is to hang two signs on the door—one for boys and one for girls. One side of each sign says STOP (to indicate the bathroom is occupied) and the other says GO.

Children will feel secure if they know that they can comfortably use the bathroom when necessary.

Learning About the School

Children who are new to the school will have to learn where important places such as the cafeteria, the library, the gym, and the main office are located. You can pair these children with classmates who are familiar with the school until the newcomers learn their way around.

Introducing children to the classroom and school environment is an ongoing task. If you try to accomplish too much in the first few days, children can become overwhelmed. Even after several weeks, expect children to still say, "Can I go to the bathroom?" or, "Where should I use this game?" or, "I forget how to find the library." A friendly reminder will be reassuring.

Teaching the Signal for Quiet

For many reasons including safety, it helps to have a way of getting children's immediate attention and achieving order in the classroom. When the noise level becomes disruptive or you have a direction or reminder to give the class, you need some way to achieve quiet. Whatever signal you adopt—raising your hand, clapping a rhythm, ringing a triangle, turning off lights—you will want to introduce it to the children on the first day.

Plan to spend time letting children practice responding to the signal. After introducing the signal and explaining its importance, you might say, "Now that you know the signal for quiet, we're going to see how it works. Whenever you see (or hear) the signal, stop what you are doing, look, and listen."

Positive reinforcement will go a long way, even if you don't achieve an immediate response in the beginning. Each time you use the signal, say something such as: "You did a good job of remembering what to do. Let's see if next time we can stop a little more quickly." Let children know that you expect them to respond immediately and affirm them when they do. Don't hesitate to wait for every child to do what you are asking. This is particularly important in the beginning when you want to convey very clearly that this is an important rule and it must be followed by everyone.

Having welcomed children into the classroom community, you can introduce them to one of the most important components of classroom life—daily group meetings.

Building a Classroom Community

Using Meetings to Build a Sense of Community

The meeting area of your classroom is the center of community life. Participating in group meetings enables children to learn what it means to be part of a community where all members exchange ideas and listen to one another. The ability to speak and listen effectively, to make choices, and to settle differences when they arise, are critically important to the functioning of any community. There will always be issues that need to be addressed; people have different points of view and will sometimes disagree. By addressing differences in a group meeting, rather than imposing solutions and rules on children, teachers show that every member of the community has a right to contribute ideas, and has a stake in the outcomes. In accepting each person's contributions and working towards consensus, teachers convey the messages that there are many possible solutions to problems and that the group can make decisions together.

Meetings provide a forum for children to engage in group discussions on interesting topics. They also enable teachers to model and actively teach communication skills such as: how to speak so others will understand, how to listen respectfully when others are speaking, and how to solve problems and contribute to the group. All these skills are necessary for successful classroom life, collaborative learning, and conflict resolution.

Types of Meetings

Teachers have class meetings whenever they want to talk with the whole group. Some meetings, such as the first meeting of the day, become part of the daily classroom routine.

Others are called for a particular lesson or event, or to handle a problem. Each type of meeting serves a different purpose and contributes to the establishment of a shared sense of community.

Meetings to Start the Day

The purpose of the first meeting of the day is to convene as a group and help children make the transition from home to school. It's a time to welcome everyone, review the schedule, and reveal specific plans for the day. During this first meeting, children may share stories from outside of school and discuss ideas related to an aspect of the curriculum.

In some classrooms, a group meeting is the first event of the day. In others, especially where children do not all arrive at the same time, teachers set out small group tasks, such as math games or puzzles, for children to do during the first ten to fifteen minutes of the morning. Other teachers have a journal writing time, or encourage children to check homework with a buddy. Group tasks such as these allow children to ease into the classroom at their own pace and work with two or three classmates before joining the whole group for a meeting.

The first meeting is a time to set the stage for the day's work. Because children this age like predictability, many teachers follow a routine that children can look forward to each morning. Welcoming routines might include:

- greeting each child in the class;
- reviewing a morning message;
- reciting a poem the group has learned or singing a song;
- introducing the next activity with a short lesson.

As children gain experience and skills, some teachers have the children take turns leading part of the morning meeting.

The morning message has become a tradition in many primary classrooms. Teachers write a different welcoming message each day, highlighting what will happen. During the meeting, the message is read by the teacher, or by the whole group together, or a different child may read each line, depending on the reading skills of the children. This can be a "shared reading" experience that allows the teacher to demonstrate that reading is purposeful, and also models journal writing. Children often use the message chart during the day as a resource, so it is a good idea to display it in a prominent place in the classroom. (The chapter on Language and Literacy describes shared reading experiences in detail.)

How the message is written and what it says depend upon the age of the children and what a teacher might want to emphasize during the meeting. In the sample message that follows, the teacher has repeated several phrases to help beginning readers identify some commonly used words.

> Good morning.
> Today is November 7, 1994.
> Today we will read.
> Today we will go to the gym.
> Today we will work on projects.
> Today we will plan our trip.

For an older group, the message would include more complex sentences. By third grade, the message might be in cursive.

> November 7, 1994
> Hello everyone!
> Check your homework with a partner before meeting.
> Think about this: What do you think our
>   neighborhood looked like 100 years ago?
> We will discuss this at meeting this morning.
> We will have music this afternoon.

The content of the meeting and the written message depend on the teaching goals for the day. If you intend to focus on patterns in math, the message might be written in a color pattern. After asking the children if they notice anything unusual about the message, you can then introduce the pattern activities. If a trip is planned for the next day, the message can remind everyone of the trip and the meeting might focus on where the group will go and what they have to do to get ready.

The first meeting of the day is an opportunity for substantive discussion around topics the children are studying. Part Two of *Constructing Curriculum* offers many examples of using meetings to involve children in the intellectual content of discussions.

No matter how you decide to conduct your first meeting of the day, keep in mind that the goal is to come together as a group and set a tone of togetherness and purposeful work.

Meetings at Transition Times

During any school day there are numerous transitions—returning to the classroom after gym, preparing for lunch, concluding a work time, cleaning up, preparing for a trip, or simply moving from one activity of the day to the next. For some children, these are difficult periods because they lack a clear sense of direction. Brief meetings at transitions help provide a bridge, making these times of the day run more smoothly.

Teachers sometimes begin a transitional meeting before everyone is in the room or sitting down. This keeps some children from waiting endlessly, and gives the dawdler a reason to hurry.

Transitional meetings may be used to review what the children have been doing, to share results of their work, or to assign specific tasks for cleaning up the room. They can also be a time to share news, play a group game like 20 Questions, talk about a math challenge, or read a poem.

Meetings for Discussions

When teachers want children to participate in a group discussion, they convene the children in the meeting area. It is important to conduct discussions so that children can talk to one another rather than simply to you. Introducing a lesson in the meeting area reinforces the idea that you want children to express ideas and learn from one another. Returning to the meeting area after work time allows children to talk about what they have done and reflect upon their learning.

Discussions related to a study might include generating a list of what children already know about a topic and what they want to find out. Meetings throughout the study are opportunities for teachers to assess what children are learning. Children can use meetings to share stories they have written or discoveries they have made during an investigation.

Meetings can also focus on issues related to community life. Topics might include:

- planning jobs for the classroom;
- establishing rules;
- discussing a problem;
- introducing a new game or set of materials;
- planning a classroom celebration.

Involving children in generating ideas and making decisions that affect the classroom community makes children feel respected and empowered.

Emergency or Impromptu Meetings

In any classroom, situations arise that need to be addressed immediately or that offer a wonderful teachable moment that merits interrupting work time to bring the group together.

If several children are breaking one of the class rules and their behavior is making it difficult for others to work, you might convene the group to discuss the problem.

> *In Ms. Crowley's second grade, several children are hoarding gold and silver colored pencils, keeping them in their cubbies. Two children who can't find the pencils they need bring this to her attention. She calls a meeting to discuss the problem. Leading a discussion on why these colors are most popular, and what children's concerns are, she reminds them that classroom materials belong to everyone. She guides them to think about how it feels when you can't find what you need. She introduces the words "hoard" and "communal."*

Impromptu meetings may be called to share something exciting and important such as an unexpected visitor who has something interesting to share with the class, or a discovery made by a child.

> *During a work time in her K-first grade classroom, Ms. Hansen calls an impromptu meeting. She explains that Marcus is having a problem with his journal writing and asks him to describe the problem. "I keep trying to write the word 'made' but it keeps coming out 'mad' and I don't know how else to write it!" Ms. Hansen writes both words on a chart and shows the children the "silent e" rule.*

Impromptu or emergency meetings are called when a teacher feels that a topic is worth the interruption. If they are called too frequently, children will experience them as a nuisance and will be less enthusiastic. When used selectively, however, they can be very effective.

Children themselves can call impromptu meetings when they want to share an important discovery or resolve a common problem. You will know that children are becoming self-directed learners when they begin to take initiative in appropriately assembling the class for meetings.

Coming Together at the End of the Day

At the end of each school day, children leave the school community and return to another community. A group meeting brings closure to the day and allows children to leave the classroom on a positive note. Teachers can use this meeting to read aloud, review the day, discuss something important that happened, and talk about plans for the following day.

Thinking about what happens in the classroom each day enhances children's learning. Discussing the events of the day also gives children something specific to talk about when they get home. Classroom discussions can be documented, thus providing a history of the classroom community.

Ms. Nguyen's third grade ends each day by gathering in the meeting area and recording responses to the day in a "Class Journal." After clean-up, she and the children spend three to five minutes talking about what they feel was special about the day. Ms. Nguyen asks the children to decide on four or five ideas that they want recorded in the Class Journal. The Journal has become a popular independent reading book. When family members visit the classroom, children eagerly share its contents.

Another way to keep a record of classroom life is on a calendar. Rather than discussing the calendar at the beginning of the day, it can become the focus of an end-of-the-day meeting to record what was significant about the day. Younger children can draw a picture of something they want to remember; older children can write down their thoughts.

The end-of-the-day meeting is also a time to evaluate what members of the classroom community liked about the day and what they might want to change. Such discussions convey a commitment to continually work to make community life more comfortable and productive for everyone. Finally, teachers can preview what children will do the next day, thus setting the stage for returning to the classroom community.

Making Class Meetings Effective

The value of class meetings can be realized when teachers take the time to teach children how to participate effectively. How children gather in the meeting area and the length of the meeting are as important as helping children develop skills in speaking and listening. Teachers must also allow for individual differences in conducting meetings; not all children participate in the same ways.

Gathering the Children in the Meeting Area

As stated earlier, one of the first decisions you will probably make in setting up your classroom is where you will have meetings. Since meetings involve exchanging ideas, a circle or square arrangement enables children to see and listen to one another. It conveys the message that each person is a part of the group and all contributions are valued equally.

It may be necessary to teach the children how to form a circle. If meetings take place on a rug, you have a natural boundary to guide children. In some classrooms, children sit on benches arranged in a horseshoe or square.

Who is sitting next to whom is an issue that will undoubtedly arise with six to eight year olds. Some children always sit together, and others tend to feel excluded. To address this issue, consider these suggestions:

- Make name cards (or have children make their own on the first day) and place them on the floor where you want children to sit. This gives you a chance to vary who sits next to whom.
- Draw a picture of the seating arrangement showing where each child is to sit, and post the picture in the meeting area. The arrangement can be changed at regular intervals. This also teaches children mapping skills.
- Establish different rules for seating arrangements. One week, have the children sit in alphabetical order by first names. Another time children might sit by last names. Invite the children to come up with their own ideas for how they might sit in the circle; they may surprise you with their creative responses to this task!

Some teachers vary the seating arrangement when they read picture books aloud. Arranging the children in three rows—using masking tape on the floor to indicate where to sit—ensures that everyone can see the book.

Limiting the Time

One way to kill the effectiveness of meetings is to allow them to drag on beyond the children's ability to stay involved. A short, effective meeting is preferable to one that is too long and tries to accomplish too much.

In the beginning of the year, 15 minutes may be as much time as children can successfully sustain attention in a meeting. A great deal depends on children's experience, their age, and how engaged they are in the topic or activity. Carefully observe children to determine what works best.

Teaching Children to Speak and Listen Effectively

Speaking and listening are essential life-long skills. Class meetings are an ideal time to teach these skills. By having daily opportunities to talk and listen to others, children can become effective communicators.

It helps to have a few simple rules about speaking and listening and to remind the children of these rules at the beginning of each meeting. You might spend one class meeting brainstorming ideas on what it means to be a good listener and speaker. As children volunteer ideas, list them on a chart. The rules that emerge might be:

- Raise your hand if you want to speak.
- Look at the person talking.
- Speak to everyone, not just the teacher.

Display the rules in the meeting area and reinforce the behaviors for effective listening by explicitly pointing out what you are doing so that children understand them.

As in all aspects of the curriculum, teachers constantly observe children to determine the amount of support and guidance each child needs. You will find that when children feel they have been listened to and when they trust that they will get a turn, they become better listeners. At first, you may have to make this explicit by saying, "Jason will go first and then it will be Shontelle's turn." This helps Shontelle listen because she knows she will get her turn. The following chart presents some specific ways in which teachers can promote children's speaking and listening skills.

What You Do	What You Might Say
Model what you want children to do.	*"Notice how I look in the direction of the person who is talking so I can hear better."*
Reinforce what you are doing by calling attention to it.	*"I'm using my loud voice so everyone can hear."* *"When I talk, I look at everyone."*
Remind children about using good listening skills.	*"It's now Nisha's turn. If you look in Nisha's direction, it will be easier to hear what she has to say."*
Give children guidance on what to do if they can't hear.	*"If you can't hear someone who is talking, raise your hand so they know to speak louder."*
When necessary, restate what a child has said to clarify.	*"Lonnie, Susan says she also thinks the Little Red Hen should share her bread. But she wants to know why you think so."*
Ask questions to encourage children to expand on what they are saying.	*"Could you say more about what you mean?"* *"Is there anything else you want to add?"*
Include everyone in the discussion.	*"Does anyone want to comment or ask a question?"*

Allowing for Individual Differences

Teachers must always be sensitive to individual and cultural differences that affect a child's level of participation in group meetings. Put any group of people together and some will speak up right away, dominating the discussion. The quiet people may be full of good ideas that rarely get shared. One of the responsibilities of teachers is to ensure that all children feel comfortable in a group meeting.

Cultural groups have various styles of communicating. Some families expect and encourage children to participate fully in discussions. Others expect children to listen and respond only when requested to speak. In some cultures, it is appropriate to talk about your personal characteristics (e.g., "I'm good at _____."); in others this is seen as bragging. Different cultures also have different modes of questioning and responding. (See the discussion on cultural differences in the previous chapter.)

Teachers must be knowledgeable about and respectful of many different styles of participation in order to nurture appropriate speaking skills in children and to communicate effectively with parents. Classroom goals may differ from home practices and these goals will have to be discussed with parents. Children who are reluctant to talk in a group may benefit from opportunities to practice one-on-one with their teacher or in a small group before they are encouraged to talk to the whole class.

Helping Children Relate Positively to Others

The ability to relate positively to others and to make friends is essential in a classroom community. A central approach to instruction is collaborative learning, and its success depends on the ability of children to work with their peers in ways that promote learning and self-esteem. Children whose lives are programmed with a regular series of activities, or who spend much of their time alone watching television, may have limited experience playing with peers and few opportunities to develop important social skills. Teachers can help children learn to relate positively to others by:

- modeling respectful interactions;
- promoting children's sense of competence;
- helping children make friends;
- teaching children how to work collaboratively.

Modeling Respectful Interactions

Children learn from what they see. Caring, empathetic teachers set a powerful example. When children are treated with respect, they are more likely to treat others the same way. If children have a positive relationship with you, they will want to imitate you.

Teachers model respectful interactions as they welcome children each morning and send them home at the end of the day. In all their interactions during the day, they treat children with the same respect they give adults. As powerful as this modeling may be, many teachers find it necessary to reinforce the message with coaching and direct teaching of respectful interactions.

Greetings and Good-byes

Your first and last contacts with children each day help set a classroom tone of warmth and acceptance. These contacts also establish a transition between school and home that gives children something to talk about.

Greet children by name when they arrive, and use a warm and welcoming tone of voice to convey that you are genuinely interested in every child. Try to think of something specific and personal to say every day.

> *"Good morning, Jeremy. I didn't realize until after you left yesterday what a good job you and Tyrell did organizing our writing tools. It will be so much easier for us all to find things. Thank you. You've both made this a better place for us all to work."*

> *"Welcome back, Cody. I know you're glad to be finished with the miserable chicken pox! We all missed you. Shannon said she wants you to join their project. She'll help you to catch up."*

"Buenos días, José. I'm looking forward to reading the story you were working on yesterday."

A good way to introduce children to the concept of linguistic diversity is to collect, display, and use greetings in the home languages of children in the class. Dismissal time provides another opportunity to model the behaviors that you want the children to learn. Some teachers like to establish certain routines in their classroom, such as shaking hands with each child as they say good-bye. This ensures that they connect with everyone. Use children's names when you address them and try to mention something that you noticed, heard, or appreciated about each child.

"Tyrell, I want you to know how much I appreciate the way you helped your reading buddy today. You have become a very good reader this year!"

"Damen, I hope your Mom is feeling better. Let me know how she likes the card you made her today."

When you say something encouraging and personally meaningful to every child at dismissal time, you send the child off with a positive message and a good feeling about life at school. Even if the day didn't go well for some children, you can offer a message of hope for the next day.

"Sonia, I know you were upset because you couldn't finish your project. Some things take longer than we expect. Tomorrow during choice time you can work on it."

"Today was a hard day, wasn't it Crystal? We'll work together to make tomorrow better."

If you don't have time to give every child a personal farewell you can praise the whole class for something they did well.

"I was so proud of the way you listened to each other during our meeting today. I know our visitor tomorrow will appreciate your good listening skills."

When children leave school every day feeling that they have accomplished something important, they feel competent. If they feel accepted by their peers and teachers, children will look forward to coming back each day.

Treating Children with Respect

The way we treat other adults, especially our friends, is a good guide for our interactions with children. Sometimes adults treat children in less than respectful ways by using baby talk, ignoring their ideas, or saying things like:

"How many times have I told you _____?"

"Can't you see I'm busy now?"

"EXCUSE ME. I was talking and you rudely interrupted me."

"I don't have time for this nonsense. Go finish your work."

If we want children to use words such as "please" and "thank you" and "I'm sorry for interrupting," then we must remember to use these terms regularly in the classroom.

When you are talking to a child or a small group and another child interrupts, you might not be able to respond immediately. Instead, you could put your hand on the child's shoulder to indicate that you are aware of the child's presence and continue with your conversation. When you are finished, turn to the child and say, "Now I can help you." If the child has trouble waiting and interrupts again, you could say, "Excuse me Sara, I'm in the middle of giving this group directions. I'll be with you in a minute. What can you do while you are waiting?" Of course there are times when an interruption is necessary and appropriate. You can teach children how to do this politely by coaching them to say: "I'm sorry to interrupt but… "

When another adult comes into the classroom and interrupts a teacher working with a child or a group of children, often the teacher immediately stops to respond. This conveys to the child that the adult's need comes first. If you feel the visitor can wait, you can say to the adult, "I'll be with you in a moment. I'm almost finished giving Allie my comments on her story." This response gives the message that your work with the child is important to you and also that you are polite to others.

Sometimes a visitor cannot wait. In this case, you can still model respectful interactions by saying something like the following: "Allie, would you hold our spot while I talk to Ms. Thompson for a minute? She doesn't have much time and I want to spend a bit longer with you." This lets the child know you believe her work matters a great deal and notifies the visiting adult that you can't take very much time.

Teaching Children What to Say and Do

Sometimes modeling is not sufficient; teachers have to be more active about teaching children how to interact in respectful ways. You might take the role of a coach, pointing out why a particular interaction may have failed and giving an alternative suggestion on the spot.

> *Ms. Richardson knew that Carly was getting frustrated when she overheard her say to Michelle and Latitia, "You've had that game too long, I want it," and she was ignored. She took Carly aside and said quietly, "Go try that again. This time, instead of demanding a turn, try saying, 'I'd like to watch you play the game. When you're finished, I want to play.' See what happens."*

Direct teaching of respectful interactions helps children develop social skills. Teachers can also send positive messages through group experiences such as the following:

- Reading books to generate discussions on the topic of being respectful.
- Doing role plays or puppet shows to illustrate disrespectful ways to talk to others or handle a conflict and respectful alternatives.
- Encouraging respectful behavior when the group eats together, acknowledging the server, and making sure everyone is served.

Teaching children what to say and do can be very effective, but only when combined with modeling. Keep in mind that teaching children to interact in respectful ways is not a one-week course; all of these approaches continue throughout the year.

Promoting Children's Sense of Competence

Experiencing success in school work can help children acquire the self-confidence they need to relate positively to others. Children who are given tasks they don't understand may feel stupid and lose confidence in themselves. In a classroom where the curriculum is developmentally and individually appropriate, children are likely to experience success.

Treating Mistakes as Part of the Learning Process

Few of us are willing to take risks if we know we will be criticized or shamed for making a mistake. When teachers view mistakes as part of the learning process and a way to understand more about a child's thinking, children learn that the classroom is a safe place to take risks. In this environment, children are not afraid to volunteer their ideas, even when they are unsure of the answer.

There are many ways to handle a "wrong" answer in a positive manner. For example, suppose a teacher asks Sally how many tens are in 54, and she replies "Four." The teacher can respond in a variety of supportive ways.

> *"Did you mean there are four tens or four left over? Take another look."*
>
> *"That's part of the answer. Show me how you decided on four."*
>
> *"You're on your way to the answer. Would you like to try again on your own or have someone work with you?"*

These responses show that the teacher respects the child's thinking and is willing to offer a way for the child to continue working on the problem.

Conveying High Expectations

Research studies and experience confirm that when teachers convey high expectations, children are more likely to be successful. This applies to promoting children's social skills as well as their academic success.

Teachers have countless opportunities to make comments or ask questions that help children see themselves as competent learners. A child who may have had a particularly frustrating time during one part of the day can be given a chance to succeed at something else later. For example, the child who was frustrated by an art project in the morning might be invited to share his story with the class during Writing Workshop in the afternoon. Children will begin to see that their teacher seeks to find the strengths in everyone.

Teachers who convey to children that they fully expect them to be cooperative and caring with one another make their values and expectations clear. This message can be reinforced in the following ways:

- Acknowledging what children do: "Thank you for helping Sloan clean out the guinea pig cage. After the long weekend, it was too big a job for one person."
- Stating rules positively to give a clear message of what behavior you want: "Be a friend" rather than "No fighting."
- Validating children's best intentions so they view themselves as people who have positive social skills: "You're the kind of person who likes to help others," or "It's just like you to be generous."

These kinds of statements will help make children feel competent and have positive interactions in the classroom.

Promoting Friendships

Peer relationships are a central social issue for children six to eight years old. Having friends can make the difference between a happy child and one who is lonely and ill at ease around others. Yet, despite the importance of friendships, many primary grade children are not skilled in making and keeping friends.

Most teachers know which children in their class make friends easily and which ones have difficulty establishing friendships. Children who do not have friends or who are repeatedly rejected by their peers are in a cycle of rejection that they often cannot break on their own. They may approach other children in ways that invite rejection: showing off, acting silly, playing too rough, bullying others, or being aggressive. The more they are rejected, the more they may exaggerate their negative behavior.

To break this cycle, children need the help of a caring adult. The younger the child, the easier it is to change the negative outcomes of being friendless. Failure to address the problem during the early years of school can lead these rejected children to engage in increasingly disruptive behavior in school and poor academic and social achievement.

Children with disabilities may need extra help developing friendships if friendships do not form naturally. Like all students, children with disabilities will use friendships as the key measure to evaluate their inclusion in the community. They weigh informal time spent with children at school, after school and weekend visits, phone calls, and being chosen for teams to measure the degree of acceptance they have among their peers. Friendship-making skills will be particularly important to children with disabilities.

The skills children learn by participating in daily class meetings—talking and listening, taking turns, solving problems, respecting the ideas of others—will also help them in making friends. However, some children will need more specific guidance because they simply do not know how to approach others in ways that will gain them acceptance. It may be helpful to know the skills children need to make friends and to learn some specific techniques for promoting friendships among the children in your classroom.

Friendship-Making Skills

There are three types of skills that help children make and keep friends. They must know how to (1) establish contact with another child; (2) maintain a positive relationship with that child; and (3) negotiate when a conflict arises (Kostelnick 1990).

Establishing contact. To be accepted initially by a peer, a child learns which behaviors will be well-received. Behaviors such as smiling, asking questions, offering ideas, inviting someone to play, or offering to share something establishes contact.

Watch a child in your class who makes friends easily. What behaviors do you notice? Next observe a child who tends to be rejected by peers. In what ways does this child attempt to establish contact? What are the results? You will probably see substantial differences in approach. Children who are rejected at the initial stage in making friends often have not learned acceptable ways to establish contact with their peers.

Maintaining a positive relationship. To maintain a friendship, children must acquire skills in cooperating, sharing, showing empathy, expressing affection, offering ideas, helping, taking turns, and expressing enthusiasm. Children who have these skills are considered by their peers as fun to be with and reliable.

The behaviors that get children in trouble at this stage include aggression, unwillingness to cooperate, showing off, trying too hard, and acting in ways that annoy others. Notice the behaviors some children exhibit that turn other children off. Through coaching and specific teaching, you can help these children see how their behavior causes them difficulties and provide them with positive alternatives.

Negotiating a conflict. Disagreements will inevitably arise in any friendship, so children must acquire the skills to resolve differences. Children who resort to violent outbursts, physical or verbal, or who withdraw from the conflict entirely, fail to maintain and deepen their friendships.

Socially successful children express their ideas, explain how they feel, listen to another point of view, and work out solutions. The classroom community offers many opportunities to practice these negotiating skills.

Steps Teachers Can Take to Promote Friendships in the Classroom

Everything you do to build a classroom community in which children develop an appreciation for differences and experience a sense of belonging creates a social environment in which children learn friendship-making skills. Because friendships are essential to children's well-being, it may also be necessary to take specific steps to overcome the rejection some children encounter.

Establish rules for the classroom. Involve children in establishing the rules for the classroom to ensure that everyone feels safe and comfortable. (A process for establishing rules is explained in the chapter on Establishing a Structure for the Classroom.)

Initiate discussions about making and keeping friends. A group meeting can be a neutral time to discuss a topic related to making and keeping friends. Reading a book such as *Tommy Goes to School* by Rosemary Wells, is a good way to introduce the subject and begin a discussion. Books such as *Leo, Zack, and Emmie* by Amy Ehrlich and *More Stories Julian Tells* by Ann Cameron can lead to interesting discussions about friends who have problems. After reading and discussing these stories, children can work in small groups to make up skits based on the plot and perform them for the class. Or children can draw a picture of one aspect of the story and write about it. Ask a librarian to recommend books on this topic that might especially appeal to the children in your class.

Pair children to work on a task. Partnering provides opportunities for children to work with peers they wouldn't normally choose. At the beginning of the year partner tasks should be simple and short. For example, partners can interview each other to find out something they each like to do after school. When they return to the meeting area, children introduce their partner to the group and describe what they learned. In completing these tasks, children relate to and develop a new appreciation for members of their class who they might not befriend on their own. Additional ideas for partner activities are outlined in the following chart.

Partner Jobs	Partner Games	Partner Art	Partner Reading	Partner Math
Fixing a snack	Concentration	"Draw and guess"	Informally looking at books	"Mirroring" in which children work to manipulate, build, and match designs piece by piece
Washing tables	Puzzles	Posters for the classroom		
Straightening books	Dominoes	Book responses	Paired reading in which children take turns reading to each other	
Stacking chairs	Simple card games	Cooperative monsters or funny animals		"Checking partners" in which children check answers with each other and help each other when answers disagree
Hanging pictures	Checkers			

Interpret children's actions. Children sometimes do not know what they are doing to alienate their peers. By verbalizing what happens, teachers can help children become more conscious of and therefore able to change the behaviors that cause them trouble: "Jessica, I notice that you do most of the talking and directing when you work with Tiffany and Michael. If you give them more of a chance to make decisions, they'll want to work with you."

Treat children's feelings with respect. Feelings invariably get hurt in the ever-changing dynamics of children's friendships. Often, in an attempt to be reassuring, adults trivialize a child's pain or upset: "Oh that's not such a big problem. He'll forget about it tomorrow." Children, just like adults, want to have their feelings acknowledged, not negated. When teachers listen to and accept children's feelings without making value judgments, they convey respect and understanding. "It's hard when your best friend is too busy to help you out. But it doesn't mean she's not your friend anymore."

In addition to these specific ideas for promoting friendships in the classroom, teaching children how to work collaboratively on their school work helps them acquire the skills for making and keeping friends and promotes their learning.

Teaching Children to Work Collaboratively

In the process of working with peers, children acquire both social and academic skills. Social skills that are strengthened through collaborative efforts include taking turns, sharing, giving help to others, and accepting help from peers. Rather than encouraging children to compete with each other for the right answers in order to "look smart," each child should have daily opportunities to contribute to the group and to learn from others. In this type of environment, children with limited social skills can still contribute their ideas to a group project and experience success. The underlying message of collaborative learning is that "in this classroom, we help one another learn."

Collaborative learning also improves academic success because children design their own questions, discuss and try out ideas, and explain their findings to others. In the process of sharing what they are learning, children clarify their own thinking and acquire a deeper understanding of the subject matter. Working together on real-life tasks improves communication among children, deepens their understanding of one another, and advances thinking.

Teachers' observations of the benefits of teaching children to work collaboratively are confirmed by research. Children's relationships with peers, especially those of different ethnic, socio-economic, and ability groups, are improved through collaborative learning (Slavin 1987). In classrooms where collaborative learning is successfully implemented, teachers find they have fewer behavior problems and children are more accepting of differences.

Collaboration Fosters Learning

When instruction is teacher-directed, the teacher gives information, teaches skills, and asks questions of the whole group. Desks are traditionally lined up facing the front of the classroom so that all children can see the teacher and the chalkboard. After lessons are presented, children practice what they have been taught, working individually at their desks. Talking among children may be discouraged.

When collaboration is encouraged, children learn from one another as well as from the teacher. The teacher may introduce a task or concept to the whole group in the meeting area and help children plan their work. Children then work with a partner or small group, which allows the teacher to assess children's progress and provide guidance and support where needed. In this learning environment, classroom life is less stressful for children and teachers.

Collaborative learning takes place formally when teachers assign children to work with one or more classmates on a project or task with specific goals in mind. Informally, collaborative learning occurs throughout the day. When children working at tables turn to their peers for help or to share ideas, when they work together to solve a problem, or when several children make a discovery and want to explore it further, they engage in collaborative efforts. Building a choice time into the schedule several times a week provides many opportunities for children to work together on their own initiative.

How Teachers Facilitate Collaborative Learning

The meetings you have every day in the classroom help children acquire the skills they need to work with a partner or in small groups to accomplish a task. However, experiences in group meetings may not be sufficient to ensure the success of collaborative learning as an instructional approach. Even children who have engaged in collaborative learning before are likely to need time to refine their skills. As one teacher put it, "I have to teach sharing before I can teach mathematics."

The increasing interest in collaborative learning has led to the development of many excellent resources to help teachers introduce it in the classroom. Several of the resources listed at the end of this chapter give step-by-step instructions and a wide range of activities that will engage children in working together. Some specific steps teachers can take to facilitate collaborative learning are described below.

Consider your basic comfort level with collaborative learning. Who you are and how you teach will strongly influence the degree of collaboration among the children in your class. Metaphors that are often used to describe the traditional role of teachers include performers or dispensers of all knowledge. When a teacher shares the responsibility for learning with the children and is open to its many variations, the tone is set for collaborative learning to occur.

Organize the classroom for collaborative learning. The way you organize the classroom and materials can support collaboration. When children work at tables instead of individual desks, peer-conferencing becomes a natural part of classroom life and collaboration is the accepted style of learning throughout the day, not just at designated times.

Sharing materials can contribute to the feeling of community in the classroom. Supplies such as crayons, pencils, glue, scissors, and tape can be stored on shelves where children can easily find them and take them to tables. Some teachers place these materials in baskets, making sure there is a basket for every table. They find this procedure avoids the problems that can arise when a child loses a color or breaks a crayon from a personal set.

Other teachers feel that some supplies, such as crayons, lend themselves to individual ownership because children have strong preferences for maintaining these materials (e.g., some like them peeled of their wrappers and broken in half, others keep them neatly stored in their original boxes all year). These teachers encourage children to borrow and lend colors with a neighbor when needed. Other supplies in the classroom are shared.

Establish the rules for working together. It's best to have a few simple rules about working together. The rules might be:

- Give everyone a turn.
- Listen when someone else is talking.
- Be responsible for your own behavior.

To reinforce the rules, post them prominently in the classroom and remind children of them before they go to work on a collaborative task. You may find it helpful to have periodic discussions on what each rule really means and what would happen if that rule were followed (or ignored).

Demonstrate collaborative skills using role plays. Use a meeting time to role play a collaborative task and illustrate the points you feel are important. For example, you could ask three children to volunteer to make a banner for the classroom. Explain that the purpose is to help us think about what it means to work together. Have a large sheet of paper in the middle of the circle and a set of markers. Ask the children to work on the banner. As they work, talk about what is happening.

> *Stefan immediately picks up the set of markers and begins to draw without consulting Meredith or Ron. The teacher says to the class, "What happened here?" One child volunteers, "Stefan just drew whatever he wanted. He didn't wait to see what the others wanted to do." The teacher then asks, "How could this have started in another way?" After discussing the need to share ideas first and then agree on what to draw, the teacher encourages the children to continue the role play. As they work out what they want to draw, share the markers, and listen to each other, the teacher invites the other children to describe what is happening.*

At the end of a role play it is important to summarize the key points about working together. List them on a chart as children volunteer their ideas. Then provide an opportunity for children to practice what they learned by working in small groups on a task.

Play collaborative games. Games reinforce a sense of community and allow children to experience the satisfaction of cooperating with others. Here are several suggestions.

- ***Musical islands.*** In this version of musical chairs, towels or rug samples are spread out on the floor as "islands. When the music plays, the children can "swim" safely in the water. When the music stops, sharks appear and the children have to stand on one of the islands for safety. Each round, another island is removed making the task more challenging. If a child falls off an island, the whole group is eaten by sharks, thus creating an incentive for everyone to work together to make a place for every child.

- ***Building a tower.*** In this game, each group of three or four children is given a set of blocks. The task is to see how high a tower they can make before the building falls. Children take turns placing the blocks on one at a time.

- ***Collaborative drawing in groups.*** Form teams of three or four children and give each a large sheet of paper and set of markers. Have children begin by talking about their favorite after school activity and then agree on ways to illustrate their activities in a mural.

The resources listed at the end of the chapter provide suggestions of collaborative games.

Use collaborative learning for instruction. The opportunities for children to work together on academic tasks are endless. Once you begin using this form of instruction, you will find it easy to encourage throughout the day.

- During ***reading*** time, children read books together; write and illustrate a story; create a skit or puppet show about a book; critique each other's writing.

- In ***math***, children work in pairs to collect, record and share data with the class related to everyday life (e.g., weather, milk count, preferences for snack); estimate the number of beans in a jar and devise a way to record and report on their findings.

- In ***science***, children study the stages of a caterpillar over several weeks, illustrating how it changes; research what they need to care for a new classroom pet; do research projects on different animals and then prepare a mural.

- In ***social studies***, during a study of the school and its environment, groups of children can make a map; create a book of information about the school that could be used to help newcomers feel at home; do research on the work of various members of the school community (e.g., the librarian, custodian, cafeteria supervisor).

Part Two of *Constructing Curriculum,* in which we describe each of the subject areas, includes many suggestions for using collaborative learning as an instructional approach.

Assign a role to each group member. If a few children tend to take over and assume all the roles for themselves, then assigning a role to each member ensures that responsibility is shared. This is particularly effective with older children. For example, if children are going to conduct interviews for a study, the jobs might include asking the questions, writing down the answers, and tape recording the interview. After completing the interview, group members discuss what they learned, record their findings, and present them to the rest of the class. A math activity might include the following roles and jobs: one person to roll the dice, one to keep score, and one to observe and report on the group's findings.

For true collaboration to take place, people have to feel equal in the roles they assume. This doesn't mean that the roles have to be the same. Different tasks lend themselves to different kinds of roles, so you will want to evaluate what is involved before deciding on the roles that need to be assigned. Not all jobs have to be active; you can help children see that observing and reporting is an important role.

Change group assignments regularly. Sometimes children choose a partner or form their own work groups. Because children tend to choose the same friends each time, it's wise to vary the make-up of groups on a regular basis. Children will be more apt to accept peers who are different from themselves if they have many opportunities to work together and to acquire an appreciation for each person's contribution.

Evaluate how collaborative efforts are working. Older children can evaluate for themselves how their group worked together—what went well, what problems they encountered, what they could do next time to improve their collaboration. Children can record their ideas on a sheet outlining these questions.

When the whole class periodically discusses the benefits and frustrations of a collaborative effort, it creates a greater awareness of the process itself. A general discussion might begin with the question, "What are some good things about working together?" The ideas could be listed on a chart.

A different approach would be to discuss, "What didn't you like about working together? What was frustrating?" To reinforce the positive, this discussion might also address what to do when frustrations arise. The children's ideas can be made into a chart to hang in the classroom as a reminder.

When you are in a group and you are frustrated, you can:

- Stop and talk about how everyone is feeling.
- Take a walk.
- Get a drink of water.

Since these discussions can raise a number of strong feelings, children may need to be reassured that working together is not always easy and that we all get frustrated sometimes. Your willingness to deal with problems and to teach children to resolve conflict when it arises will help make collaborative learning successful in your classroom.

Teaching Children to Resolve Conflicts

onflict resolution is gaining increasing attention nation-wide from educators and parents. In some schools, conflict resolution training is offered to everyone and is implemented on a school-wide basis. This is an effective approach because everyone in the school community supports the goal of managing conflicts peacefully. If families are invited to participate, then children receive consistent messages at home and in school.

When teachers are asked, "If you could teach only one thing, knowing that it would be learned, what would it be?" the most common responses given are: self-esteem, respect for others, communication skills, and the ability to solve problems non-violently. Given the importance of social competence, it is surprising how little time is allocated in the curriculum to teach children how to solve problems non-violently.

"One more thing to fit into our already full day," many teachers say. The reality is that if you do not help children learn how to handle their anger without resorting to aggression, the disruptions that occur will occupy more of your energy and time than teaching children how to manage conflict in the first place.

The Value of Conflict Resolution

Helping children handle intense emotions, including anger, without resorting to aggression, and to resolve conflicts so that all those affected feel their views have been heard and agree to the solution, is a challenging task. Conflict resolution is particularly appropriate in the primary grades for three reasons: it responds to important developmental issues, it is one way to reduce the increasing level of violence in today's society, and it gives children the skills to handle exclusionary behavior.

How Conflict Resolution Responds to Developmental Issues

Conflict resolution addresses many important social and emotional issues of children six to eight years old. This is a particularly volatile stage of development. Children come to school with a mixture of feelings and they often react emotionally to what happens each day in the classroom and on the playground. When children's emotions are involved, they may lose whatever impulse control they have acquired and resort to striking out.

Many primary grade children are just learning to put their feelings into words—an essential skill in learning to handle conflicts. Even those who do have well-developed language skills may lose their ability to express themselves in the heat of anger or hurt feelings. While they are cognitively capable of seeing a situation from another person's point of view, this ability is often lost in the midst of a conflict.

The conflicts and developmental issues that children bring to the teacher's attention can be irritating: whose turn it is to be first in line; getting in each other's "space"; who is friends with whom; who took someone's belongings; who got something first. Such issues are important to children, and they want their teachers to stop everything and resolve the problem. It can be tempting to resolve problems for children: deciding who is right in a disagreement and dictating the solution, sending the offending child to a time-out chair, negating the seriousness of an issue or depth of a child's anger. A more enduring approach is to use problems as opportunities to help children acquire the skills to handle their conflicts independently.

A Way to Reduce the Level of Violence

We need conflict resolution skills today more than ever before. Statistics on the level of violence, the number of children involved in violent crimes, and the impact on communities and families are staggering. The United States is now the most violent country in the industrialized world, leading other nations in homicides, rapes, and assaults (Dodd 1993). Marian Wright Edelman, President of the Children's Defense Fund (1993), alerts us to the fact that "gun-related violence takes the life of an American child every three hours, and the lives of 25 children every three days." An estimated 100,000 children bring guns to school every day, threatening the lives of peers, staff, and themselves. Many of these children say that carrying a gun is the only way they feel safe.

In a national survey to determine the effects on children of violence in the media and toys, 91% of teachers who responded reported increased violence among children in their classrooms (Carlsson-Paige and Levin 1991). The message children receive every day is that violence is an acceptable response to perceived insults, conflicts, and any person who impinges on their space. By teaching children alternatives to violence, we can help reduce the level of violence in children's lives and in our country.

Addressing Exclusionary Behavior

It is not enough to simply value diversity. History has demonstrated that people's experience of differences leads to conflict. This conflict may arise because people feel threatened by differences. For example, name-calling, overt or covert exclusionary behavior, teasing, and physical barriers may arise between disabled and non-disabled children, or among children from different ethnic groups.

One way to address exclusionary behavior is to confront it directly in the classroom. If, for example, a child with a disability is being teased, the teacher can intervene by supporting the child, assessing whether the child has internalized low self-esteem from current or previous conflicts, providing accurate and developmentally appropriate information about the disability to the class, having class discussions on how it feels to be excluded or teased, and clarifying or reminding children of the class rules on conflict and respect.

It's also important to explore the ideas and feelings of the child who name-calls or excludes. While explaining how the behavior hurts the child in question, seek the underlying reasons for the behavior by asking "Why do you think that?" or "Let's investigate that idea," "Let's ask the nurse/doctor/special educator about that," or "Let's ask Sarah's parents."

Incorporating Conflict Resolution Into the Curriculum

Everything you have done to create a positive sense of community in your classroom also works towards minimizing conflicts and behavior problems. In a classroom where children experience a sense of belonging, where they know that their ideas and feelings are respected, and where collaborative learning takes place, children learn to handle disagreements before they escalate out of control. Yet even in these classrooms, conflicts will emerge and children will experience intense feelings of anger.

Conflict resolution is not a quick fix; it's a process learned over time and enhanced by continual practice. Children can be helped to see that people have different opinions, that we have to listen to one another and learn to compromise, and that adults can help arbitrate when tempers flare. If teachers see conflict resolution as an opportunity to strengthen their classroom community, children will be more likely to approach conflicts with a healthy attitude.

Modeling How to Handle Anger

All of us feel angry at times; anger is a common human emotion. It's how we handle anger that is important. Teachers can model for children ways to deal with angry feelings without resorting to aggression.

> *"I'm feeling really disappointed right now. I'm angry and I need some quiet time to collect my thoughts. Then I'd like to talk to the class about what just happened in the lunchroom."*

Occasionally even the best teachers lose their tempers in front of the children. When this occurs, it's best to acknowledge what happened and use the incident as a learning experience.

> *"I lost control when I shouted at you and I'm sorry. There was a reason I got angry, but I am sorry about how I behaved. Let's talk about what happened and why it made me so angry."*

Similarly, teachers can give children specific suggestions on what to do when they feel upset, frustrated, or hurt before these feelings turn to anger.

> *"When you feel yourself getting angry, stop and count to 10. Take 5 deep breaths. Think about what has made you upset."*

Using Class Meetings to Discuss How to Handle Conflicts

Class meetings are an excellent forum for teaching children the skills to manage conflicts. Discussions can take place when the atmosphere is calm. In the midst of a conflict, it is natural to fall back on old patterns and habits.

Role plays can be used to teach conflict resolution skills. When teachers participate and are willing to ham it up, children are also willing to join in. You might take a real example of a conflict or one from a book you and the children have read together. To highlight the importance of listening to one another, you could establish the rule that each member of the role play must listen to the statement of feelings made by another member and restate them before explaining their own feelings. This can be done in a "fishbowl" with the rest of the class observing and discussing what they saw afterwards.

Puppets can also be effective for acting out a situation and generating discussion. Children's books with stories about feelings and conflict situations are excellent discussion starters. At the conclusion of a discussion, write the key points on a chart to remind everyone.

Some specific strategies and skills you can teach children in meetings to help keep conflict to a minimum are outlined below.

- Have periodic discussions about feelings, especially anger. Brainstorm a list of words that describe feelings and keep them on a chart so children can refer to them. This gives children the language to describe what they are feeling. During a writing time, you might use a mini-lesson to read a story about an emotion, and then encourage children to write their own.

- Have discussions about stereotypes, where they come from, and the impact they have.

- Teach children how to use "I statements" in describing a situation. "I feel ____ when you ____ because ____." This changes the way they describe an event and helps avoids accusations and finger pointing. "I statements" can often help to defuse strong feelings.

- Generate, with the children, a simple set of steps they can follow when they are not happy with what someone says or does. Then when children come to you for intervention, you can refer them to these steps. Post them prominently in the room.

  If you don't like what someone does:

  1. Ask a question.
  2. Make an "I statement." (I feel____because____.)
  3. Make a reasonable request of the other person. (Will you please ____?)

You will have to discuss and practice these steps with the children until they begin to follow them independently.

Many excellent resources, such as those listed at the end of this chapter, describe practical activities and cooperative games that teach children how to resolve conflicts and problems. Trying out these games with the children is one way to begin incorporating conflict resolution into your curriculum.

Handling Conflicts Between Children

What children fight about tends to vary with their age (Carlsson-Paige and Levin 1992). The younger the child, the more likely the argument will be about actions or things: "He took my book," or "She pulled my hair." As children get older, their conflicts center more broadly on peer relationships: "They won't let me in the game," or "He always calls me a bad name." Few teachers have the time or patience for constantly arbitrating disputes between children.

Whenever possible, try to head off a conflict before it escalates. As soon as you hear voices rising, try to become a stabilizing force by getting close to the children involved. Ultimately, you want children to have the skills to resolve the situation on their own, but at first you will need to take an active role to help them learn the steps for conflict resolution described below. By following these steps consistently, children will internalize them and apply them with increasing independence.

Help Children Calm Down

When emotions are hot, it's not useful to try to have a discussion. It is best to defuse the situation so children can hear one another. You might suggest a cool off time first, or describe what you think the children are feeling so that they know they have been heard and feel that their concerns are valid:

> *"I can see you're having a hard time waiting for your turn. It is hard to wait. You seem to be feeling impatient and angry."*
>
> *"This is hard for both of you. You're really upset right now."*
>
> *"Let's take a few minutes to calm down. Take a few deep breaths."*

If children are still intensely angry, it's too soon to try to identify the problem. Generally, it's not advisable to force the process before children are ready.

Identify the Problem

Children will be more open to discussing solutions if they feel their views are understood. The goal of this stage is to give each child a chance to speak and be heard.

> *"We can hear better if one person talks at a time. We'll take turns. When Marcus is talking, Carrie will listen without interrupting. Then it will be Carrie's turn to talk and Marcus will listen without interrupting."*

Putting your hand on each child's shoulder or waist conveys that you will guide them and help them resolve the problem. Open-ended questions allow children to identify their view of the situation.

> *"What do you think happened?"*
>
> *"Now tell us what you think."*
>
> *"It looks like... Am I right?"*

Children often have trouble hearing one another, or even looking at each other when they are intensely angry. The teacher's role is to help children hear each other's point of view. Many childhood conflicts arise out of confusion or misunderstandings.

> *"Did you hear what he said?"*
>
> *"Do you need to hear it again?"*
>
> *"Do you have a question to ask him?"*

It's important to stay calm and neutral, even if you have strong opinions. Listen with your eyes as well as your ears and let children know that you want to hear both sides. Repeat what you hear so children know they have been heard and they have a chance to correct any misconceptions.

> *"So you're saying... "*
>
> *"And you're feeling... "*
>
> *"What I hear you saying is... "*

Have children restate what they heard. Then review each step of what happened, who did what, how each action made the other person feel, and what resulted.

Generate Solutions

If the children cannot come up with a solution, help them by asking questions.

> *"What can we do about this?"*
>
> *"Do either of you have any ideas?"*

Brainstorming is a valuable tool for problem solving. Come up with as many ideas as possible. If the same type of conflict took place recently, or you have role played or discussed a similar situation during a class meeting, you can refer children to the solutions they generated.

> *"Remember last week when...? Think about what you did then and see if that gives you an idea for solving your problem."*

If children are stuck, you might have to suggest some ideas, or ask if they would like help.

> *"What do you think would happen if... ?"*
>
> *"What do you think about... ?"*
>
> *"Do we need more information about... ?"*
>
> *"This is a tough problem. Would you like other class members to suggest things that have worked for them?"*

Agree on a Solution and Implement It

The goal is to arrive at a solution that everyone can live with, so that all those involved feel that their needs have been met.

> *"What is good about this solution?"*
>
> *"What might be a problem?"*
>
> *"Would another solution work better for you?"*

Evaluate and Share the Results

Once the solution is agreed upon and implemented, it's a good idea to check how it's working. If it's a particularly good example of problem solving, or you simply want to give the children recognition for their work in resolving a conflict, you might invite them to share what happened with the class at a meeting time.

Encourage Children to Resolve Problems on Their Own

As children acquire the skills to resolve problems, encourage them to work out solutions on their own. Sometimes you can't just stop what you are doing to mediate a problem between two children. You can make suggestions:

> *"I just can't help you right now. Think about it for a while and check with me in 15 minutes."*
>
> *"Go look at the chart about what to do when you don't like something someone does."*
>
> *"Remember this same problem came up last week? Try to remember what you did then. Go to the book area and talk about it. Report to me after you do."*

For older children, it often defuses the situation if they write down what happened or what they would like to have happened. Always remember to check with the children to see if they have resolved the issues. As children become increasingly able to handle conflicts on their own, the teacher's time spent resolving conflicts is minimized.

Provide a Place in the Classroom to Calm Down

Group life is demanding for adults as well as children. Everyone needs a break at times. Establishing one or two places in the classroom where children can go to cool off, relax, or take a break gives children a positive alternative to acting out or falling apart during a conflict.

A calm-down place might be the classroom library, the meeting area, a loft, or listening area. The designated area ideally will contain soft furniture: a rocking chair, bean-bag chair, rug, covered mattress or pillows. Just flopping onto a bean-bag chair, curling up with a book, staring at tropical fish, or listening to a favorite tape can be calming. Sometimes just being near a teacher is the best calming down place.

A place to calm down where children can choose to go is very different from a "time-out chair." Children learn very little from sitting in a time-out chair and too often it is used punitively.

At first, you may have to tell children when they need to retreat and cool off. The goal is for children to recognize their own uncomfortable volatile feelings and know when they need to take a break in a quiet space. In this way, children become responsible for their own feelings and behavior.

Conflicts That Affect the Whole Class

Some issues affect the whole class and require problem solving as a group. Involving all the children in discussing the problem, generating solutions, and deciding on a plan teaches children that we are all responsible for each other and we can solve problems together. This is an important part of learning to function as members of a community.

The class meeting is an appropriate time for teachers to lead children in uncovering and resolving a problem. The following steps, which may require several class meetings to follow, can guide this process:

- discuss the situation;
- generate possible solutions;
- make a plan;
- implement the plan;
- assess progress.

To illustrate the steps in resolving conflicts that affect the whole group, we will use an example from a third grade classroom where recess has become unmanageable. Children fight continuously over game rules, some do not get involved in any activities, and after recess children complain and tattle endlessly. Many children have expressed the desire to stay inside during recess, rather than deal with the unpleasant atmosphere. Ms. Strickler, the teacher, decides that she will involve the children in improving the quality of the recess period.

Discuss the Situation

In the initial discussion, uncover the issues and have children describe the events leading to the problem. The tricky part of this discussion is to encourage children to describe the situation without resorting to blaming and fingerpointing.

Providing ample opportunity to discuss the situation, whatever it is, lets children know that their opinions are important. Because children at this age can be rigid about their opinions, discussions may become heated. The temptation may be to end a discussion by saying something like, "Unless you can talk calmly, the discussion will end." It's important to acknowledge the strength of children's opinions and remind them that the purpose of the discussion is to hear all points of view.

Ms. Strickler sets up a chart in the meeting area. On one side she writes, What's Good about Recess and on the other she writes, What's Bad about Recess.

"Everyone has strong opinions here and that's understandable. Let's work at taking turns talking and try very hard to listen to each other so we can see all sides of the issue."

"Let's make a list of both the good and bad points of recess on this chart. Feel free to say whatever you wish about recess."

As the children express their opinions, she listens, modeling that this is what children should be doing as well. As each child finishes sharing, she asks,

"What should I write on the chart?"

For about fifteen minutes the children brainstorm ideas; the list of bad points is getting quite long. Ms. Strickler acknowledges this, saying, "Hmm, I notice there are quite a few negatives. Does anyone have any ideas on what's good about recess?"

The process of engaging in discussion helps children both to clarify their thinking and hear the ideas of others. Sometimes it's helpful to review all the ideas so children hear them at one time.

Generate Possible Solutions

The next step is to brainstorm possible solutions to the problems raised. You may do this at the first meeting if interest is high and the children are still involved. Alternative approaches might be to:

- categorize the problems, break into teams to address one problem, and then report back to the entire group;
- ask children to write about possible solutions in their journals or for homework and then share ideas in a meeting the next day.

In this example, Ms. Strickler moves right into brainstorming possible solutions.

"Let's start brainstorming some solutions. I'll put up another chart. Who has ideas about what might make recess time more pleasant?"

A list of ideas is generated. Ms. Strickler decides that the children need more time for reflection and discussion before they can make a plan.

"You have done a lot of really good thinking. While you are out on the playground for recess today, think of yourself as an observer. Consider some of these ideas and whether you think they would work. See if you can come up with any others. We'll talk about this again at our meeting tomorrow."

During the second meeting on the recess issue, the children come up with a list of ideas for solutions, including having three organized games each day with a sign-up sheet for each game; playing one big organized game that the class votes on for a week; having a team of four children be recess mediators who serve in the job for two weeks; and dividing the playground into three sections for the different kinds of activities that take place, establishing a set of rules for each area.

After the list has been generated Ms. Strickler says, "This afternoon we'll break into small groups to discuss each of these ideas and begin to outline what each idea might be like if we implemented it. Your group can decide to evaluate all of the ideas or just pick one or two." Ms. Strickler assigns children to groups of four, tells each group to pick a recorder, and reminds them to collaborate in order to come up with the best plan. She encourages the recorder to take good notes to share in the discussion the following day.

Make a Plan

Discuss the alternatives and then either come to consensus or vote on a plan. A plan is most likely to be successful when children have a stake in making it work; ownership of the ideas leads to having a stake in the outcome.

Each of the four groups presents their ideas. There is a great deal of overlap. Ms. Strickler orchestrates the discussion to help children see how their ideas mesh.

"Let's take a minute to think about how the suggestion made by Jonah's group might work with the plan we heard from Ariana's group."

They formulate four possible plans by combining several ideas into one. Ms. Strickler suggests that they reflect on these plans for homework and decide which one they want to try. She reminds them that they can always change their plan if it doesn't work.

In anticipation of the next day's meeting, Ms. Strickler records the four options on a new chart. When the class meets again, they vote on the plans. The chosen plan is to have three organized game areas: two for big groups playing soccer and tag, and a third for kids who want to play 4 square, jump rope, or other games that involve only 3 or 4 children. Some children agree to design a sign up sheet so that each morning before meeting children will sign up for their choice.

Implement the Plan

The next step is to allow children to try out their solutions. It can be helpful for the children to role play the plan prior to actually trying it out.

On the day the plan is to begin, Ms. Strickler hangs a chart describing the plan. She also has the sign-up sheet ready for children to use when they arrive. She reminds children of the sign-up sheet on the morning message.

"Today we will begin our new recess plan. Think about what you want to do at recess today. Talk your plan over with a friend. Once you have signed up, you have made a commitment for today. I am inspired by the new plan. You've done some excellent problem solving."

Assess Progress

Even in situations where it's obvious that the plan is working well, it's important to let children discuss how things are going at many intervals. Often when their plan doesn't work out immediately, children want to make drastic revisions or try something else. Teachers can help children modify the original idea and try it out again before abandoning a first attempt too quickly. Remind children that new ideas take time to work. Your patience helps children understand that results may not be immediately obvious.

Establishing a classroom environment where conflicts are kept to a minimum, and where children acquire the skills to handle conflicts when they emerge, helps children feel that they are in control. They learn that their feelings and concerns are respected and that together, they can solve problems and make the classroom a peaceful place to work.

The School as a Community

Once you see children thriving in a caring classroom community, you may begin to look beyond the classroom to the school. It follows that classes can work together to make the school a caring community and that teachers would also benefit from belonging to a supportive, inclusive community. Ideally, the message everyone receives from the school community is, "We care about all members."

When the entire school shares the values and approaches described in this chapter, everyone benefits. The school principal or a school improvement team can promote a sense of community throughout the school. Just as the classroom teacher initiates the process of community building in the classroom, the principal can involve everyone in developing and achieving a shared vision.

Sometimes one teacher, or a small group, can begin the process of building a sense of community in the school by thinking of projects classes can do together or alone that will benefit the school as a whole. Here are some ideas:

- Plan a school beautification project and invite each class to make a plan (for example, maintaining the playground, planting flowers or bulbs, making signs, making maps for visitors, painting a number line on the floor of a hallway).

- Involve families in projects that classes do together. If there is a lunch program for seniors in your community, seniors may welcome visits from children who can share songs, poetry, or art projects.

- Think of a community service project such as making sandwiches once a month for an organization that feeds homeless people. Ask a local grocery store to donate the ingredients and organize a time when classes get together to make sandwiches.

- Set up partner classes and do special projects together. Older children can come and read to their partners, help them with projects, or go with them to the library to help with a research project. Singing is a wonderful joint activity.

Teachers also benefit from belonging to a supportive community. It's very difficult to be an excellent teacher all alone. No matter how committed to the children a teacher might be, good teaching takes an enormous amount of energy, creativity, and knowledge. Teachers need opportunities to share their ideas, struggles, and solutions with one another. They feel less alone and thus have the energy needed for children and for the art of teaching.

Sometimes one teacher can begin the process of building a community of teachers. Here are some suggestions.

- Invite other grade level teachers to meet regularly—perhaps over lunch or dinner —to talk about curriculum issues and share ideas.
- Seek other teachers who can help you with a problem or share an approach they have successfully implemented. Ask for their help and advice. Offer to share ideas and resources with them.
- Suggest regular potluck get-togethers where staff can socialize. Take turns planning a topic for discussion.

Finally, take time for yourself. Your own professional development is as important as your health. Join professional organizations where you can meet other dedicated teachers and administrators. The conferences and resources you will have access to can provide a sense of renewal as you strive to construct curriculum that is meaningful for your children.

Closing Thoughts

When a classroom functions as a community, children can feel safe and accepted and make positive connections with others. The opportunity to participate as a contributing member of a community helps children to become successful learners, problem solvers, and decision makers. Teachers build a classroom community by welcoming children, using meetings to promote a sense of community, helping children to relate positively to others, and teaching them to resolve conflicts. In order for a community to work, a clear structure is essential.

Resources for Building a Classroom Community

Children in Danger: Coping with the Consequences of Community Violence. Garbarino, et al. San Francisco: Jossey-Bass Publishers, 1992.

Collaborative Classroom, A Guide to Co-operative Learning. Hill, Susan and Tim Hill. Portsmouth: Heinemann, 1990.

The Cooperative Sports and Games Book: Challenge Without Competition. Orlick, Terry. New York: Pantheon Books, 1978.

Creative Conflict Resolution: More Than 200 Activities for Keeping Peace in the Classroom K-6. Kriedler, William J.. Glenview: Scott, Foresman and Co., 1984.

Designing Group Work Strategies for Homogeneous Classrooms. Cohen, Elizabeth. New York: Teachers College Press, 1986.

Educating for Character: How Our Schools Can Teach Respect and Responsibility. Lickona, Thomas. New York: Bantam Books, 1991.

Everybody Wins: 393 Non-Competitive Games for Young Children. Sobel, Jeffrey. New York: Walker & Co., 1984.

Greater Expectations, Overcoming the Culture of Indulgence in America's Homes and Schools. Damon, William. New York: The Free Press, 1995.

Teaching Children to Care: Management in the Responsive Classroom. Charney, Ruth Sidney. Greenfield, MA: Northeast Foundation for Children, 1992.

The Friendly Classroom for a Small Planet: Children's Creative Response to Conflict Program. Prutzman, Priscilla, et al. Philadelphia: New Society Publishers, 1988.

The Resilient Self: How Survivors of Troubled Families Rise Above Adversity. Wolin, Steven and Sybil Wolin. New York: Villard Books, 1993.

The Tone of Teaching. Van Manan, Max. Ontario, Canada: Scholastic-TAB Publications, 1986.

References

Benard, Bonnie. 1991. *Fostering Resiliency in Kids: Protective Factors in the Family, School, and Community.* Portland: Northwest Regional Educational Laboratory, 9-14.

Bredekamp, Sue and Teresa Rosegrant, eds. 1992. *Reaching Potentials: Appropriate Curriculum and Assessment for Young Children, Volume I.* Washington, D.C.: NAEYC.

Carlsson-Paige, Nancy & Diane E. Levin. 1991. The Subversion of Healthy Development and Play. *Day Care and Early Education,* 19(2), 14-20.

_____. 1992. Making Peace in Violent Times: A Constructivist Approach to Conflict Resolution. *Young Children*, November, 7.

Clark, Reginald. 1992. *African American Male Students in Bakersfield City Schools: An Assessment and Proposals for Action.* Claremont, CA: Reginald Clark and Associates.

Clark, Reginald. 1990. Why Disadvantaged Students Succeed: What Happens Outside School Is Critical. *Public Welfare,* Spring.

Dodd, Senator Christopher. 1993. Testimony before the Joint Senate-House Hearing on Keeping Every Child Safe: Curbing the Epidemic of Violence, March 10, 1993.

Edelman, Marian Wright. 1993. Testimony before the Joint Senate-House Hearing on Keeping Every Child Safe: Curbing the Epidemic of Violence, March 10, 1993.

Jorgensen, Cheryl M. 1992. Natural Supports in Inclusive Schools: Curriculum and Teaching Strategies. In *Natural Supports in Schools, at Work, and in the Community for People with Severe Disabilities.* Dover, NH: University of New Hampshire Institute on Disability.

Kostelnik, Marjorie. 1992. Social Development: An Essential Component of Kindergarten Education. In *The Developing Kindergarten: Programs, Children, and Teachers*. Edited by Judith Spitler McKee, Ed. East Lansing: Michigan Association for the Education of Young Children, 170-172.

Lickona, Thomas. 1992. *Educating for Character: How Our Schools Can Teach Respect and Responsibility*. New York: Bantam Books.

Maslow, Abraham H. 1955. Deficiency Motivation and Growth Motivation, Nebraska Symposium on Motivation. Edited by M.R. Jones. Lincoln: University of Nebraska Press.

Pelligrini, A. D. and Carl D. Glickman. 1991. Measuring Kindergartners' Social Competence. *ERIC Digest.* Urbana, IL: ERIC Clearinghouse on Elementary and Early Childhood Education.

Rutter, Michael. 1979. Protective Factors in Children's Responses to Stress and Disadvantage. *Primary Prevention of Psychopathology, Volume 3: Social Competence in Children.* Edited by M. W. Kent and J.E. Rolf. Hanover: University Press of New England, 49-74.

Slavin, Robert. 1987. Cooperative Learning: Can Students Help Students Learn? *Instructor* (March): 74-78.

Werner, Emmy. 1990. Protective Factors and Individual Resilience. In *Handbook of Early Childhood Intervention*, ed. by Samuel Meisels and Jack Shonkoff. New York: Cambridge University.

ESTABLISHING A STRUCTURE FOR THE CLASSROOM

Each community has its own structure—a set of rules, common understandings, and systems that all members agree to follow. Without a predictable structure, people often feel insecure and unsafe because they don't know what is expected or how to act appropriately. When the structure is clear, it is easier for everyone to work and to feel productive.

In a collaborative community, power is shared. All members of the community contribute to creating the structure that governs community life. As described in the previous chapter, classrooms are also communities in which children can experience a sense of belonging and know that they are valued members. When classrooms operate like communities, children have an investment in building and maintaining the quality of community life. They understand the rules and systems because they help to create them, and they are willing to re-evaluate and change what does not work for the good of all. Teachers can work with children to create a sense of order based not on power, but on shared understandings.

Children six to eight years old need to feel autonomous and powerful. Teachers would like children to develop self-discipline, share responsibility for keeping the classroom neat and orderly, and become self-directed learners. The structure you build in your classroom will enable you to achieve your goals and also address children's needs. Structure comes from a well-organized classroom environment, a daily schedule and routines that are predictable, and clear expectations about behavior in the classroom. Making the structure clear to the children is a critical step.

Why the Structure Has to Be Clear

The type of structure that helps children become self-directed learners may not be immediately obvious to children or to adults who visit the classroom. Therefore, teachers cannot assume that children will understand the classroom structure they have created unless they make the structure explicit to children. For example, although a well-organized classroom conveys the message that materials are valuable and everything has a place, children won't automatically use materials well and help maintain order. Teachers have to reinforce this message by systematically introducing the proper use of materials and explaining the systems for using and returning them.

In the classroom described below, the teacher has established a structure that the children understand. If you were a visitor to this classroom, here's what you might see.

> *When you enter the classroom, you hear a steady hum of activity. At first you don't see the teacher; she is sitting and talking with one of several small groups of children working on a variety of math activities at tables arranged in different areas of the room. Each group has three to four children and they seem intent on the materials they are using together. Children are talking in lively voices about what they are doing, explaining their ideas, giving directions, asking questions, challenging one another and laughing. You sit down near one group of four children using geoboards and rubber bands. "Tell me something about what you are doing," you say. One child immediately volunteers: "We are finding out how many ways we can make different shapes. Look, we've made triangles, squares, and diamonds," he says, pointing to each one. Another child adds, "And I've made a hexagon. I know because it has six angles and six sides." You then ask, "How did you know what to do?" A third child explains, "We had a meeting and talked about different shapes we knew. Then each group got different things to use. We got the geoboards, that group got popsicle sticks, over there they have tangrams. Look around and you'll see." Just before you leave, the teacher calls the children together in the meeting area so each group can report on what they did and what they learned.*

To some, this classroom might seem noisy and lacking in structure. There's a lot of activity in all corners of the room—materials are out, and children's voices can be heard everywhere. But the noise and activity are not chaotic. Children are engaged in tasks that have meaning for them. They know what they are expected to do and are self-directed. The structure is clear; the teacher has planned it and children understand it.

The structure in this classroom has been established in three ways. First, the teacher has organized the physical environment so that children know where to find what they need and how to help maintain a sense of order. Second, the teacher follows a consistent schedule and set of routines so children know the day is predictable. And finally, there are clear expectations about behavior; the teacher has established these expectations by involving children in creating rules for the classroom, by identifying jobs for maintaining the classroom, and by offering children opportunities to make choices during the day.

The Physical Environment

T he most obvious form of structure is the classroom itself—how you arrange the furniture, select and organize materials, and what you have on the walls. The physical environment conveys strong messages to children from the first time they enter the room. It can reassure them that their classroom is a place where they will be safe, comfortable, and where they will do interesting things.

Messages Children Receive from the Environment

A good place to start in designing your classroom is to think about what messages you want children to receive as soon as they enter the room. You might begin by pondering questions such as the following:

- How will children know that this is a place they can trust and that they will be safe here?
- How do I show children that the classroom belongs to them?
- How can I make it easier for children to work together and share materials?

The chart below offers some suggestions for communicating positive messages.

Positive Messages	How the Environment Conveys These Messages
This is a safe and comfortable place.	• Room dividers and shelves are at children's eye level; they can see everything and the teacher can see the children. • There are properly-sized places to work, rugs, and comfortable furnishings for relaxing. • There is space to move around; the room is not crowded and congested. • There is a safe place for each child's personal belongings. • Children can see the teacher at all times. • The furniture is solid, clean, and well-maintained. The room has a clean, neat appearance.
I belong here and I am valued.	• Pictures and materials in the room reflect the children's families and communities. • The environment has been adapted for children with disabilities. • There is display space reserved for children's work. • Children can find their names posted in several places in the classroom.
I can make friends and share.	• Areas of the room are set up for small groups of children to work together. • There is a rug in a meeting area large enough to accommodate the whole class. • Materials are grouped for shared use (e.g., baskets of pencils, markers, and crayons for writing) and there are sufficient quantities. • There is a message board or mail boxes where children can leave messages for each other.

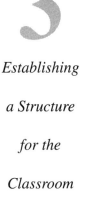

First impressions are powerful. Think about how you react when you enter another person's home. You may make assumptions about how they live. Think also about how you have organized your own home. Each room serves a different function and is organized so that you can find what you need. Your home is a statement of who you are and what kinds of activities you enjoy. You can function efficiently and easily in your home because its organization makes sense to you. In the same way, the classroom's organization is most effective when it is well designed and makes sense to everyone.

Positive Messages	How the Environment Conveys These Messages
I know what I'm expected to do.	• Everything is neat and labeled so children can find things easily. • Materials are within reach. • There is a chart listing job responsibilities for the upkeep of the room. • The weekly and daily schedules are posted at children's eye level.
I can do interesting work here.	• The room and materials are organized in attractive ways. Everything looks inviting. • There are sufficient quantities of books, objects, games, and collections for children to explore and investigate—enough to go around, but not so much that it is over-stimulating. • There are writing tools, blocks, art, and construction materials to encourage children to build, draw, write, and paint about what they are learning. • The displays change on a regular basis. • There are math and science tools (measuring devices, magnifying lenses, microscopes) for investigations.
I can find what I need and put things back where they belong.	• Materials are logically organized and labeled. • Games with small pieces and manipulatives are in containers so they won't get lost. • Shelves are labeled to show where materials belong.
I can make choices.	• Materials are placed on shelves where children can reach them. • There is a choice board and time in the schedule for children to choose their own activities.

Taking a Look at Your Classroom—First Steps

Begin with what you have. In your classroom you most likely have desks or tables, chairs, books, board or wall space, and different amounts of supplies. Organize what you have in ways that will make each day go smoothly. When possible, you can add materials to enhance your program.

Because the meeting area is the center of community life, it should occupy a well-defined place in the classroom. For children to work cooperatively on projects, and select and return materials, they will need tables to work on and convenient storage places throughout the classroom. Display space can serve many important purposes. And children, like all of us, want a safe place for their belongings.

Meeting Area

The meeting area is where the class gathers to have discussions, listen to a story, learn about new materials, participate in a lesson, make a transition to a new activity, get directions, or summarize an experience. The meeting area should have a prominent place in the classroom—a place that says, "This is where we come together and do important work."

As you look around your classroom to select the best place for meetings, consider the following recommendations:

- Allow sufficient floor space in the meeting area to accommodate all the children and adults in a circle or square, either on the floor, on chairs, or on benches. Using the floor means that chairs don't have to be moved every time there is a class meeting. Benches can define the area and also serve as cubbies or storage space.

- Make the space big enough so that children can wiggle without disturbing those around them.

- Define the meeting area and provide for children's comfort with a rug, or sewn together carpet squares to give every child a soft place to sit.

- Decide whether you will sit on the floor, a chair, or a bench. If you have a special chair, children can use the chair when they are conducting the meeting. Whoever reads aloud to the class can use it also.

- Include in the meeting area displays you will want to refer to such as the daily schedule, morning message, choice board or list, job chart, and calendar.

- Locate the meeting area near a chalkboard for group lessons, and have available chart paper and a sturdy stand or easel, magic markers, pocket charts to manipulate words and lines from a poem or book, and individual clip or chalk boards.

Arrangement of Furniture and Tables

In a classroom where collaborative learning is encouraged, tables that accommodate four to six children are preferable to individual desks. If you do not have tables, you can group individual desks to accommodate four to six children. Some teachers who use this approach still have assigned seats so children can store their personal supplies and books inside. If you want to be more flexible about where children work, then you will have to provide separate storage places for children's work and explain that all classroom materials are shared and accessible to everyone.

A few individual desks can be used as study carrels when children prefer to work alone, which is not unusual at this age. Providing other quiet places in the classroom such as bean bag chairs in the library or a loft with soft cushions also helps to address the need for privacy.

As you organize your furniture, keep these guidelines in mind.

- Separate noisier areas from quieter ones (e.g., blocks away from the classroom library).

- Plan traffic patterns that will prevent children from interrupting one another as they move around the room, invite moderation in speed (no "runways"), and allow you to move freely between groups and individual children.

- Make sure you can see all areas without obstruction.

Organization of Supplies and Materials

In selecting supplies and materials for your classroom, a good rule to follow is "less is more." Classrooms that are cluttered with materials, walls completely covered with displays, and overflowing storage bins contribute to chaos. For some children, too much visual stimulation makes settling in extremely difficult and choosing activities and materials almost impossible. The task of cleaning up seems overwhelming when there are too many things to put away and it's not clear where everything should go.

Children are more likely to be responsible about caring for and returning materials if they understand the order you have established and if they have participated in establishing this order. When materials are arranged logically and in designated places, then children don't have to ask their teacher for everything they need. They can find materials independently and they know where to return them when they are finished. Because the organization is clear, children can take pride in helping to maintain an orderly classroom.

Consider these guidelines as you organize the materials in your classroom:

- Locate materials in logical places, as close as possible to where children will need them for their work (e.g., art materials near water, manipulative math materials near tables).

- Keep shared materials such as pencils, crayons, markers, erasers, and scissors in small baskets or plastic food containers—one for each table.

- Label all containers to indicate that there is a proper place for everything. When children help make these labels, they see the importance of labeling.

- Label shelves to show where containers belong.

- Keep materials within children's reach so they can use them independently.

Following these suggestions will enable you to establish a sense of order in the classroom from the very first day, thereby making the statement that everything has a proper place in the classroom. If it becomes evident that some of the arrangements are not working as well as they should, solicit the children's ideas for addressing the problem(s). Children who are invited to think of solutions to a problem are more likely to support its resolution.

Display Space

Classroom displays represent what the children are studying and who they are. When commercial materials or art projects that all look the same dominate the classroom, children receive the message that everything has to be done a certain way. In contrast, when children see their own work displayed, they learn that their creative work is valued and the classroom belongs to them.

It's a good idea to leave plenty of empty space in your room at the beginning of school. An empty wall tells children that there is more to come. Some teachers simply label the space to indicate what will soon be featured: "Pictures of Us" or "Who We Are."

Bulletin boards, shelf tops, easels, room dividers and walls can be used to display children's work. Allocate special space for works-in-progress where children know their projects will be safe and accessible until the next day. Trays can keep projects organized and moveable.

Include in your classroom displays a variety of children's work such as writing, art, inventions or other constructions, math patterns, computer discoveries, and signs. Be sure to include the work of all students. In addition to individual work, you might display charts that have been developed in meetings with the children (e.g., "What We Noticed at the Construction Site" or a graph summarizing the children's findings after conducting a survey on favorite books).

Not all displays have to be items made by the children, but they should reflect the interests of the children. You might consider:

- books on various subjects (a book about ants in the science area, a book about numbers near where you store math materials);
- pictures that relate to a collection or project;
- newspaper articles on a community event or topic under study;
- objects that are relevant to a topic the children are exploring (shells if you are studying patterns, clocks if you are studying time);
- materials children bring from home that relate to an interest or study.

Displays of children's work reflect what the class is studying and therefore should be kept current. Charts that remain on the wall too long are ignored.

Personal Belongings and Work

Finding safe and accessible places to store personal belongings is a concern in all primary classrooms. In allocating storage space for children's personal belongings, think about when and where children need access to their possessions. For example, if children leave the room to go to a cafeteria for lunch, then a good place to store their lunches might be on a shelf near the door. If your classroom has direct access to the outdoors, you will want clothing stored near the exit. Backpacks and special objects from home should be near work areas since children may need to retrieve items during choice time.

If children don't have assigned desks, then they need places to keep their work. Math journals, writing folders, and children's portfolios can be stored in plastic crates, library boxes, dish pans, or partitioned shelves.

Making Your Classroom a Place for Active Investigation and Representation

Children learn best when they can explore and investigate objects, events, and places. The classroom environment is enriched by allocating space and organizing materials that encourage these active investigations. Opportunities to write, draw, paint, and construct representations of ideas and concepts are essential experiences that promote learning for children in the primary grades. As they write, draw, build a model, or engage in dramatic play, children construct their own understanding of new concepts. If the materials in the classroom are well organized, attractively displayed and labeled, children know where to look for information and locate materials to help them investigate and represent their learning.

In this section we offer suggestions on how to organize space and materials for:

reading	games	cooking, music, dance, and drama
writing	science	art and construction
math	social studies	block building
computers		

Setting Up a Library

When the classroom features an attractive library area filled with a collection of good books, the message is that literature and reading are valued. Children will be more likely to use the area if it also contains comfortable seating and if it looks attractive.

Organizing the Space

If you have moveable bookshelves, you may want to use them to define a library area. Try to allow sufficient room so children can read alone, with a partner, or with a small group of children. A soft carpet, a small (crib-size) mattress with an attractive cover, pillows, bean bags, or a rocking chair make the library area a restful retreat when children need a break from other classroom activities.

Walls or the top of a shelf can be used for displays that highlight certain types of books or display children's work related to reading. Here are some ideas:

- Display books related to your social studies or science projects.
- Showcase books by a certain author or illustrator you are studying.
- Make a poster with suggested titles to read.
- Hang the art work that books inspired children to create.

Stocking the Library with Good Books

You can make your classroom library an exciting place for children by having a wide selection of books that will appeal to many different interests and reading levels. In selecting books for your library, be sure that they reflect ethnic, gender, age, and ability diversity. Consider the following categories:

poetry collections

picture books

chapter books

books related to our study

biographies and autobiographies

information books (e.g., sports, animals, weather, machines, solar system)

reference books (e.g., dictionaries, thesauruses)

magazines and newspapers

To help children find and return books independently, a library should be organized logically. You can group books by category in bins, buckets, baskets, or cartons, and label the shelves or mark the bindings with different colored tape for each category. How you plan to use books will dictate the way you want to organize them. Here are some possibilities:

- Categorize books by reading level (e.g., from easy to challenging).
- Group books by author.
- Create categories according to topics that interest your children (e.g., insects, mystery, sports, adventure, sea creatures, space).

You will need multiple copies of books that you plan to use for small group reading lessons. Because children's interests change and their skills improve during the year, new books should be added to the library throughout the year. Most school or public libraries allow teachers to check out a good selection of books for long periods of time.

A nice addition to a classroom library is a tape recorder with headsets so children can listen to books on tape. If you have several sets of headphones, try to have enough copies of each book for every listener.

To encourage children to care for books, include a "first-aid kit" for books in the library so that when a book is damaged, a child can easily patch it. A sturdy shoe box or pencil box works well for this purpose. Include transparent tape to repair torn pages, cloth tape to repair the spines of books, gum erasers to remove pencil marks, correction fluid to cover ink and crayon marks, and a pair of scissors. Children can be taught to make repairs on their own, thus learning the importance of caring for and maintaining books.

Displaying Books Throughout the Classroom

In addition to a classroom library, you may want to place book bins in other strategic areas of the classroom to further convey the message that books are important. For example, a few books about different kinds of buildings, cities, and bridges can be placed in the block area. Several books related to math concepts might be displayed with the math manipulatives. Books, magazines, and posters about science topics and inventors could be featured with a science display. How-to books and books about famous artists can be placed near the art supplies. The judicious placement of books in strategic areas inspires children and shows them how books are related to all aspects of the intellectual life of the classroom.

Storing Materials for Writing

Writers must have easy access to supplies for writing and illustrating their work. Because writing takes place throughout the classroom, the only space requirement is for storage. The designated space for storing writing materials can also be a place to display "published" books, stories, or poetry the children have written.

Supplies for writing and illustrating work include items that are available in most classrooms:

> standard pencils, colored pencils, markers;
>
> skin color markers, crayons, paper, paint;
>
> erasers, pencil grips (especially helpful for children with limited fine motor skills);
>
> stapler, staple remover;
>
> scissors, paste, tape, hole punch;

paper—white, manila, construction, newsprint—in a variety of sizes;

lined paper—one half inch for younger children and regular-ruled paper for older children;

story paper with space for pictures;

posterboard;

a folder/file system in which to store finished and unfinished work;

a date stamp and stamp pad;

shelves, bins, or baskets to hold writing paper and writing tools;

wastebaskets, recycle bins;

book-binding materials (e.g., thread, yarn, needles, paper fasteners, a binder machine, cardboard).

Think about the messages you want to give children about writing. Children will be more likely to write independently when teachers take steps such as the following:

- Honor children's writing by displaying work on a book rack or on the bulletin board for others to read.

- Make sufficient quantities of writing materials available so children know there is enough for everyone.

- Display a chart that describes what happens at each stage of the writing process, so children can work independently.

- Provide reference materials such as alphabet charts, dictionaries, word lists and, for third graders, thesauruses.

- Select and share library books for inspiration and clarification.

Writing materials can be stored in plastic crates if shelving is limited. You can also use crates to store children's writing if you place hanging file folders in them.

Supplies and Space for Exploring Math

It is a good idea to put all math materials—manipulatives and games—in one place. This helps children to find materials efficiently. It also enables them to consider a variety of options for using materials. For example, a child who wants to measure the length of the classroom might go to the math shelf and decide to use cubes or colored rods. Board games, poker chips, dice (number cubes), and playing cards all encourage logical thinking and therefore could be stored together.

Children are more likely to share, explore, create, and acquire skills and concepts with these materials if you take the following steps:

- Provide sufficient quantities for several children to work at a time.
- Display a range of children's work with different materials.
- Give each child a math journal to record ideas, questions, and problem-solving strategies.
- Keep the materials neatly displayed, organized, and available at all times during the day.

As you expand the number and variety of materials, try to avoid cluttered shelves. Make sure children have enough room to use the materials successfully. Sometimes large projects (e.g., measuring with links) may take up the entire classroom. Small projects that children want to preserve for a period of time (e.g., a pattern block design) can be safely stored on a tray.

Materials that invite explorations in math include collections and commercial manipulatives. Children also need supplies for recording information.

Collections

Collections of household objects can be used for counting, estimating, and sorting. The children can help you gather these from their homes. Some suggestions are:

Buttons	Spools of thread
Plastic bottle caps	Screws, nuts, bolts
Assorted seeds	Shells
Keys	Wallpaper or fabric samples
Ribbons	(with patterns)

Children will use these collections to sort, organize, weigh, design patterns, trade in place value, estimate, and for many other math tasks. For storage, you can use dishtubs, shoe boxes, and plastic containers that can be purchased inexpensively at any variety store. For sorting, you can use trays, bowls, egg cartons, meat trays, and margarine tubs to hold sorted items.

Commercial Manipulatives

There are many excellent materials to inspire children to explore mathematical concepts. If you are just beginning to stock your math shelves and have a small budget, we recommend that you invest in the following materials:

Colored Links	Colored Cubes
Cuisenaire Rods	Pattern Blocks
Unifix Cubes	

Other basic and inexpensive materials for math that will enrich your program include the following:

Beans and Sticks	Yard sticks, meter sticks,
Dice	and clear plastic rulers
Calculators	Playing cards

When your budget allows, you can expand your supply of math materials. Many of the materials listed below can be found in school supply catalogs.

Blocks

Attribute blocks	Base Ten blocks
Multilink cubes	

Calculating and Counting Materials

Play money	Hundreds boards
Plastic counters	Dominoes
Chip trading - tills and chips	

Drawing Tools and Measuring Devices

Stencils	Compasses and protractors
Trundle wheel	Even arm balance
Deep dish simple scale	Clear plastic containers with metric delineations
Measuring cups and spoons	Money stamps
Clock stamps	Clocks and stop watches

Geometric Materials

Geoboards	Tangrams
Geometric solids	Polydrons
Pentominos	Templates for tangrams and pattern blocks

Supplies for Recording Math Discoveries

To record discoveries in math, supplies such as the following can be used:

pencils, markers, crayons

graph, grid, and dot paper

ruled, unruled, and colored paper

chalk and 4 to 6 individual chalk boards

adding machine paper

tape, string, and rulers

vinyl graphing cloth

Math materials and supplies, particularly those with small pieces, can be stored in dish-tubs, buckets, or boxes and labeled with the name and picture. If you also label the shelf or table where each item belongs, children will know how to clean up independently.

Collecting Games

Games can enhance learning in all areas of the curriculum, particularly math and reading. When children play games, they develop important social skills and practice winning and losing. Games are ideal for choice time. Because games may be played in many areas of the room, the only space required is a cupboard or shelf for storage.

Children will enjoy both commercial and homemade games and puzzles. If you tape the corners of boxes when they are new, they will last longer. Some games can be stored in large self-sealing plastic bags. Directions can be typed in large letters or enlarged on a copier and placed on the box cover or inside the bag. Sometimes children like to rewrite the directions given in commercial games. Directions can be preserved if they are pasted on cardboard and laminated or covered with clear contact paper.

Commercial Games/Puzzles

Many games promote mathematical and strategic thinking. They provide an enjoyable way to reinforce the acquisition of basic math facts in addition, subtraction, multiplication, and division. Some popular games for young primary age children are:

Uno	Connect Four	Sorry!
Rack-O	Dominoes	Twister
Stack	Checkers	Mancala
Chutes and Ladders	Parcheesi	

For older primary grade children, the following games can be added:

Backgammon	Rummicub	Junior Boggle
Chess	Junior Scrabble	Othello
Monopoly Junior	Yahtze	

Playing cards can be used for all sorts of games that reinforce math skills (see Resources).

Jigsaw puzzles give children an opportunity to collaborate with partners. A sheet of cardboard, plywood, or a tray will make the puzzle moveable. In choosing puzzles of interest to your group of children, you may also want to think about subjects that relate to social studies or science projects.

Homemade Games

Children take great pleasure in inventing their own games to practice skills such as times tables, addition and subtraction facts, and spelling. You and the children can make games with a few basic materials such as the following:

old workbooks to cut up

index cards of many colors

magnetic letters to manipulate for word construction

posterboard of various sizes and colors to make game boards

stickers to decorate boards

blank dice on which you can write letters for spelling games or numbers
for math games

Invented games can be an excellent culminating project for a study. For example, after studying the neighborhood, children might replicate their community and make up a game similar to Candyland. It could incorporate what children learned about mapping, directions, keys and legends, and provide practice in reading and math. Work on regrouping might be encouraged by "trade-in" games like Race to 100 (also known as Win a Hundred). Other trading or renaming games can be devised to work in bases other than ten.

Organizing Science Materials and Tools

How you decide to organize science experiences in your classroom will dictate how you organize the science environment. You may have work times when all of the children are engaged in science activities. You may also want to have a shelf or an area equipped with tools for investigations in science and offer this as a choice activity. Since math and science materials are often used together (e.g., scales, measuring cups, rulers), consider storing these materials near each other. A table located close to the science materials may be sufficient for science explorations. If the whole class is involved in a scientific study, then other work tables or the floor can be used.

Materials that will inspire scientific investigations include any of the following:

rocks and minerals	batteries, bulbs, and wires
magnets	plants
fish tank	shells
seeds and nuts	terrarium
meal worms	pets (guinea pig, bird, rabbit, hermit crabs)
ramps and balls	pendulums
straws and bubbles	

Tools for scientific investigations and for recording observations may include:

magnifying glasses	binoculars
microscopes	balance and bathroom scales
writing tools	medicine droppers
tweezers	measuring spoons and cups
drawing and graph paper	

Children will be more interested in using science materials and tools if they also see books, charts, diagrams, and posters relevant to the things they may explore. In addition, science studies for children will have more success if children:

- know how to handle the materials, insects, or other animals properly;
- understand and follow safety rules;
- have a place (e.g., Scientist's Journal) to record observations and questions;
- see their work displayed.

While including materials and tools for science explorations will enrich your curriculum, don't ignore what's right outside your windows. Rocks, plants, bugs, construction projects, bodies of water, and weather can all be part of science.

Materials for Social Studies

Learning the concepts and content of social studies involves both active investigation and representation of new information. How this occurs amidst daily classroom life is discussed in the chapter on Social Studies. Supplies and materials that support investigation and representation activities are, for the most part, those described in other parts of this chapter.

- Books about people and places are included in the library or highlighted in other areas of the classroom.
- Art and construction materials are necessary for children to make models, paint pictures, and create murals of people and places.
- Blocks are used to recreate places children have visited; block building helps children develop geographic thinking and map-making skills.
- Appropriate software for the computer can encourage social studies thinking.
- Cooking experiences (e.g., making bread after a trip to the bakery, or preparing foods related to a study) can extend learning in science, social studies, math, and reading.

When thinking about social studies and the physical environment, also consider:

- space for displays of children's project work;
- space for the display of artifacts related to studies;
- an area for dramatization (the meeting area is often sufficient).

Finally, taking trips to experience people and places first hand is an essential aspect of the social studies curriculum. Trip boards (paper on clipboards or stapled paper on cardboard) enable children to record their observations during trips.

Organizing Art and Construction Materials

You will find it helpful to designate a place for storing art and construction materials so children have access to what they need. Depending on the project, children will use different kinds of work surfaces including tables, standing and wall easels, and sometimes, the floor.

If you have a sink in the room, store the art supplies near it. Find space away from the line of traffic in order to avoid interruptions and accidents. It's wise to choose an area that is not carpeted and make that the main area for painting and other "messy" work. If the entire room is carpeted, a vinyl drop cloth, taped to the carpet, creates a space that says, "It's okay to be messy here." Hang smocks or old shirts in the area for children to wear over their clothing.

A modest supply of basic materials will allow children to paint, draw, put things together, cut, mold, and clean up. Art supplies can be organized in three categories: painting materials, drawing and sketching materials, and construction materials.

Painting Materials

Liquid tempera lasts long and produces vibrant colors; however, it is costly. Powdered tempera is less expensive, but it must be mixed to the right consistency. If you choose to use powdered tempera, add a few drops of rubbing alcohol or oil of wintergreen to keep the mixture from spoiling. Ivory Snow also improves the consistency of tempera and makes it easier to remove from clothes. Water-color sets give children yet another painting experience.

The best brushes are those with metal bands and no seams. Large brushes are good for easel painting, murals, construction projects, and painting at the table. Smaller brushes are best for water colors.

Include a variety of types and sizes of paper:

manila paper	newsprint (18" x 24")
butcher paper	construction paper
glossy fingerpaint paper	

An excellent alternative (or addition) to easels is using aluminum cookie sheets as paint palettes. "Tray painting" (originated by Lois Lord at Bank Street College of Education) allows each child to have an individual set up for painting that includes:

1 aluminum tray

5 plastic furniture coasters—each with a spoonful of red, yellow, blue, black and white paint

2 bristle brushes (1" and 1-1/4" widths)

1 damp sponge

1 plastic water container

Painting Procedure

① Get a piece of newspaper and spread it out on the table.

② Set up your tray for tempera paints or a watercolor set.

③ Select the paper for your painting and sign your name and the date on back of it.

④ Paint!

white blue yellow red black cup brushes sponge

Supplies for tray painting can be stored on a shelf, preferably near the sink. You will want to show children how to prepare and use the trays as painting palettes, and how to clean up when they are finished. The procedures can be illustrated and posted near the sink as a reminder.

If you don't have a sink in your classroom, have two buckets available, one with clean water and an empty one for dirty water. One of the advantages of tray painting is that children need only the three primary colors plus black and white paint. They learn to create other colors by mixing the paints on the tray and discovering for themselves that blue and red make purple, yellow and blue make green, and so on.

Drawing and Sketching Materials

Children will draw pictures and sketch if you simply provide paper and writing tools. Sturdy manila paper is ideal. In addition, stock the shelves or place baskets on each table with the following materials: markers, crayons, chalk (white and colors), chalkboards (from the math area) and colored pencils.

Construction Materials

Materials for construction include: scissors (high quality ones serving both left- and right-handed children), different kinds of paper, and glue (both white glue and glue sticks). Keep a supply of "junk" scraps for collages that you and the children (and their families) can collect, including fabric scraps, yarn, wallpaper, junk mail scraps, catalog pictures, and natural items (acorns, pine cones, seeds, etc.).

Water-based clay and plasticine can be used effectively by primary age children. Clay will last a long time and remain consistently soft and malleable if covered with a wet cloth and stored in a plastic container with a tight cover.

Block Building

If you have blocks in your classroom, children will discover many opportunities for experimentation related to structure and design. They can create three-dimensional representations of what they are learning, experiment with balance and weight, and measure and compare the size and shape of constructions.

First graders may use blocks to re-create their experiences—a trip to the zoo, the supermarket, or the harbor—and then they move into dramatic play. By second and third grades, the building itself is of interest to the children. Children learn about mapping as they create representations of their neighborhood around school or the market they have been studying.

Unit blocks are wonderful materials for children of all ages. If space is limited, you can offer children building opportunities with smaller blocks that can be used on a table or rug.

Unit Blocks

Hardwood unit blocks are durable, have smooth edges, and are easy for children to manipulate. Unit blocks come in proportional sizes that help children acquire math concepts. There are at least 25 different sizes and shapes of unit blocks. A set of 390 unit blocks is recommended for one classroom. This total should include a wide range of sizes and shapes, such as ramps, curves, and cylinders. The more types of blocks children have access to, the more creatively they can explore. If you store unit blocks on labeled shelves and group them by size and shape, clean-up will be efficient.

The size and location of the area for unit blocks will affect its success. Children need sufficient room to build, a clearly defined space, and appropriate flooring. The area for building activities must accommodate a small group and the building project itself. Tape on the floor, shelves, and/or a carpet can define the area. Large projects may sometimes be difficult to accommodate in the classroom. You may want to inquire about using a hallway occasionally, and then find ways to protect the construction from passersby.

Props and Accessories

Props and accessories for block building are essential in a preschool or kindergarten classroom. They inspire children to use blocks to reconstruct their experiences. In the primary grades, children are less dependent on commercially made props. In fact, they will be more imaginative and inventive if you simply provide blocks and encourage them to develop their own props using art materials and manipulatives.

When children are building and express a need for props, you can say to them, "Let's think about what we have in the classroom that you can use." Encourage them to solve the problem creatively, for example, by making fruits and vegetables out of plasticine, traffic signs from construction paper and sticks, furniture out of colored inch cubes, and so on. If you have organized your classroom materials so children know where to find and return them, using them temporarily for a building project will not be a problem.

Table Blocks

There are a variety of small block sets that can be stored in plastic basins and used on tables or the floor. Among the most popular are Castle Blocks, Legos®, and construction blocks in logically ordered colors, sizes, and shapes. Children in the primary grades can spend hours constructing elaborate buildings and designs. Often these constructions lead children into dramatic play.

Look through supply catalogs to find architectural blocks, dominoes, or unit block sets that are scaled down to be used on a table. Children this age love to build structures as tracks for marble runs or domino structures which tumble down when pushed. They will do this over and over again.

Providing for Cooking, Music, Dance, and Drama

It isn't necessary to have designated areas for cooking, music, dance, or drama in your classroom in order to offer these activities for children. Cooking can take place at a table; music, dance, and drama can occur in the meeting area or outdoors. These activities are not isolated but relate to the subject areas of your curriculum. Part Two of this book offers many examples of how children can use these experiences to explore curriculum content.

Since these activities take place in a variety of places, you only need a place to store supplies. Boxes with covers, laundry baskets, or buckets all serve this purpose.

Some teachers keep ***cooking supplies*** in the classroom; others bring supplies out as needed. A group of teachers can get together and share supplies such as these:

    Cookie sheets

    Measuring cups and spoons

    Muffin tins

    Bread and cake pans

    Electric frying pans

    Mixing bowls

    Cooking utensils

    Hot plate and toaster oven

    Pots and pans

    Sieves

For **music and dance**, you need only your voice and children who like to sing and dance. It is also helpful to have the following:

> Tape recorder and cassette tapes
>
> Musical instruments (e.g., bells, drums, xylophone, triangles, castanets)
>
> Song books
>
> Strips of fabric and scarves

Again, these items can be shared among several classrooms.

For **drama**, children like to dress up when they act out scenes from books or those related to social studies topics. It's not necessary to provide many materials. Children can make them and bring in appropriate props and dress-up clothes from home.

Including materials in your classroom for writing, drawing, painting, constructing, cooking, music, dance, and drama will enable you to provide children with a wealth of opportunities to represent their learning.

Arranging a Computer Area

Computers can be tools for exploring, creating, solving problems, organizing data, reading, and writing in your classroom. They belong in your classroom, rather than in a computer lab, so that computer use can be integrated into your daily classwork. To ensure children's comfort, computers should be on low tables with keyboards at children's elbow level and monitors at eye level. Whether you have one or more computers in your classroom, try to arrange the space so two children can work together comfortably at each computer. If the monitors face outward toward the center of the room, other children can see what is going on and work can be shared.

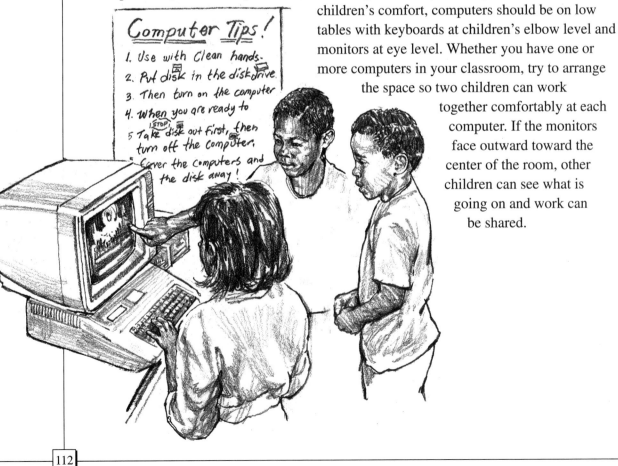

Additional points to consider in locating your computers are listed below.

- Locate the computers away from water or messy activities.
- Avoid placing the computers where the lighting causes glare on the screens.
- Locate the computers near an outlet and use a power strip so all equipment can be turned on/off with a single switch.
- Provide storage space for printing paper.
- Use nearby wall space for displays of children's work and for information about how to use the area.

Computer *hardware* refers to the physical equipment. The programs you choose to run on the machines are called *software*. Some software programs available for children provide little more than a workbook or coloring book on a computer screen. If your software is developmentally appropriate, computer use can be a shared activity that extends children's thinking and offers opportunities for children to solve problems together. Good computer programs also reinforce and extend math and reading skills in enjoyable ways.

The information in the chapter on Arts and Technology will assist you in thinking about how children might use computers and in making judgments about software that meets your goals.

Planning for Children's Physical Needs

It is very important to take children's physical needs, and your own, into consideration in planning the physical environment of your classroom. If you have ever been to a workshop where you had to sit for hours on hard furniture sized for preschool children, you know how your discomfort can affect your learning!

Addressing Basic Needs

It's a great advantage to have bathrooms adjacent to your classroom. If you are not this fortunate, try to avoid the need to line children up to go down the hall and use the bathrooms several times a day. You can do this by establishing a system for children to use the bathrooms independently. (We suggested some possible systems in the previous chapter when we discussed introducing children to the classroom community.)

Children get hungry and thirsty during the day. If you do not have a drinking fountain or sink in the classroom, an alternative is to set up a pitcher of water and cups in a convenient place so children can help themselves. Try arranging (with the school or with parents) to offer children a snack of crackers, fruit, raw vegetables, and juice to sustain them until lunch time. You can set up a "snack bar" in the classroom where children can help themselves if you do not have time in the schedule to stop. However, allocating time for a snack contributes to the feeling of community.

Creating a Comfortable Environment

Far too many classrooms contain only hard furniture. Sitting on hard furniture all day can be tiring and often causes restlessness by late morning or afternoon. When the environment offers alternate, more accommodating spaces and materials, children are more comfortable, better able to concentrate, and more likely to work cooperatively with others.

You can make your classroom more comfortable by including rugs or a small mattress covered with a colorful fitted sheet where children can stretch out. Adding large pillows, bean bag chairs, or an overstuffed chair to a reading or listening area provides a place for children to curl up with a book and relax when they need a break. Think about what you need to be comfortable such as an adult-size chair and safe a place for your belongings.

The environment becomes more friendly when you have plants, a lamp in the library, and pets that children can hold and love. Living things also require care which generates jobs and promotes a sense of community.

Making Accommodations for Children with Special Needs

If you have a child or children with a diagnosed disability, you may need to make changes to the physical layout of your classroom to ensure accessibility and comfort. If, for example, you have a child confined to a wheelchair, you will need to look at traffic patterns to determine if the child has access to materials and working spaces. At least one table in the classroom should be at an appropriate height to accommodate a child in a wheelchair. An alternative is to provide trays for the chair. Some children may need adaptive equipment for standing, or bolsters for floor work.

It is not the classroom teacher's responsibility to obtain any special equipment needed or to make structural changes to the physical environment. As stated in the first chapter on Knowing the Children You Teach, teachers who include children with disabilities in their classroom are entitled to support from a specialist who is knowledgeable about the particular disability.

Offering Places to Be Alone or to Calm Down

Get-away places within the classroom can provide a respite when tempers flare or children just need to be alone for a few minutes. These areas might be designed for other purposes but can double as neutral territory when two children need to work through a conflict in a quiet place. The library, for example, could be a place where children can go to discuss a problem and resolve a conflict.

Privacy in the classroom can be achieved by building lofts, filling an appliance box or an old bathtub on legs with pillows, or using shelves and furniture to define a space where children know they can go to be alone. These alternatives are more useful than a "time-out chair" which often is used punitively without achieving a positive result.

Creative Solutions to Common Problems

Very few teachers start with everything they need. If you are committed to enriching your classroom but your resources are limited, here are some solutions to common problems. You can probably add many of your own ideas.

What if you have individual desks in your classroom and no tables?	• Four desks can be grouped together to make a table. You can turn the open ends toward the center if it doesn't hinder seating, and provide other places for children to store their work. • Let administrators, custodial staff, and other teachers know that you are interested in obtaining tables whenever they become available. • Provide spaces where children can work on the floor.
What if you do not have any bookcases or shelves in the room?	• Boards and bricks or cinder blocks can be used, but need to be safe and stable. • Check with a high school shop program to see whether they could make bookcases for you. • Scout yard sales and search second hand furniture stores. • Provide plastic stacking bins or milk crates. • Ask parents for donations. • Check discount or used furniture stores.
What if the shelves in your room are too high for children?	• Lay them on their sides and find bins to use in vertical spaces. • Cut them down if this is possible. • Create shelving using milk crates and boards. • Use window ledges.
What if you don't have a rug for a meeting area?	• Ask people you know if they are replacing carpets in their home. • Visit carpet stores and seek donations. • Ask for discontinued books of carpet samples and sew squares together. • Call people who install carpets and ask them to save any used carpeting for you. • Check thrift or discount stores.

What if you don't have the materials suggested?	• Save common household junk objects (buttons, bottle caps, keys, plastic bread tabs, seeds).
	• Use a camera to create pictures portraying accurate ethnic/disability/ gender groups.
	• Purchase at yard sales.
	• Ask for donations from community groups, friends, and parents. Holidays are an especially good time to ask for donations. Children can bring a "present" for the class (new or old) and open it at a class meeting.
	• Become a partner with a school or another teacher who is willing to share.
	• Put a notice in a school or community newsletter.
	• Approach shopkeepers in the neighborhood to help. (A hardware store might have lots of discarded keys they could save for you, and a wallpaper store will have discontinued books of wallpaper samples.)
	• Get a teacher's library card and ask the librarian to help select books for your class.
	• Find out whether there is a teacher resource store in your area.
	• Use your budget to purchase manipulatives and other materials that will last for many years.
What if you don't have enough display space in your classroom?	• Cover the chalkboard with paper and use it for display.
	• Ask permission to hang art in the hallways, cafeteria, or administrative offices.
	• Hang displays from the ceiling or tape them flat on the ceiling.
	• Display art on "laundry lines" strung across the classroom.
	• Use ends of shelves or dividers.
	• Drape paintings across windows.

The Daily Schedule and Routines

The schedule and routines reflect the way you want children to spend their days. A predictable schedule and clearly understood routines help children feel safe and become independent, confident workers in the classroom. Just as a properly designed physical environment is conducive to learning, a well-planned schedule gives children a sense of order and makes the day run smoothly.

Considerations in Planning the Daily Schedule

An appropriate schedule is based on an understanding of child development and the specific needs of a particular group of children. Eager for increasing independence from adults, children six to eight years old benefit from having informal, social times during which they can make independent choices. They are active and energetic, yet they tire easily. Therefore, it is a good idea to plan for variety in the day—times to sit quietly and times to move around—and opportunities to run around outdoors.

The amount of time you schedule for activities will vary. For example, meeting times will last longer with older children and their ability to sustain reading and writing times will also increase.

Every schedule should include blocks of time for meetings, writing, math, reading aloud, silent and small group reading, choice time, projects or studies, outdoor time, snack and clean-up. Some of these activities might be grouped together, for example when children are working on projects or a task that involves several content areas.

In planning your daily and weekly schedule there are several issues to consider. What factors must you include? What are your priorities? How will you balance children's need to make choices with your knowledge about what they need to learn? And finally, what are the difficult times for children (and you) each day? Once you have answered these questions and planned your classroom schedule, you will also want to think about how you will make it clear to children.

Starting with Fixed Times

There are some times during the day over which you have little control or choice. These include:

- arrival and departure times;
- mealtimes (lunch and sometimes breakfast);
- special classes (physical education, music, art, library);
- recess;
- individual children's schedules (special services);
- assemblies and other required school functions.

A good way to start is to make a chart of the week and fill in the times of each day that are fixed. By doing this you can see where you have big blocks of time and consistent time slots each day.

Sometimes, even the fixed times of the day are not carved in stone. For example, if special classes or the time allocated for recess don't work for you, try trading times with another teacher. Or invite special teachers to come into your classroom and help with projects, rather than having the children go out. Another alternative is to have half of your class join another for special classes, thus giving each of you more time to work with a small group in the classroom.

Determining Your Priorities

Your priorities may change from one year to the next but they are important factors in determining a workable schedule. Some questions to consider are:

- How do I balance the importance of consistency with the need for flexibility?
- When will meetings take place?
- When will group lessons and work times be scheduled?
- When can I schedule large blocks of time for projects?
- When will the children have outdoor time?
- How can I schedule time for a snack?

Consistency vs. Flexibility

An effective schedule is one that allows for both predictability and variety, but is also realistic. Because you want to help children become increasingly independent, it is a good idea to schedule some activities at the same time each day. The fixed times in your schedule provide some consistency already.

When you know what experiences you want children to have on a regular basis, you can put those into the schedule. For example, if children know that they have writing every day after lunch, or math in the morning, or a free choice time every Tuesday and Thursday before lunch, they can anticipate those activities and know what to expect. If you have several special classes each week in which the children have to leave the classroom, it may make sense to schedule reading, writing, and math times only four times each week.

Rather than attempting to fit everything into every day, you can schedule several substantial work times a week. For example, if children have physical education two days each week, you may decide to schedule outdoor times on the other three days.

Meetings

Different types of meetings occur in the classroom—some that are scheduled every day and others that are called for a specific purpose. It may not be possible to have a meeting first thing every day. For example, if your class is scheduled for music or has to attend a school assembly every Thursday morning, you may want to schedule a meeting later in the day.

If you decide to end each day with a fifteen minute meeting in which you read a story to children, and you want children to spend about ten or fifteen minutes each day cleaning up the room, then you have to anticipate that the work of the day will end a half hour before school does. The kinds of decisions you make about scheduling meetings are based on your priorities and your goals for the children.

Different Kinds of Work Times

Within the course of each week, there will be a variety of work times. They often begin with a group meeting where the teacher introduces something new to children and then has them work independently or in small groups on a task. For example, Monday's math time may be an hour long. For the first 15 minutes a new concept is introduced to the children in the meeting area. For the next 30 minutes children work in small groups on tasks related to the new concept. Then the children regroup in a meeting for 15 minutes to share their discoveries. Subsequent math experiences during the week may either be scheduled, integrated into other curricular areas, or completed during a work time in which children complete a variety of tasks.

It may be helpful to plan one day each week for each subject in which you introduce a new concept or skill. When you decide to teach something new, think about whether it would be best for the whole class to be together or if children would be more successful learning it in small groups.

Projects require large blocks of time because children often have to set up and clean up materials when they are finished. We recommend selecting one or two times during the week for longer, uninterrupted periods (about an hour or an hour and a half) during which children can work on projects in science or social studies.

Outdoor Times

Unless it is raining hard or the temperature is severe, young children need outdoor play time every day. Even when the weather isn't perfect, a five or ten minute break outdoors in the middle of the morning and again in the middle of the afternoon can refresh tired children and increase their ability to concentrate on classroom tasks.

An increasing number of children in the primary grades return to empty homes where they must stay indoors until family members return. They have little time to play outdoors. This makes it especially important for teachers to provide outdoor time for the children on a daily basis.

While many schools have scheduled recess times for an entire grade or several grades after lunch, having class times outdoors is also desirable. During these times the rules of your classroom community are taken outside. Children have the opportunity to play in groups with your guidance and support. Lessons can also take place outdoors. Social studies trips or science expeditions provide an outdoor break. Art projects or measurement activities can also be done outside. As they explore and make discoveries outside, whether about nature or garbage, or play games, they continue the classroom lessons of establishing rules, solving problems, cooperating, negotiating, and talking.

Snack times

Whether and when you schedule a snack time will depend upon your children's arrival and departure times, and lunch time. In addition to providing important energy, snack time can also be used to reinforce social skills and build community. Healthful snacks may be brought from home or provided by the school. Snack time can be combined with outdoor time in nice weather or used to celebrate a birthday or other special event.

The Difficult Times of the Day

In planning your daily schedule, give some thought to the difficult times during each day and how you can make them less stressful. Major transitions include arrival, going to and returning from lunch, and departure times. Additionally, there are numerous smaller transitions during the course of the day as children change from one activity to another: from writing time to recess, snack to a group lesson time, choice time to clean-up.

Many children lose focus and purpose during times of change. This can be especially true for children with certain kinds of disabilities. If you establish a clear transition process, it will be helpful for all children. For example, some teachers have short meetings in the meeting area to wind up the last activity and prepare for what comes next. Involving the children in planning what to do often leads them to have a greater investment in the procedures. Ask children for their ideas about what they might do while waiting for another activity to begin.

Transitions work more smoothly if set procedures are followed consistently. When children have helped to create the procedures, they are more likely to follow them.

Arrival

In some schools, children gather on the playground first and then go to their classrooms as a group. In others, children may ride the bus and arrive earlier or later than children who walk or who are driven to school. In some schools, children may attend a breakfast program before classes begin.

Whenever the children arrive, they each come from a different setting and have to make the transition to school. First thing in the morning is probably not the best time to teach something new or even to expect all children to sit still and focus on a morning discussion. Having a fifteen minute transition time in which children can play quiet games, draw, or write in a journal enables children to settle down, socialize and adjust to the classroom community. It also gives you a chance to talk individually with children as they go about their transition activity. Try not to plan something that children have to make up if they are too late to participate.

Lunch Time

Hungry children do not learn well. Right before lunch may be a good time to read aloud, offer a "free choice" time, have children write in journals, or finish up work. Having children gather in the meeting area prior to lunch provides a time to help them get settled, remember cafeteria and recess rules, and think about what will happen when they return to the classroom.

After lunch can be equally difficult. Children may have just had to negotiate all the issues that are hardest for them: socializing, fairness, games with rules, cheating, and aggression. When they return to the classroom, they are almost always filled with energy. If tempers are hot, you may need to have a discussion to address conflicts. This is also a good time to plan a calming activity such as read-aloud or quiet reading. Children can reconnect with the positive feelings of their classroom community. You will have to observe your group's temperament to determine the most suitable activity for the period after lunch.

Clean-up

Clean-up after a choice or project time can be challenging. It's important to give children a warning. Give the class signal for quiet and tell children how many minutes remain so they can mentally prepare themselves for closure. If children have assigned jobs for clean-up, you can remind them at this time.

Some teachers find it helpful to allow children a little time between work and clean-up. They call a brief meeting where children can share what they have been working on, and then make plans for clean-up.

Departure

If you want children to leave feeling good about the day, try to arrange some time for them to wind down. Gather the children together in the meeting area to talk about the day, participate in an activity, read from a chapter book, and/or distribute papers.

Making the Schedule Clear to Children

Children often ask, "What's next?" A predictable daily schedule minimizes the need for this question and helps children feel secure. If you can refer children to a written schedule to figure it out for themselves, it reinforces their independence. When children can "read" the schedule and use it as a guide, they are more likely to feel a sense of control over their day.

Settle in
Morning Meeting
Writing Workshop
Outdoors
Snack
Shared Reading
Morning Work Time
Lunch and Recess
Story and Quiet Reading
Math or Science Activity
Choice Time
Jobs
Meeting

A good place to post the daily schedule is in the meeting area, where you can review it with the children every morning. You can make daily schedule cards in five different colors (for each day of the week) to distinguish the days of the week. These cards can record the unchangeable elements of each day. The special activities for the day can be written on the morning message (described in the previous chapter) and read with the children during the first meeting of the day.

In summary, the day's structure needs to include sufficient time for active learning, teacher-initiated activities, and children's self-directed activities. An effective schedule for children in the primary grades offers a balance of large group activities, small group activities, individual work times, outdoor and snack times, quiet and noisy times, and active and sedentary times.

Establishing Classroom Routines

Routines are procedures that ensure the effective use of time and space. The regular daily routines, as well as those special routines and events that are particular to your class, help establish a structure for classroom life, and contribute to the positive sense of community. Routines give children the message, "This is our way of doing things."

The routines of your class are often what make the year special for children. They help create bonds within the classroom community. Special routines might be a particular way you start and end the day, the songs you sing, or an activity that is unique to your class such as a special snack on Fridays or being reading buddies with the kindergartners. Knowing that third graders love to tell jokes, one teacher scheduled a twenty-minute joke time every Friday after lunch. Often teachers don't know something is a ritual in the class until the children ask, "Why aren't we doing it anymore?"

What Routines Are Needed

In planning the routines for your classroom, think about all the things you want children to do, and how you can establish procedures that will enable them to work with increasing independence. These may include:

- Putting away and later retrieving coats and lunches;
- Getting quiet;
- Going to the bathroom;
- Coming to meeting, sitting, and taking turns talking;
- Cleaning up after work times and at the end of the day;
- Lining up;
- Getting and eating a snack;
- Doing something constructive during arrival time in the morning;
- Putting away finished work and works in progress;

- Turning in and receiving homework;
- Working in groups;
- Using and cleaning up art and construction materials;
- Storing journals;
- Following procedures for math, writing, and reading activities;
- Collecting and dating samples of work for portfolios.

As you review this list, it becomes increasingly clear why it may be difficult for many children to negotiate their day, especially at the beginning of the year. It's also a challenge for the teacher, especially a new teacher, to create the necessary routines and communicate them to the children! Clearly defined routines, however, are an extremely important aspect of the classroom structure. When children know in advance what is expected of them, they feel in control.

Once you have identified the routines you need, think about what must be in place so children can be successful in following the procedures you establish. Some questions to consider are:

- What will children need for the routine (e.g., folders, signs or charts with instructions, bathroom passes, meeting seat chart, attendance cards)?
- What do I have to get ready (e.g., for writing workshop I have to have folders, boxes to store the folders, and labels on the boxes)?
- How can the children help (e.g., label their own folders, suggest where to display the books they write)?

If you are using storage boxes for the children's folders (for math, writing, reading, or homework), you can label the storage boxes in advance. Written directions can be reviewed with the children at a meeting and then posted near the storage boxes as reminders.

Teaching Routines to Children

Routines will truly become routine if they are made explicit to the children. You may help children learn routines by introducing them at a meeting, helping children remember by reminding and practicing, and giving children reasons for following them.

Using Meetings to Introduce Routines

When you introduce children to a routine such as your procedure for going to the bathroom or lining up, you will need to explain it clearly and model the steps to be followed. You can introduce it by asking children for their ideas on how to best line up. A simple role play can add humor: have the children watch you proceed to the door by running, pushing chairs aside, in order to get there first. Ask the children to assess what was wrong and why it might be dangerous. After the discussion, ask for volunteers to show the group a better way to line up.

Open-ended questions are an effective way to begin a discussion on a new procedure. For example, suppose you are going to introduce homework to children. You might begin by asking children what they know about homework. Depending on their age and experience, children will have a variety of thoughts. Some might say, "My sister does homework every night for hours," or, "We had homework last year on Wednesdays."

A discussion about a routine serves many purposes. It enables children to express concerns and expectations. It allows you to get to know the children better. And it is likely that children will say things you can build on.

> *"Jason, you mentioned that you had homework on Wednesdays. Now that you are in third grade, we will have homework on two nights. One will be the same, Wednesdays, but we will also have it on Mondays. Who remembers how you brought homework back and forth from school last year?"*

Children this age often say things with great bravado such as "Ugh, I hate homework," or, "Do we have to have homework two nights? Second graders are so lucky." Comments such as these are typical. Most children are both excited and a little afraid about whether they can meet the expectations of a new grade. They need opportunities to express these feelings.

Whether or not you are going to tell children what is expected or invite them to participate in establishing the method, it's a good idea to take time for discussion. Once the routine has been introduced, children will need regular reminders to conform to it.

Helping Children Remember

You probably already know or suspect that taking time to discuss the routine doesn't mean that everyone will remember it. Children need a great deal of practice and reminding. If they sense they are being criticized, they will often resist doing what they are asked or told. The following examples illustrate how teachers can help children remember what to do in a positive way:

> *"We're going to get in line now for lunch. Close your eyes and think about what you have to do. Get a clear picture in your mind. Are you ready? Okay. If your birthday is in a month that begins with J, please get your things and get in line."*

> *"Who can demonstrate for us how to set up for writing workshop? Debra? Okay. Let's all watch closely. She's going to the folders. She finds hers in the box that has her name on it. She goes to the pencil can. She takes some yellow lined rough draft paper. She goes to a seat. Good job, Debra. Is everyone else ready? The people sitting from Janet to Shana can go get their writing folders."*

> *"We are about to get ready to go home. Tonight is a homework night. Let's brainstorm all the things you have to do to get ready to go home. Think about what you will need. Who wants to start?"*

Each of these ideas requires taking some time to discuss and practice the routine. However, it is time well spent. Everyone is involved. Of course some children will still have difficulty and need a friendly reminder from time to time: "Nina. Do you have your backpack? Is the note about the PTA meeting in it? Do you have your homework folders?"

Providing Reasons

Children in the primary grades often have difficulty waiting for turns or doing things an adult tells them to do. The minute the adult gets impatient, the child may become increasingly stubborn. Rather than waiting for a conflict to arise, explain your thinking in simple ways.

> *"I know that you are really thirsty and it's hard to wait to get a drink. But if everyone rushes to the water fountain at once, what will happen?" Provide children with time to respond. "Yes. There will be pushing and shoving and someone is likely to get hurt. So the reason I am calling only three people at a time is to avoid an injury."*

Children may not agree with our reasons, but they are more likely to cooperate once they understand them.

You may think that the reason for something is obvious, but it is often not obvious to children. For children, the actions of adults can seem arbitrary and confusing. Offer an explanation like: "Not everyone can use the paper maché materials at once because it is messy. I decided that five children would work with paper maché today. Everyone will have a turn sometime during the next two weeks. I realize that this is frustrating. Paper maché is a wonderful but very messy material." Explaining your reasoning to children helps them become logical thinkers. It also enables them to move from self-centeredness to cooperation. When you explain your reasoning and children see that you will let everyone have a turn, they grow to trust you. Teachers have to try to be fair. For children, wanting and waiting can be the hardest part of school.

Evaluating the Effectiveness of Routines

Sometimes even when you have thought through the routines for your classroom, things don't run smoothly. A procedure may work for one group of children and the next year be totally ineffective. Do not assume rules and routines can be carried over year after year. If a particular routine is not working, try to pinpoint where the problem is. Ask yourself the following questions:

- Do the children understand what they need to do?
- Are there too many steps involved?
- Am I sending too many children at one time so that things get chaotic?

Once you have located the problem, try to identify two or three ways it can be addressed. Pick the one you think will work the best. Explain to your class why you are changing the routine and why you think the new one will work better. After you have tried the new routine for a few days ask your class whether they notice a difference.

> *Ms. Pope was feeling frustrated because at the start of every writing time her students were falling all over one another as they reached for their supplies. She decided a change was needed. The next day she carefully observed this period of time. She noticed there were too many children going to the supply shelf at one time. She also saw that if she moved the paper supplies away from the writing tools it would naturally divide the writers. The next day for her mini-lesson, Ms. Pope explained what she had observed and what she decided to change. She asked her class to observe how the beginning of writing time felt and to plan to talk about it tomorrow.*

Involving children in the evaluation process helps them understand why you want to make a change. It is also more likely to engage their support.

Offering Children Choices

When children have choices in school, they are likely to feel competent and independent about their work. Whether the choices are small—what snack to eat, which game to play—or large—selecting a topic for a story, planning a skit about a study—children are more motivated to pursue a task or idea they have chosen. Teachers who provide genuine choices on a daily basis convey an important message: "I respect your ability to make decisions about what you will do and how you will do it." In these classrooms, children feel empowered to pursue something of interest to them, to take on a project because they have questions to explore, and to be in charge of their learning.

Choice times are a wonderful opportunity for teachers to assess children. By noticing and documenting what kinds of choices children make, the children they work with, what materials they gravitate toward, and how they complete a task, teachers learn a great deal about individual children that helps them in planning the curriculum. Choice times also allow teachers to interact one-on-one with an individual child, either by playing a game or talking informally.

Teachers who find ways to provide children with daily opportunities to make choices soon find that some of the behavior problems they experienced in the past—short attention spans, children who act out and disrupt the class—are minimized. Children interested in what they are doing are less likely to be bored and disruptive.

Types of Choices

There are countless opportunities for children to make choices during the day. Choosing a book to read, the type of manipulative to use to solve a math problem, or who to sit next to at lunch are all meaningful choices. When you talk with children about the rules or jobs needed in the classroom (described in the next section), you are offering them an opportunity to make choices. When you plan a lesson in which children work in groups of four to investigate a topic, children feel that they have a choice in deciding how they will proceed with the task.

There may be specific times during the day when you offer children open choices. Some teachers call this "choice time" or "free choice" and offer a specified number of options: painting, games, blocks, computers, cooking, and so on. Open choices allow children to apply the skills they have learned to tasks and projects that particularly interest them. When children are encouraged to pursue their own interests, teachers can learn a great deal by observing them.

A particularly good time of day to plan an open choice time is in the afternoon, toward the end of the day, when children may be getting restless. In the beginning, you may decide to have every child try each activity at least once so that they understand their options.

Helping Children Make Choices

If children are not accustomed to making choices, they may need specific guidance in the beginning. At a meeting, teachers can introduce the choices that are available.

> *"Today during choice time, you have five options. As I describe them, think about what you would like to do. I'll be asking you in a few minutes for your choice. The choices are: games, tray painting, computers, drawing and writing, and working on social studies projects. When you have decided what you want to do, raise your hand so I know you have a plan."*

Before children leave the meeting area, the teacher hears from each child or small group about their plans. Thus, a clear structure for making choices is established.

It's very important to respect the choices children make during an open choice time. Many teachers wonder if they should be concerned if a child always selects the same activity. It's tempting to say:

> *"You've chosen games every time we have choice. Why don't you try something new?"*

This statement, however well intentioned, belittles a child's selection. Another way of responding that is more respectful is:

> *"You really like games. I guess you like them better than anything else in our classroom."*

This validates the child's choice, and lets the child know that you are aware of this personal preference. It also reinforces the idea that other choices are available.

If you determine that a child is stuck, and perhaps uneasy about trying something new, you may want to be a little more forceful. You could say something like the following:

"It's wonderful that you have a favorite choice, but part of school is trying new things. Next week, I'd like you to try a different activity. I'll help you get started."

"Who has not tried the Tangram puzzles? I would like the three of you to try them today. Tomorrow you can make a choice again."

Inviting children to talk about what they have done during choice time at a meeting will often inspire reluctant children to try something new.

Listing Choices

To further structure the process of making choices, some teachers find it helpful to have a choice board in the meeting area. The board lists the activities that are open and tells how many children can be involved in each activity. Children state their choices and indicate on a choice board where they intend to work. Choice boards can be made in a number of ways:

- Turn a chalkboard that attracts magnetic tape into a choice board. You will need cards for each of the choices, and name tags for each child with magnetic tape on the backs.

- Use a peg board with cards to indicate the choices for that day. Next to each choice card, place a specific number of pegs to show how many children can select that activity.

- Insert hooks into piece of plywood and use it as a peg board. Write children's names on round tags with holes.

- Hang library pockets on hooks to show which choices are available. Children put their names in the pocket of their choice.

A choice board must be introduced to the children. At a meeting you can discuss the system: how the number of pegs or hooks indicates the number of children who can choose each activity; where children put their name tags; and how they can change their choice if they decide to try another activity during choice time.

Keeping track of choices reveals children's preferences. A class list on a clipboard can serve this purpose. Older children can be responsible for recording their own choices on a monthly record sheet.

A form for recording choices makes a good portfolio item to share with parents to illustrate a child's interests. Children can also observe their own patterns which helps them to gain greater self-awareness.

If you have not tried including a choice time in your schedule, you may want to plan it one day a week, perhaps on Friday afternoons, and see how it goes. The children's enthusiasm for this opportunity may inspire you to offer choice time more often.

Choice Record

Name: _____

Week Of	Monday	Tuesday	Wednesday	Thursday	Friday

Clear Expectations About Behavior

The third way that teachers establish structure in the classroom is by conveying clear expectations about appropriate behavior. Children feel safe when they know how they are expected to behave, when they understand the reasoning behind classroom rules, and when rules are consistently enforced. Teachers communicate these expectations from the first day of school by:

- involving children in creating classroom rules;
- sharing responsibility for maintaining the classroom;
- introducing the proper use and care of materials.

Involving Children in Creating Classroom Rules

Every classroom needs rules so children know what behavior is expected and what will not be tolerated. Teachers who involve children in creating the classroom rules are helping them develop a sense of responsibility for their own behavior.

You may feel that you already know the rules you want for your classroom and you don't want to take the time to involve children in the process. Establishing rules for community life is a good social studies lesson and teaches children about living in a democracy. Children are more likely to abide by rules and develop self-control when they have participated in generating rules that they understand and agree to follow. Although you begin this process on the first day of school, you will find that throughout the year it will be necessary to revisit the list of rules, modify them, and have discussions about how they are working.

Generating Rules

At your very first meeting you can begin involving children in identifying rules for the classroom. There are a number of ways to introduce the idea of having rules and to involve children in deciding what rules are needed to make the classroom a hospitable place for everyone. You can use the suggestions below to design an approach that is comfortable for you.

Introduce the need for rules at a meeting: "I want to welcome all of you to our classroom. We will be together for the whole year. This is our classroom community and it's important for everyone to feel safe and comfortable here."

Lead a discussion about why we have rules: "We will need some rules for our classroom community. Let's think about how we define the word rule. Any ideas? Does anyone know what a rule is? What kind of rules do we have for crossing the street? Why are those rules important? What might happen if we don't follow the rules about when to cross the street safely?" Relate the discussion to children's experiences. "What would happen if we wanted to play kickball and there were no rules?" Discuss issues of safety, fairness, and comfort.

Ask children for their ideas: "I want you to help me decide what our rules will be. If we make the rules together, it will be easier for all of us to remember them. Because we want our classroom to be a safe place, we'll start with rules that will help us feel safe. Let's take a few minutes for each of us to think about what would make us feel safe here." Invite children to raise their hands when they have an idea. As they share their ideas, write them on a chart, repeating each word as you write it. You may need to ask more probing questions such as, "How do you want people to treat you?"

Help children be specific: A child may suggest the rule, "Be nice." This would be a hard rule to follow because it is not specific. It doesn't let children know what to do. To help children focus on behavior, you might say, "Let's think about that rule. What does it feel like when people are nice to one another? Can anyone think of an example of being nice?"

State rules positively: This increases the likelihood that children will follow the desired behavior. When we say "Don't run," children tend to focus on the word "run" rather than the desired behavior. If we state the rule positively, "We walk when indoors" then children have a positive image of what is expected.

Give examples to illustrate your points: "Let's pretend that someone just shared an idea in one of our meetings and another person said, 'That's a stupid idea.' How would the first child feel? What rule do we need to make sure everyone feels comfortable sharing their ideas in our classroom?" Guide children in developing a rule such as, "We help each other."

Summarize a group of ideas that are related: Children may have offered a series of ideas such as, "Don't push. Don't hit. Don't pinch." Read these back to the children and ask, "How can we say this positively in one rule?" The children might come up with a rule such as "Don't do anything to hurt anyone." Encourage them to say it positively, for example: "We treat each other kindly."

Discuss where the rules should be posted: After you have a list of rules, explain that you will put all their best ideas on a chart and bring it to the next meeting. Ask the children where to keep the list so everyone can refer to it. One teacher made the rules into a classroom pledge. The children read it together most mornings and have discussions about what each rule means.

You may not be able to get through the whole process of generating rules in one meeting. This will depend on the age of the children and how familiar they are with

> *Our Classroom Pledge*
>
> Because our classroom needs to be a safe, peaceful, and comfortable place, I will do my best to:
>
> 1. Be helpful to others.
>
> 2. Solve problems with words.
>
> 3. Keep the room neat and organized.
>
> 4. Move slowly.
>
> But most of all, I will try to follow the golden rule:
>
> Treat others the way you would like them to treat you.

participating in a discussion. For some groups, you will need several meetings before you complete your classroom rules.

To further clarify the meaning of each rule, you can ask the children to draw pictures of what each rule means. The children can also make up skits to show what it would look like if each rule was followed.

Reminding and Reinforcing

Rules will sometimes be broken, and everyone will need reminders about the rules and how to follow them. In fact, one community building rule might be, "We remind our friends if they forget the rules." This keeps the responsibility for order within the group and not just with the teacher.

In *Teaching Children to Care*, Ruth Charney states that in order for children to feel safe, they have to know that they are seen (1992). The author recommends that for the first month or two of school, teachers focus on the three Rs of classroom management: Reinforcing (letting children know that they are noticed), Reminding (asking children about rules and procedures), and Redirecting (letting children know what they should be doing at a given time). She states that appropriate comments are:

- *Encouraging*—They support children's efforts.

  "That problem you've been working on is tough. I'm so impressed with how you all are working hard together. Let me know if you need my help."

- *Specific*—They name a behavior or accomplishment and avoid general labels of "good" and "bad."

  "I see that many of you are remembering to look at the person who is speaking. We can listen better when we look at the speaker."

- *Positive*—"Show me what you will do..." rather than "Don't do that."

  "Show me where we keep our journals."
  "Remind me how we respond if someone makes a mistake."

By commenting in positive terms on what you see, you let children know that you are always aware of what everyone is doing in the classroom. Positive reminders can be very effective in encouraging the kind of behavior you want to see and in making children feel safe.

Consequences for Breaking the Rules

Instead of punishments, think about logical consequences when children break the rules. Consequences must be concrete and straightforward. A particularly effective strategy is to involve the children in determining the consequences. You might ask, "What do you think we should do when someone forgets to put things back when they have finished using them? How can we help one another remember?" By involving the children in determining consequences for breaking a rule, accepting the consequences becomes a choice for them and not a power struggle.

Sitting alone with a child and discussing why the rule was developed and what it means can help. "Do you remember why we have that rule? How can we help you remember it?" Sometimes a child needs to spend time practicing and role-playing the helpful behavior if she has wasted class time and upset the constructive atmosphere of the classroom.

When you stay calm and speak in positive terms to children about breaking the rules, you show them that you dislike their behavior but you will provide time for them to practice more positive behavior. Public embarrassment or ridicule makes children feel bad and does not help them change their behavior. Instead, it is best to speak to a child privately. This gives children the message that you care about their feelings and that you want to help them to keep trying to be successful in following the rules of the classroom.

Sharing Responsibility for the Classroom

While it is important to have the room organized with a clear plan in mind for the first week of school, there are compelling reasons for leaving some things until after the children arrive. You don't have to spend your summer vacation making beautiful labels for everything in your classroom and preparing elaborate job charts and bulletin boards. You can involve children in making labels for materials, and in deciding on what jobs are needed for the classroom. The process of involving children in these tasks sends a very important message: "This classroom belongs to all of us and we will decide together how to take care of it."

Generating Jobs for the Classroom

Sometime during the first week of school, a class meeting can be used to discuss the need for classroom jobs. You may begin this discussion by asking children:

"Why do we need a neat classroom?"

"What would happen if we left the classroom a mess every day?"

"What are some of the jobs we need to keep our classroom clean and neat?"

List the ideas children offer on a chart. You can include the name of the child who offered each idea.

Jobs We Need to Do in Our Classroom	
Danna	– We clean up rubber bands.
Arben	– We clean up blocks.
Franny	– We clean up markers with the tops facing up.
Shantelle	– We clean up the paints.
Pavel	– We clean up crayons and markers.
Bailey	– We need to take care of frogs and hermit crabs.
Zara	– We have to clean up paper.
Tommy	– We clean up our books.

If children are not thinking of all the jobs you know are needed, you can ask leading questions such as the following:

> *"Let's suppose we were finished painting and there were dirty brushes and paint holders on the table. What would we need to do?"*
>
> *"If no one was responsible for watering our plants, what might happen?"*
>
> *"What kind of job do we need to make sure the tables are cleaned before snack time?"*

Once you have a list of the jobs, you can have the children vote on how many children it will take for each job. Job-sharing is a good way to have children get to know their peers and learn to collaborate with others.

In making the job chart, keep in mind that it is beneficial to have everyone's name on the chart all the time. If there are not enough jobs to go around, you can have a category called "Week Off" to acknowledge that even when children don't have a job, they are still part of the classroom. Special tasks can be assigned to these children during job time such as helping the teacher file work or preparing for the next activity.

Classroom jobs need to be re-evaluated periodically. After trying the agreed upon jobs, the class can discuss questions such as the following:

- Are the jobs being done well?
- Do we have the right number of people assigned to each job?
- Are other jobs needed?

Once children have had the experience of deciding on jobs for their room, they are likely to think of new responsibilities and roles. Some of the most popular jobs involve leadership roles. For example, one class decided to have a "Meeting Starter." The job entailed giving the class signal for quiet, gathering the children in the meeting area, and having the class read the morning message. In another class, the children decided in the middle of the year that they needed a "Clean-up Manager" to keep everyone on task. Another year, the children decided to have a "Floater" who circulated during clean-up time asking if anyone needed help and offering assistance if needed. One teacher established a "Math-board Data Collector" to record daily counts for the class. The possibilities are endless!

Making Signs and Labels for the Room

Some teachers prefer to make all the signs, charts, and labels themselves because they want everything to look attractive and neat. This is a perfectly valid reason and may be particularly appropriate if you teach younger children.

If you teach second or third grade, consider having the children make some of the signs and labels for your classroom. Even first graders can write their names and label their own cubbies. It won't look as neat, but children learn that the classroom belongs to them.

Introducing the Proper Use of Materials

In the previous chapter on Community, we suggested that at the beginning of a new school year, teachers should limit materials to ones that children are able to handle. To establish a structure for the use of materials, it's important to give some thought to how you want children to use the materials, where you want them stored, and how you want them maintained. Children will then learn that you want them to be responsible for their own actions, and that they are trusted members of the group.

Using Meetings to Introduce Materials to the Class

Meetings are an ideal time to introduce classroom materials to the entire class. Present the material in an interesting way by hiding part of it, giving a clue about it, and asking the children to guess what it is. Engage the children in a discussion about the material and its use in the classroom. Next, invite several volunteers to make something with the material and talk about the different and creative uses children can invent for the materials. Discuss all the safe and purposeful ways to use the material in the classroom. Ask children for their suggestions about the care of the materials. This encourages collaboration and respect for each other's ideas.

Each time you introduce new items, take time to talk about them with the children. Encourage children to think of new ways to use and care for all materials.

Listed below are the kinds of questions you can ask children when you introduce new materials. Taking time to have children share their responses to these questions helps to insure satisfying learning experiences as children begin to work independently in the classroom:

- What materials do you see?
- How many objects look the same? How many are different?
- Can you name all the things that you see?

- Do you see anything familiar in front of you? Is there something you have never seen before?
- Do you see anything that looks like something you used at another time?
- What could you do with this…?
- What would happen if…?
- Do you see something you would like to try to use?
- Where can we keep these materials?
- Where can we put your finished work?
- How will we know whose work it is?

It is important to give children an opportunity to ask questions themselves, and to keep instructions simple. Here is an example of how you might introduce tray painting to the children during a meeting time.

Before the meeting, prepare an aluminum tray as a paint palette as previously described. Place the tray where everyone can see it and spark the children's curiosity by saying, "I've collected all these things on the tray from our art area. Can you tell me what you see on the tray?"

After the children name the items, continue with a series of questions to extend their ideas:

"How many paint colors do you see? Can you name them?"

"What if we need a color that's not here? Does anyone know how we can get colors we don't see?"

"How can we keep the colors from getting all mixed up?"

"Can you think of why there are different sized brushes here?"

"Why do we need a container of water?"

"What ways will we be able to use the sponge?"

"When your painting is finished, how should you clean up? Where do the materials belong?"

Each question encourages the children to consider ways in which the painting tray can be used as an independent classroom art activity, while it also anticipates their needs.

Introducing all classroom materials in this way generates interest and teaches children how you expect them to use materials. By inviting children to think about all the ways they could use the materials and by accepting their suggestions, you model respect for ideas, encourage logical thinking and problem solving, and help children learn to use materials thoughtfully.

If you have begun the year without introducing materials to the children and you find that you are unhappy with the way they are using and caring for materials, it's not too late to start over. Remove the materials that are being poorly used or abused. At a class meeting, introduce each set of materials to the children as described above. Many teachers find that this approach works very well, even if children are already familiar with the materials.

Involving Children in Introducing New Materials

Once you have introduced all the basic classroom materials and discussed their use, where they go, and how to keep them orderly, it may not be necessary to introduce every new addition to the classroom during a class meeting. An alternative is to teach a small group of children how to play a new game or use a new set of manipulatives and then have these children teach the others.

Suppose, for example, you want to introduce a new card game such as Uno. You could offer this as an option during choice time by saying, "I have a new game for our class and it's called Uno. I can teach it to four children during our choice time today. Who is interested?" If some children already know how to play the game, you can have them help you teach the rules. In this way, the teacher's job is made easier and children reinforce the proper use of materials for one another.

Whether the teacher introduces materials or children teach one another, it is important to convey the message that materials are valued and must be used with care. You will find that the benefits of introducing all materials are well worth the time involved.

Closing Thoughts

An explicit classroom structure enables teachers to teach more effectively and children to become self-directed learners. Children who know how to use and care for materials, who understand the rules of the classroom, and who are able to make choices experience the power of being in control of their learning. It then becomes the teacher's job to guide the learning process.

Resources for Establishing a Structure for the Classroom

Deal Me In! The Use of Playing Cards in Teaching and Learning. Golick, Margie. New York: Jeffrey Norton Publishers, Inc., 1973.

Serious Players in the Primary Classroom: Empowering Children Through Active Learning Experiences. Wasserman, Selma. New York: Teachers College Press, 1990.

Reference

Charney, Ruth Sidney. 1992. *Teaching Children to Care: Management in the Responsive Classroom.* Greenfield, MA: Northeast Foundation for Children.

GUIDING CHILDREN'S LEARNING

All teachers want children to become confident, competent learners. A competent learner understands the processes of learning: how to define a problem, find information needed to solve problems, put ideas together in an organized way, and apply knowledge to new situations. The most important message children can receive from adults is "I have confidence in you. You can learn. Trust yourself."

> Students respond to their own expectations of what they can and cannot learn. If they believe they are able to learn something, whether solving equations or riding a bicycle, they usually make headway. But when they lack confidence, learning eludes them. Students grow in self-confidence as they experience success in learning, just as they lose confidence in the face of repeated failure. Thus, teachers need to provide students with challenging but attainable learning tasks and help them succeed (Rutherford and Alhgren 1990, 187).

The early childhood and elementary school years establish a foundation for life-long learning.Therefore, **how** teachers guide children's learning is as important as **what** children are learning.

The fourth strategy for constructing curriculum describes the teacher's role as a guide in the learning process. Underlying this approach to teaching is an understanding of how children learn best and a set of principles that guide teachers in planning curriculum that is meaningful to children. Teachers design classroom activities so that children can construct their own knowledge by actively investigating real problems, representing their growing understandings in a variety of ways, and reflecting on what they have learned. They use an integrated approach that allows children to apply skills they are learning across the curriculum in math, reading, writing, science, social studies, and the arts and technology.

How Children Learn

To construct curriculum that is responsive to the needs and interests of a group of children, teachers base their decisions about instruction on a well-defined philosophy of education. This philosophy emerges in part from a teacher's own experiences, and also relies on the work of psychologists and learning theorists.

In the first chapter, Knowing the Children You Teach, we provide an overview of what several respected theorists have taught us about how children learn. Piaget observed that children's thinking changes over time and that they continually construct their own knowledge. Vygotsky described the important influence of social interaction on children's development and learning. Erikson explained how children in the primary grades are at the stage of Industry during which they enjoy the challenge of new ideas, are capable of collaborating with peers, and like to use tools to produce products. And Gardner's work alerts us to consider all types of intelligence in planning learning experiences so that every child can feel confident and experience success.

Based on the work of these theorists, we highlight four central concepts about how children learn: (1) children actively construct knowledge; (2) children learn by interacting with others; (3) play engages children in active learning; and (4) learning takes place in stages in which children move from a concrete, personal understanding to a symbolic, and more conventional one.

Children Construct Knowledge

Children are doers—they explore the world around them to learn how things work, and what will happen if they try an experiment. They strive to make sense of their experiences, to relate new information to what they already know, and to acquire understanding.

Children's natural tendency to explore and figure out how things work is active, not passive. Using all of their senses to examine and work with objects and materials, children form understandings of the physical properties of things: they are hard or soft, flat or bumpy, rough or smooth, straight-edged or round. They learn about relative sizes and weights, cause and effect, and that different objects behave in different ways. A trip to observe firsthand how pizza is made—the tools, ingredients, and techniques used—gives children a chance to think about all the processes needed to create a product. When they return to the classroom and follow a recipe for making pizza, or paint a mural of what they saw in the pizzeria, they make their own meaning from the experience. Children learn by doing, not simply by listening or looking.

Learning is a process of building new and deeper understandings about the world, and acquiring and refining skills. The human brain strives to make sense of experience, to find patterns and construct meaning. When children actively engage in the learning process, they "construct knowledge." This means that children apply information they already have in order to interpret what they observe and make sense of the new experience. They revise their theories and form a clearer understanding based on their previous experiences and observations.

> *Six-year-old Petey looks at the fish tank in the classroom and announces, "We have to put more water in the fish tank because the fish are drinking the water." His teacher asks how he knows this is happening, and Petey replies, "Two reasons. First, they keep opening and closing their mouths. And second, the water used to be up here," pointing to the water line at the top of the fish tank, "now it's down to here," pointing to the current water level.*

Petey makes his best guess as to why the water level is decreasing. The teacher could use this observation to explain evaporation, or, preferably, set up an experiment to allow Petey to construct his own understanding of the phenomenon he has observed. For example, by observing the water level in another tank or jar without fish, Petey can see whether the level stays the same or changes. Other experiments might include painting on the blackboard with water and making chalk lines around puddles after a rain. Based on these experiments, the teacher can guide Petey in developing new theories about what happens to the water.

> *Eight-year-old Simone is adamant that she can explain why the stars shine brightly at night. "The earth is like a ball and we live inside the earth. When it is dark inside the earth, it is light outside. There must be holes on the outside of the earth that let in the light and that's what we see when we look at the sky."*

Simone has some information about day and night—that when it is night where she is, it is day somewhere else. Although she seems to know that the earth is round, she has not yet grasped that people live on its surface. Using the information that she has, she is thinking hard to find an explanation. A skillful teacher observes how Simone thinks and recognizes that Simone needs additional information, experience, and time in order to acquire understanding. Given Simone's explanation, simply telling her the facts is not likely to increase her understanding. Discussion and a variety of appropriate experiences can provide the scaffolding she needs to construct an increasingly accurate explanation. Observing the night sky, making maps of imaginary places, working with a globe, reading myths about the earth, and writing some of her own stories will stimulate continued and revised thinking about her theory.

The process of forming and revising explanations based on experience is the way that children (and adults) learn; it is the construction of knowledge. As children grow and gain a larger repertoire of experiences, they move toward increasingly logical explanations. Carefully listening to children as they describe their thinking enables teachers to perceive how children understand their world. Teachers also learn about the types of experiences that can lead children to more accurate understandings.

Children Learn by Interacting with Others

Learning is a social experience. Most of us are eager to talk with someone else when we learn something surprising, read an interesting book, or acquire a new skill. Children also like to share what they know with others.

Just as children construct knowledge as a result of their active explorations with materials, they also learn by interacting with adults and other children. From infancy, even prior to their acquisition of language skills, children interact with their caregivers. The give and take of sounds, facial expressions, and body language is the beginning of communication. Long before they use words, children understand their meaning. With the expansion of language comes the ability to put thoughts and feelings into words and to communicate effectively with others.

In a classroom where children are encouraged to work collaboratively to solve problems and to create representations of what they are learning, there are countless opportunities for children to learn from others—their peers as well as adults. Working collaboratively with their classmates, children are exposed to ideas that may be unfamiliar to them. They acquire new concepts and understandings when they have opportunities to share information with others, ask questions, and work together to achieve new insights.

Ms. Sanders' class is studying the river in their city. As part of the investigation, the children explore bridges, mills, and dams. Ms. Sanders organizes many research materials for the children to use. Today, at an early stage in the research process, the children work in small groups, organized by topic, to locate the materials they will use. Gina's topic is the Memorial Bridge. She finds pictures of it in several books. Hannah, who is researching the 14th Street Bridge, finds a book on the Arlington Memorial Bridge. She calls to Gina saying, "I found something on your bridge." Gina argues that it's not the same bridge, because the name isn't exactly the same. Together they look at pictures of the bridges in both books and determine that sometimes this bridge is referred to one way, sometimes another.

In the process of talking about what they know, children unravel problems they encounter together and clarify their own thinking. As a result, they acquire a greater comprehension of the concepts and contribute to others' understanding.

Play Engages Children in Active Learning

Children learn naturally through play. Their play is often spontaneous, imaginative, and engaging. Block building holds children's attention and offers endless opportunities for creative problem solving. Spontaneous and planned dramatization in response to literature or a trip enables children to develop language skills and express feelings. Card, board, computer, and dice games help children develop logical thinking and mathematics skills.

Sara Smilansky identifies four different kinds of play: functional play, constructive play, socio-dramatic play, and games with rules. Each type of play contributes to children's growth and learning (1990).

Functional play occurs when children explore and examine the functions and properties of objects and materials. By handling, experimenting, observing, listening, and smelling, children make discoveries. As children express what they are doing in words or pictures, they both recognize and articulate what they are learning. Working with pattern blocks, for example, leads to numerous discoveries—they are flat and can be stacked, when placed on edge they form walls, and they fit together in different ways to make stars, flowers, towers, and tunnels.

Constructive play involves using materials to shape a representation of something— either real or imagined. To study the neighborhood around the school, some children construct a map of the area using blocks, or create a model out of boxes and collage materials. In constructive play, children represent their understandings concretely and in so doing, reveal their interpretation of their experiences.

Socio-dramatic play entails pretending or make-believe. When children engage in socio-dramatic play, they re-enact experiences they have had, observed, or imagined. When first graders recreate a trip to the restaurant by building a restaurant with blocks, and then using the block people for different roles—cook, server, cashier, customer—they are engaged in a cognitive task that requires them to do the following:

- remember the actions of workers and customers;
- select relevant details of particular events to incorporate in the scene;
- use real or imaginary props;
- display in gestures and words that they are playing the roles appropriately.

When children in a third grade class act out different scenes about life in early America based on museum trips, books, and discussions, they are using dramatization to construct an understanding of a time and way of life that is unfamiliar to them. The act of dramatizing helps make the newly learned content personally meaningful for them.

Socio-dramatic play is important for children in the primary grades because it supports the development of abstract thinking. When children engage in socio-dramatic play, they develop the ability to substitute symbols for real objects and events. When they dramatize a story they have read, their play may have imaginary qualities, or it may serve as a means for children to express their understanding and interpretation of the story.

Dramatizing stories leads to many valuable problem-solving tasks: who will play each part, what props will be used, how to summarize the story, and how to remember cues. By replaying experiences with other children, they gain new understandings about a topic they are studying.

Games with rules are board games, many computer games, sports, or any type of play governed by a set of rules that everyone understands and follows. In board games such as checkers or Connect Four, children have to keep the rules in mind as they invent strategies to win. Children practice math skills in games that require dice-rolling or score-keeping. By playing card games, children compare quantities and apply mathematical thinking skills.

Playing games with rules provides opportunities for children to learn how to deal with competition and the feelings generated by winning or losing. Teachers can help children learn to cope effectively with competition if this occurs in the context of a supportive community with clear rules and expectations for behavior. Providing a safe setting for competitive play helps children learn to handle feelings of anger, aggression, and competition (Greenspan 1993).

Many different factors can affect the level of children's play and what they gain from play activity. These factors include family background, individual personality, environment, and gender. Children with learning disabilities or a physical handicap may play differently—their ability to use play to learn new skills or to generalize new concepts may be restricted. They may need to be taught specific play skills such as where to find materials, how to play with them, and how to involve other children in their play, before they begin to learn through their play (LAUSD 1990, II-1).

Learning Takes Place in Stages

Reaching Potentials (Bredekamp and Rosegrant 1992) describes learning as a four-stage process in which children move from a concrete, personal understanding to the conventional understandings of society. All learning begins with awareness and exploration and moves to the stages of inquiry and utilization. To learn, children have to:

- be exposed to concepts and ideas (*Awareness*);
- have opportunities to interact with these concepts and ideas on a personal level (*Exploration*);
- be supported in their efforts to achieve mastery (*Inquiry*);
- use and refine their skills and understandings in real situations (*Utilization*).

All learners, regardless of age, go through these stages when learning something new. And in any classroom, there will be children at different stages in the learning process.

Exposure to Concepts and Ideas (Awareness)

The best time to teach children something new is when they are ready to understand the concept or value the skill. This is why it is important to select content for study that is relevant to children. Content should relate to their own experiences so that they can make connections with what they already know.

The teacher's role is to observe what children already know and set up an environment in which children are exposed to concepts and ideas that are important for them to learn.

- To foster language and literacy learning, teachers fill the room with a variety of interesting books, read stories and poetry to children daily, record children's words and ideas on charts, and put a selection of writing tools and paper on shelves accessible to children.

- To foster mathematical thinking, teachers make materials such as scales, rulers, measuring tapes, thermometers, calculators, and various kinds of graph paper accessible to children. They encourage children to explore with different kinds of dice, a variety of manipulative materials, and measuring tools. They use meetings to discuss mathematical problems. Children are given time to play mathematical games.

While some children are ready to use the materials a teacher sets out, others may not be. Children who have been read to at home or who have seen older children and adults reading and writing are often eager to become readers and writers themselves. Similarly, children who haven't been read to, or haven't had occasion to observe people reading, may not seek out books. Lacking first hand experience, they may not understand why it is worthwhile to become a reader. Although they may gradually recognize letter-sound relationships, or learn sight words by rote if teachers require it, they are unlikely to feel a sense of purpose and motivation in the process. Hearing stories read aloud and watching a teacher write on charts is a first step to helping children with little experience gain awareness of the value of literacy skills. Learning to read is made purposeful when the learner has an awareness of the advantages of reading and writing.

Interacting with Ideas on a Personal Level (Exploration)

Once children have been exposed to new ideas or skills, their natural curiosity usually takes over. During this stage in the learning process, they seek understanding by exploring and investigating on their own. At this stage children don't want to be told how; they may not be aware that there is a "right" or conventional way of doing something. They want to jump in.

> *Theresa takes a familiar book and "reads" through each page using the pictures as cues. While she does not yet recognize printed words, she is demonstrating an understanding that books contain words and tell stories, and that reading proceeds from the beginning of the book through the end. By interacting with books, she is developing an understanding of what reading is all about.*

> *Jesse is drawing a picture of his cat who is quite fat. On the bottom of the page he writes "mi kt s ft." He reads his story to his teacher: "My cat is fat." Jesse is inventing his own way of spelling and demonstrating an awareness of the sounds letters symbolize. He has no trouble reading his own story perfectly.*

Adult encouragement during this stage of exploration is essential for children to acquire their own understanding of skills and concepts.

Efforts to Achieve Mastery (Inquiry)

In the third stage of learning, children gradually realize that conventional methods may differ from what they are doing. They want to know the "right" way and often ask for help. Sometimes they may be ready to learn a more effective technique, but don't know it exists. Because children are motivated at this stage, it is often the optimal time to teach new concepts and skills directly. Teachers can sense when children are ready to learn conventional techniques by carefully observing and listening to children as they work. Knowing when to introduce new ideas and skills is part of good teaching.

> *After Jesse has had some time to experiment with invented spellings for simple words, Ms. Lane has a conference to show Jesse some conventional spellings of words. She uses a book she has just read aloud to the class and points out the correct spelling of the word "cat." Ms. Lane asks Jesse to observe the difference between the two spellings—his in the story and the one in the book. She then suggests that Jesse might want to use "the book spelling" in his story.*

> *In Mr. Cory's first grade class, Mei is trying to figure out how many unifix cubes there are in a bucket. Mr. Cory notices that while she has formed stacks of ten cubes, she starts at one to count the whole amount. Having observed previously that Mei knows how to count by tens, he shows her how to apply this strategy to a new problem.*

In each example the teacher uses careful observation to assess when the child is ready to learn a new skill. Jesse and Mei are both ready to respond to some simple direct instruction from their teachers.

Skillful teachers continually assess the skills and understandings each child has acquired in order to avoid trying to teach something that may be beyond a child's ability to understand. When teaching matches a child's readiness to learn, that child is likely to experience success and develop self-confidence.

Using and Refining What They Have Learned (Utilization)

Once children (or adults) have acquired a new skill, they want to use it. When children apply what has been learned in an authentic context, they refine their new skills and understandings. Because primary grade children are increasingly interested in creating products (Erikson's Stage of Industry), the classroom can be a place where children become productive, purposeful workers, using skills and tools in meaningful ways as they engage in the learning process. The following examples illustrate how children use and refine what they have learned.

- Reading books for pleasure and information involves children in practicing their reading skills. Doing research reports provides children with a focus for reading for information.

- Writing stories, messages, charts, notes, letters, and scripts helps children become competent writers. Publishing stories, collections of poetry, or a class newspaper enables children to feel a sense of accomplishment at creating a written product.

- Working with patterns, shapes, and measuring tools to solve interesting problems helps children become mathematical thinkers. Children utilize mathematical thinking by recording strategies in a math journal, creating graphs, making up games that incorporate skills, or designing LOGO inventions on the computer.

- Collecting specimens, using scientific tools, making observations, and sharing what they've learned all involve children in the work of discovery. Older primary children often enjoy working on science projects and reports.

- Participating in a classroom community and acting as a responsible member of that community helps children to increase their social awareness and social competence. Applying these skills and knowledge to larger communities by participating in a recycling project or helping to put up a handicap access at school enables children to expand their sense of community responsibility.

- Drawing, painting, and sculpting enable children to refine their artistic skills and to demonstrate concepts learned in other areas. Children demonstrate their learning by setting up art exhibits, or producing a play.

Teachers should be aware that the learning of a child with disabilities may require compensating strategies to "go around" a deficit. Technology, a peer, or a classroom assistant may be helpful. Most children with disabilities learn according to the same developmental stages as other children, but be aware that you may have to teach something in a different way if a deficit prevents a child from participating in certain learning experiences. Sometimes significant growth in a skill area can occur after some specific coaching and instruction has been given.

The more teachers know about the children they teach, the better they can plan experiences that support each child's learning. Because in any classroom children bring diverse experiences, have a wide range of interests, and learn at varying rates, you can assume that their receptivity to learning will also be different across all areas of the curriculum. When learning experiences are interesting and leave room for children's input and interests, children can participate in ways that have personal meaning. In the process, children begin to see themselves as successful and competent learners.

Principles that Guide Teachers in Planning

Teachers constantly make decisions as they plan curriculum. Some decisions are made in advance and involve scheduling work times for various subjects or long-range planning for studies; other decisions are made on-the-spot as a "teachable moment" arises in the classroom. Whether the decisions are about teaching a specific skill, a new concept, or introducing a long-term study, you can most effectively guide children's learning if you apply the following four principles in your planning: (1) learning should be purposeful and relevant to children's lives; (2) meaningful learning is integrated; (3) communication is central to learning; and (4) learning takes time.

Learning Should Be Purposeful

Think of a time when someone was trying to teach you how to do something in which you had very little interest. Despite an energetic manner, what the person said probably went in one ear and out the other. In contrast, recall a time when you either wanted or had to know something and you eagerly sought the answer yourself. Perhaps you looked in a book, or struggled with the ideas until finally they made sense. Having a reason and desire to find something out increases our willingness to learn.

Children are more motivated to learn when they are challenged to solve real, interesting problems. When children pursue answers to questions of interest to them and apply their learning to something they care about, they are more likely to remember what they have learned than if they are taught skills out of context. As you think about the new skills and content you want to introduce, look for ways to build on children's interests and help them to see the relevance of what they are learning to everyday life.

Responding to Children's Interests

Children's personal observations and interpretations of an experience can be a marvelous stimulus for introducing new information. A teacher who takes advantage of a child's interests by encouraging further investigation helps that child clearly understand the purpose of the task.

> *After a ferry trip to a nearby island, Sherri, a second grader, asserts the theory that islands float in the water. Some of her classmates agree while others argue that this isn't so. Ms. Kallen asks them how they could find out and the children offer many suggestions. They form groups to test out their ideas. Sherri's group suggests using plasticine and a tub of water to test the theory that islands float. Repeated experiments lead to many sinking balls of plasticine. When finally the ball is big enough to stick out over the top of the water, Jeremiah points to the top and exclaims, "Is this part the island?" Following this, Ms. Kallen sets up other activities for the children to continue their explorations of land forms.*

The teacher could have responded to Sherri's statement by giving her the information that islands do not float. Instead, Ms. Kallen builds on Sherri's curiosity about islands. She encourages exploration that can lead to answering Sherri's question and simultaneously captures the interests of other children. She allowed the children to construct their own understanding by encouraging them to generate and test their theories. It didn't take much encouragement because the children were investigating a topic of genuine interest to them. Because they made their own discoveries and came to their own conclusions, they are likely to retain what they learned.

Teaching Skills in Context

Most children are practical: when they learn something new, they want to use it. When children use newly learned skills in practical ways, they are more likely to remember them.

> *Committed to capturing the excitement he is feeling about a camping trip with his family, eight-year-old Brian makes several revisions to the rough draft of his story before deciding he is ready to "publish" it. In the final editing stages of his writing, Ms. Asche observes that his story contains lots of dialogue. She shows him how to use quotation marks and why they are important. Brian readily uses them because he wants to make his story perfect for publication.*

Skills taught in isolation usually have little meaning for children. Skills taught in context—where children can immediately use what they learn—make sense to learners. When Ms. Asche told Brian that quotation marks help the reader know who is talking, she made the purpose of Brian's learning explicit. Giving a reason to learn a new skill that made sense to Brian motivated him to learn it.

Teachers can use moments such as the one with Brian to present new information to everyone in the class. Brian might share his writing with the class during story sharing (discussed in detail in the chapter on Language and Literacy), at which time Ms. Asche can point out to the class how Brian incorporated quotation marks into his story to make it clear to the reader who was talking. At first, she may use the term, "talking marks," until she is sure the children understand what a quote is. Using chart paper, she might write a part of Brian's story large enough for the entire class to see. In this way other children can learn from Brian's experience.

Meaningful Learning Is Integrated

Integrated curriculum means planning activities that enable children to gain knowledge and apply skills across many disciplines. Teachers have long recognized that children are more likely to learn and remember new skills and concepts when they use them in a meaningful context. Because children in any classroom are at different stages in the learning process, integrated learning experiences offer a wide range of possibilities so that all children may participate successfully.

An Integrated Approach Reflects Real Life Experiences

In our everyday lives we do not have experiences that are "math experiences" or "literacy experiences" or "social studies" experiences. We utilize a broad range of knowledge and skills from many disciplines. Shopping in the supermarket is an example of this process: we may select items to buy based on our knowledge of nutrition and good health; determine quantities to buy based on knowledge of weights, measures, and costs; move throughout the store guided by our understanding of categories of organization; and speak with store clerks using our language skills. Shopping is an "integrated experience;" we use skills and knowledge from many different disciplines to accomplish our goals.

Curriculum is naturally integrated. For example, language and literacy includes speaking, listening, reading, and writing. We teach these skills in an integrated way all the time. Children listen and speak as they discuss stories they have read and math problems they solved. In exploring who works in the community, or investigating the life cycle of a butterfly, children use speaking, listening, reading, and writing skills. Mathematical skills are used to answer science and social studies questions: "How many of the eggs in our incubator will hatch?" or, "What are the different jobs in our school and how many people do each job?"

Integrated learning experiences already take place in most classrooms. For example, after reading a story, a teacher may have children draw pictures or make puppets of the characters, create maps of the setting, write about a character, or create a sequel. In each of these choices, children use a range of skills. When curriculum is integrated, children can see connections between the skills they are learning and how to use them.

- To follow a recipe, children realize they have to measure and therefore need a measuring cup and a teaspoon.
- To send a letter to the senior citizen center arranging a visit, children appreciate the importance of writing neatly and using a business letter style.
- To build a model of the city, children measure, consider scale, draw a plan, and research what to include.

Organizing curriculum around real topics and problems enables children to make connections which are a critical part of learning.

Integrated Curriculum Facilitates Planning

Teachers often feel pressured because there is so much to teach and not enough time. Finding ways to integrate curriculum effectively addresses a range of curriculum objectives at once. In thinking about the possibilities for integrating your curriculum, ask yourself the following:

- Do children use math skills as they work on science or social studies projects? Could they?
- During math and science lessons, do children read, write, and discuss? Could they?
- Are children using dramatics and art to represent their interpretations of literature or what they are discussing in social studies? Could they?

Long-term studies are an effective way to integrate curriculum because a teacher can use them to teach skills, process, and content.

Communication Is Central to Learning

Communication—the exchange of knowledge, ideas, and opinions with others— reinforces children's understanding. As children investigate problems or topics of interest, teachers encourage them to talk about what they are learning. In doing so, children learn to value their own thinking as well as to respect the ideas and opinions of others. Effective communication is an important feature of a learning community.

Talking Clarifies Thinking

When children try to put their ideas into words to explain them to others, they must describe, explain, evaluate, and clarify their own thinking. Informal talking around learning tasks takes place in classrooms all the time.

> *Mei and Ben, two first graders, work together on a math problem. Mei, having just learned to count by tens, makes a suggestion: "Let's make stacks of ten, like this (pointing and counting) so we can count by tens." Because Mei attaches words to her thinking, Ben learns a new strategy for counting.*

A more formal way for children to talk with others takes place in meetings. Participating in group discussions promotes the development of critical thinking skills as children express their own thoughts and evaluate the thinking of others. For example, before a work time, several children talk about the model they are going to make. They discuss what size the people will be and therefore how tall the buildings should be, how many to include, the size of doors, and so on. In the process of describing it and making their building decisions, they organize and clarify their thinking and learn to make decisions as a group. Another example of how teachers encourage children to talk about their work is to call a meeting after a writing time so children can share their stories and ask for the questions and comments of their peers.

Just as children bring their individual learning styles to investigating and representing information, they also bring varied comfort levels and styles of speech. Some children readily speak in discussions while others prefer to listen. Some have learned how to engage in discussions at home while other children may have been taught not to express their opinions or ideas in a public setting. By offering options—working in pairs, small groups, one-on-one conferences, or group meetings—teachers demonstrate respect for children's individual preferences and learn more about what each child knows. Based on their observations, teachers can ask questions and offer information to extend children's thinking.

Open-Ended Questions Extend Thinking

Teachers use questions to find out what children know and to encourage children to reflect on their ideas. Depending on their goal, teachers ask one of two types of questions: closed and open-ended.

Closed questions have only one right answer. They simply tell us whether or not a child knows a fact: "How many sides does a triangle have?" or "What is the main idea of the story?" In closed questions, the teacher knows the answer and the child's response is either right or wrong.

Open-ended questions enable children to respond with many possible answers. Rather than asking how many sides the triangle has (a closed question), a teacher might ask, "What do you notice about this shape?" This way, the teacher will find out whether or not children know the number of sides of a triangle as well as their other thoughts and observations.

You can use open-ended questions and comments to help children:

- *label and organize their thinking:* "Tell me about how you estimated the number of jellybeans in the jar," or, "What would you like to happen to the character in your story?"

- *describe what they already know:* "What do you already know about the public library in our town?" or, "What do you know about caterpillars?"

- *anticipate and wonder about what they will see or do or what might happen:* "Let's think about what we might see when we visit the telephone company," or, "Based on the picture on the cover of this book, what do you predict this story will be about?" or "What will happen to each of these fruits if we slice them and leave them on the windowsill for the week-end?"

- *reflect on an experience:* "What did you see on our visit to the court house?" or, "Tell us about the part of the story that you remember," or, "Tell us more about how the machines worked at the bread factory."

Guiding

Children's

Learning

- ***think about possible ideas or solutions to problems:*** "What jobs will we need in our classroom in order for it to remain clean and orderly?" or, "Let's make a list of the ways we can represent a favorite part of the story we just read," or, "Tell us how you solved the problem. That's a good approach. Can anyone think of another way?"

Listening to children's responses to open-ended questions and comments gives teachers vital assessment information and helps them plan appropriate next steps. For example, after asking children what they expect to see when they visit the harbor the next day, a teacher realizes from their responses that several children have not visited a harbor before and have no idea what to expect. She decides to read *Harbor* by Donald Crews, to prepare children for the upcoming trip.

As discussed in the first chapter on Knowing the Children You Teach, it is important to keep in mind that children react differently to different kinds of questions, depending on the experiences with questions they have had previously. Many teachers find that children not familiar with open-ended questions may be hesitant to respond because they wonder what answer the teacher really wants. With experience, these children will become more comfortable as they realize there are no "wrong answers" and the teacher is genuinely interested in their ideas. With open-ended questions, children have room to interpret the question their own way.

Learning Takes Time

Meaningful learning can't be rushed. It doesn't always fit into fifteen or thirty minute time slots. Frequently, the necessity of scheduling the day into brief time periods arises from pressures to "cover the curriculum" and manage the schedules of specialists and resource teachers. Many teachers complain about not having enough time and feeling pressured by scheduling demands. Scrambling from one activity to the next increases the level of stress in the classroom for everyone and is not conducive to learning.

Three ways teachers can allocate time for learning are: (1) scheduling extended work times each day so children can become involved in tasks; (2) recognizing the importance of giving children time to revisit concepts that have been taught; and (3) giving children time to think about and play with ideas.

Schedule Extended Work Times

Each day, try to schedule work times of at least 45 minutes to an hour so children get involved in an activity. Once or twice a week, it's beneficial to plan even longer periods for projects such as model making, murals, or working on skits. Combining subjects means you don't lose time making the transition from one work time to another.

This may sound impossible at first, but it can work if you adjust your schedule by rethinking time allocations. For example, if a work time will involve children in exploring more than one subject (e.g., math and science, or language and math), try allotting an hour for one activity rather than 30 minutes for two separate ones. (See the chapter on Structure for suggestions on planning the daily schedule.)

Children, like all of us, become frustrated when they are busy at work and we expect them to stop and quickly make a transition to the next activity. When you have no choice but to end a work time when the children are engrossed in what they are doing, it helps if you say something like, "I know it's really hard to stop what you are doing when you're so close to finishing. We just don't have a choice today. You can put your things on this tray and get back to work first thing tomorrow morning."

Encourage Children to Revisit Ideas and Concepts

Simply because you have presented a concept or skill to children does not mean that everyone will now understand and be able to use what you have taught. Some children may already know what you introduced; others will have varied levels of understanding. Like adults, children often need time to come back to an idea, to revisit it in other contexts, and to construct their own understanding.

> *During a discussion about birthdays, Ms. Wong talks with the children about their birthdays. Jenny says, "Tomorrow is my half-birthday." Several children ask her what she means. Ms. Wong asks the class if they know why Jenny says it is her "half-birthday." One of the children volunteers that there are 12 months in a year and 6 months in half a year. The children use the calendar to figure out when their half-birthdays occur. The following week in the midst of a math activity related to money, Ann-Marie says to Ms. Wong, "I just figured out that my quarter birthday is next week. I'm going to ask my parents to give me a quarter for my quarter birthday." Ms. Wong realizes that Ann-Marie has continued to mull over the discussion from the previous week. She applied what she learned to solve a problem of interest to her that relates to money, time, and fractions.*

This example provides insight into the importance of allowing children to stay with topics over time and to revisit them.

Give Children Time to Think

Group discussions highlight children's individual differences. In response to a question or statement, some children will immediately raise their hand, bursting to share their thoughts; other children will ponder the question or the concept presented, trying to assemble their thoughts before raising their hands. The eagerness of their classmates often interferes with their ability to think. As a result, they may lose their own train of thought and therefore the opportunity to contribute to the discussion.

Allowing children time to "think about their thinking" is a teaching technique that addresses children's individual learning styles and makes it possible for all children to participate equally. Here are some ways teachers can provide children with thinking time:

- After posing a question during a discussion, say "Take a minute to think of an idea. Don't say anything yet. Close your eyes and just think."
- Before inviting children to share their ideas in the group, invite them to share with a neighbor. "Turn to the person next to you and talk about what you are thinking."
- Model for children your own ways of taking time to think before talking. "That's an interesting question. Give me a minute to think about it. I have lots of ideas and I need to sort them out."
- Prior to sending children off to work after a meeting, check to see if anyone needs more time or help. If so, encourage those children to stay for a minute or two, to talk with each other or with you, until they feel sure and ready to get to work.

When you model the importance of slowing down to think, you reinforce the value of careful thought as part of the learning process.

In this section we have discussed the importance of making learning purposeful, integrating the curriculum, fostering communication, and providing ample time for learning. These four principles can be applied to planning learning experiences that enable children to construct their own knowledge.

Ways Children Construct Knowledge

For learning to be meaningful for children, they have to be given time and materials to construct knowledge so they can make sense of their experiences. To do this, teachers plan experiences that allow children to investigate a problem, represent their thinking, and reflect on what they are learning.

Active Investigations

Learning experiences that enable children to question, explore, and research respond to how children naturally learn. Investigation allows children to see, hear, touch, smell, and therefore extract personal meaning from their experiences.

Investigation experiences can take many forms. Children investigate when they:

pose questions	explore problems using computers
explore materials	study pictures, maps
conduct interviews	form hypotheses
have discussions	create experiments
observe objects/events	take trips
watch videos, slides	listen to speakers, tapes
read books, articles, diaries	

Not all children participate in investigations in the same way and with the same enthusiasm. Depending on their individual styles, some may eagerly ask questions and rush to gather information. Other children may be more watchful, carefully taking things in before getting involved. Teachers who offer a range of investigation experiences allow for these differences. As children participate in investigation activities, teachers can observe their responses and learn more about the children's individual learning styles.

The examples you will find in the content chapters of *Constructing Curriculum* emphasize engaging children in investigations. Active investigation can take place as part of a scheduled work time in any subject or in the context of a study. (Long-term studies will be discussed later in this chapter.)

Active Investigation During a Work Time

In planning a work time, think about ways children can investigate a topic. Open-ended tasks have many possible outcomes as opposed to lessons limited to a single objective. Open-ended tasks increase the chances that all children will learn something and be able to contribute.

In the two examples that follow, teachers use geoboards so that children can explore concepts in geometry. However, there is a difference in the kind of investigation each teacher promotes.

Ms. Parker, a second grade teacher, shows the children how to construct triangles and squares using rubber bands and a geoboard. Then she has the children practice making triangles and squares of different sizes on their geoboards following the instructions she has written on task sheets.

Ms. Hernandez introduces geoboards and rubber bands to her second grade class. They discuss the attributes of the materials and how to use them carefully. She assigns the following: "Work with a partner to see how many shapes you can make and how many different ways you can construct them. Keep a record of the shapes you make in your math log."

In the first classroom, Ms. Parker has a clear sense of her objectives and expectations for the children. The structure of the lesson allows little room for free exploration and discovery. The children who understand and follow her directions exactly will succeed, while others may be confused. Children who already have knowledge of simple shapes may get bored quickly and ask, "What should we do now?"

Ms. Hernandez encourages the children to be active investigators. She, too, has clear objectives which include recognition of shapes. However, the way she has organized the lesson encourages children to learn different things, depending on what they already know and what they learn from their investigations. Children can continue their investigations, inventing their own next steps. She builds the possibility of surprises into her lesson structure. She observes what each child takes from the experience so that she can plan additional challenges or extra support.

Active Investigation in a Study

Making active investigation a central part of learning content and acquiring skills means that teachers encourage children to wonder about something, to generate their own questions, and to seek the answers. The two teachers in the following examples take different approaches to a social studies project.

> *Ms. Jones' third grade class studies immigration using their social studies textbook as the primary source of information. The chapter they read describes the reasons people leave their homelands to move to a new place. The children answer questions at the end of the chapter. Ms. Jones suggests that the children draw pictures of something they remember from the chapter.*

> *Ms. Parks approaches the study of immigration with her third graders by first reading* Letters from Rivka, *by Karen Hesse, a story about a family who leaves their homeland. The children tell and write personal stories about moving to a new house, going to a different school, and moving to a new city, state or country. Many of the children's parents and grandparents were born in different countries. Ms. Parks asks the children to think about people they know who are "experts" on the subject of moving from a birth place. The children decide to interview people in the community, including family members, who immigrated to the United States. They form small groups to plan interview questions.*

Children in the classroom described in the second example are actively investigating the topic of immigration. Ms. Parks allows ample time for the study. She structures the experience by:

- sparking children's curiosity;
- encouraging children to think about what they already know;
- getting them to generate questions that will guide the investigation.

Ms. Parks involves children in research so that they can extract personal meaning from their experiences.

The process of investigation can encourage children to be active and purposeful as they seek answers to interesting questions. When given opportunities to represent new information and ideas, children begin to internalize what they learn.

Representing Ideas

When we learn something new and then describe it in our own words, draw a picture of it, or act it out, we solidify our understanding of the concept. Offering children a variety of ways to represent their learning contributes to the effectiveness of guiding children's learning. As children investigate and make discoveries, they process new information—

either accurately or not so accurately—and relate it to what they already know. When children represent their ideas in drawings, constructions, writing, or clay models, they take ownership of the information.

Vehicles for children to represent their learning include:

drawings	puppets	writing (stories, letters,
constructions	murals	journals)
skits or plays	graphs	diagrams or charts
songs	dances	dioramas
models	mobiles	clay models

In the previous example with geoboards, Ms. Hernandez suggests that the children use the rubber bands to construct shapes on the geoboard and then record what they make in their math logs. She recognizes that by having the children record or represent their work, they can learn the symbolic representations of the shapes and the shapes' attributes as well as the differences between shapes.

Representing newly acquired information helps children grasp complex concepts and gain new understandings.

> *Following a trip on the commuter train, first graders construct a model which includes the two train stations, the tracks, the bridge they traveled over, and the train. The construction of the model engages them in learning how trains can go in two directions on one set of tracks, how the bridge is constructed, and how the train cars connect.*

Encouraging children to record and represent what they are learning gives teachers another source of information about each child's thinking. These insights help teachers ask appropriate questions, give clarifying information, and guide children's thinking to a higher level.

Allowing for Differences in Interests and Learning Styles

Because children have different ways of expressing and representing their learning, it is essential to offer a range of possibilities for children to represent their ideas. Some children may be more comfortable writing while others more readily express their thinking through artwork. Similarly, children personalize the meaning they get from experiences. When offered choices about what to describe and how to do it, children often surprise us with what they have learned and the aspects of a topic that interest them most.

> *In studying bridges, Delante expresses his understanding of the function of bridges by building with blocks. Cynthia achieves a similar understanding by painting a picture in which two cars move across a bridge while a boat passes underneath it.*

> *After a trip to the science museum, Roger writes about seeing the diorama of underground life, describing in detail the roots, worms, and different colors of soil. Eli is enchanted with the architecture of the museum and uses Lego® blocks to reconstruct the arches and ramps of the main lobby.*

The first two children have different ways of revealing what they understand about bridges. The second two children have extracted different meaning from similar experiences.

Children are the best source of ideas about ways to represent what they are learning. Asking them in a group discussion how to proceed puts children in charge of their learning. You might ask, "How can we show what we saw at the museum?" or, "How can we record our observations of the chameleons?" or, "How can we show our interpretations of the story we just read?" If children have choices about how they want to show what they have experienced, they will have more of an investment in their work than if they are told what to do.

Reflecting on Learning

An important but often overlooked part of the learning process is reflection—stepping back and thinking about what has been learned and evaluating the process itself. Children become thoughtful learners when teachers provide a forum for reflection by encouraging children to ask themselves:

- What did I learn?
- What do I know now that I didn't know before?

- What questions do I have?

- Am I confused? About what?

- What do I think of the work I've just done? Is there something more I want to do? Do I like it? Was it hard? Why?

Allowing time for reflection doesn't come naturally to many teachers, particularly at first. However, once you make it a part of learning experiences, either after a work time or as part of a study, it will be easier to see how to include it as an ongoing part of classroom life.

Reflection After a Work Time

In the section on investigation, we provided an example of a geoboard lesson in Ms. Hernandez's classroom. In that example, reflection could be included in the following way:

After the children complete the activity, Ms. Hernandez has them come to the meeting area to share their work. Using their math logs for reference, and drawing on chart paper, the children take turns describing the discoveries they have made. At the end of the meeting, Ms. Hernandez asks the children to think about the discussion, look over their work in their math logs, and then write down something they have learned or understood in a new way.

Reflection as Part of a Study

Recall the example, described in the section on representation, of the class that took a trip on the commuter train. The teacher of this class encourages reflection at several stages of the children's learning.

After the children return from the trip, the teacher asks them to think about what they saw. As a group, they share memories and information which the teacher records on a chart. She helps them plan their model by asking them to think about what they need to include in it. While the children build, they continually reflect on what they saw and grapple with concepts—how the trains fit on the tracks, how the tracks form curves, how the bridge is constructed. Throughout the building process, the teacher listens to what children say and do. She asks questions to help them reflect on their learning. When the model is completed, the teacher photographs it with the six builders standing next to it. She has each child write about the experience of building the model which she attaches to a photocopy of the photograph. These reflections and representations of the work are excellent examples of children's learning for their portfolios.

Encouraging children to reflect on their learning helps them become more aware of what they have learned and how they learned it. Including time for reflection helps children become self-directed learners.

Putting It All Together: Organizing Your Curriculum

How can you put all these ideas and principles together in an organized way? We have talked about how children learn, and proposed four principles that guide teachers in planning curriculum: learning should be purposeful; meaningful learning is integrated; communication is central to learning; and learning takes time. We suggested that to help children construct knowledge, teachers provide experiences that allow children to investigate actively, represent, and reflect on their learning. The missing element is how teachers apply these principles as well as what they know about child development and individual children in order to meet curriculum guidelines and standards. Teachers need a plan.

In planning your curriculum—how you will address the content and skills for all subjects—you will probably rely on one or more resources. They may include:

- the scope and sequence guides of your school district;
- textbooks that outline the standards for each discipline;
- assessment tools that outline what children can be expected to understand and learn at a given age;
- standards published by various disciplines (e.g., *Curriculum and Evaluation Standards for School Mathematics*, National Council of Teachers of Mathematics, 1989; *Benchmarks for Science Literacy*, American Association for the Advancement of Science, 1993; *Dance, Music, Theatre, Visual Arts: What Every Young American Should Know and Be Able to Do in the Arts*, National Standards for Art Education, The Consortium of National Arts Education Association, 1994);
- resource books (such as those listed at the end of each chapter in Part Two).

These resources can help you think about reasonable expectations for children's learning at a given stage. They can provide some direction for planning what you will introduce to the children during a given year. When and how you will address the curriculum content is organized in three ways.

The first way we recommend that teachers organize curriculum is to plan long-term studies. Studies integrate many different subjects and allow children to acquire skills and content as they explore a topic for an extended time. Secondly, teachers schedule daily work times. Work times often begin with a mini-lesson followed by time for children to explore a topic or practice a skill in one or more subjects. Finally, recognizing that learning occurs all day long, teachers use "teachable moments" to address various components of their curriculum.

Planning Long-Term Studies

Long-term studies enable teachers to guide children's learning of skills, content, and processes across various subject areas in the primary grades. Studies can make curriculum planning efficient and more interesting for teachers and children. Instead of striving to explore a wide range of topics during the year, a few well-selected studies allow children to uncover and explore aspects of the topic that are beneath the surface. Within any broad topic, children can explore many smaller topics.

The content for a long-term study often comes from the social studies and science curriculum. These content areas provide appropriate topics for studies because they address real people, places, objects, and events that children can investigate first-hand. For example, a second grade class in a rural community studies how foods are grown and/or raised in their community. Their research includes in-depth investigations of an apple orchard and a dairy farm. In the process of their study, children explore questions that address both social studies and science concepts, including:

- What jobs do people do at each of these places?
- How do apple orchards and dairy farms affect our community?
- How do these foods get transported to stores?
- How do apples grow and change?
- What is the life cycle of cows?
- How is fruit preserved?
- How is milk pasteurized?

During a study, teachers encourage children to develop questions, theories, and explanations. They conduct research, try out their ideas, and evaluate them. As children learn more about the topic, they are able to revise their theories. They begin to see themselves as competent learners and budding "experts."

The Length of a Study

The length of a study depends on the age and interest level of children as well as the scope of the topic. A teacher may plan a month-long study, but in the process of investigation, children come up with a slightly new direction, so the study goes on longer. On the other hand, sometimes a study is initially intended to last for several months, but for whatever reason, the topic doesn't click and so it is best to end it sooner.

This approach has advantages for teachers. When children explore a topic over time, they gain a broader understanding of the world around them. Studying a few topics in depth also enables teachers to address objectives in all curriculum subjects within an interesting context. The more time allocated to explore a topic, the more likely that teachers learn along with the children. And when children work together to become experts about a topic, it strengthens the sense of community within the classroom.

A Sample Study That Integrates Curriculum

The following example illustrates how one teacher, Mr. Phillips, plans a long-term study that permits enough flexibility to accomplish many areas of study outlined in the school's goals for social studies (e.g., people, work, geographical relationships), science (e.g., water, machines, pollution), math (e.g., measuring, graphing, patterns, geometry, problem solving), literacy (e.g., reading, writing, researching, speaking, listening), and the fine arts (visual arts, music, dramatics). Mr. Phillips allows children to explore their own interests within the structure of this study. He creates a broad plan for the study which includes several trips. Class meetings are used for discussions and planning sessions with the children, thus supporting the goal of creating a sense of community in the classroom.

As you read the example, note the variety of investigation, representation, and reflection experiences. Think about how you might adapt a study like this to the neighborhood in which you work.

Mr. Phillips' class of first and second graders is doing a study of their city, a capital located on a coastline with a large harbor. He divides the study into three parts: the harbor, factories, and public buildings.

He begins the study with a trip to the harbor, a place where people work and spend leisure time. He talks with the children about the trip by posing open-ended questions in a meeting to find out what children already know and what questions they have about the harbor. They generate a list of questions they want to answer on the trip.

Mr. Phillips assigns the children to research groups. Each group will investigate specific aspects of the harbor. The children have some choice in selecting the focus for their group project. He gives each child a "trip board" made from a sturdy piece of cardboard with paper stapled to it so the children can record what they see. They can choose to sketch or write about points of interest to them.

During the study, children take additional trips and interview people who work at various jobs at the harbor. They represent their findings in many ways:

building with blocks   *making milk carton constructions*
drawing and painting   *reading and writing stories about harbors*
making graphs   *engaging in continual discussions*
creating skits

Throughout their work on these projects, Mr. Phillips uses open-ended questions to engage the children in critical thinking and problem solving:

"Why would people want to build factories close to water?"

"Why would our city be selected the capital of our state?"

"What problems might result from having so much industry along the waterfront?"

The children regularly share their thinking with one another and also with other children in the school. The research skills they develop during the first part of the study are used again as they move through the study of factories and other public buildings in the city. The children make maps of the places they visit. During the study of factories, they learn about machines, creating some of their own.

By continuing the study over an extended period of time, children are able to ask questions, come up with explanations, and revise their thinking based on new information. The study described in this example draws on the children's immediate environment. They study a harbor because a harbor is in their city. They study the public buildings in their community as a way to think about community workers and city government.

Once the children become experts about their immediate surroundings, they can begin to think about life in other places. What if they didn't have a harbor? How would their city be different? What are harbors like in faraway cities? Literature and videos can extend children's thinking about differences and similarities between their lives and the lives of other people in other places.

Steps for Planning Studies

A good study takes both advance and ongoing planning. The teacher provides the overall framework for a study and gives some thought to the content, experiences, and materials needed. Once a study is underway, teachers involve children in the planning process by asking them what they already know about a topic and what they want to find out.

As you read the following ten steps for planning a study, think about how they apply to a topic that would be of interest to you and the children you teach. Consider the environment right around your school and what's available for children to see and investigate.

1. Select an Appropriate Topic

As stated earlier, the science and social studies curricula are excellent sources for long-term studies. The topics children can explore in these subjects relate to the physical, natural, and social world and address questions such as:

- why things are the way they are;
- how events happen;
- how and why people live as they do;
- how things work;
- who performs a certain job and how;
- how things change.

Studies related to self, families, and the community can provide rich content for social studies. Science topics can be drawn from natural and physical phenomena immediately observable in the children's environment. This allows children to engage in investigation, representation, and reflection on topics that they already know something about.

For example, if the second grade science curriculum in your school calls for a study of water, habitats, and living things, ask yourself, "What nearby body of water can children observe and study over time?" If there is a lake close by, then organize all three of these topics around the study of a lake. If there is a stream or pond, then make this the focus for learning about your required topics. If there isn't a body of water close by, begin with habitats of living things that children can observe. Then think about how to set up a water environment for snails, fish, or hermit crabs in your classroom.

Guidelines for Determining Suitable Topics

- The topic permits children to think, question, and solve problems as they investigate.
- The topic allows me to teach the required objectives of my school's curriculum.
- The skills and knowledge that children acquire from studying the topic can be applied to future living and learning.
- The topic is real, relevant to children's experiences, and is age-appropriate. The topic begins with phenomena that children can observe directly.
- Resources and materials related to the topic are readily available. They might include people to talk to, places to visit, books to read, and artifacts to examine.
- A wide variety of skills can be applied to the topic.
- The topic can be explored in various ways over an extended period of time.

---

2. Brainstorm Ideas About the Content of the Study

Once you have selected a topic that meets the criteria above, take time to brainstorm the possibilities the topic offers. Ways to begin brainstorming a study include talking with colleagues, making lists, webs, or calendar plans. Looking at books on the subject or taking a field trip by yourself may spark more ideas. If you can interest a colleague in collaborating with you, the planning and implementation will be easier to manage and more enjoyable.

Some teachers find it useful to begin with a web to map the possibilities for a topic. As they learn more, they add to the web. The web on the next page shows how Mr. Phillips organizes his thinking about the harbor, one topic in his class's year-long study. By making this web, he generates a range of possibilities for the study and extends his own thinking. The children will not actually investigate all of the concepts.

3. Become Familiar with the Subject

Brainstorming gives you a sense of the directions the topic might take. You may decide that you have to learn more about the subject. This might involve taking preliminary trips, locating books and materials, and talking to people. Exploring the topic on your own

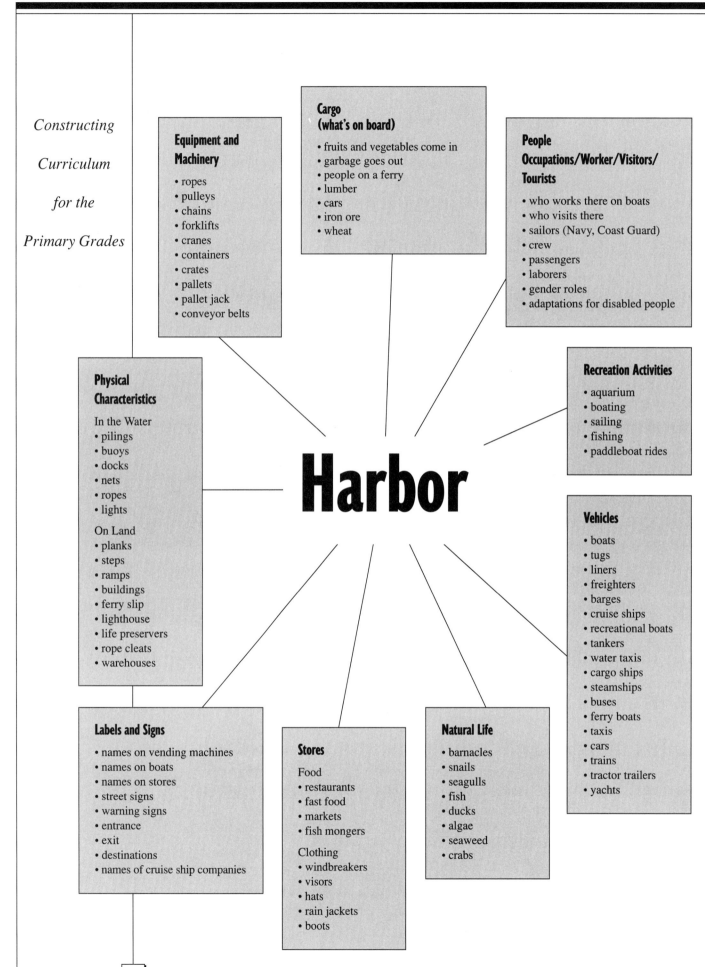

Equipment and Machinery

- ropes
- pulleys
- chains
- forklifts
- cranes
- containers
- crates
- pallets
- pallet jack
- conveyor belts

Cargo (what's on board)

- fruits and vegetables come in
- garbage goes out
- people on a ferry
- lumber
- cars
- iron ore
- wheat

People Occupations/Worker/Visitors/Tourists

- who works there on boats
- who visits there
- sailors (Navy, Coast Guard)
- crew
- passengers
- laborers
- gender roles
- adaptations for disabled people

Recreation Activities

- aquarium
- boating
- sailing
- fishing
- paddleboat rides

Physical Characteristics

In the Water
- pilings
- buoys
- docks
- nets
- ropes
- lights

On Land
- planks
- steps
- ramps
- buildings
- ferry slip
- lighthouse
- life preservers
- rope cleats
- warehouses

Harbor

Vehicles

- boats
- tugs
- liners
- freighters
- barges
- cruise ships
- recreational boats
- tankers
- water taxis
- cargo ships
- steamships
- buses
- ferry boats
- taxis
- cars
- trains
- tractor trailers
- yachts

Labels and Signs

- names on vending machines
- names on boats
- names on stores
- street signs
- warning signs
- entrance
- exit
- destinations
- names of cruise ship companies

Stores

Food
- restaurants
- fast food
- markets
- fish mongers

Clothing
- windbreakers
- visors
- hats
- rain jackets
- boots

Natural Life

- barnacles
- snails
- seagulls
- fish
- ducks
- algae
- seaweed
- crabs

helps you anticipate children's interests and questions. It enables you to plan how to guide children toward their own discoveries by organizing investigation experiences.

Imagine that you selected machines as the topic. You have visited several factories in your community where workers use different types and sizes of machines. Now you have to decide where to take the children. Should all of the children see all of the machines? Can you arrange small group trips? Which places can best help children answer their questions? You can answer such questions most effectively after you have familiarized yourself with the subject.

As you research the topic, consider the open-ended questions you can ask children during the study. Open-ended questions and statements enable children to think and wonder about a subject. For example, a teacher who visits a textile mill prior to taking the class on a trip might say to them, "Let's think about reasons why the factory is located on a river."

4. Think About How You Can Address Curriculum Objectives

As you review the long list of skills, concepts, and content that children are expected to acquire during their year in your classroom, it is helpful if you can assemble it in an organized and logical way.

Think about how the topic you selected can address a broad range of curriculum objectives. The web of the harbor gave you a sense of the many directions a study could take. Focus on the directions that relate well to other learning areas. The Harbor Study chart (on the following page) shows the range of possibilities. During the study, as you work with the children and incorporate their ideas, you will make specific decisions about time, materials, and different ways to explore the topic.

With the list of ideas for a harbor study, Mr. Phillips can prioritize activities. He can begin to find books to read aloud as well as books with a range of difficulty for the children to read independently. He can ask other teachers for ideas about books, songs, and computer programs; he can collect tape recordings of songs, look for jigsaw puzzles about sea animals, and think about the materials, books, and supplies he wants to organize for classroom resources.

5. Begin Collecting Materials Related to the Topic

Gather pictures, books, and artifacts to stimulate discussions and elicit children's questions. Children's individual interests and learning styles will lead them to different materials, so try to offer a variety of choices.

Children, as well as their families, may contribute materials relevant to the topic. When you establish a partnership with families and keep them informed about classroom life, you will greatly expand the resources available for your study.

Harbor Study

Social Studies

- Location of the harbor
- Different kinds of work/jobs
- Goods that meet people's needs
- Skills and tools used
- Issues related to the environment—transportation, housing
- Area around harbor—mapping

- Different kinds of cargo ships
- The harbor today and in the past
- Outer harbors—similarities and differences
- Unloading and transporting cargo
- Rules for harbor use—quarantines, dumping, safety

Science

- Sea gulls, snails, barnacles, fish
- Cycle of the moon
- Boats
- Sounds of the harbor
- Machines, ramps, pulleys

- Water, currents, tides, pollution
- Why objects sink, float
- Inventions
- Water
- Concept of leverage

Math

- Notice patterns, textures
- Classify boat sizes
- Depth of water
- Number of workers
- Recognize shapes
- Things that float, sink
- Graph types of people, cargo, boats

- Describe boats
- Count things around the harbor
- Amounts of cargo
- Length of boats
- Notice symmetry, water reflections
- Nautical time—24 clock hours
- Making predictions about cargo

Language and Literacy

- Poetry to read aloud
- Letters home from a long trip
- Journals, diaries about life at sea
- Spelling words
- Vocabulary words
- Interviews of workers

- Books: read aloud, picture, non-fiction, fiction
- Read and write advertisements around harbor
- Poems about sounds, smells of the harbor
- Research projects about workers, machinery
- Research skills needed to get information
- Letters to cargo, ocean liner companies for more information

Arts and Technology

- Water colors of harbor
- Fish prints
- Songs about the sea
- Using computer for data collections, statistics, writing, and research
- Pulleys, simple technology
- Act out observations

- Mural scene of harbor
- Skits on different harbor scenes/workers
- Building small boats that float
- Navigational instruments like depth sounders, radios, and latitude and longitude
- Play about going to the sea

6. Plan Experiences That Will Help Children Become Experts on the Topic

Before introducing the study to children, anticipate their questions and draft a plan. To prepare, ask yourself:

- What kinds of questions will children have at first?
- What information will help them ask in-depth questions?
- Can we take a trip?
- Can we invite an expert into the classroom?
- How can children represent the information they are learning?

Review the goals and objectives of your curriculum for all subjects. Think about the activities and experiences you can plan so children will develop and practice skills across a variety of domains. For example, after reviewing your math curriculum, consider whether children's investigations can involve measuring, recording patterns, and preparing graphs. Can you fit these experiences into the study in a logical way?

During the study, children share their knowledge and raise new issues they want to explore. You may find that scheduling an additional trip or inviting a local expert to visit the class can respond to the growing interests of children. In order to involve children in continually evaluating their learning, teachers have to remain flexible in their thinking and planning.

7. Introduce the Study to Children

Introduce studies by finding out what children already know and what they want to learn. You can inspire children's curiosity by putting a few hints around the room: books, a chart, a question, a few interesting pictures. In an introductory meeting, ask children if they noticed something new in the room that might indicate what the next study will be. Then ask questions such as the following:

"What do you know about (the topic)?"

"What do you want to find out?"

"How can we find answers to these questions?"

When you record children's ideas on a chart you validate the knowledge and experience they bring to the study. If they have misinformation, you may say something like, "That's interesting. We may find more information about that. Let's put a question mark next to it to remind us that we want to know more about it." Although you may teach the same topic for several consecutive years, each group of children will have their own unique set of questions that interest them.

Very often children need time to think about their questions. Giving them time to talk with peers or to write down questions for homework is beneficial. You may want to encourage them to talk with family members.

Invite children to contribute materials related to a study. Suggest that they get books from the public library or bring in books, pictures, or other artifacts they may have at home that are related to the study.

8. Invite Families to Participate in the Study

Parents and relatives can be wonderful helpers and resources. Family members can participate in trips, talk with the class about their work, assist with projects, or share a special skill.

Sending home brief newsletters or notes describing the study and inviting participation keeps family members up-to-date on classroom activities. Throughout the study children can involve family members by bringing home surveys, interview questions, opinion polls, or work they have created in class. (See the chapter on Building a Partnership with Families for additional suggestions.)

9. Listen to and Learn with Children

Throughout the study, pay close attention to what children say and how they respond. Observe and record children's comments and questions. Note the level of their involvement with projects, their successes, and their confusions. Think about the amount of time you allot to activities. Finally, pay attention to the level of children's enthusiasm for the study, as well as your own.

Allow time in the study to help children reflect on their learning. Refer to the questions they raised at the beginning of the study. Identify those that have been answered and those that merit further investigation.

Include children's representations—dioramas, models, writing, drawings, paintings, graphs, or photographs of their work—in their portfolios. Encourage children to evaluate their learning regularly. (This will be discussed in detail in the next chapter on Assessing Children's Learning.)

Documenting the activities of the study along the way can be invaluable for future planning. Take notes about what you might do differently next time. Keeping a journal or log in which you record books read, trips taken, and people contacted will enable you to repeat the study with another class with greater ease.

10. Think About Concluding the Study

Some investigative studies last for a month and some for several months. The length of time depends on the nature of the study, the age of the children involved, and the level of interest the children exhibit.

Marking the end of a study with an exhibit of the children's work, a play, a class book, or a breakfast with parents, provides closure to a study. A culminating event unites all the parts of the study, enables children to see how much they have learned, and promotes children's sense of pride in their accomplishments.

These steps can serve as a beginning guide for planning studies. Interesting topics studied over time excite teachers and children and contribute to the feeling of community in the classroom. Children take pleasure in becoming experts on a subject. Teachers can share the responsibility for planning experiences with children and relax in the realization that they do not have to know everything about the subject in advance. Teachers and children look forward to the surprises that unfold along the way.

Remember that it is not possible to teach everything through a long-term study. Many times, material that must be taught does not fit into the study. You can plan work times to focus on particular skills or content using the principles and processes presented earlier in the chapter.

Scheduling Work Times

Scheduling work times each day enables teachers to address specific content or skills related to one or more subjects. As described in the chapter on Establishing a Structure for the Classroom, most teachers schedule times for math, small group reading, independent or silent reading, reading aloud, writing, and sometimes an open choice time when many different activities can take place. Work times will vary depending upon whether you introduce a new concept or material or continue a previous investigation.

Introducing Concepts or Skills

In order to pursue certain activities related to a study, children may need to be introduced to particular skills that have not yet been taught. Thus, a study can help you think about what new concepts or skills to address during work times. For example, in his study about the harbor, Mr. Phillips considers that children will see many kinds of vehicles and that collecting data about various types can lead to making graphs. He plans a work time in which to introduce graphing as a way of organizing and comparing collected data.

Teachers often begin a work time with a mini-lesson. At a meeting, the teacher introduces a new skill or a concept that the children will explore in small groups immediately afterwards. Examples of mini-lessons include:

- talking about a spelling rule (e.g., how to add "ing" to words);
- introducing the concept of paragraphs before a writing time;
- demonstrating a technique for using a piece of science equipment prior to an activity;
- teaching a strategy for counting or measuring that children will use in solving a problem.

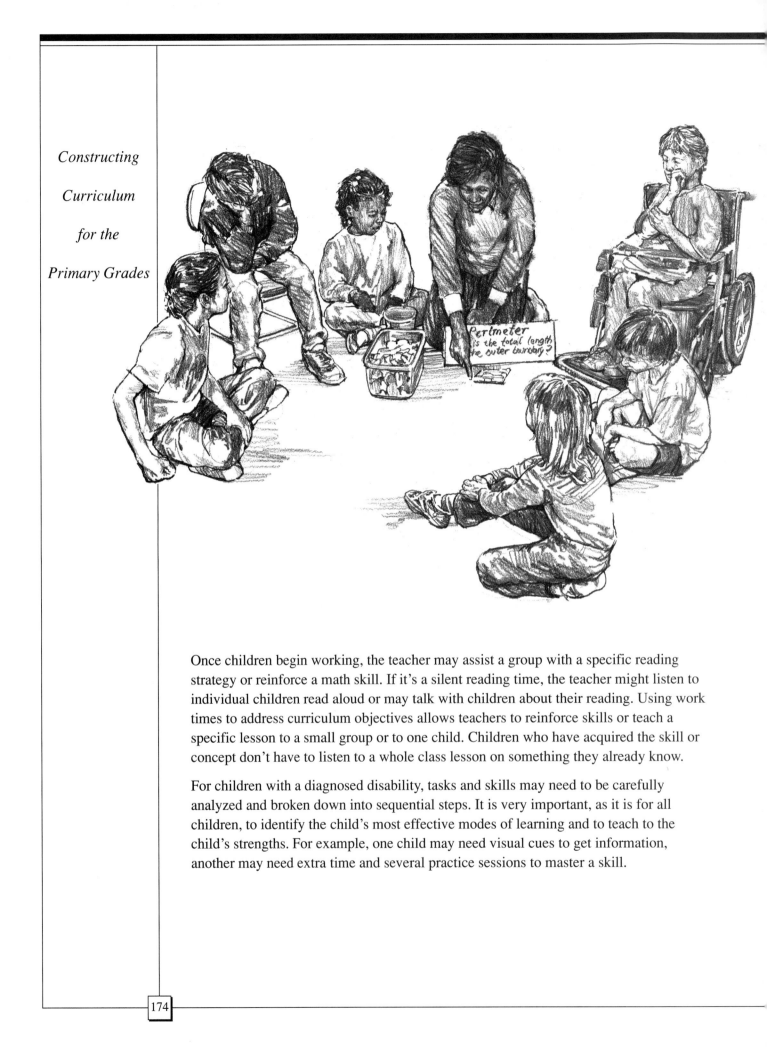

Once children begin working, the teacher may assist a group with a specific reading strategy or reinforce a math skill. If it's a silent reading time, the teacher might listen to individual children read aloud or may talk with children about their reading. Using work times to address curriculum objectives allows teachers to reinforce skills or teach a specific lesson to a small group or to one child. Children who have acquired the skill or concept don't have to listen to a whole class lesson on something they already know.

For children with a diagnosed disability, tasks and skills may need to be carefully analyzed and broken down into sequential steps. It is very important, as it is for all children, to identify the child's most effective modes of learning and to teach to the child's strengths. For example, one child may need visual cues to get information, another may need extra time and several practice sessions to master a skill.

Addressing Multiple Objectives in a Work Time

When children engage in active investigations, teachers can address multiple objectives within one subject or across subjects. The whole class may be involved in the same subject, but the teacher's objectives for different children vary. For example, during a writing work time, some children might compose letters, some edit a story, while others talk to the teacher about what makes an effective story ending. The teacher has considered what each child knows and has identified different objectives and activities based on individual needs.

The following example of a work time shows how a lesson on using the dictionary can address multiple objectives within one subject area—language and literacy. The teacher structures an activity to allow children to actively investigate, represent, and reflect on what they learn.

Ms. Richards wants to introduce dictionary use to her third grade class. She observes that the few children who have attempted to use a dictionary ignored the guide words at the top of the page. She constructs a lesson that involves children in learning more about the dictionary and how to use guide words. She reviews the skills from her third grade scope and sequence that could be addressed in an investigation about dictionary use, including:

alphabetical order   *using the dictionary as a resource*

syllabication   *guide and entry words*

spelling rules   *suffixes*

vocabulary words

To begin the lesson, Ms. Richards brings a large dictionary to the class meeting. She poses several open-ended questions and statements, allowing time for children to respond to each one and share their knowledge:

"Let's think about how this book is used."

"What do you know about dictionaries?"

"When have you used a dictionary?"

"Let's consider some ways dictionaries can help you."

Ms. Richards records the children's ideas on a chart. Following the meeting, the children work in teams of three or four as "dictionary detectives." Each group has its own dictionary. She gives the following directions:

"Study the book. Record what you observe about how the book is organized, and what it has inside it. Notice as many details as you can. Pick one person on your team to record your observations and your questions on paper. Later we'll share what each team learns."

As they examine the book, the children record the items they find interesting. Working in small groups, each child has a chance to discuss something and to share information. Ms. Richards moves around the room, listening to and observing the children at work. She asks open-ended questions to find out what they are learning and to extend their thinking. At the end of the work period, they report their findings in a class meeting. This allows Ms. Richards to further assess each child's learning and gives the children an opportunity to learn from each other.

Following this exploration time, the teacher incorporates dictionary use as part of everyday life in the classroom. She places one in the meeting area and suggests that children take turns looking up unfamiliar words they find during discussions and stories. She plans other investigations during work times to focus on particular aspects of dictionary use: she sends the children on a dictionary scavenger hunt for four syllable words, and asks the children to see if they can discover rules for how words are divided.

Ms. Richards could have taught a lesson on guide words by demonstrating their location using a dictionary, and asking the children to complete a practice worksheet of duplicated pages from a dictionary. Instead, she presents the task in a meaningful context, structures it so children investigate the topic and record what they learn, and allows time for them to talk about and reflect on their discoveries.

Questions to Consider in Planning Work Times

- Keeping the key objective(s) in mind, what investigation task can children do that requires them to explore, experiment, collect data, or gather information?
- What other skills/concepts might children use/acquire (within and across subjects/disciplines)? In what ways can I extend the task to foster the use of these skills/concepts?
- How can children interact with one another most effectively in this task? As a full group? In pairs? In small groups?
- In what ways can the task be constructed so that children invent and design their own strategies for gathering information?
- How can children record and represent their process of thinking and their work?
- How can children reflect on their work?
- How can I encourage children to talk with others to organize and clarify their thinking?
- How can children apply what they learn to real-life or simulated situations?

By asking yourself these questions as you review your objectives for children's learning, you may begin to see natural connections within and across disciplines. Carefully structuring work times will allow children to explore extensively, think deeply about ideas, invent solutions, and record what they have learned. These experiences help children become successful life-long learners who can think, solve problems, and work independently or collaboratively with others.

Using Teachable Moments

Children learn all the time; not everything that happens in the classroom is planned. The whole day is full of opportunities to teach because there is always something happening, whether it's serious investigations, telling jokes, playing a game, or transitioning to another part of the day. Here are some examples:

- After having a conference with a child who uses dialogue in a story, a teacher writes part of the child's story on a chart and uses it to teach the class about quotation marks.

- In the process of cutting oranges for a snack, a teacher conducts a mini-lesson on fractions.

- In reading the morning message, "We will share stories after lunch…," one child points out that the word "stories" is missing a 'y.' The teacher uses this observation to teach the spelling rule about changing the 'y' to 'i' and adding 'es.'

- While reading a story a teacher points out how the illustrator used borders. Later that day, several children use this technique in illustrating their stories.

- A child brings in baseball scores from the newspaper and the teacher suggests making a class graph.

- When a child makes a clothespin person and it's bigger than the door in her diorama, the teacher conducts a lesson on scale.

Teachers can use "teachable moments" effectively if they keep in mind the various components of each subject and observe skillfully. We teach some of our most successful lessons on the spur of the moment, or as a follow-up to a child's question or need.

Closing Thoughts

Teachers are constantly making decisions about curriculum. Sound decisions are based on knowledge of how purposeful learning occurs. Teachers guide children's learning by designing classroom experiences that are integrated and allow children to construct knowledge by actively investigating, by representing their understandings, and by reflecting on what they have learned. By observing and listening to children, teachers modify curriculum experiences to respond to individual children's needs and interests. When children learn by doing, the process of assessing learning takes on broader and richer dimensions.

Resources for Guiding Children's Learning

Creating Curriculum: Teachers and Students as a Community of Learners.
Short, Kathy G. and Carolyn Burke. Portsmouth, NH: Heinemann, 1991.

Engaging Children's Minds: The Project Approach. Katz, Lilian G. and Sylvia C. Chard.
Norwood, NJ: Ablex Publishing, 1989.

Learning and Loving It: Theme Studies in the Classroom. Gamberg, Ruth, et al.
Portsmouth, NH: Heinemann, 1988.

*Serious Players in the Primary Classroom: Empowering Children Through Active
Learning Experiences.* Wasserman, Selma. New York: Teachers College Press, 1990.

Teaching and Learning in a Diverse World: Multicultural Education for Young Children.
Ramsey, Patricia G. New York: Teachers College Press, 1987.

Valuing Diversity: The Primary Years. McCracken, Janet B. Washington, DC:
NAEYC, 1993.

References

American Association for the Advancement of Science. 1993. *Benchmarks for Science
   Literacy, Project 2061.* New York: Oxford University Press.

Bredekamp, Sue and Teresa Rosegrant. 1992. *Reaching Potentials: Appropriate
   Curriculum and Assessment for Young Children, Volume I.* Washington, DC: National
   Association for the Education of Young Children.

Consortium of National Arts Education Associations. 1994. *National Standards for Arts
   Education.* Reston, VA: Music Educators National Conference.

Greenspan, Stanley, I. 1993. *Playground Politics: Understanding the Emotional Life of
   Your School-Age Child.* Reading, MA: Addison-Wesley Publishing.

Los Angeles Unified School District (LAUSD), Division of Special Education. 1990.
   Special Needs Supplement to The Creative Curriculum for Early Childhood. Los
   Angeles, CA.

National Council of Teachers of Mathematics. 1989. *Curriculum and Evaluation
   Standards for School Mathematics.* March 1989. Reston, VA: National Council of
   Teachers of Mathematics.

Rutherford, James F. and Andrew Ahlgren. 1990. *Science for All Americans.* New York:
   Oxford University Press.

Smilansky, Sara and Leah Shefatya. 1990. *Facilitating Play: A Medium for Promoting
   Cognitive, Socio-Emotional and Academic Development in Young Children.*
   Gaithersburg, MD: Psychosocial and Educational Publications.

ASSESSING CHILDREN'S LEARNING

Assessment is the process of gathering information about children in order to make decisions about their education. Teachers obtain useful information about children's knowledge, skills, and progress by observing, documenting, and reviewing children's work over time. Ongoing assessment that occurs in the context of classroom activities can provide an accurate, fair, and representative picture of children's abilities and progress. To obtain a well-rounded picture of each child's growth and development, the materials used for assessment must be comprehensive.

> The root of the word evaluation is "value," and authentic assessment includes understanding what students value and then building from there. Authentic assessment is inside-out rather than outside-in. It is an attempt to get away from sorting a mass of students and closer to the teacher's question: Given what I know now, how should I teach this particular student (Ayers 1993, 113)?

Assessment is the fifth strategy for constructing curriculum. When teachers have a method for collecting information on children's development and learning, they can design curriculum and plan instruction so that every child experiences success. This chapter discusses the different purposes of assessment, identifies some of the problems with standardized testing, and describes the type of assessment that is appropriate for planning curriculum. It focuses on methods of assessment that inform instruction and describes specific approaches for assessing children's progress.

Understanding Assessment

Currently, there is much debate about assessment. What are the purposes of assessment? What methods of assessment are best? What role do standardized tests play? What is performance assessment and is it a viable alternative to traditional testing? To determine the type of assessment that is most appropriate, we must first know its purpose and how the results will be used (Hills 1992).

Purposes of Assessment

A critical purpose of assessment is to inform curriculum and keep track of children's achievement. Teachers need a way to determine what children know and what they have learned. Observing and documenting children's work in the classroom is one way to obtain this information. Traditionally, schools have relied more on paper and pencil methods of assessment—either graded worksheets, end-of-unit tests found in textbooks, or standardized tests.

A second purpose of assessment is to identify children with special needs who may require additional educational services or interventions. Observations of the child, input from family members, and the use of screening instruments and diagnostic tests are appropriate for this purpose. Developmental screening instruments identify children liable to be at risk for school failure. Screening instruments do not identify the nature of a problem, but rather, indicate whether it is necessary to seek additional information. Diagnostic tests are designed to confirm the presence and extent of a disability.

Finally, assessment is used for the purpose of program accountability and evaluation. Assessments designed for this purpose attempt to determine whether educational programs achieve their goals. Typically, standardized tests have been used for this purpose. Unfortunately, the use of standardized tests has often had negative effects on children, on teachers, and on the curriculum.

Problems Associated with Standardized Tests

A standardized test is one administered under controlled conditions. Not all standardized tests are bad. Standardized tests that are individually administered and used to determine eligibility for special education services can be very helpful for teachers and children. Most teachers, however, are more familiar with group administered, multiple choice, norm-referenced achievement tests. These tests are problematic because they raise issues of fairness, they have a narrowing effect on curriculum, and the consequences associated with these tests make them "high stakes" (Meisels 1992 and 1993; Sheppard 1989).

Issues of Fairness

Group administered, norm-referenced, objectively scored tests raise questions about fairness. When tests are norm-referenced, a child's performance is compared with the performance of other children. This assumes that the experiences of the children taking the test are comparable to the experiences of the children on whom the test has been "normed." Unfortunately, this is often not the case. Group administered multiple choice tests cannot take into account the wide range of experiences, knowledge, and skills of individual children. Children from diverse backgrounds often interpret questions and express their knowledge differently.

Experts have also raised concerns as to whether or not group administered achievement tests are, in fact, "standardized" tests. Research has demonstrated that such tests are often not administered under standard conditions. Teachers provide children with unequal amounts of preparation time and different verbal cues to help them perform successfully.

Criterion-referenced assessment instruments present an alternative to norm-referenced tests. Such assessments use a fixed standard or criteria for measurement—the person being evaluated is measured against a standard of mastery.

Narrowing the Curriculum

A second serious consequence of standardized testing is that it tends to narrow and even dictate the curriculum. In an effort to ensure that children perform well on tests, teachers may stop teaching meaningful curriculum and instead use the time to prepare children for the test. Curriculum then focuses only on those basic skills that can be measured by multiple choice questions.

Group administered, multiple choice tests cannot measure some of the most important goals and objectives of the primary curriculum. It is difficult to effectively assess a child's critical thinking skills using multiple choice tests. A child's confidence, self-esteem, or ability to make friends and resolve conflicts cannot be measured on multiple choice tests. Cultural pride and awareness of oneself and other cultures cannot be measured through such tests. Multiple choice tests miss the many different ways children express and represent their thinking.

High Stakes Consequences

Norm-referenced, group-administered, multiple choice tests of achievement are often called "high stakes" tests because the results of these tests are used to make important decisions about student promotion or retention, teacher salary increases, or the allocation of resources to schools. The pressure to perform well on the tests creates stress on teachers as well as children. The high stakes consequences of these tests often lead to negative feelings and lost confidence on the part of both the test giver and the test taker.

Because of the problems associated with group administered tests of achievement, there is much research and discussion about alternative methods of assessment. Early childhood educators have long believed that the most effective way for teachers to know how children are doing is to observe them, document what they see, and review children's work carefully. Individual classroom teachers as well as entire school districts are beginning to adopt new approaches to assessment with an eye toward supporting the teaching and learning process.

Appropriate Assessment

Appropriate assessment relies on an approach that outlines reasonable and age-appropriate expectations for children. These expectations are based on knowledge of child development and on curriculum goals. Teachers plan curriculum with these expectations in mind and they assess children's growth and learning by looking at children's performance in terms of specific milestones. The information obtained from assessment also enables teachers to plan learning experiences that respond to the particular needs and strengths of each child. In order to assess children accurately, assessment procedures should be ongoing, in context, and comprehensive.

Assessment Is Ongoing

We often think of assessment as coming at the end of the learning process to conclude a unit, marking period, or the year's work. Teachers translate the results into a grade or a category ranging from "needs improvement" to "outstanding." When assessment comes at the end of the learning process, a teacher cannot use the information to adapt instruction, therefore there is little benefit for the child.

Ongoing assessment guides instruction. Teachers begin assessing children's learning and development at the outset of the year so that they have a basis for shaping their curriculum. As they observe children at work, they modify learning experiences to meet the individual needs of their children. Teachers share assessment information with children so that the children know how they are doing and can trace their own progress.

Assessment Is in Context

Current thinking about assessment emphasizes finding out what children know and can do, rather than on what children do not know. If we want to know what children can do, then we have to watch them complete tasks in familiar contexts where they have many different opportunities to demonstrate their knowledge and skills, rather than relying on tests.

Tests provide only a single snapshot of children's abilities (Meisels, 1993). Asking a child to solve a math problem using subtraction on a paper and pencil test does not necessarily reveal whether or not a child has problem-solving skills or can use the operation of subtraction to solve a problem. Further, a child who doesn't feel well on the day of the test is unlikely to score well. Ongoing assessment in the context of daily classroom life allows children to reveal their knowledge, skills, and abilities in many different situations and over the course of time.

Performance-based assessments are those in which children carry out specific tasks that simulate or represent real-life tasks. Sometimes performance assessments are conducted in test-like settings. Authentic assessment is a type of performance assessment that occurs in the context of actual classroom experiences.

Assessment Is Comprehensive

Comprehensiveness refers to both the range of information teachers have and the types of data collected. To get a fair and accurate picture of each child's growth and development—a picture of the whole child—teachers assess children's social, emotional, cognitive, and physical development.

Teachers also collect information on all aspects of the curriculum. Collecting samples of work in only a few subject areas (e.g., children's writing or their work in math) does not provide a full picture of what the child has learned. Children who are talented artists or strong scientific thinkers may not have documentation of their special strengths if only written work is collected.

Comprehensive assessment also means that teachers collect many different kinds of data and use a variety of approaches.

> *Assessment utilizes an array of tools and a variety of processes, including, but not limited to, collections of representative work by children (artwork, stories they write, tape recordings of their reading), records of systematic observations of teachers, records of conversations and interviews with children, and teachers' summaries of children's progress as individuals and as groups (Bredekamp and Rosegrant 1992, 10).*

Systematic observation of children as they go about classroom tasks gives teachers information about how children think, what they know, what they are confused about, and how they approach learning tasks. Reviewing samples of children's work reveals the quality of children's thinking and learning. Comparing children's work over time enables teachers to evaluate progress. Summarizing the collected data gives teachers a way of sharing information with parents. Appropriate assessment that is ongoing, in context, and comprehensive both supports instruction and enriches curriculum planning.

How Assessment Supports Instruction

The foundation for constructing curriculum is knowing the children you teach. The more information teachers have about what each child knows, the more effectively they can plan instruction that builds on children's strengths and addresses individual learning needs. A comprehensive approach to assessment provides this information. It allows children to become involved in setting goals for themselves and enables them to see visual proof of their progress. When assessment is tied closely to curriculum, the information teachers collect and share with families offers an in-depth portrait of what the child is learning in school and how the child is progressing.

Using Assessment to Plan Curriculum

Assessment is a critical first step in planning curriculum. If the assessment approach you use is compatible with the goals and objectives of your curriculum, then information obtained from assessment helps you know what to teach, when children are ready to learn particular skills and concepts, and how to structure learning experiences.

Assessment at the beginning of the year provides preliminary information about each child. Ongoing assessment enables you to determine how children are growing and developing and when to modify the curriculum to meet individual needs.

Assessment at the Beginning of the Year

Most teachers start the year with an overall plan for their curriculum based on their knowledge of child development and appropriate curriculum goals. Child development knowledge provides a set of reasonable expectations about what content and skills children are able to learn at certain ages. Because all children grow and develop at different rates, it is necessary to observe children carefully to determine what they already know and exactly what they are ready to learn. The assessment teachers do at the outset of the year determines how teachers shape instruction by providing answers to questions such as the following:

- What skills do children already have?
- What are children ready to learn?
- What are the particular interests and learning styles of this group of children?
- What are the special strengths and needs of each child in this class?

The first four to six weeks of school can be viewed as a time to get to know each child's abilities, prior knowledge, and individual approach to learning. Conversations with family members and the child's former teachers can help you learn about each child's special strengths and talents.

Assessment at the beginning of the year serves as "baseline" information and later helps evaluate children's progress. Having appropriate and realistic expectations about what each child can do is essential to ensuring successful learning experiences. Recognizing that uneven development is normal and expected also allows teachers to assess children fairly.

How Ongoing Assessment Informs Instruction

Ongoing assessment helps teachers to monitor what and how children are learning and to be responsive to children's needs. Teachers observe how certain children respond to particular learning tasks and use that information to structure new experiences.

Sometimes teachers plan an activity thinking that children already have had certain experiences and understandings. Once into the activity, they realize their assumption was wrong.

> *Mr. Johnson's third graders are learning to solve problems with two and three digit numbers using estimation and counting strategies. He places a jar filled with buttons on a table and suspends a clothesline with clothespins across the blackboard. On the left he places the numeral "0" and on the right the numeral "500." The morning message tells the children to estimate the number of buttons in the jar, write their estimates on a card, and hang the card along the number line in numerical order. Mr. Johnson assumes that the children understand the concept of numerical order—greater than and less than— because they have worked on it before. However, as several children begin hanging numbers incorrectly (e.g., 230 after 320) he senses that he has to make some adjustments in his lesson plan. First, he decides to postpone the next step of having children count the buttons in the jar. Instead he will have the children work in their groups to review the number line and identify places where numbers are out of order. Each group is encouraged to offer an explana- tion of why a number is out of order and where it belongs. Later, they will resume the estimation activity.*

By observing children in the context of an activity, this teacher realized that for all children to feel successful, he had to modify his plan. By having them work in small groups, he provided a way for everyone to participate equally. Careful observation enables the teacher to identify those children who are confused about numerical order and then to plan a small group lesson to teach this skill.

Individualizing Instruction

Ongoing assessment in the classroom helps teachers to individualize the curriculum and plan instruction that is responsive to children's needs and builds on their strengths. Observation in a variety of situations often leads to ideas for alternate instructional approaches.

Because Jeremy, a third grader, struggles as a reader, he dislikes quiet reading time each day. Other than relying on picture cues, he has very few strategies for getting meaning from print. During a choice time Ms. Keats observes him looking at a baseball magazine. She notices that he studies each picture carefully and tries to read the captions beneath the picture, pointing to each word with his finger and mouthing the sounds quietly. The next day she brings in a biography about Jim Abbott, the baseball player, by Greg Lee. Although she senses that the text will be challenging for him, she suspects that the content will sustain his interest so that she can continue to work with him on acquiring reading strategies.

Observing children in a variety of settings gives teachers many occasions to look for children's strengths. A child who isn't able to demonstrate knowledge in one situation may be able to do so easily under different circumstances. Teachers must consider children's diverse learning styles, rates of learning, cultural influences, and fluency with English.

The class is studying the night sky. Following a trip to the planetarium, Janine barely writes one sentence during a writing assignment. Ms. Bernard wonders if Janine learned anything from the trip. The next day during a work time, she suggests that Janine draw a picture of the constellations exhibited at the show the day before. By looking at the details in Janine's picture, Ms. Bernard discovers that, in fact, she learned quite a bit during the trip but needed another way to demonstrate her knowledge.

During the course of the year, you may find that you are having difficulty meeting the needs of certain children. If attempts at alternate teaching strategies are not effective, it may be helpful to talk with parents, consult the previous year's teacher, or obtain the advice of a specialist. For a child with a diagnosed disability, you can also refer to the child's Individual Education Plan (IEP) which outlines specific goals for instruction.

Increasing Children's Investment in Their Work

Parents and educators become concerned when children lack motivation and do not seem involved in their work. One reason may be that children don't know what criteria are being used to evaluate their work. Letter grades do not provide specific information on the quality of work or progress. An approach to assessment that involves children addresses this problem. Children's investment in their learning and the quality of their work increases when teachers involve them in setting personal goals and evaluating their own progress.

Helping Children Set Goals

Children want to know the expectations and standards their teachers and parents have for them, how they are being evaluated, and how they are doing. Encouraging children to set their own goals helps them become self-directed learners. By modeling the language and process of setting and striving for personal goals, teachers foster self-directed learning.

Goal setting activities occur throughout the year in different ways. At the beginning of the year, teachers can help children think about:

- Which of my skills improved last year?
- What can I do very well? What are my personal strengths?
- Which skills can I improve?
- What is one thing I really want to work on this year?
- What do I hope to learn this year?

When teachers pose such questions, children become involved in self-assessment. By recording their thoughts and goals in a journal, children can return to them later in the year and reflect on their progress. This also gives children an opportunity to re-examine their goals and set new ones.

Other opportunities for children to set personal goals include the following:

- Before beginning a long-term study, encourage children to write in their journals in response to the question, "What do I really want to learn during this study?"
- Before editing a story, ask a child: "What editing skill do you want to work on? What do you want to get better at as a result of editing this story?"
- At the outset of a week, ask a child, "What do you want to work on this week?"
- Before a field trip, have children respond to the question: "What do you hope to see and find out?"
- To focus positive attention on a difficult time, ask a child, "How would you like to act during this activity (e.g., in the lunchroom, at recess, during music or physical education) and what will help you to be successful?"

Reflecting on and Evaluating Their Learning

The importance of reflecting on learning was discussed in the previous chapter on Guiding Children's Learning. Children become aware that they have accomplished something—that they know something now that they didn't know before—when teachers provide opportunities for them to think about what they have learned. In the process of reflection, children may observe that they have tried something for the first time. When they review samples of their work over the course of the year and see the progress they have made, they have concrete evidence of their growing competence.

Too often, teachers and children focus on "best work." However, there are many ways to evaluate work besides "best" and "worst." In the beginning, children need help from their teachers about how to reflect on and evaluate their work. Their first and most natural responses are likely to be "I like this" or "I hate this" or "This was so easy." You can guide children to evaluate their work more critically by asking specific questions such as:

"What do you like best about your drawing?"

"How do you decide if you like a story you write, or a picture you draw?"

"What did you enjoy most about this project?"

"Which math problem was frustrating? Why?"

"What was most difficult for you to do? What was easy to do?"

"Did you try using a new technique in writing your story?"

"What's the hardest part of working in a group?"

The more practice children have in setting goals, discussing, and evaluating their work, the more they take responsibility for their learning. When children are involved in the assessment process, they learn to think critically about their work and take pride in their accomplishments.

Communicating with Families

All families want to know what their children are doing in school and how they are progressing. Although all families do not convey their expectations and dreams in the same way, they all want their children to become competent learners.

When family members attend conferences or receive written reports about children's progress, they typically ask:

"How is my child doing?"

"What are you teaching my child?"

"What can I do to help my child?"

Family members appreciate specific examples of children's progress. It is more meaning-ful to see their child's work than to receive a grade of "B+" or "Satisfactory." Showing actual examples of work collected over time enables parents to personally assess their child's progress: "Oh. She can write sentences now. Earlier this year she could only write single words."

A comprehensive approach to assessment that is tied to your curriculum enables you to share children's progress in a meaningful way. Parents will have a much better picture of the child's progress when they see concrete evidence of the child's work.

How Teachers Assess Children's Learning

Teachers continually monitor children's growth and learning. Every day teachers talk with children about their work, observe children interacting with others and with materials, and review the products children create. To assess children fairly, teachers have to observe with a purpose in mind. Without a focus for observation, it is easy to be sidetracked by other characteristics that may "take center stage." For example, suppose a teacher is leading a small group discussion about a story the children just read. One child offers an explanation of the character's motives. The teacher observes that the child uses non-standard grammar and corrects him. By criticizing his use of language, she fails to recognize or acknowledge the child's comprehension of the story content and his ability to conceptualize. The child has received a negative message—which may squelch his motivation and self-esteem—and no recognition for his abilities.

In reviewing a child's work, it is equally important to remember the purpose of assessment. A child's drawing of a hermit crab, for example, might reveal that she knows all the names of the body parts and that she observed and documented many details. The teacher might focus on the child's inaccurate spelling and weak fine motor skills, thus failing to recognize the child's skills in making detailed scientific observations.

A framework for assessing children or a formal assessment instrument can help to ensure that observations are focused and that all areas of a child's development and learning are assessed. Observation and documentation in the context of classroom activities reveal extensive data about children's knowledge and skills. The collection and review of their work over time illustrates the quality of their thinking and their progress. Summarizing the information provides an efficient and comprehensive way to report to families.

Using a Framework to Support Assessment

A framework for observation and work collection should outline developmentally appropriate expectations for children's learning. When an assessment instrument is linked to the goals and objectives of your program, it helps you focus your observations and serves as a reminder to address all aspects of your curriculum. A comprehensive assessment tool provides a complete picture of every child.

As the interest in appropriate assessment has grown, the demand for assessment tools has also increased. Some tools that are currently available to teachers include the following:

- *The California Learning Record* is a yearly portfolio of information on a child's progress, development, and achievement from kindergarten through 12th grade. It includes a collection of teacher observations and samples of children's work.

- The Centre for Language in Primary Education has created the *Primary Language Record* which helps teachers assess language and literacy development.

- The High/Scope Educational Research Foundation has an assessment instrument called the *Child Observation Record*, or COR, which is designed to focus observations. Although it is currently available for use with children through age six, it is being extended to address assessment of older children as well.

- The Minnesota Department of Education provides teachers with a basis for observation using outcomes in all domains of development for children through age nine. This instrument is called the *Model Learner Outcomes for Early Childhood Education*.

- *Project Construct* has been developed by the Missouri Department of Elementary and Secondary Instruction. It outlines an assessment framework for children up to age seven in three domains: sociomoral, cognitive, and language development.

- *The Work Sampling System*, developed at the University of Michigan, is a comprehensive assessment system designed to assess children in preschool through fifth grade in seven different domains. It includes a developmental checklist with guidelines, a structured approach to portfolio collection, and a method of summarizing information for reporting to families.

In the Resources section at the end of this chapter, you will find information on where to order these assessment tools.

Observation and Documentation

Teachers watch children all the time. Some observations are informal while others are focused to determine whether or not a child has acquired specific skills and understandings. Together, informal and formal observations of children give teachers a representative picture of each child's knowledge and abilities.

How does a busy teacher find time to observe all the children in the class and to document these observations? Establishing a routine for observation and documentation makes this process manageable. It's not necessary or possible to observe and record everything that children say and do. Organizing a plan for what and how to observe and record, and then spending a few minutes a day doing so, yields a wealth of valuable information.

Making Observations Part of Daily Classroom Activity

Observation is part of everyday life in the classroom. During work times, when children are engaged in investigation and representation activities, teachers move around the room watching what children do, listening to what they say, and talking with them about the products they create. When children work collaboratively with others, teachers learn about children's thinking by listening to what children say to each other. By asking children questions teachers gain information about children's thinking.

In the chapter on Guiding Children's Learning, an example of a geoboard lesson showed how children use active investigation, representation, and reflection to construct knowledge. Their teacher, Ms. Hernandez, has opportunities to assess individual children in the context of that lesson. She notes what children say in the introductory meeting; comments about shapes and their attributes give her some ideas about children's prior knowledge and experience. As she moves about the room during the work period, she carries a clipboard with her. On it is a photocopied paper with each child's name on the left hand margin. At the top of the page she writes the date and next to it, "Shapes and Attributes." Occasionally she jots down a note or two to help her remember what children are doing. Later, she will review the children's math logs and add to her list of notes.

Week of: 10/14	Shapes and Attributes
Amy	able to make attribute train / 3 attributes
Arona	
Brendan	in mtg. said " two triangles can fit together to make a square"
Brian	
Chris	
Celia	
Denise	sorted collection of attrib. blocks by shapes/color
Elisha	
Greg	
Gerard	
Hector	
Kim	resumed geoboard work at choice times
Leonard	
La Shon	
Nathanial	
Raashon	working w/ blocks – used "square rectangle triangle, cylinder "to describe constructions
Richie	
Rondelle	
Sherise	
Steven J.	
Steven R.	
Tony	
Vanessa	
Zack	

Conferences with children offer another way to observe them. For example, during writing workshop a teacher might have two or three minute conferences with children to discuss what they are doing and observe how they are working. These conversations between teacher and child usually provide insights about the child's thinking. Regularly scheduled reading or math conferences enable teachers both to gather information and to individualize their instruction.

Many teachers find it helpful to inform children that part of a teacher's job is to observe children at work. At a meeting, you might pose the question, "What are some ways you think I can learn about what you know and can do?" Give children time to think about the questions and share their ideas. As children often do, they may surprise you with some ideas that you did not expect. Explain that one of the ways you learn about them and their abilities is to observe them carefully. Tell them that sometimes you may want to observe them without being interrupted. For example, you might say, "When I carry my clipboard it means I need five minutes to observe. Ask someone else if you need help. If it is an emergency, of course you can interrupt me."

The Importance of Documentation

Collecting observations made at various times of the day, over time, and in many situations gives you a great deal of data for reflection. One observation may not be typical of a child's skills or behavior. After reviewing written notes from several observations you may be able to find just the right strategy to support a child's learning. The documentation you have from ongoing observations helps you to make instructional plans for children and gives you information needed to report to families and complete school reports.

Documenting observations enables you to detect patterns in a child's behavior. For example, by recording the choices children make, whom they choose to work with, the books they select, or the topics they write about, you may discover that certain children are stuck. You can make suggestions to expand their choices and ideas: "I've noticed that you have chosen to work with blocks during choice time for the past week. Perhaps today you would like to draw some pictures of your structure," or, "You have written several stories about your dog during writing workshop. Would you be interested in reading a book about a dog? I know a chapter book that I think you'll really enjoy."

When teachers take the time to document their observations, they often detect the source of a problem, devise a plan, and monitor the plan's effectiveness. The examples that follow show how two teachers were able to pinpoint and appropriately address problems based on their documented observations.

> *Ms. London notices that after meetings, while other children readily start their work, Kim invariably wanders around the room. Noting this same behavior on several occasions, Ms. London suspects that Kim is unable to follow the directions she gives to the whole group. She decides to have a one minute conference with Kim at the end of each meeting to help Kim get started on her work. To her surprise, Kim is able to tell Ms. London exactly what is expected of her. In fact, she listens carefully during the meeting. However, she needs the chance to say the words back to Ms. London in order to get focused on the next task.*

> *Observing that Janet is consistently unable to settle down during morning work time, but does so easily after lunch, leads Mr. Sparks to investigate whether Janet is eating breakfast in the morning. He learns that Janet's bus is often late and that she misses the school breakfast program because she doesn't want to come into the classroom after meeting has started. He arranges to have another child pick up Janet's breakfast and bring it to the classroom. After a few days, there is a noticeable improvement in Janet's ability to settle into her morning work.*

Documented evidence of children's development is important because it is often difficult to remember what a child was or was not able to do earlier in the year. Having recorded observations can be invaluable in cases where a child may need additional support.

Recording Actions Not Impressions

One of the hardest aspects of observing children is documenting their actions and words, rather than our impressions of them. It is normal for our interests, culture, beliefs, and experiences to influence our observations. However, when we observe children for the purpose of assessing them, we need to make every effort to guard against our biases by focusing on actions and avoiding judgments about behavior.

To illustrate the difference between an objective and biased observation, consider these two examples of anecdotal records about Natalya. In each, the anecdote was written while observing the child, and the teacher used abbreviations.

Example 1

March 6; 1:15 p.m.

Natalya is reading on the rug with Cherise. Cherise is trying to concentrate for a change, but N is bugging her. C is reading aloud. N looks down at the book for a second and then starts talking to C again. N is fiddling with C's hair. N seems bored by the story. She is more interested in socializing.

Example 2

March 6; 1:15 p.m.

It is read-with-a-partner time. Natalya is sitting next to Cherise on the rug. C is holding the book. C is reading. N looks down at the book, touches the corner of the page. She puts her hands in her lap. She looks at C. She says something to C (which I can't hear). She touches C's hair for a few seconds, then looks at the book. She says something else. C keeps on reading. N puts her arm around C.

Take a moment to think about your reactions to these two records of the same observation. In Example 1, the teacher's irritation and judgment of Natalya is very apparent. She interprets Natalya's actions as "bugging Cherise." She labels the touching of Cherise's hair as "playing with it." After reading the first anecdote, one would probably conclude that Natalya is misbehaving.

In the second anecdote, we may have several interpretations of the incident. Perhaps Natalya is listening to the story and taking pleasure in Cherise's reading. Or possibly Natalya is unhappy about something and needs the comfort of being close to Cherise.

When only the child's actions are recorded and judgments are omitted, it is possible to consider a variety of explanations for behaviors and to be open to different ways of interpreting a child's motives. Therefore, in recording and observing, try to write down only what you see and hear. Questions and concerns can be documented separately.

Techniques for Recording Observations

It is easy to understand why many teachers say, "I watch my children all of the time and I know what they can do. I just don't have the time to write things down. There's too much else going on in the classroom." Classrooms are busy, hectic places with constant demands for a teacher's attention. Some practical techniques for observing and recording children's work make this task more manageable: creating a system for recording observations, allocating time to document observations, and using a checklist to structure your observations.

Creating a System for Recording Observations

Different types of records serve different purposes. Systems for recording observations include anecdotal records, running records, descriptive notes, and quick classroom notes.

- *Anecdotal records* are brief reports of behaviors recorded after the event has occurred. They can provide rich and detailed descriptions of the child's abilities and approach to learning.

- *Running records* are actual accounts of what a child says or does, recorded at the time of the action. Running records effectively document a child's reading abilities, expressive language, and interactions with others.

- *Quick notes on a class list* are made during a busy work time to keep track of what children do. Teachers review these periodically to complete checklists or to write more detailed anecdotes or narratives about a child.

Post-it notes, sticky mailing labels, or index cards are useful for collecting records. Some teachers carry a clipboard with dated class lists on it.

It helps to review periodically the records you collect. Some teachers have a file folder for each child or a section of a looseleaf binder in which they gather all of their notes. This can make it easier to review information prior to conferences or when writing final reports.

Allocating Time to Record Observations

Observing and recording take time. To ensure that these processes happen regularly, identify periods of the day when you can set aside a few minutes for the task. Ideas include:

- 10-15 minutes during a project or work time, 2 or 3 times a week;
- half of each silent reading period, 3 times a week;
- during a time that children share stories after writing workshop;
- during reading and writing conferences;
- 1 or 2 times a week as children arrive in the morning;
- once every two weeks during a special subject class;
- once a month during gym or recess.

Having a realistic schedule helps make the job of observing and documenting systematic and manageable. Some teachers find it helpful to spend twenty minutes immediately after school once a week to write down one thing they have noticed about each child.

Using Checklists

Checklists can provide a structure for observing children by identifying the range of specific skills, knowledge, and behaviors that children may be expected to acquire at particular ages. Many curriculum guides list discrete skills for children to learn within a particular subject area. It is both challenging and limiting to try to piece these together to create a comprehensive checklist.

At the end of this chapter, we list currently available assessment tools that include comprehensive checklists. Useful checklists reflect the development of the whole child by including personal, social, and physical development, as well as all aspects of cognitive development. It is also important that the checklist show a continuum of development because children's growth and development does not proceed at fixed intervals.

Collecting, Reviewing, and Evaluating Children's Work

The work children create each day in the classroom as they investigate, represent, and reflect on their learning, provides concrete evidence of what they are learning. Collecting, reviewing, and evaluating children's work on a regular basis is important for three reasons:

- Children are more motivated when they receive specific feedback about their work.
- Studying the products children create helps you learn about how children think, what they know, and what they are ready to learn next.
- Samples of children's work can be organized into a portfolio to create a portrait of the child's growth and progress.

Giving Children Feedback

The type of feedback children receive about their work can significantly affect their attitudes towards their learning. Many children believe that they do their school work for teachers. They may say things like, "Well, you didn't say it had to be my best work" or, "It doesn't matter if my homework is neat. The teacher doesn't look at it anyway." Constructive and supportive feedback often leads children to a stronger ownership of and commitment to learning.

How, when, and in what form should feedback be given? The answer to these questions depends in large measure on the nature of the work. A story that a child spends several days writing, a model of the neighborhood that a group of children work on for two weeks, or a first attempt at painting a mural deserve a different type and amount of feedback than a series of math problems solved for homework. Children can get feedback on their work by:

- reading a story they wrote and inviting other children to give comments and ask questions at a meeting;
- getting comments from an audience after dramatizing a scene from a book;
- having a conference with the teacher to make a plan for next steps in a story or to review a book report;
- receiving written comments and/or questions on a journal entry, a collaborative social studies project, or on a science observation;
- comparing strategies used to solve a math problem with a peer.

Sometimes the feedback comes directly from the teacher; at other times children receive feedback from peers as they collaborate on a project. There may be times when more than one type of feedback is appropriate. For example, children may share strategies for solving math problems in a group discussion and get feedback from both the teacher and their peers in the process. However, the teacher may also want to review children's math logs to find out more specifically how they handled the task. In reviewing the work, a teacher may make a comment or pose a specific question that validates the child's work or helps to extend the child's thinking. For example, next to Jason's math journal entry his teacher writes: "Jason, it was a good idea to group the Unifix cubes by tens before you counted."

Studying Children's Work

In the previous chapter on Guiding Children's Learning we described how children represent their learning by drawing, writing, making models, dramatizing, and creating charts and graphs. Observing children in the process of creating representations and then reviewing their work informs teachers about children's skills, knowledge, and approach to learning tasks. It helps teachers know what children are ready to learn next.

Different types of representations reveal different aspects of children's thinking and learning.

- José's block building of the hospital shows how well he observed during the class visit to the hospital. His building includes an underground garage, signs showing patients and visitors where to park and how to get to the emergency room, and stretchers to carry the patients through the halls. The building also reveals José's spatial thinking; his construction is symmetrical and includes doors and windows.

- Theresa's story has no clear beginning or end; it is mostly a string of conversations. She uses lots of dialogue but does not know how to include the transitions that show who is talking or how the action got from one place to another. If she could focus more on how to convey who is talking, what leads up to the conversation and how it ends, she will be more aware of the concept of sequence.

- Yana's painting of sea creatures is incredibly detailed. She has included both fish and plants. She obviously remembers a great deal from the fish study earlier this year. She found some books about sea life in the class library in order to make the creatures look realistic. Her painting reveals that her fine motor skills are well developed and she has learned to mix paints to make a wide variety of colors.

- A third grade class has been collecting information to determine which grade in the school has the most children. Working in teams, they add long columns of two-digit numbers. The teacher uses this activity to assess whether children demonstrate number sense, recognize patterns, and see combinations of ten.

Sometimes teachers observe children's work as they are creating it. They notice aspects of children's learning and take notes as described in the section on observation and documentation. At other times teachers reflect on children's work during a conference with the child. In both of these cases teachers talk with children about their thinking. Studying children's work when the child is not present also gives teachers opportunities to be reflective. They can take time and learn a great deal from the work as they begin to consider appropriate next steps for the child's learning.

Portfolios: Portraits of Children's Growth and Progress

Portfolios are purposeful collections of a child's work. They tell the story of a child: what the child can do, the child's special interests, and how the child thinks and solves problems. A portfolio is not simply a scrapbook or folder of children's work. It is a tool that is organized in such a way that the teacher, the child, and the child's family can learn about the quality of the child's work and observe progress over time.

Because a portfolio is a collection of a child's work that reveals its quality as well as the child's thinking, it should include a range of samples, including some that the child feels were hard, easy, enjoyable, frustrating, and successful. Examples of work in a child's portfolio might include the following:

- samples of writing (e.g., stories, poetry, journal entries, reports, letters, signs for projects, scripts for puppet shows);
- examples of solutions to mathematical problems (e.g., diagrams with written descriptions, photographs with narratives, drawing and writing, pages from a math journal, charts or graphs);
- documentation of science observations (e.g., stages in the transformation of a caterpillar to a butterfly, findings from a study of shadows);
- drawings, paintings, collages or photographs of three dimensional constructions;
- photographs of a project (e.g., skits, models, presentations) with written narrative.

Portfolios can be a valuable assessment tool when they are organized according to a plan. While some teachers collect samples of children's work only in math and writing, to create a comprehensive portrait of the whole child, the portfolio should include work samples across all aspects of the curriculum. When you structure portfolio collection so that similar types of work samples are collected at intervals during the year, you will observe growth and change in children's thinking and abilities. For example, if a sample of writing is collected in the fall and again several other times during the year, it is possible to see a child's growth as a writer (*The Work Sampling System* 1994).

Methods for Work Collection, Review, and Evaluation

The process of collecting, reviewing, selecting, and storing work in portfolios is only manageable if you have a well-organized system. Teachers cannot do this alone; children must be involved. Teachers do the initial planning and then engage children in discussion to get their ideas as well.

Establish a Place to Collect and Date Work

A place to collect work that may eventually be placed in the portfolio is essential. Some teachers have collection bins with a section for each child's work. Children should have easy access to collecting bins so they can regularly place work in the folder.

In order to use collected work for assessment purposes, each item should be dated. You can help children get in the habit of dating work by making date stamps available in the classroom.

Schedule Time for Children to Review Their Work

To provide children with feedback and encourage them to reflect on their work, teachers must allocate time in the schedule. Some teachers like to do this at the end of the week and allot 45 minutes every Friday for a work review period. One way to introduce a work review session is to invite children to talk about the projects and activities they have been doing as a class. As children begin to go through their collections of work, you might suggest they sort items into categories: "easy" and "hard."

During the work review time, you can circulate and conduct individual conferences with children as they select the work they want to save for their portfolios. Older children can write comments on their work to explain the reasons for their selection. Creating a comment sheet that children can attach to each sample of work helps to focus children's thinking. Questions might include:

- What was the assignment?
- Why did I select it?
- Did I work alone or with others?
- What did I learn from doing this work?

Provide Storage for Portfolios

The portfolio itself can be an accordion folder, a large sheet of construction paper folded and stapled, or pocket folders. Some teachers find it beneficial to divide the portfolio into sections according to subject areas. The portfolio can be stored in milk crates or in a filing cabinet. Unlike the collection bins, children do not need to have daily access to their portfolios.

Send Work Home

When children review work at the end of the week, they can take home the work that is not being saved for portfolios. Having an organized method for children to take work home helps family members to feel connected to the child's life at school. When primary grade children take work home every day, it often arrives crumbled in a backpack and families never get to see it. Saving it in the classroom and then sending it home in a folder often helps children take pride in their work.

Summarizing Information to Share with Others

When teachers have conducted observations in an ongoing way and collected samples of children's work over time, they have extensive assessment information to share with families or others who need to know about children's learning.

Reviewing the notes collected about a child and examples of the child's work helps you to think carefully about your work with children. What do you know about the child? What are the child's primary interests? Strengths? Weaknesses? Who are the child's friends? What materials does the child particularly like to use? What part of the long-term study interested the child most? Reflecting on individual children also influences how you think about your own work as a teacher. Have you provided each child with sufficient challenges and opportunities for success? Are there children with whom you are having trouble connecting? What other ways might you try to reach the child? What information might you try to obtain from the family?

Many teachers find it useful to have conferences with children prior to writing reports and having conferences with families. They encourage children to reflect on the goals they have set for themselves, review work together, and discuss progress. Children describe ways they feel they have grown and what new goals they have. Teachers explain the information they will be sharing with families so that children are not surprised by what their family members hear.

Some teachers have found it valuable to include children in their conferences with families. It is an excellent way to encourage family members to attend and it helps children develop a sense of responsibility for their school work. During the conference the child describes the work in the portfolio and why that work was selected.

Written Reports to Families

Most, if not all, school systems send written reports home to families. In some instances the written report accompanies the conference. In others, a written report is sent home three or four times during the year. Written reporting methods differ from one district or school to the next.

Some school districts are moving away from using grades to report the growth and learning of young children. Letter grades and ratings such as "Very Good," "Satisfactory," "Unsatisfactory,"or "Needs Improvement," do not provide sufficient information for families about children's growth and progress.

If you are tied to a reporting system that requires you to use summarizing words that you feel are unsupportive of children's growth and development, or the categories that you have to rate do not reflect the goals, objectives, and instructional techniques you are using, you may want to consider writing an addendum to the report form, offering parents a brief explanation of terms. If, for example, one of the categories on the report card for first graders is "Spelling" it might be helpful to clarify your expectations for children's spelling.

> *Because we want first graders to become confident writers, we encourage them to guess the spelling of a word. We refer to this as "invented spelling." This helps children to be independent as writers. Gradually children's spelling progresses to look more like conventional spellings.*

Or, for "Science" you might write:

> *During the last two months we have been studying insects. The study has helped children learn to observe, write about what they are seeing, and make predictions about living things. Children have learned about different kinds of insects, the body parts of insects, and how and where insects live.*

In addition to sending home copies of this addendum, you can add a specific comment about the child's progress. For example, "Larry worked particularly hard on his model of a cricket. The details on his model show what good observation skills he has acquired."

Whatever system of reporting you use, the information you have to share with families will be broad and detailed if your assessment methods are comprehensive, ongoing, and they document the children's work in your classroom.

Putting It All Together—One Teacher's Experience

When assessment supports instruction effectively, the teacher's documented observations, the samples of children's work collected, and written reports reflect the curriculum in the classroom and what children actually do as they learn. For example, the children in a class studying local bridges would have different work samples than children studying immigration.

Charlotte Stetson, a first/second grade teacher participating in our Brattleboro, Vermont Follow Through Project illustrates how she has linked this approach to curriculum with *The Work Sampling System* of assessment (1994). In her own words, she describes how she learned about children's progress.

> *In the fall, children explored the question, "How do animals prepare for winter?" We examined our own preparations for winter and discovered that our activities fell into several categories: keeping warm, having food, and moving around. Using prior knowledge, books, other media, and a guest speaker, we began to expand and consider what various creatures do to prepare for winter. It seemed obvious to all of us to compare and contrast human and animal preparations. A field trip to the top of a nearby mountain to watch the hawk migration was the high point of our investigations. Subsequently, looking at what creatures need in order to survive winter led us to explore the concept of habitat, our next focus.*

> *The outcome of all of these investigations was lots of children's work. Children's portfolios included some or all of the following: journal excerpts about our investigations; a book response to* Blueberries for Sal; *a photo of a clay sculpture of a bird of prey; a drawing of a child's personal habitat; a map of how to get from our school to Putney Mountain; an estimating task from our acorn collecting walk; a response to a visit by a local naturalist; and a sketch of the scenery from the top of Putney Mountain.*

> *This combination of content matter and activities gave me extensive opportunities to observe children's abilities and skills in all seven domains of development as identified on* The Work Sampling Checklist. *The boldface phrases are particular performance indicators from the* Checklist. *As I observed children involved in the activities that grew out of our study, I noticed many aspects of growth and learning.*

> • *In the domain of Personal and Social Development —When children spontaneously write stories and poems or draw pictures about the winter habits of various creatures, I know they are* **"showing eagerness and curiosity as a learner."** *Or, when children repeatedly go to the library asking for books on hawks, I'm witnessing a* **"sustained interest in work over time."**

- *In the domain of Language and Literacy —When I hear children discussing how to make a curved beak out of clay, I say to myself, "Aha, these children* **'listen for meaning in discussions and conversations.'"** *Or, when a child draws and writes about what the people and creatures in* Blueberries for Sal *are doing to prepare for winter, I'm seeing a child* **"understand and interpret information from a story or other text."**

- *In the domain of Mathematical Thinking —When I watch various children figure out a quick way to count 50 acorns and hear some simply speed up their counting while others group by 10's, I'm looking at children* **"using strategies to solve mathematical problems."** *Or, when children guess how many acorns are in each size jar—small, medium, and large—I get a good sense of their ability to* **"make reasonable estimates of quantities."**

- *In the domain of Scientific Thinking —When a child is sent on a nature walk to collect some good winter nesting materials for a mouse and returns with long grasses, fluffy milkweed down, and crinkly leaves, that child is* **"observing characteristics and/or behaviors of living and non-living things."** *And, when a child draws a bear inside a large black circle and writes, "bears sleep," I know that the child can* **"communicate scientific information in various ways."**

- *In the domain of Social Studies —When I interrupt a song with the lyrics "People affect the whole world with their bad habits" to ask what this means, and a child offers an explanation like "they push their old cars over banks" I know that child is* **"recognizing how people affect their environment."** *And when a child draws many lines through an odd shaped outline and dictates to me, "This is a map of birds migrating," I have ample evidence that this first grader shows an* **"early understanding that maps represent actual places."**

- *In the domain of The Arts —When a child works tenaciously at the easel painting and labeling a gorgeous red-tailed hawk and pulls me over by the arm to see it, I have a great example of a child* **"using the arts to express and represent ideas, emotions, and experiences."**

- *In the domain of Physical Development —When a child sketches, cuts out, and puts together all the parts of a bird of prey and then punches a hole in it and ties it on a string, I can say with confidence that the child* **"uses strength and control to accomplish fine motor tasks."**

I use the Checklist *to guide and focus my observations of the children. I do these observations continually and in an ongoing way in the context of the daily activities of the classroom. The combination of my observations and the work collected in the portfolio provide me with a comprehensive picture of what children know and can do. I summarize this information using the* Work Sampling System Summary Report. *In my conferences with families, I share the* Summary Report *and particular examples of work from the portfolio.*

A comprehensive approach to assessment speaks to all the players in the education process. It speaks to children because it focuses on them and their work. It speaks to teachers because it focuses our vision of developmentally appropriate education and provides a lens through which we can look at individual children. It speaks to administrators because it offers them knowledge of classroom practice and children's progress that is based on authentic, first-hand information and it speaks to parents because they can relate a teacher's assessment of their child to their child's work. They no longer must implicitly trust that what the teacher says about their child is true. The child's work holds the supporting evidence.

Closing Thoughts

Assessing children's learning is vital to making informed decisions about their education. Teachers gather information about children through observation, documentation, and careful review of their work. To obtain an accurate, fair, and representative picture of children's abilities and progress, the process of assessment must be ongoing, comprehensive, and in the context of classroom activities. A comprehensive approach to assessment enables teachers to share children's progress with families and others in a meaningful way.

Resources for Assessing Children's Learning

Assessing and Guiding Young Children's Development and Learning. McAfee, Oralee and Deborah Leong. Des Moines: Allyn and Bacon, 1994.

Observing the Development of the Young Child, 2nd ed. Beaty, Janice. New York: Macmillan Publishing Company, 1990.

Portfolio Assessment in the Reading-Writing Classroom. Tierney, Robert, Mark Carter, and Laura Desai. Norwood, MA: Christopher-Gordon Publishers, 1991.

A Practical Guide to Alternative Assessment. Herman, Joan, Pamela R. Aschbacher, and Lynn Winters. Alexandria, VA: Association for Supervision and Curriculum Development, 1992.

Ways of Assessing Children and Curriculum: Stories of Early Childhood Practice. Genishi, Celia. New York: Teachers College Press, 1992.

Ways of Studying Children. Almy, Millie and Celia Genishi. New York: Teachers College Press, 1979.

Assessment Tools

Center for Language in Primary Education (1989). *The Primary Language Record: Handbook for Teachers*. Portsmouth, NH: Heinemann Educational Books, 70 Court Street, Portsmouth, NH 03801, (800) 541-2086.

High/Scope Educational Research Foundation (1992). *High/Scope Child Observation Record (COR) for Ages 2 1/2-6*. Ypsilanti, MI: High/Scope Press, 600 N. River Street, Ypsilanti, MI 48193-2989, (313) 495-2000.

Minnesota Department of Education (1990). *Model Learner Outcomes and Early Childhood*. St. Paul, MN: Author, Minnesota Department of Education, Curriculum Services Section, 626 Capitol Square, 550 Cedar Street, St. Paul, MN 55101, (612) 296-2358.

Missouri Department of Elementary and Secondary Education (1989, May). *Project CONSTRUCT: Curriculum and Assessment Specifications, Validation Survey Edition*. Jefferson City, MO: Author., Director of Early Childhood Education, PO Box 480, Jefferson City, MO 65102, (314) 751-2095.

The Work Sampling System (1994). Meisels, Samuel J., Judy R. Jablon, Dorothea B. Marsden, Margo L. Dichtelmiller, and Aviva B. Dorfman. Ann Arbor, MI: Rebus Planning Associates, 317 South Division Street, Suite 155, Ann Arbor, MI 48104, (800) 435-3085.

References

Ayers, William. 1993. *To Teach: The Journey of a Teacher*. New York: Teachers College Press.

Bredekamp, Sue and Teresa Rosegrant. 1992. *Reaching Potentials: Appropriate Curriculum and Assessment for Young Children, Volume I*. Washington, DC: NAEYC.

Hills, Tynette W. 1992. Reaching Potentials Through Appropriate Assessment. In *Reaching Potentials: Appropriate Curriculum and Assessment for Young Children in Volume I*. Edited by Sue Bredekamp, and Teresa Rosegrant.Washington, DC: NAEYC. 43-63.

Meisels, Samuel. 1993 Remaking Classroom Assessment With the Work Sampling System. *Young Children*. V. 48, 34-40.

Meisels, Samuel. 1993. Doing Harm By Doing Good: Iatrogenic Effects of Early Childhood Enrollment and Promotion Policies. *Early Childhood Research Quarterly*. V.7, 155-174.

Sheppard, Lorrie A. 1989. Why We Need Better Assessments. *Educational Leadership* (April): 4-9.

Constructing

Curriculum

for the

Primary Grades

6

BUILDING A PARTNERSHIP WITH FAMILIES

F amilies and educators share the same goals: to help children become successful learners and socially competent members of their community. The primary educational setting for children is the family. In the home environment, children first develop language, the ability to relate to others, and attitudes about learning and school. When children see that their teachers and families share common goals and can work together in positive and mutually respectful ways, they feel more comfortable at school.

Research and anecdotal evidence convincingly show that parent involvement in their children's school life benefits everyone. Children at risk of school failure improve their performance and continue to achieve throughout their schooling when someone in their family becomes involved. Parents who develop a partnership with their children's teachers feel accepted in the school community and more confident about their parenting. Teachers gain needed support and respect from parents and find that children are more cooperative. Schools that view families as partners in the educational process become better schools (Henderson 1987).

The sixth strategy for constructing curriculum addresses the importance of building a partnership with children's families. Throughout this chapter we refer to parents and families interchangeably. While most children live with one or both parents, other family members may be primary caregivers and therefore most involved in the child's school life. The critical factor is that someone of importance in the child's home life—a parent, relative, or another significant adult— develops a positive relationship with the child's teacher, and that this person supports and feels supported by the school community.

Setting the Stage for a Positive Relationship

People build relationships based upon trust. To establish trust we sometimes have to begin by eliminating fears. Many parents have expectations, and often fears, about school. These may be based on their own experiences or the ways they have been treated in the past by teachers and administrators. If these experiences were not positive, families have no reason to trust that you will be open to building a different kind of relationship with them.

Teachers also have past experiences that affect both their openness to building relationships with families and their expectations of what can be accomplished. If previous efforts to involve families have failed, making new efforts may seem futile. It's easy to get discouraged when parents seem unresponsive or negative.

Perhaps the best place to start is to consider the perspective of a parent. As one teacher said, "I was always a good teacher, but now that I'm a parent myself, I've become a great teacher." Setting the stage for a positive relationship with the families of the children you teach means understanding parents' feelings and the influence of culture, and developing the ability to communicate effectively.

The Parent's Perspective

James Hymes captured the parent-child-teacher relationship well when he said:

> …parents are your friends. Show your interest in a child and parents are on your side. Be casual, be off-handed, be cold toward the child and parents can never work closely with you… To touch the child is to touch the parent. To praise the child is to praise the parent. To criticize the child is to hit at the parent. The two are two, but the two are one (1974, 8-9).

James Comer reinforces this view when he describes a child as a "parent's handiwork" (1989). Teachers who keep these views in mind tread carefully and respectfully in all their contacts with parents. They are more willing to give up old ideas about parent involvement and adopt new beliefs to guide their interactions with families.

All parents want their children to succeed. They care about what happens while their children are at school. Parents, however, have different ways of conveying their expectations and becoming involved in their children's education. Not all parents will attend school events or participate in their children's classroom activities. Many are raising children alone. For some families, coping with everyday life is a struggle, and basic responsibilities—getting their children up, dressed, fed, and to school—represent major accomplishments. These parents are involved in their children's education to the greatest degree they can achieve at the time. Their efforts need to be appreciated and acknowledged as sincerely as the efforts of parents who participate in the PTA, in decision-making, or in classroom activities.

As educators, we have a responsibility to find ways to help all families feel that they are contributing to their child's education. Parents tend to respond positively to a teacher who conveys respect and appreciation for *whatever* they do to support their child's life at school.

Changing the Focus of Parent Involvement

The traditional view of parent involvement focuses on getting parents to participate in school activities or fund-raising efforts. Success is often measured by how many parents attend a school event or donate their time and resources. Given the number of working parents and non-traditional families in today's society, these measurements fail to assess family involvement realistically. Consequently, we may be discouraged by the failure of our efforts to achieve a high level of attendance and may blame families for a lack of interest in their children's education. A promising alternative focuses on **collaboration** and **outreach** rather than on "educating parents" and "getting them into the schools."

Teachers can involve parents in the educational process of their children at many different levels. Not all parents have the capacity or desire to be involved in traditional ways. The range of involvement might be characterized in the following ways:

- Basic obligations: parents meet the child's needs for safety, security, nutrition, health care, and discipline.
- Responsive communication: parents consistently respond to school notices, invitations, meetings, forms, and progress reports.
- Volunteers: parents or family members assist classroom teachers and/or school administrators with school tasks and attend events and/or workshops.
- In-home follow-through: parents help their children at home with learning activities coordinated with the children's classwork.
- Decision-makers: parents are involved in school governance and advocacy through the PTA/PTO, advisory councils, school board, or other decision-making committees or groups.

As with many critical aspects of school life, administrators play a key role in supporting positive school-home relationships. The value of parent involvement must be conveyed by all school personnel: the principal, vice-principal, counselors, office staff, custodians, and health staff. By creating a school atmosphere that welcomes parents and all family members, and by recognizing the importance of effective relationships with parents, administrators enable staff to feel positive and enthusiastic about involving parents.

Understanding the Influence of Culture

Understanding cultural influences helps teachers build strong relationships with families. Children define themselves in relation to their families, and culture plays an important role in how families raise their children. A failure to understand and respect parents ultimately affects a teacher's relationship with the child.

As discussed in the chapter on Knowing the Children You Teach, culture is defined as that which forms the knowledge, perceptions, and understandings each of us brings to a situation. Culture, language, and ethnic origins are a major part of our identities. The foods we eat, the ways we celebrate holidays and life events, and our child-rearing attitudes and practices reflect our cultural heritage. Regardless of how long ago our ancestors came to the United States, our cultural roots influence our attitudes, thoughts, and behaviors.

When the culture of the school is entirely different from the child's culture at home, the child may be confused and uncomfortable at school. It is too much to ask children to bridge the gap between these two very different cultures. What often happens is that these children identify most strongly with their home culture and reject the school culture because it is so unfamiliar. In so doing, they also reject the goals and values of the educational setting. It is the teacher who must take the initiative to bridge the gap between home and school (Lightfoot 1978).

Cultural Differences that May Affect Relationships with Families

When working with families from diverse cultures and backgrounds, it is extremely helpful to know something about traditional values and attitudes that may influence your interactions. Cultural values and norms can vary greatly along many dimensions including the following:

- orientation to time
- importance of individualism and privacy
- attitudes toward competition/cooperation
- degree of formality in interactions
- respect for adults/authority
- reflecting on questions before answering
- orientation toward work, achievement, and materialism
- spirituality and religious orientation
- gender roles
- child-rearing practices
- comfort with physical proximity
- expectations for the future

Family cultural values may conflict with school expectations. For example, some families have a relaxed attitude toward time and do not view punctuality as especially important. The teacher may view tardiness as a sign of disrespect.

> *Ms. Wheelock prepares for conferences with family members. In order to see all the parents, she has to schedule conferences twenty minutes apart. She knows that some family members may not be comfortable with this schedule and want a more relaxed or informal way to talk. To help her keep on schedule and to alert families to the need to keep to a schedule, she posts a chart on the door to her classroom listing conference times. She addresses the issue early in the conference by saying, "I wish we had more time to get to know one another and talk about Hannah. If we don't get a chance to talk about everything that's important to you today, we'll schedule another time to get together."*

In some cultures, a fatalistic acceptance of life circumstances may mean that special help or assistance for a child with special needs is unlikely to be pursued. A willingness to accept "what is," including the possibility of a limited future for a child, does not mean that the parent does not love the child and want the best life possible for the child, but that the parent views the situation differently.

> *Mr. Sherwin is concerned that Anthony's language development may be delayed. He wants to get some additional information by scheduling an evaluation with a specialist. When he speaks with Anthony's parents about this, they are resistant to the idea of involving a specialist. Based on their response, Mr. Sherwin realizes that the intervention he proposes is offensive to Anthony's parents. He decides that a better approach for now is to encourage them to play a game at home that will enhance Anthony's language skills. He offers to send home the materials and suggests that the parents let Anthony teach them the game he learns at school.*

These two examples highlight the importance of understanding and respecting cultural values and norms in order to communicate effectively and build positive relationships with families.

Self-Awareness Is an Important First Step

An understanding of culture begins with gaining awareness of our own cultural background and influences. Listed below are questions about messages you may have received, and experiences you may have had when you were growing up. Take some time to think about the impact they may still have on your attitudes, assumptions, and expectations about children's families. Ask yourself, "What stayed?" "What changed and why?" and "What do I wish would go away?"

- How was your racial/ethnic identity described to you? Were there any characteristics of your group that were described as special?

- What were the early messages you received about other ethnic/racial groups?

- How has the media's labels of different groups influenced you at different times during your life?

- What messages did you receive about your family's socio-economic position?

- What types of exposure did you have to people with mental or physical disabilities? What were you told about these people? How did you feel when you were around them?

- What messages did you receive about "being smart?" Were certain groups of people smarter than others?

- How important was the ability to express yourself verbally? Was it acceptable to interject your opinion when others were speaking?

- Was it okay to be noisy and physically active in your home/community?

- Were you exposed to families that did not have a traditional familial structure (husband/wife)? What were you told about non-traditional family structures?

It is helpful when teachers know something about the specific cultures represented in their community and among the families in their class. At the end of this chapter and the first one, we list resources that can help you learn about the influences of culture. Remember that no family will necessarily share every belief and value attributed to their cultural background. The length of time the family has lived in the United States, their social class (in their country of origin), and various other influences can all affect the family's values and practices. Each family should be viewed as unique with its own personal history and background and treated accordingly.

Communicating Effectively with Families

Transmitting information accurately is an essential component of building relationships with families. Communication involves both the sending of messages and the understanding of messages received. Though fundamental to human understanding, communication is often fraught with misunderstanding. Many factors influence the effectiveness of communication: language, literacy levels, listening skills, voice tone, cultural expectations, values and beliefs, and body language.

Schools traditionally rely upon written communication in the form of letters, memos, and newsletters sent home with the children. Written communication is not the most effective way to exchange information. This is true for all families but especially for those with poor literacy levels or stressful living conditions. Written forms of communication should be reinforced with personal contact.

Personal contact, through home visits, conferences, or visits to the school promotes good communication and relationships with families most effectively because body language and voice tone communicate more powerfully than words themselves. But, as with written communication, one-on-one communication is being filtered through the receiver's and the sender's values, beliefs, past experiences, and expectations as illustrated in the following diagram (Espinosa 1994).

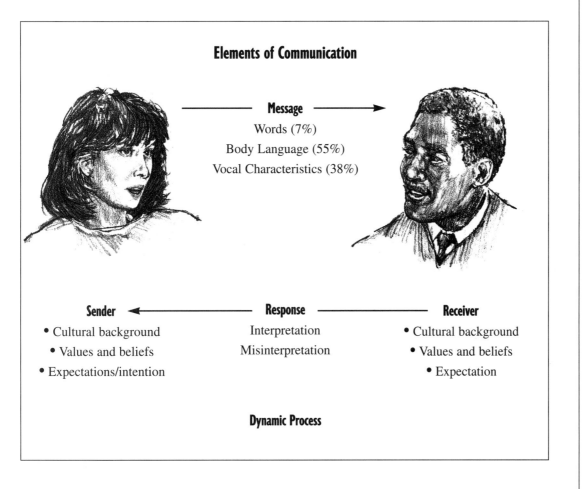

Elements of Communication

Message
Words (7%)
Body Language (55%)
Vocal Characteristics (38%)

Sender
• Cultural background
• Values and beliefs
• Expectations/intention

Response
Interpretation
Misinterpretation

Receiver
• Cultural background
• Values and beliefs
• Expectation

Dynamic Process

Effective honest, respectful, and open communication takes time. The following suggestions may be helpful:

• Give total attention to the communication process when interacting with parents. Look directly at the person, smile, nod, and use body language to convey your interest and respect.

• Make sincere attempts to understand the parent's point of view. By listening carefully, restating, clarifying, and checking what you've heard, you demonstrate a genuine desire to understand. Listen carefully to the stories parents want to tell you.

• Suspend judgment about what the parent says. Although you may disagree with the parent's viewpoint, avoid making quick judgments about whether you feel they are right or wrong. Keep in mind how much you can learn from parents.

- Use simple, clear language and avoid educational jargon. Keep in mind that most parents have not been trained as educators, so words that have a specialized or professional meaning may be foreign to them and interfere with good communication. Avoid trying to "educate" the parents.
- Convey respect for other cultures. Parents' views about child-rearing or school involvement may differ from yours. By communicating an open mind and a willingness to listen, you convey respect.
- Always leave parents with a sense of confidence in their child. Avoid saying anything that will undermine a parent's sense of hope for their child's future. Close a conference by telling parents about their child's recent accomplishments.

When you do send home written notices, make sure parents will be able to understand them. Literacy organizations make the following recommendations (Weinberg 1990.)

- Use short, easy, familiar words.
- Avoid long introductions—get to the point.
- Keep sentences short (no more than 20 words) and try to avoid words with multisyllables.
- Write in logical order (who, what, where, when, why, and how).
- Be direct—use "you" instead of "parents."
- Use the active voice—"Please join us" rather than "Your participation is encouraged."
- Avoid jargon or abbreviations that parents might not know.
- Use pictures and headings to break up text.
- Have written communication translated for families who do not speak English.

Acquiring the skills to communicate effectively both within one's own culture and across different cultures is a lifelong process. The trust that good communication with families builds makes it worth the effort.

Eight Approaches to Involving Families

I n this section we describe eight approaches to involving families. We have focused on those approaches that an individual teacher can implement. However, we recognize that much more can be accomplished when everyone in a school believes in and promotes a partnership with families.

Before-School Contacts

The unknown often makes us feel uneasy. Before entering your classroom, parents wonder if you will like their child, recognize their child's special talents and interests, and if you will be a good teacher. You may wonder if parents will like and support you. Will they respond to your efforts to communicate? Follow through on requests for assistance? Convey appreciation for your efforts to help their child succeed in your classroom? A friendly contact before school begins frequently puts everyone at ease and starts the year on a positive note. Here are some suggestions.

- Write a brief note or postcard to each child and family welcoming them and conveying your enthusiasm about the coming year. School administrators can support this effort by providing stamped and addressed postcards or envelopes, or at least the names, addresses and phone numbers of the children and families in your class. (Try to have all school-home communication translated into the family's primary language whenever possible.)

August 19, 1994

Dear Families,

Welcome to Second Grade! I look forward to meeting you and getting to know your children. Because families are so important, we plan to begin the school year by learning about families. Please have your child bring a picture of your family so we can include it on our bulletin board. If you don't have a picture available, I'll have a camera ready on the first day of school and will be glad to take a picture of you with your child.

I will send home bulletins every two weeks to tell you about life in our classroom. Your questions and concerns are very important to me. I encourage you to come by the classroom, call, or write to me at school. I will be in our classroom, Room 123, all day on September 1 and on the afternoon of September 2. Please feel free to stop by with your child to say hello.

You are an important member of our classroom community. I look forward to working with you and your child to make this a successful school year for everyone.

Sincerely,

- Make a phone call to each family the week before school starts. This personal contact allows you to begin the partnership on a one-to-one basis. You can use this call to introduce yourself, talk a little about your program, and find out if the parents have any questions or concerns. If language will be a barrier, ask someone to help you who can translate the conversation.

  "Hello, Ms. Carter? My name is Margaret Eliot. I will be Latita's teacher this year. I just wanted to tell you personally that I am looking forward to having Latita in the third grade and getting to know her family. I understand from Ms. Smith, her teacher last year, that Latita is quite an artist. Has she done any draw-ings this summer? Ask her if she would like to bring some of her art work to school to share. If you have any questions please feel free to leave a message for me at school and I'll get back to you."

- Have an informal open house prior to the beginning of school so families can stop by with their children. This friendly gesture helps reassure both children and their families that they are welcome at school.

- Arrange a home visit to each child's family. A half-hour visit is usually sufficient to go over some of the plans you have for the year and ask about the parent's expectations and hopes. You will learn a great deal by observing how the child and family members interact with one another. Parents who might feel uneasy in the school setting often are relaxed and more open at home. On the other hand, if families feel they are being judged, the visit will be uncomfortable and unnatural. Therefore, be careful not to infer too much from this brief glimpse of family interactions. If the families do not want you to come to their home for any reason, it's important to respect their decision and suggest an alternative place to meet.

- Visit the community where your children live, particularly if you are from a differ-ent community. Walk through the neighborhoods, visit cultural institutions, busi-nesses, and recreation facilities. Learning about the community provides valuable insights into the cultures and life circumstances of the children in your classroom. It will also be helpful in planning your social studies and science curriculum.

You may think of other ways to establish contact with children's families. Talk with colleagues to find out what approaches work for them. These initial contacts are so important because they set the stage for all future interactions between you and the families of the children you teach.

Informal Contacts

Every day you have many opportunities to communicate informally with families. You can use the times when children are brought to or picked up at school by a member of their family to build relationships.

One of the primary reasons that parents avoid coming into the school building with their children is that they aren't treated well. They feel that administrators and teachers ignore them or convey the impression that they are too busy to talk. Many parents feel unwelcome and out of place.

Teachers who take the time to greet each family member with a smile and a friendly welcome can often put even the most wary parent at ease. You may be too busy to talk at length, but in just one minute, you can convey a positive message to anyone who enters your classroom.

> *"Good morning, Mr. Washington. I bet Lionel wants to show you his caterpillar diary. Please come on in and spend some time with us this morning. Lionel, you know where we keep the science journals. I'm sure your grandfather will be interested in what you recorded yesterday."*

> *"I'm so glad you stopped by, Ms. Morales. Let's set up a time when we can talk. I have free periods on Tuesdays and Fridays from 2:00 to 2:45. Would you be able to meet with me at one of those times, or would you prefer a time before or after school? I'd welcome the opportunity to talk to you about Miguel."*

A smile, a handshake, and a brief communication can go a long way towards making family members feel welcome.

In schools where children arrive and leave by bus, you have fewer opportunities for informal communication with families. The telephone is the next best means for communicating on a regular basis. Once a month you might call each family to chat informally about school life and say something positive about the child's progress. Not all teachers are willing to give out their home phone numbers, but those who do find it helpful to identify specific times when parents may call and discuss any questions or concerns they have. Some schools set up a dedicated phone line so parents can call anytime, day or night, to get a brief message on current events or announcements.

Informal, positive contacts—whether in person, on the phone, or through brief notes—build trust and keep parents informed.

Back-to-School Night

Most schools have a back-to-school night so parents can visit their children's classrooms and hear about the curriculum. This is an excellent opportunity to give parents a tour of the classroom and to share the highlights of your curriculum. If your school does not have a back-to-school night, you may want to initiate a plan to have one. Find a few interested teachers and collaborate.

Attention to logistics makes a big difference in attendance at these events. Schools located in neighborhoods where people don't feel safe coming out at night sometimes schedule the event in the late afternoon or on a weekend. The school could also arrange for extra security in the parking lot and neighborhood and publicize the measures taken to ensure everyone's safety.

The availability of child care often has a major impact on attendance. Many parents can't attend events because they have no one to look after their young children. Ensuring accessibility for disabled parents and arranging for a sign-language interpreter for deaf parents will assure all families they are welcome. An evening potluck meal or coffee and dessert at the school also increases participation in school events.

Prior to the event, send home an announcement and a brief agenda so parents know what you plan to discuss. Arrange the chairs in a circle or horseshoe to convey that you want everyone to feel part of the group. Be sure that what you display in the classroom includes samples of every child's work.

Here are some suggestions for conducting a meeting with parents on back-to-school night:

- Begin with the parents themselves. Suggest that everyone turn to the person next to them and introduce themselves. Ask them to think of their own school experiences, such as a time when a teacher really helped them to feel successful and competent as a learner, or a time when they were truly happy in school. Invite them to share their experiences with their partner. Then ask for volunteers to share what they discussed. Make a list of the key characteristics that are identified. Use this list to explain your approach. (If you try this introductory exercise, limit the time to approximately 10 minutes so you have ample time to talk about your program.)

- Provide a brief overview of child development, focusing on a few typical behaviors of children in your grade level. You might begin by asking parents about developmental characteristics they've noticed. (You can base your presentation on the characteristics we discussed in the first chapter on Knowing the Children You Teach.)

  "I enjoy working with seven year olds because they are such social beings and get so serious about their work. Because each of you lives with a child this age, you are also experts on what they are like. Let me read to you some of the typical characteristics of sevens. Think about whether this fits with what you know about your child."

  Usually parents can relate well to what you have to say about developmental characteristics. It is immensely reassuring to parents to know that the behavior of their child is not unusual.

- Highlight key points about curriculum. Share your approaches to teaching reading, your views on invented spelling, hands-on math, and any other aspects of the curriculum you want parents to understand. Reinforce the importance of parents reading with the children every evening, if possible, instead of watching television.

- Explain your rules about materials, jobs, and routines. Some of the issues you may want to discuss are whether children should bring personal supplies from home, what happens on the days children go out for special classes, when they need to wear sneakers, and whether they need smocks for art.

- Discuss homework—its purpose, how it's assigned, how long it should take, and how you want to involve parents. Ask about the best days to send work home. Invite parents with older children to share what has worked for them in the past.

- Show slides or a video of children working at school. Point out how children work collaboratively, how they use and care for materials, and how they acquire skills and concepts as they investigate, represent, and reflect on what they are learning.

- Develop a handout on the topics you will explore in long-term studies. Talk about the activities you plan for the year and when you expect to take trips. Invite families to contribute their talents and ideas.

- Share your commitment to establishing good communication with families and invite input on how to make this happen. Invite parents to let you know if they welcome phone calls, prefer notes, want to volunteer in the classroom, and so on.

You probably have many tried-and-true approaches of your own. Other teachers in your school can provide additional suggestions. Also, keep in mind that not all of these suggestions will be appropriate or successful for every group.

Bulletins/Newsletters

Regular written communications keep families in touch with classroom life. They need not be elaborate or beautifully typed and formatted; a simple handwritten newsletter or brief, one-page bulletin can accomplish much with very little time or effort.

You can print a supply of "Good News Bulletins" with space to write a personal message to each child's family. (Again, have these messages translated into the family's home language if possible.)

Good News Bulletin

Date: *October 12, 1994*

Dear *Mr. and Mrs. Riley,*

Timothy **and I have some good news to share with you**.

This week Timothy completed a final draft on his story and he will bring it home on Friday with his work folder. I think you will enjoy reading it together. He also helped two other children edit their stories. He is learning a lot about good writing.

Timothy and I have selected samples of his work for his portfolio. We are looking forward to portfolio night when we can show you how much he has accomplished this year.

Sincerely,

A general message that goes to everyone in the class might address specific aspects of the curriculum.

October 12, 1994

Dear Families,

We are studying time. In order to help the children become more aware of when things happen, I have asked them to choose 5 activities that they do in a typical day. These could be: waking up, brushing teeth, eating breakfast or dinner, homework time, bedtime, or doing a particular chore. I have enclosed a chart for the children to use to write the activities and keep track of when they happen each day.

Please help your child fill out the chart for any two days next week. I'd like to have all the charts back by the end of the week. Thank you for your help.

Sincerely,

Some teachers find it helpful to send home bulletins/newsletters on a regular schedule so parents know when to expect them. If you number these bulletins, parents know if they receive all of them.

Invitations to Participate in the Classroom

There are many ways in which having families participate in the classroom can be an asset—for the child, for the family member, and for the teacher. Children love to have someone from home see what their life is like at school. When a Cambodian child's grandmother comes to school and two other children who speak Cambodian have a chance to speak their language with her, they feel that a special part of their life experience is valued. At the same time, the grandmother makes an important connection with her grandchild's world. And for the teacher, involving families in classroom life provides extra help.

Families can participate in the classroom in a variety of ways: as the audience for a play or assembly, as guests at a holiday party, as assistants on trips, or as volunteers to share their talents and skills. An extra hand to help a group with a project, listen to children read, play games, or assist writers can free a teacher to work with individual children or a small group. Several adult volunteers on a trip can help supervise children to ensure their safety.

In any group, you will find family members with special skills and talents to share with the children. An open letter offering a range of options for participating in the classroom may inspire some volunteers.

Dear Families,

Our classroom community includes children's families. We hope you will be able to volunteer your talents and services. Please indicate any areas that interest you.

Name: _____

Phone Number: _____

- Assist children in working on tasks during choice time (Mondays, Tuesdays, Wednesdays, Thursdays, or Fridays)
- Volunteer occasionally for special projects (e.g., walks in the neighborhood)
- Help on field trips
- Share a special hobby or area of expertise with the class
  Please indicate area(s) _____
- Interested in reading to the class or telling stories
- Available for home assignments such as sewing costumes (if we have a play), or book binding
- Willing to bake for classroom celebrations, or to supply juice and snacks
- Other? Please indicate: _____

Please return this to me by: _____

Thank you very much!

Sincerely,

When you send home an invitation to participate, explain to the children what the letters say so that they can help convey the message to family members. Have the letters translated if you know the family has limited English proficiency. Always follow up when a parent responds to your request for volunteers. Parents get discouraged when their offers to assist are ignored.

Although there are many benefits to encouraging this kind of family involvement, there may also be worries or difficulties associated with opening your classroom to family members. Some teachers are uncomfortable asking for help, or they worry about being watched and not looking good. Others are concerned that parents might not do something correctly. Teachers who are helping children to become more self-sufficient may worry that having family members around encourages children to be clingy. While there are no easy answers to these concerns, the benefits of making your classroom an inviting place for families are worth trying to overcome these difficulties. It may be helpful to reframe your idea of parent involvement. Parents can be partners and collaborators in teaching children.

Conferences with Families

Individual conferences with children's families provide time for an in-depth exchange of information. Teachers can explain aspects of the curriculum of interest to a child's family, and ask questions that solicit valuable information about a child's special interests and family background. Parents frequently have specific questions and concerns to raise with their child's teacher.

The best use of the first conference of the year is to discuss goals that you and the parents have for the child. Let parents know ahead of time that you hope to use the conference to learn more about their child, discuss the expectations they have for the year, and respond to their questions. Then parents can think about what they would like to learn and discuss during the conference.

Conferences later in the year can focus on reviews of children's work and progress. To enrich the conference, have actual examples of children's progress to share and discuss (e.g., the portfolios discussed in the previous chapter on Assessing Children's Learning).

In planning for conferences with families, consider the following suggestions:

- Schedule conferences at convenient times for families and for you, so no one will feel rushed.

- Make a plan for conducting the conference and outline a few specific questions you want to ask. Send home a form listing your questions so parents can prepare as well. In this way you will be able to use the time most efficiently and effectively.

- At the start of the conference, establish a relaxed and comfortable tone. Allow time for social conversation and a tour of the classroom if parents have not been there before.

- Ask for parents' opinions about how their child likes school and the changes they have seen in their child.

- Make positive statements about the child. Convey sincerely how much you like having their child in your classroom. Parents tend to like and support a teacher who genuinely likes their child.

- Discuss social as well as academic progress.

- Share examples of the child's work such as a book the child can read, paintings, math work, journals, or a computer program the child enjoys.

- Discuss parents' goals for the child, share your goals, and develop a plan identifying what each of you will do to help the child achieve these goals.

- End by discussing with the parent how you will maintain communication.

It is quite normal to feel somewhat anxious about an upcoming conference. Some conferences are more difficult than others. If, for example, you are planning to meet with the parents of a child who is having a particular difficulty, or you know a parent tends to be defensive and argumentative, try to be especially positive in your approach.

> *"I'm a parent myself so I can sympathize with what you are going through. My oldest son was just like Patrick. I want you to know that I am absolutely committed to Patrick's success. I know that you are committed as well and that's why you are here today."*

An approach like this reinforces for the parent that you share the same goals—to help their child learn and experience success.

Prior to a conference you expect to be difficult, it may be helpful to discuss your concerns with another teacher, preferably someone who knows the family, or with your principal. Ask yourself, "What's my biggest fear?" Then develop some strategies for handling what worries you so you feel more prepared for the conference. Role playing how you plan to handle a conference can also help.

Parent Meetings and Workshops

Schools and individual teachers sometimes plan meetings or workshops for parents about the curriculum. For example, if you have started a new math program in your classroom, introduced a writing workshop, or added computers and want to share new software with families, you might plan a workshop to share these approaches.

Rather than conducting these meetings on your own, consider collaborating with other teachers in the same grade to conduct a series of workshops. When child care is a consideration, some teachers may offer to share this responsibility during a meeting so that more parents can attend.

In planning and running parent meetings and workshops, consider the following suggestions:

- Arrange for simple refreshments for the meeting. This sets a friendly tone and makes parents feel relaxed.
- Survey families about the topics they would like to hear about (e.g., drug education, sex education, literacy) and then work with your principal or PTA to try to accommodate their interests.
- If a parent asks too many questions and dominates the meeting, you may consider saying something like, "You have so many ideas to share with me, I'd like to set up an individual conference with you."
- If parents ask no questions, it may be useful to say, "Last year many parents wanted to know…" or "A frequently asked question is…"

It's very likely that some parents who have an interest in the topic being presented simply cannot attend. If possible, make an audio or videotape of the presentations and lend copies to parents who express an interest.

Workshops or seminars on a school-wide program such as conflict resolution can involve parents and staff learning together. Getting support for such programs at home and school promotes teamwork and increases the chances for a successful program.

Family Gatherings

In addition to meetings and workshops for parents, family gatherings involve both the children and their families. At the end of a project, such as the study of machines, the children might want to invite their families to come see the machines they created in the classroom and to celebrate the conclusion of their study. Some teachers have an "Authors' Breakfast" when children share their published work with family members. Family meetings can be held during the school day, in the afternoon or evening, depending on when most families can attend.

If you only have one conference each year, consider planning a family gathering mid-year. You might plan a family portfolio night, for example, where children can share their school work with family members. You can talk about how children have been saving work samples and how they reflect the work you have been doing together. While children share their portfolios with their families, you can move from one group to another and answer questions or make comments.

How Involving Families Supports the First Five Strategies

We recognize that building relationships with families takes a great deal of time and effort. Most teachers find, however, that when they are successful in building relationships with families and involving them in the educational process, it makes their job easier and more rewarding.

We conclude this chapter on families by showing how developing a partnership with families based on trust and mutual respect supports each of the strategies described in the previous chapters: knowing the children you teach, building a classroom community, establishing a structure, guiding and assessing children's learning.

Getting to Know the Children You Teach

In the first chapter we stated the dimensions to knowing the children you teach: who they are developmentally, individually, and culturally. You can learn about child development from books and your own teaching experience. In order to learn about each child as an individual and about how culture and family background influence the child's communication and interaction styles, your greatest resource is the family.

In parent conferences, home visits, or informal conversations at school or on the phone, you can ask for information that will be helpful in understanding your children. Let parents know that you are always open to hearing what their children say about school, concerns they have, and insights they wish to share with you.

Talking with Parents About Their Child

You may want to begin these discussions by sharing a little about yourself, such as why you went into teaching, what you enjoy most, your own experiences as a child in school or as a parent. When teachers share something personal, parents are more likely to share a little about themselves.

You might explain that each year you adapt and build the curriculum around the specific needs and interests of the children. Therefore, you are eager to know as much as you can about each child so that you can best meet their learning needs.

To learn more about the child's position in the family, temperament, talents and interests you might ask the following:

- Does your child have siblings?
- How does your child help at home?
- When are you most proud of your child?
- How does your child respond to new people or situations?

- Does your child have any special interests (e.g, sports, games, nature, art, music, dance, computers)?
- Do you have any concerns about your child or about school?
- What kind of school experiences do you wish for your child this year?

Another area in which parents can provide useful insights is in defining their children's preferred learning styles and strengths. In the first chapter we described Howard Gardner's expanded view of intelligence, and how we have often judged children as not being very "smart" because they did not excel in language or math skills. It can be very reassuring to families to learn that their child, who may excel in other areas such as music, art, physical skills, and relationships, has special strengths that you appreciate and will build upon.

To learn more about each child's learning and interactive styles, you might pose a few of these questions:

- What is your child's favorite activity?
- Does your child like to have friends over or to go to other children's homes?
- How does your child approach other children? Does he hang back and watch a while, or does he join right in?
- What kinds of activities does your child enjoy doing for extended time periods?
- Have you ever seen your child take things apart and put them back together to figure out how they work?
- Do you have to repeat directions several times or does she grasp what she hears the first time?
- How does your child respond to books and stories?
- How do you know what your child is thinking or feeling?
- Does your child watch television? Do you notice any ways in which television affects your child positively? Negatively?

Understanding Cultural Expectations

As previously stated, culture has a profound influence on children. The greater the difference between the teacher's cultural background and those of the children in the class, the more effort the teacher must make to understand children's behavior and expectations. Your contact with families can help you learn what they value most, the expectations they have about school, and the behavior considered appropriate and respectful at home. This understanding can give you valuable insights and keep you from seeking changes that would be inappropriate in the child's culture. Consider the following story.

Ms. Robinson, a teacher who values choice time and encourages children to work collaboratively at tables, is concerned about Lee Ming's behavior in the classroom. He constantly runs in the classroom, picking up toys and materials and dropping them everywhere. When he paints he spatters all over the table. At a parent conference, Ms. Robinson describes Lee Ming's behavior at school and the problem it is causing. She learns that at home, the child is expected to be very quiet and to respect his father's need to study and read. The parents explain that they give Lee Ming coloring books and workbooks which he uses on his own for long periods of time. Ms. Robinson discusses how important it is for children to go outdoors every day and have opportunities to be active. She suggests some activities that Lee Ming can do with his mother or on his own. The parents work out a plan that will allow Lee Ming to be more active at home, while still respecting his father's need for quiet. Ms. Robinson realizes she needs to focus more on helping Lee Ming develop self-control and allocates time to teach him how to use materials appropriately. Within a few weeks, there is a dramatic change in Lee Ming's school behavior.

This example illustrates the importance of close communication between school and home in resolving problems created by different expectations.

Consulting with Parents about Special Needs

Parents are a teacher's greatest resource, especially for a child with a diagnosed disability. These parents have often spent years consulting with experts to diagnose the problem and find out the best strategies for promoting their child's growth and development. Teachers who welcome children with disabilities in their classrooms will gain the trust and support of their parents.

Get to know the parents' view of the disability, their current responses to the disability, their interpretation of the educational/medical counseling they have received, their membership in support/advocacy groups, their home goals for the child, their school goals for the child, and their views of key elements in their child's school success. It may take quite a bit of time to gather such extensive information from parents. Many have faced misinformation, prejudice, and undervaluing by professionals before they met you. Listen to their stories to learn how this family has coped with a disability. You will learn about the highs and lows of parenting this individual child. This information will help you formulate the best approaches to fully including the child in your classroom.

Including Families in the Classroom Community

Families are already part of your classroom community. Children do not enter into your classroom alone; they bring their families with them. Think about what children share at meetings, and what they are bursting to tell you when they arrive each day. Most often they share stories about family members, something that happened to someone they love, or a family event. Children need to see that their families are accepted in their school community.

Teachers convey this message by being open to what children share, by accepting their stories, respecting their concerns, and celebrating good news. This affirmation enables children to see the strong bond between their two worlds and to experience acceptance in both.

Teachers need to guard against being judgmental in responding to what children bring into the classroom about their families. Some of the experiences children share may be shocking and distressing: having a family member arrested or shot, or seeing physical violence in the home, for example. If our own discomfort leads us to say that those stories do not belong in school, we negate a part of children's lives. Thereafter, they may hide this part of their lives and lose their sense of belonging at school. Teachers can help children by being good listeners and responding to how the child is feeling: "That must be very upsetting. I'm glad you're safe."

Just as children share family stories at school, they also talk about school experiences at home. The meetings you have every day, in which children talk about topics that are of interest to them and participate as members of a community, give children information that they can take home and share with their families. Sharing information reinforces the link between home and school.

To make families an integral part of your classroom community, consider the following suggestions:

- At the beginning of the year, display pictures of children and their families on a bulletin board as a focus of study. If photographs are not available, have children draw pictures of their families. Children can conduct interviews, draw and write stories, and have discussions about all kinds of families, even those that may not exist in your class. Read some of the wonderful children's books on families and encourage children to borrow them to share with their own families.

- When you conduct parent meetings or an open house, arrange the chairs in a circle as you do for all class meetings. You can model the way you conduct meetings with the children: greeting everyone, reading a morning message, going over the agenda, asking if people have anything they want to share, and involving everyone in the discussion.

- Encourage family members to enrich your curriculum by sharing their own talents and special interests with children. The notes you send home to invite their participation can be reinforced through informal communication. If possible, try to arrange the schedule so that choice times take place when family members are available to help.

- Use class projects that focus on the community or on different kinds of jobs to provide opportunities to involve family members in the classroom. Children might visit their parents' places of work or invite members of their family to school to be interviewed about their jobs.

- Think of activities for families who can't come to school (e.g., making phone calls, collating papers, sending in the snack). Acknowledge their contributions by describing how they have helped the class.

- Plan a special workshop on conflict resolution so that parents can learn about this approach, how it works in your classroom, and how they can help their children handle anger and conflicts non-violently at home.

- Invite family members into the classroom to read to the class, bring a special object to share, or contribute to a class newsletter. Show appreciation for their contributions by having children write thank-you notes.

- If your school has a home-school liaison, you can ask that person to follow through with a particular family that you have difficulty contacting.

Families want to experience belonging to a community as much as children do. The best schools truly serve the community around them. This sense of community can begin in your classroom.

Reinforcing the Classroom Structure

The structure you create in your classroom—by organizing the physical environment, designing the schedule and routines, and involving the children in establishing rules for classroom life—helps children develop responsibility and a sense of their own competence. Reinforce this structure constantly so that children know what is expected of them. Parents can be your best allies in making the structure work.

Explaining Your Classroom Structure to Families

To support the classroom structure you create, parents must understand what you expect and why, and how they can support their child. At an open house, parent meetings, or parent conferences, you can explain the various aspects of structure. Weekly bulletins and newsletters give you an opportunity to provide a little bit of information at a time and to reinforce what you previously shared in person. Older children can help present this information to their families.

In explaining your classroom structure to families, select topics critical to the success of your classroom. The suggestions listed below may prompt ideas of your own:

- Make a map or floor plan of your classroom. Attach a simple explanation of how it's organized, why you label materials, the purpose of shared materials, and how children help to maintain the classroom. Invite parents to contribute furniture or materials you may need such as computer paper, beautiful "junk" for collage and construction, collections for sorting and counting, books, plant cuttings, cooking utensils, a fish tank, shelf, or rug for the meeting area.

- List the rules you develop with the children and why you include children in this process. Discuss how you help children remember them, how children remind each other, and the consequences for not following the rules.
- Give each family a copy of the daily schedule and highlight the times you need volunteers most. Discuss why children need a snack mid-morning. Ask for contributions if this is appropriate.
- Share your list of jobs, how children help identify the jobs needed, and the importance of everyone having a job each week. Invite parents to share what jobs their children have at home.
- Demonstrate how you introduce materials to children so that they learn to respect and take care of them.
- Explain how children can catch up if they are ill and miss several days of school.
- Share a list of board games that help children develop social, reading, and math skills. (This is especially appreciated during the holiday season.)
- Discuss the importance of going outdoors, even in cold weather, and the need for children to dress appropriately. You might suggest having a box in the classroom for extra mittens, sweaters, hats, and scarves for children who forget these items. Families are often willing to donate outgrown or extra clothing for this purpose.
- Describe the structure of choice time and the reasons it is valued by children and teachers.

Parents often say that their children do not talk about what goes on in school. When asked, "What happened in school today?" they respond with a shrug or, "Nothing." The more information parents have about the daily program, the easier it will be for them to frame specific questions and get a response that can lead to more conversation. For example, families who understand your structure might replace the question above with something like, "What did you do at choice time today?"

A Structure for Homework

Often, homework becomes "homewar" and the results can be disastrous for all involved. Children may not understand what they are supposed to do and fail to complete the assignment. Some parents do not know how to help. They may feel incompetent, frustrated, or they may even do the homework for their child. It's important to think about why you assign homework, what you expect, and to help parents so they can help their children successfully complete assignments.

Why do teachers in the primary grades assign homework? In addition to reinforcing skills and concepts learned at school, homework reinforces and strengthens the school-home connection. When children do schoolwork at home, parents learn about the curriculum and can talk to their children in a meaningful way about what they are learning. Another reason for giving homework is to teach children responsibility and good work habits.

When teachers plan homework thoughtfully, it can achieve these positive outcomes. Here are some suggestions for informing parents about homework:

- Explain (and repeat if necessary) that it is **your** responsibility, as the teacher, to be clear in assigning homework. If parents find that their child doesn't understand what to do, they should send it back unfinished and let you know. An important goal is to make homework a successful experience.

- Make homework assignments age-appropriate. In first and second grade, children begin to develop a pattern regarding homework: taking work home, doing it, and bringing it back to school. For many, it's best to give assignments that involve family members, such as reading together or counting the number of windows in the house. Send home a brief note explaining the requirements. Allow enough time for the assignment in case parents are not available in the evenings. By third grade, children can be encouraged to do their homework independently, to develop consistent habits about when and where they do homework, and to keep track of their papers.

- Limit homework to between 15 and 30 minutes, depending on the child's age. Let parents know that if it's taking more time, their child can stop. Parents should write you a note about it. Reassure them that you will help the child if needed.

- Establish a schedule for sending homework. For example, let parents know that every Monday and Wednesday their child will bring home a work folder and their homework will be due two days later. You might first discuss the convenience of this schedule at a parent meeting. Parents may prefer having a weekend to work with their child on something like spelling.

- Make suggestions that will help parents develop their own structure for supporting homework. These might include: establishing a consistent place in the house to do homework, preferably a quiet place; turning off the TV; keeping incomplete homework in a designated place; posting a schedule on the refrigerator as a reminder of when homework is due; keeping completed homework in a backpack the child takes to school each day; reviewing homework with the child; signing the homework folder each week.

To reinforce the guidelines about homework and to promote good communication, some teachers have found it helpful to use a consistent system, such as the one described in the following letter to parents.

Building a

Partnership

with

Families

233

September 13, 1994

Dear Families:

Today marks the beginning of regular homework assignments for the class. On Mondays children will have spelling work and on Wednesdays a math assignment.

I select spelling words from each child's journal writing. This week I have only identified three words for each child; eventually the children will have five to seven words per week to study. Every Monday the children receive a card listing their spelling words. The homework will be to write a sentence for each word and underline the spelling word. (Don't worry if other words in the sentence are misspelled.)

The math homework assignments will usually be some problems to solve based on something we've been working on in class.

All of the work will be contained in a red folder which I hope you will help your child remember to bring back to school after completing assignments. Establishing a routine for time, place, and care of homework is important for third graders.

Thank you for your support.

Sincerely,

Supporting Children's Learning

One of the most important messages we give children is that they are competent learners who are acquiring a great deal of knowledge about the world around them. When children's families understand the curriculum and value the skills being developed, children receive positive messages about their growing competence.

It's extremely important to explain your instructional approaches to parents. For example, if you encourage children to invent their own spelling when they are writing stories, it is a good idea to prepare parents for this or they may question whether their child will ever learn to spell correctly. Similarly, if you are encouraging children to count on their fingers as one strategy for solving math problems, you will want to let parents know that they need not discourage this practice at home.

Topics for long-term studies come to life when children take home what they are learning at school or when they bring to school what they learn at home. Homework assignments can focus on interviewing family members about what they know about the topic under study. Families can be invited to join investigations and contribute their ideas. Here are some examples of ways that children can include their families:

- While studying the neighborhood, children might ask their families where they shop and why.
- During a science study about food spoilage and mold, children could ask family members to predict what will happen to foods left out of the refrigerator.
- Children can invite family members to come on a trip.
- While studying inventions, children can interview older relatives or neighbors about the types of machines they had as children in their homes.
- While working on surveying and graphing information in math, children can select a question and survey family members about their preferences or opinions.

Long-term studies, as described in the chapters on Science and Social Studies, involve many discussions with children about what they already know about a topic, and what they want to find out. The charts that you develop during these discussions can be typed and sent home to share with families.

Dear Families,

The third graders of Room 312 are beginning a study about life in our town one hundred years ago. We will be visiting many of the town's landmarks and studying old photographs and maps. The children have discussed what they know about our town's history and what they want to find out. Here's what they said.

We think we know:

- There were only dirt roads a hundred years ago.
- Some of the buildings on Main Street were already built.
- There were no TVs back then.
- The bridge that crosses the river wasn't built but there was a ferry.
- There were no cars; people rode horses and used carriages.

What we want to find out:

- How many people lived here?
- Where were the schools and what were they like?
- Were there telephones a hundred years ago?
- When was the bridge built?
- Where did people go if they were sick?
- Before the mall was built, where did people go shopping?

The children will be interviewing you and other relatives to find the answers to their questions.

Sincerely,

A proven approach to involving families in promoting their children's reading skills is to have children read school books at home. This type of program leads to improved communication between children, family members, and teachers as well as substantial gains in reading skills. Here's how one first grade teacher began such a reading program with her class.

Dear Families,

Your child is learning to read! Beginning this week, I will send home books for your child to share with you. Each book will be sent home in a plastic, sealable, storage bag. This is to help protect the book and to serve as a reminder to return it by the date listed on the card. You can help your child develop responsibility by finding a place at home to keep the book.

Shared reading experiences are an important part of our reading program. You will see lots of signs that your child is using new skills in reading. For example, notice if your child:

• uses pictures in the book to get ideas about words;

• points to some words;

• "reads" the story with expression and enjoyment.

Your encouragement will help your child see that reading is important. If you have any questions, please let me know.

Sincerely,

Programs such as this, where children read to their parents every night, have been implemented in many schools in the United States and in England. Because the child is reading to the parent, parent literacy skills are not an issue. The results have been very positive. Children's reading ability improved dramatically and parents became more involved in their children's school life without having to come to school (Nurss, Huss, Hannon 1993.)

Parents do not have to be well-educated to make a difference. "The motivation and impetus for learning begins in the home," says Beverly Langford Thomas, Executive Director of the Head Start Program in the District of Columbia Public Schools. "It's not a set of skills. It's the values, desires, determination, and belief that it can happen." Ms. Thomas cites the experience of a colleague, now a professor at Johns Hopkins University, whose mother was concerned that he and his brother were clowning around too much in elementary school. The mother required the boys to read to her every night, and to write weekly book reports for her. They didn't know at the time that their mother could not read. What they learned from her was that reading was valued in their home.

Involving Families in Assessment

Earlier, we described how parents can help you learn more about their child. Through personal contacts, and by asking specific questions about the child, you can gain valuable insights. This information, along with your observations of the child, provide a comprehensive picture of the child's abilities. Involving families in all phases of the assessment process can promote mutual understanding, generate a joint commitment to achieving the goals for each child, and keep parents informed about any concerns.

Promoting Mutual Understanding

Teachers cannot assume that parents understand how children's work is assessed at school or the teacher's expectations for work quality. When papers come home with invented spelling, reversed numbers, or incorrect math problems, it can raise concerns that a teacher is not teaching children the "correct" approaches or valuing right answers. Even if you share your approaches during back-to-school night (as described earlier), you may find that it helps to remind parents of when and how you evaluate children's work. It is valuable to you as well as to children and their families to be clear about your expectations and methods for evaluating work.

Take time to explain any of the following approaches you use in your classroom:

- when you correct spelling and when you do not;
- how children edit one another's work and what they learn from this process;
- when you expect work to be perfect, when you do not, and why;
- why children are encouraged to count on their fingers in doing math;
- how you mark children's papers and what the marks mean;
- why you don't use red pens to correct work or give stickers as rewards.

The portfolios of children's work, as described earlier, provide a rich resource for sharing both the quality of a child's work and progress over time. Parents can contribute samples of their child's work to the portfolio—work that you might otherwise not have seen. Portfolios give parents a better understanding of the topics and projects the class is studying and allow parents to ask specific questions about their child's work in your classroom. Particularly for parents who are not entirely comfortable speaking in English, portfolios do not rely on words and therefore provide concrete evidence of your curriculum content and how their child is learning.

Involving Families in Establishing Goals

One of the primary purposes of assessment is to establish realistic goals for children in order to plan your curriculum. Parents will want to know your goals and how you plan to help their child achieve them. By involving parents in the process of formulating goals and identifying strategies that will help the child, you will find that you have strong allies in achieving these goals.

Ms. Woodburn is having her first conference with Nancy's mother, Ms. Fowler. She describes how one of Nancy's goals for herself this year is to write longer stories, and asks Nancy's mother what she hopes Nancy will learn in second grade. Ms. Fowler says, "I'm concerned about her spelling." Ms. Woodburn responds, "I feel that it is an important goal for Nancy as well. Nancy and I will come up with words each week from her writing, make a list, and these will be her spelling words for the week. She'll have some time to study them in class, but it will help Nancy if you can practice them with her at home as well."

Keeping Families Informed

Parents often want to know how their child measures up to the school's expectations. Is their child achieving at grade level? Does the teacher have any concerns about their child? A comprehensive approach to assessment linked to your curriculum allows you to convey an accurate picture of the child's progress and to discuss any concerns either of you have. All parents have a right to know this information and feel reassured when they learn that you have a plan for helping their child if there is a problem.

In any given year, you may have children whose progress is of particular concern to you and/or the parents. You may suspect that a health problem, a hearing loss, poor eyesight, or a learning disability is impeding the child's progress in your class. If you have established a relationship with the parents and have discussed each of your concerns, parents are likely to be open to suggestions that they have their child examined by a specialist. Problems identified early can often be corrected or addressed before the child experiences too many failures.

It's critically important not to wait until the end of the year to let parents know if their child is not progressing according to your expectations. Nothing is more upsetting to a parent than learning that there is a problem when it's too late to address it. Sharing any concerns early in the school year allows teachers and families to work together on behalf of the child right from the beginning.

Families in Need of Special Services

Building a

Partnership

with

Families

For some families and in some communities, it may be especially challenging to establish close, trusting relationships on behalf of the children. The children who need the most help academically and socially often live in impoverished and unstable home environments. A concern voiced repeatedly by teachers of young children is that they are increasingly being called upon to "do it all." They feel that many of their children and families have complex needs that must be addressed before successful learning relationships can be established.

Community-based family support programs that link the adults as well as the children to formal agency services and informal community support can help teachers in their efforts to reach out to families in need. Providing new immigrant families with information about how the school and social services systems work, preferably in their own language, can involve teachers, families, and members of the community in joint support efforts.

Most family support programs work in partnership with parents, or other significant adults in the child's life, to build the family's capacity to respond appropriately to the developmental needs of its children. Program staff acknowledge and address the contexts in which families live, appreciating and valuing each family's community, culture, individual traditions, values and lifestyles. The process of establishing trust and creating positive communication is particularly difficult when families are accustomed to an adversarial relationship with schools or community services.

In communities where school-home collaborations have been the most successful, the schools have taken an active leadership role. A cadre of teachers or an active principal has taken the initiative to personally create effective partnerships. These partnerships often include services such as: school-based medical and dental services, drug and alcohol abuse counseling, family crisis counseling, child care, parenting classes, employment training and counseling, and transportation. Services are provided at the school site or near the school.

An increasing number of schools, and almost all those receiving Title 1 funds, have a home-school liaison. This staff person is often in the best position to work with the principal and the community to explore how most effectively to acquire more family support services. Currently there are federal and state grant opportunities as well as private foundation funding possibilities. An essential first step is for teachers and administrators to make the decision that they want to work more closely with their most vulnerable and challenging students and families.

Closing Thoughts

Teachers and families share the same goals and therefore the responsibility
for building a partnership that brings the child's school and home life together.
The teacher must take the initiative for making this a positive partnership. Using
the eight approaches to working with families described in this chapter will
enable you to learn more about the children in your classroom, build a classroom
community, reinforce the classroom structure, and both support and assess children's learning. Teachers who take time to build a partnership with each child's
family have gained critically important allies in creating exciting classrooms and
confident students.

Resources for Building a Partnership with Families

The Art of Crossing Cultures. Storti, Craig. Yarmouth, ME: Intercultural Press, 1989.

At Risk Families and Schools Becoming Partners. Liontos, Lynn Balster. Eugene, OR: ERIC Clearinghouse on Educational Management, University of Oregon, 1992.

Beyond the Bake Sale: An Educator's Guide to Working with Parents. Henderson, Anne T., Carl L. Marburger, and Theodora Ooms. Washington, DC: National Committee for Citizens in Education, 1986.

Black Children: Their Roots, Culture, and Learning Styles. Hale-Benson, Janice. Baltimore: Johns Hopkins University Press, 1986.

The Conditions of Teaching. Carnegie Foundation for the Advancement of Teaching. Princeton: Carnegie Foundation for the Advancement of Teaching, 1988.

Developing Cross-Cultural Competence: A Guide for Working with Young Children and Their Families. Lynch, Eleanor and Marc Hanson. Baltimore: Paul H. Brooks Publishing Co., 1992.

"Families as Partners on Educational Productivity." Walking, H.F. *Phi Delta Kappan* 65(1984): 397-400.

"Parent Involvement and Reading Achievement: A Review of Research and Implications for Practice." Beecher, R.M. *Childhood Education* 62 (1985): 44-49.

Parents as Partners in Education. Berger, Eugenia. New York: MacMillan Publishing Co., 1991.

References

Comer, James. November 2, 1989. Keynote address at National Association for the Education of Young Children Conference. Atlanta, Georgia.

Espinosa, Linda. 1994. Facsimile to author, January 31.

Henderson, Anne T., ed. 1987. *The Evidence Continues to Grow: Parent Involvement Improves Student Achievement.* Washington, DC: National Committee for Citizens in Education.

Hymes, James. 1974. *Effective School-Home Relationships.* Sierra-Madre, CA: California Association of Young Children.

Lightfoot, Sara Lawrence. 1978. *Worlds Apart: The Relationships Between Families and Schools.* New York: Basic Books.

Nurss, Joanne R., Rebecca Huss, and Peter Hannon. 1993. American Parents Hearing Children Read: Trying a British Approach. *International Journal of Early Childhood, Volume 25, No. 2,* 20-26.

Weinberg, Pamela. 1990. *Family Literacy and the School: How Teachers Can Help.* New York: New Readers Press.

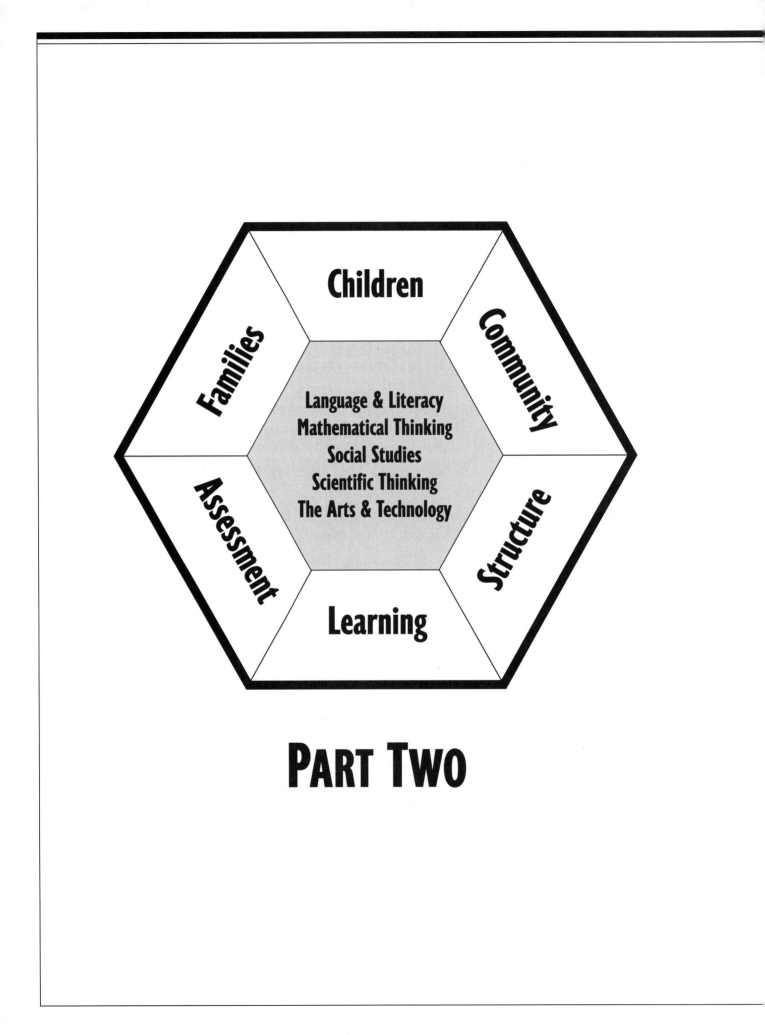

Children

Community

Families

Language & Literacy
Mathematical Thinking
Social Studies
Scientific Thinking
The Arts & Technology

Assessment

Structure

Learning

PART TWO

Introduction to Part Two

Part Two of *Constructing Curriculum* presents the content that is taught in the primary grades. It shows how language and literacy, mathematical thinking, social studies, scientific thinking, and the arts and technology are taught within the *Constructing Curriculum* framework.

The six strategies described in Part One make the subject matter of the classroom come alive. Knowing your children helps you plan where to begin, which materials to choose, and what questions to ask. The classroom community that you create enables children to work in small groups, to share supplies, and to feel safe taking risks. The structure you establish enables children to work independently because they anticipate the day's events, understand classroom rules, and know how to find, use, and put away materials. Applying the approach to guiding children's learning will assist you in helping children construct their own understanding within each subject area. The approach to assessment offers you many ways to find out what children are learning so that you can modify instructional approaches in order to address individual needs. Involving family members in homework projects that call for real-life application of skills and concepts enhances children's learning.

The chapters in Part Two are not meant to provide everything a teacher needs to know within a discipline; they offer a way to think about each subject area. The overviews of content and specific skills in each subject reflect child development research and national and local standards and were derived in conjunction with the development of the *Work Sampling System.*™ These chapters show how concepts and skills are taught not only in the context of long-term studies or regularly scheduled work times, but also by taking advantage of teachable moments. The sample resources listed at the end of each chapter offer you additional ideas about how specific activities can best be incorporated into your curriculum.

As you read each of the subject chapters in Part Two, you will notice that children are having discussions in meetings, working in small groups to conduct active investigations, and representing their learning in a variety of ways. Teachers provide children with daily opportunities to reflect on their learning. The classroom doesn't change with each subject area. The framework remains constant and it is this framework that enables teachers to make learning meaningful for children.

LANGUAGE AND LITERACY

anguage and literacy skills are central to communication and to learning. Communication includes the ability to obtain information, clarify concepts and feelings, and convey ideas in ways that others understand. Whenever we talk on the telephone, read the newspaper, write a letter, discuss books and movies, or find out what time a store opens, we use language and literacy skills. Children need these skills to become successful learners who can read for understanding, enjoy literature, and experience the power of putting ideas into print.

Young children come to school with a wide range of experiences and ideas about language and literacy. In infancy, they are surrounded by the sounds of language; they babble and adults respond, including them in conversations. Children see print all around them: they notice that cars come to a halt at the big red STOP sign; they see labels and signs in the supermarket; they listen to story books being read. Teaching language and literacy means building on these early experiences in ways that convey our confidence that all children can learn to read, write, and express their ideas effectively.

An important goal in the primary grades is to help children see that language and literacy learning has a purpose. When children acquire language and literacy skills as part of meaningful activities, they see connections between what they are learning and their everyday lives. Classrooms can be places where listening, speaking, reading, and writing are integrated into all activities. Children can learn and use these communication skills on a daily basis.

Children Acquiring Language and Literacy Skills

Teachers who surround children with books, give them interesting reasons to write, and use meetings for in-depth discussions make language and literacy experiences a vital part of classroom life. Consider the following examples of classrooms in which teachers provide purposeful experiences for children.

> *In a **first grade**, Ms. Wallen reads several "how-to" books to her class in order to encourage the children to write their own how-to books. They identify a range of topics, including "All About Skateboarding" and "How to Bake Cupcakes." After making a list of ideas for their books, they interview their classmates for additional ideas. The children record the suggestions in their writing folders.*

Ms. Wallen models a specific type of writing for the children in order to support their growth as writers. She allows time for discussion and peer interaction. After listening to and talking about books that exemplify the "how-to" genre, the children are eager to become authors themselves. Because their knowledge is valued, they want to communicate it. Each child makes an independent choice about what to write. Through activities such as these, the children practice reading, writing, speaking, and listening.

> *In a **second grade** classroom, Mr. Sanders and the children are gathered in the meeting area. They are discussing how each character in the stories they have read has a major obstacle to overcome. Mr. Sanders suggests that each child spend a few minutes jotting down ideas about how a particular problem was solved. When the discussion resumes, they notice similarities in the solutions and chart them, making three categories. The first column lists stories in which a miracle occurs. In the second, a new character enters the story and saves the day. In the stories listed in the third column, the characters consistently solve the problems on the third try.*

Mr. Sanders encourages the children to talk about the problem-solving aspect of each story. He models an organized way for children to record their ideas. Group discussions help the children clarify their thinking about the stories and learn strategies for analyzing story content.

> *A small group of **third graders** reads* Charlotte's Web *in a literature group. The teacher opens the discussion by asking, "What is your reaction to the characters?" Peter comments that he likes the character of Templeton, the rat. Others agree. Ms. Weiner suggests that they find some examples of how E.B. White describes Templeton. The children thumb through their individual copies of the book to find favorite selections about Templeton.*

In this classroom, the children eagerly discuss literature they have read together. The teacher guides the discussion in a way that encourages the active participation of each child. The children can competently seek information and contribute their own opinions. The children are aware of the purpose of their work and therefore highly engaged in the process.

Language and literacy teaching is exciting for both teachers and children in these classrooms. The teachers emphasize what children *can* do, rather than what they don't know. The teachers foster social interaction because it is a vital part of language and literacy learning. They know that children learn from one another as well as from books and adults. Experiences are planned that expose children to the joy of listening to and reading good literature. Teachers engage children in making discoveries about books as a source of information, about writing as a way to share experiences, ideas and information, and about talking and listening as important ways of learning. When children have choices in their reading and writing selections, they are likely to become self-directed learners. With this type of motivation, they can then be taught skills to help them become more effective communicators.

Goals for the Language and Literacy Curriculum

Many teachers today have concerns about children's poor communication skills. Blame is placed on hurried lifestyles, too much television being watched, and a lack of opportunity to play informally with peers. Whatever the reasons, it is important for children to learn the art of conversation, experience the pleasures of storytime, and enjoy the satisfaction of being listened to when they have something to say.

The National Council of Teachers of English and the International Reading Association are two of many organizations that advocate an expanded view of the language and literacy curriculum. These organizations encourage us to broaden our thinking about teaching language and literacy, and to think in terms of life-long goals. Goals for the language and literacy curriculum include helping children to:

- clarify their own ideas and feelings;
- share their ideas and thoughts with others, orally as well as in print;
- use literacy skills to obtain information;
- develop a love for literature.

These four goals address the long-term benefits of acquiring language and literacy skills, along with the desire to use these skills to continue learning. An understanding of the value of these goals helps guide our curriculum decisions.

Clarifying One's Own Thoughts and Feelings

Putting complex ideas and emotions into words allows us to gain a deeper understanding of them. Because children are capable speakers before they are writers, talking about their ideas before they write them is often beneficial. For beginning writers, teachers may take dictation from the children, then read aloud what the children have said.

By articulating their feelings and putting their ideas into print, children can take pleasure in seeing how much they know about a subject. Teachers provide support by suggesting that children continue writing, even after they think they have said everything. When encouraged to write more, they often learn more.

> *Ms. Tyler overhears a group of third graders having a heated argument about which combination of baseball players would make the best team. She proposes that the children list their ideas for teams and explain their choices, including each player's merits and weaknesses. Following their writing, the children share their work. After presenting his proposal to the group, Pavel exclaims, "I really* do *love baseball!"*

Putting their thoughts and feelings in words enables children to make sense of events in their lives. After reading a story about someone who has moved to a new home, a child may better understand her own feelings about a move her family is about to make by learning how someone else responds to an event that is both exciting and terrifying. She may discover a phrase or passage in the story that describes her own feelings. Reading that one character writes letters to former classmates, she might decide to do the same. Personally connecting to a story in this way can help a child to overcome difficult feelings.

Sharing Ideas and Thoughts with Others

Because language and literacy learning affects how we communicate ideas, thoughts, and feelings, it is both personal and social. When something important happens, we phone our closest friend and share it. When we observe a terrible accident, we talk about it with anyone who will listen. When our best friends relocate, we are eager to receive a letter or phone call so that we can learn about what they are doing. It is natural for people to want to communicate with others.

When children have the words to describe their feelings, they are better able to cope with what is happening.

> *"I know you miss your mother while she's in the hospital," says Mr. Jenkins to Amelia. "She misses you too, and she probably wonders what you're doing at school. Would you like to write her a letter to tell her about the project we've been working on? I bet it will make her feel better just to read something you wrote for her."*

Children who can read and write about their experiences, express ideas clearly, and listen to the responses of others are equipped to take control of their learning. For this and many other reasons, communication skills are powerful.

Using Literacy Skills to Obtain Information

It is essential that children's school experiences demonstrate the purpose of learning skills. Opportunities to ask questions, listen for information, read, and write as a way to make discoveries lead children to appreciate the reasons for having a repertoire of literacy skills. Children learn to use literacy skills to obtain information when they have interesting problems to solve and when they want to pursue answers to their questions. Their natural curiosity leads them into situations that require the use of language and literacy skills.

> *Following a research project on hurricanes, Carly wants to read more about weather. She learns how meteorologists measure rain and decides to conduct an experiment about rainfall by setting up a rain gauge outside the classroom. The class gets involved in estimating and measuring how much water will be collected each time it rains. Carly writes a report on rainfall, which she shares with the class. Her classmates decide to continue the research by tallying monthly rainfall.*

Through reading and writing, children connect with people—near and far, real and imaginary, current and historical. Reading and writing biographies give children access to intriguing people—those they know and some whom they may never meet.

After reading a biography of Jackie Robinson, Mario decides to write a biography about a sports hero of today, Jim Abbott. In the process of doing the research, he learns about physical disabilities and how one man overcame his disability to become a successful Yankee pitcher.

Teachers can help children recognize their ability to reflect on events in history and make personal connections to them.

Developing a Love for Literature

Children who are read to, who enjoy the sound of poetry, and who learn to love stories and books are motivated to become readers themselves. Teachers cultivate a love of reading in children in many subtle ways. The way a teacher holds a book while reading, shares a tidbit about the story to pique children's interest, reads with great expression and enthusiasm, all convey to children the value and excitement of books.

Children develop a love for literature by listening to and reading books that are full of surprising language and fascinating plots. Stories that reflect children's cultural backgrounds and home life help them see how books relate to personal experience.

Tatiana browses through the book shelves in her classroom library, trying to find a book for quiet reading. She discovers the book A Chair For My Mother *by Vera Williams. "Look!" she says. "This book has a mother, a grandmother, and a girl living in the same apartment—just like me!"*

Books can encourage children to bring their personal experiences to the classroom. Once children begin to identify with story characters, they also vicariously experience the lives of many different people, not just those like themselves.

With these broad goals in mind—clarifying thoughts and feelings, sharing ideas and thoughts with others, using literacy skills to obtain information, and developing a love for literature— it is evident how all aspects of the language and literacy curriculum are integrated. Talking about ideas and books helps children expand their vocabularies. Language is intricately woven into reading and writing. Children who are encouraged to write are also learning to read. Often their writing is enhanced by what they read in books.

Components of the Language and Literacy Curriculum

Reading and writing have always been central to the primary curriculum. It is critically important for children to develop the abilities to read with understanding, write with increasing accuracy and clarity, express their ideas articulately, and listen with understanding to what others say. The skills of language and literacy, so necessary for communicating and learning, are organized into four components:

- listening
- speaking
- reading
- writing

Each of these components include particular skills for children to learn during the primary grades. The following chart provides an overview of the language and literacy curriculum.

Overview of the Language and Literacy Curriculum

Components	Children Learn to:
Listening	• Listen for meaning in the ideas of others (e.g., in conversations and discussions) • Listen with understanding to stories (e.g., discuss what happened; identify problems and solutions) • Follow directions • Reflect on and relate relevant personal experience to what is heard • Listen to other points of view (e.g., take turns and respond)
Speaking	• Speak easily to convey ideas (e.g., in conversations, in small or large group discussions, during play) • Ask and answer questions (e.g., differentiate between questions and statements) • Use language for a variety of purposes (e.g., self-expression, play, questioning, humor, drama) • Use language in imaginative ways

continued on page 252

Overview of the Language and Literacy Curriculum, *continued from page 251*

Components	Children Learn to:
Reading	• Sustain interest in reading activities • Understand and interpret information from a story • Use a variety of strategies to construct meaning from print (e.g., context cues, visual cues) • Use a variety of strategies to figure out unknown words (e.g., letter-sound relationships, context cues, pictures, structural cues) • Make logical predictions about stories (e.g., guess what will happen) • Respond to literature in a variety of ways (e.g., act out a role, draw a picture, make a diorama, keep a reading journal) • Select independently a range of books for a variety of purposes
Writing	• Use writing to convey meaning for a variety of purposes (e.g., persuasion, humor, description, feelings) • Recognize conventions of print (e.g., use of capital letters, punctuation, spelling) • Compose stories with a logical progression • Reflect upon and revise writing (e.g., edit for style, content, conventional spelling) • Sustain interest in writing activities • Develop legible handwriting

Weaving these components into learning experiences for children is the teacher's task. Because the components are interrelated, there are many ways to guide learning. The following sections describe each component.

Listening

Listening skills involve hearing what has been said and relating it to personal knowledge. Children develop listening skills when they have opportunities to:

- participate in a discussion and respond appropriately;
- follow oral directions, first with one or two steps, then with more;
- repeat increasingly complex messages to a third person;
- concentrate in an effort to understand what is being said and ask questions or make relevant comments;

- receive descriptive, positive feedback about what good listening looks like (e.g., "I noticed that you were looking right at Mindy when she was talking.");

- receive clear feedback about the results of good listening (e.g., "Your question shows how much you learned and what else you want to know.");

- comment on similarities and differences between two books;

- listen carefully for interesting language in books.

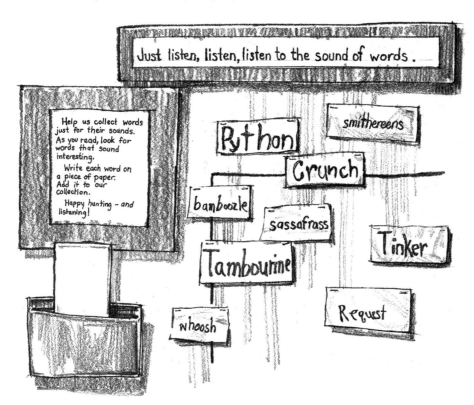

Children develop listening skills when there is something worth listening to and when they have good listening behaviors modeled for them. Teachers model listening behaviors by looking at someone who is talking, by asking questions, making comments, facilitating discussions, and taking turns.

Teachers can also help children recognize how words sound and how they make us feel. Some passages in books make us cry and some make us laugh. A classmate may say something that is comforting or hurtful. Teachers can encourage children to become observant about the tone of language. It is not just the words we hear but how the message is conveyed that affects our ability to listen.

In a second grade classroom a teacher helps Irene to think about how she makes a request. "I'm going to ask Julian if I can borrow his scissors. I'm trying to decide how to do it. Which one do you think he'll say yes to?" says Ms. Brown. "GIVE ME THOSE SCISSORS!" or "May I borrow your scissors for just a minute? I'll bring them right back."

Children know they are being heard when they receive an appropriate response to what they share. When their classmates are attentive, they experience both the emotional and physical impact of being heard. When they provide that kind of support to others, they become good listeners. Children become more aware of listening behaviors when these skills are discussed. Meetings provide many opportunities to practice and discuss listening skills and behaviors.

Speaking

As children become better listeners, they develop more sophisticated speaking skills. Speaking skills include the ability to convey ideas and questions in discussions and conversations, and to use language for a variety of purposes. Children develop and demonstrate speaking skills when they:

- participate in discussions by sharing their own thoughts and feelings;
- describe what they are doing or thinking in response to open-ended questions and encouragement;
- ask questions that are relevant to a story;
- make up word games, riddles, and poems;
- use imaginary language and new vocabulary in stories they write and read aloud;
- present an oral report or read a story they have written.

To share what they are learning, children may need help organizing and expressing their thoughts. When they are encouraged to talk about their experiences and use new words, they are better able to incorporate those words into their permanent vocabulary. A more refined vocabulary helps children to gain greater control over a conversation by describing ideas and events in a way that a listener understands.

During a discussion of a class trip to a vegetable packaging plant, Bernard, a first grader, describes how the people worked together to get the tomatoes packed. He says, "You remember, they were all in a row and each person had just one job to do." Ms. Harris, his teacher, says, "Bernard, that's a great description of an assembly line. When people work like that they work on an assembly line." Later that day Bernard builds in the block area. He constructs a factory with an assembly line. He says, "Put these block people in a row along that long block. They are going to work on the assembly line to get those veggies out to the city!"

Children can learn vocabulary and they also can learn that there are different styles of communication. We talk to family members, to doctors, to teachers, and to one another in the classroom or on the playground with different voices, depending upon the relationship and where we are.

With experience children become aware that communicating clearly takes time, skill, and patience. Listening and speaking skills are fostered in many ways throughout the day and are an integral part of literature and reading activities.

Reading

Allocating time every day to read quality literature aloud to children—especially books and poetry that children may not yet have the skills to read on their own—is the most important way to promote a love for literature and reading.

During the primary grades, teachers can introduce children to a wide variety of reading materials: animal stories, mysteries, fairy tales, science books. Teachers can help children discover that books can be sad, humorous, delightful, puzzling, and enjoyable. By reading and talking about a variety of books, children learn that books can make us laugh and cry. Books can be scary and informative. Books can take us to places not yet explored.

Often children like to hear and read books over and over again. Sometimes books on a particular subject inspire children to seek more information or make something.

> *Ms. Snow, the school librarian, notices Jaime checking out his fourth book on woodworking and says, "You must really like carpentry." "I do," replies Jaime, "My grandfather loves it. I'm trying to learn as much as I can so that the next time I visit him, he'll be really surprised. He promised me that I could help him build a bookshelf."*

Children who enjoy reading reflect on the ideas in stories and often talk with their friends and families about what they are reading. Children can be encouraged to respond to books they have read together with classmates by doing projects.

> *After noticing the map in the front of* My Father's Dragon *by Ruth Gannett, a second grade class decides to make a study of books with maps. They find as many books with maps as possible. Next, they write a group story that involves following a map of their school to solve a mystery.*

Reading can offer a greater understanding of the world. First graders read non-fiction books about the local animals they are studying. Second graders hear stories about how families from many cultures live and work. They learn about the similarities and differences among people. Third graders read the newspaper to find the latest information on a proposed new city playground.

The Whole Language Perspective

When teachers encourage a love of literature and create an environment that promotes reading, most children begin to see themselves as readers. Motivation is a central factor in learning how to read. The "whole language" perspective towards teaching language and literacy is built on this principle. The whole language movement grew out of teachers' knowledge of what works best for children and is based on extensive research about how language is learned. Goodman, Goodman, and Hood, in the *Whole Language Evaluation Book*, explain:

> Whole language teachers use a range of authentic, natural, functional materials to build literacy. They integrate oral and written language development with conceptual learning. That is, they believe you learn to read and write while you read and write to learn (1989, xi).

The whole language philosophy meshes with the *Constructing Curriculum* approach because it emphasizes creating a classroom environment that integrates learning and promotes communication skills all the time. Instead of focusing on the parts of language such as letter sounds or word recognition as a prerequisite to reading, children actively read and write across the curriculum, and in the process, learn particular skills.

Learning language is a process in which children first become aware of how, where, and when people listen, speak, read and write. Then they have multiple opportunities to explore in each of these areas before finally becoming competent users of all of these skills. Educators now speak of "emergent literacy" as a way of recognizing that language and literacy development is a process that begins with a baby's first awareness of language and continues with the child's early attempts at reading and writing. Children have to know the purposes and pleasures of reading to be motivated to learn the skills involved.

Beginning readers first must understand that print tells a story and has a message. You will see evidence of this understanding when children:

- listen with interest to stories read aloud;
- notice that the labels on shelves identify things;
- write notes to friends;
- make signs for block buildings.

The goal of reading instruction is for children to be able to read for meaning. Once they are familiar with the idea that print conveys a message, children are ready to learn the strategies that readers use to make meaning out of text. Teachers guide children to develop strategies for reading at increasing levels of comprehension. We all use different strategies to make logical guesses about unknown words. These are called cueing systems.

How Children Learn to Use Cueing Systems

When readers come across an unfamiliar word, they need a strategy for figuring out what it says. These strategies are called "cueing systems." As you observe developing readers in your classrooms, you will probably see examples of children who:

- find all the names of classmates that begin with the same letter;
- use the pictures in a book to identify words;
- recall familiar words from their environment or other books and read them in a new context;
- sound out words based on their knowledge of initial and final consonants, vowels, and vowel combinations;
- know that certain words can be skipped if not known because they are not needed to get the overall meaning of the text.

The strategies children used in the above examples have been categorized into three cueing systems and described by Marie Clay (1979):

- meaning/semantic cues
- syntactic cues
- visual and grapho-phonic cues

Meaning/Semantic Cues

When readers use their understanding of the text to figure out a word they don't know, they are using meaning or semantic cues. Children who use their memory of experiences in everyday life to read a previously unknown word are also using semantic cues.

> *Ammar pores over a book on spiders. He looks for information on how spiders catch their food. He comes to the sentence, 'Some spiders catch insects by throwing a silk net over them.' He reads, "Some spiders catch bugs by throwing a silk net over them." His teacher, Ms. Swanson, says, "Ammar, bugs does make sense in that sentence. You know that spiders eat bugs. Let's look closely at that word. Does the word bugs start with an 'i'? What word could that be?" "Insects," says Ammar proudly.*

Syntactic Cues

Many children enter first grade with a strong sense of the structure of language. They intuitively know the grammatical structure of sentences. When they make use of this knowledge about the forms of our language to read an unknown word, they use syntactic cues. This can be observed when a reader replaces an unknown word with the same part of speech for that word. For example, a young reader may read, "I can ride a car," instead of "I can ride a bicycle." She has replaced a noun with another noun.

Visual and Grapho-Phonic Cues

When readers see a word in print, immediately recognize it, and say it out loud, it is called automatic word recognition. Children who rely on remembering whole words, without sounding them out, are known as **sight word readers**. They use the visual cues of the letters to read the word.

Children who rely on sounding out words are known as **phonetic readers** and use grapho-phonic cues. This means they recognize individual letters, groups of letters, and the sounds represented by the letters.

> *Six-year-old Miriam looks at the sentence 'Here comes the school bus.' She reads, "Here comes the school b-b, sss, bus." Ms. Fay says, "Miriam, you are looking closely at that word and thinking about what letters are there and what they sound like. Good for you. You read that new word."*

A strong reading program provides opportunities for children to increase their sight word vocabulary and phonetic awareness by using books that specifically support reading development. Knowledge can start with individual letters and expand to letter combinations and the sounds represented by those letters. One effective way to make the alphabet meaningful to beginning readers is to place each child's name next to the letter it starts with and to write the first letter of each name in a contrasting color.

There is much discussion today about the appropriate place of phonics instruction in reading programs. The fact is that children do benefit from knowing the sounds made by letters and letter combinations. However, we believe that teaching children phonetic cues comes after children see themselves as readers. In our complex language, readers use phonetic cues as secondary—rather than primary—cues in decoding words. This is different from an earlier belief that children depend on phonics in order to read.

Self-Improving System

To become successful independent readers, children need to practice reading all the time. It is very important, therefore, for children to develop techniques that enable them to improve on their own. Marie Clay calls this a "self-improving system." She says,

> The end-point of early instruction has been reached when children have a self-improving system, which means that they learn more about reading every time they read, independent of instruction… They engage in "reading work," a deliberate effort to solve new problems with familiar information and procedures. They notice new things about words… The newly-noticed feature(s) of print, worked upon today, becomes the reference point for another encounter in a few days (1979, 141).

Teachers can help children to become aware of the strategies they use to puzzle out new words. When teachers foster independence and self-confidence, children can figure out words they don't know. With each guess, children learn to ask themselves if their guess makes sense, if it looks right, and if it sounds right. If it does, they continue reading. If it does not, they should try again. Children use cueing systems to self-correct. They may ask themselves, "Did what I just read make sense?" (meaning), "Did what I just read sound right?"(syntax), or "Did what I read look like what I said?" (grapho-phonic cues).

As you read with children, carefully observe their reading behaviors and use of cueing systems. Tell children what you see them doing so they become aware of their own strategies and thus increase their reading independence. After you have labeled the strategies for them, it is appropriate to ask children how they figured out an unknown word.

> *Gabriel, a first grader, reads a book about pets. When he comes to the sentence,* Here are the puppies, *he says, "Here are the dogs. No, I mean, here are the puppies." Ms. Wilson says, "That was great reading. How did you know to change dogs to puppies?" Gabriel responds, "At first I thought it was dogs because the picture kinda looks like dogs, not puppies. Then I noticed the word was long and it had a lot of p's so then I knew it was puppies."*

There are many ways to weave reading experiences into the classroom day. These will be discussed later in the section on organizing the language and literacy curriculum. Knowing about cueing systems enables you to integrate the teaching of these skills into many classroom activities.

Writing

Young children learn to write by writing. Most first graders have some idea of what writing looks like and understand that meaning is contained in print. When children scribble, draw, and "pretend" to write, the writing process has begun.

Most children have a natural desire to write because they want to belong to the adult world of literacy. They learn the value of writing by seeing adults write for a reason. When you send a note to the office, fill out a form, or write a reminder note to yourself on the blackboard, you show children that writing serves a purpose.

To become effective and powerful communicators, children must believe that they have something important to say and that their thoughts and experiences are worth recording. When children are motivated to write, they will struggle through the process of presenting their ideas. They are more willing to work at making their thoughts as clear as possible.

> *Jane, a second grader, complains about how the school play yard is always full of litter. The yard is used for a flea market on Sundays and it is not always cleaned by Monday morning. Jane reports this to her teacher who suggests that she make signs to ask the market workers to clean up after themselves. Jane interviews her classmates for appropriate slogans. When she makes her signs she uses bright colors so they won't be missed. To Jane's delight, it works! There is great improvement in the condition of the yard.*

How Children Learn Writing Skills

Children need many opportunities every day to write for reasons that make sense to them. Teachers incorporate a variety of writing activities in their classrooms to show the range of purposes for writing, and to give children more opportunities for success.

Children use writing to **convey meaning** when they:

- make signs for their block constructions;
- use a message board or mailbox to send notes to classmates or the teacher;
- label drawings;
- make lists;
- write a report about something they have studied;
- write in a journal about a feeling, an event, or an observation;
- conduct an interview and record the information gathered.

Children develop awareness of the conventions of print and learn the **mechanics of writing** when they:

- edit their writing for use of capital letters and punctuation;
- underline the words in their writing that they think are misspelled;
- read their writing aloud to hear where the punctuation belongs and add the missing punctuation;
- re-read a story and find an omitted word;
- find and correct misspelled words.

Children learn to **compose stories** when they:

- choose the topics they want to write about;
- call on personal experiences for story ideas;
- read their stories to classmates and get suggestions for improvement.

Children learn to **revise and change their writing** as they:

- read a story they have written, decide a detail is missing and add it;
- experiment with the arrangement of sentences and phrases;
- work on a story over time and make changes along the way;
- revise a story by taking out unnecessary information.

The Link Between Reading and Writing

Writing helps children learn to read, and as children become more proficient readers they notice the conventions of print. As children become more accomplished writers, they notice how authors carefully craft their books. They begin to use punctuation in their stories. Exposure to varied and interesting literature improves children's writing.

Mr. Jackson picks up the basket containing a number of poetry anthologies. He reads several poems and then responds to a child's request to hear a poem he read the day before. After finishing, Mr. Jackson says, "We've been reading and talking about poetry for a while. What are some of the things that you've noticed?" Lia raises her hand and says, "Some rhyme and some don't." Dana adds, "One poem had a line that was repeated three times." Joey says, "Some poems talk about two things and say how they're different." Mr. Jackson writes down the different ideas children identify and suggests that everyone try writing a poem. Equipped with models of poems to think about and rich discussion to draw on, the children set to work.

Providing children with opportunities to become aware of and imitate a number of writing forms helps them appreciate what they are reading.

In addition, to guide children as readers and writers, we must be aware of the different skills they need in spelling and handwriting.

How Children Learn Spelling Skills

When spelling is taught as part of an integrated approach to language and literacy, children see spelling as a tool for writing and not as a prerequisite. Learning how to spell is integrated into children's writing through opportunities to write about something that is personally important. By incorporating writing, and therefore spelling, throughout the school day and in all subjects, children will learn to spell the words they need.

Many teachers and parents wonder how spelling skills can possibly develop if children are encouraged to write without attending to spelling and punctuation. It may help to think about how children learn to talk. Infants babble, experimenting with the sounds that surround them, as a way to learn to talk. In a short period of time they put these sounds together to form real words. We wouldn't think of telling them not to talk until they learn how to speak correctly. They learn to talk by talking. Before long they are able to use strings of words.

Children who are given the same opportunities to experiment with spelling develop confidence as writers. Using "invented spelling" can be thought of as encouraging children to "babble on paper." Children may begin by using a variety of letters, using the same letter over and over again, or they may use many letters in a random order. They are experimenting with print in the same way they experimented with the sounds of the spoken word. Young writers may not hear or use all the letters. "Went" may be recorded as "wnt" and "dog" as "d" or "dg."

Ms. Santos wants to encourage William, a first grader, to write. "William, you really noticed many details about our guinea pig in order to draw this picture. Now slowly say the words that go with the picture. Listen closely for the sounds in those words. Put down the letters that you hear. Do the best you can. When you're finished you can read it to me."

In addition to thinking about sounds, teachers encourage children to write a word the way they think it looks. This enables children to use what they already know about words they have seen in their environment. Many times children will remember a place where they have seen a particular word before and go back to find it. Children use their visual memories of words that surround them in books, posters, wall charts, and signs, and incorporate those words into their work.

In addition, direct spelling instruction can take the form of discussions about unusual, tricky, or hard-to-remember words.

> *A third grade class gathers in the meeting area. Two columns of words are written on the chalkboard in front of them. The first has words that have the long a sound represented by -ay, the second by -a-e. Michael raises his hand and says, "While I was reading I noticed the word* rain *has the long a sound but we don't have a column for it. I think we need an -ai- list."*

Children will begin using vowels after they understand that words have vowels. Teachers highlight this concept by showing children how longer words have more letters. Gradually children make the connection between word length and syllables.

Through observation, experience, direct instruction and reminders, children apply the spelling system of our language. They become more skillful in identifying both the separate sounds in each word, and the letters and groups of letters representing those sounds. Encouraging children to use invented spelling does not mean they are never expected to learn and use standard spelling. Just as infants grow from saying "ba-ba" to "bottle," children will learn correct spelling. Explaining this process can reassure family members.

> *Ms. Ward keeps a sample of her second graders' work to share with families at conferences. When Jessica's mother expresses concern over seeing a number of stories with words that were not "correct," Ms. Ward points out how Jessica's spelling is developing. She focuses on the word* phone. *Over a month it changed from* fon *to* fone *to* phone. *She explains that Jessica is not only learning the rules about spelling, she is gaining confidence in her own abilities as a writer.*

As in all areas of guiding learning, teachers need to be excellent observers to know just when a child is ready to learn something new. Although some spelling lessons can be taught to the entire class, spelling lessons are likely to be most effective when they respond to individual needs.

How Children Learn Handwriting Skills

Neat and legible handwriting makes it easier for the writer to read what has been written, and ensures that the reader gets an accurate message. When children copy their own words neatly, they also improve their spelling skills because, as they record the word, they form a clear visual picture of it in their minds.

In the primary grades, children's fine motor skills are still developing and, therefore, forming small letters can be a difficult task. Close observation of children's skills will help you to recognize what an individual child is capable of attempting.

Many schools choose to teach manuscript letters in first and second grade and cursive in third grade. Some schools have adopted a combination of manuscript and cursive (the D'Nealian method) to make the transition into cursive easier.

There are many ways that teachers support children's acquisition of handwriting skills as part of the writing and reading program. Talk about handwriting as you write. Anything posted in the classroom that is written by the teacher should be neatly written in the same manuscript form that is expected of the children. In a third grade class where cursive is taught, the morning message can be written in cursive.

To combat the tedium of handwriting practice, many teachers keep it in the context of meaningful writing. Children can concentrate on letter formation when they write stories that are important to them. In reviewing a story, the teacher might ask a child what letters were difficult to write or to read.

After Ms. Allen talks with Eduardo about his story, the two of them scan the text together. "Eduardo, are there any words you had a hard time reading to me?" asks Ms. Allen. "Yes" says Eduardo, "This one, the word car. *The* a *looks like an* o *and an* i *because I didn't write the two parts touching." "Yes, I see what you mean. I think that would be a good letter for you to spend some time practicing. What do you think?" says Ms. Allen. "O.K., so other kids can read my story," says Eduardo.*

Following this conference, Eduardo might practice letters in a handwriting book or on paper designed to help children learn neat penmanship. In this way, he is in charge of his learning and is invested in writing legibly.

Organizing the Language and Literacy Curriculum

Having read about the many ways to guide children in acquiring language and literacy skills, you may now be wondering how to implement them. The six strategies you read about in Part One provide the framework for promoting language and literacy learning in your classroom. Having taken the time to know your children, developmentally and as individuals, your knowledge of their interests and individual reading and writing skills will enable you to gauge the kinds of experiences most suitable for them. Your classroom community supports language and literacy development every time you have class meetings. During meetings, children have opportunities to develop listening and speaking skills and to hear new ideas. Grouping children at tables and allowing them to talk about what they are doing promotes literacy as well.

You may want to reflect on the structure of your classroom. Consider whether you have included interesting books and other reading materials in places where children can read and write and talk about topics that interest them. The signs you or the children make, the schedules and lists you post, and the daily messages you write make the structure explicit to children while allowing them to see real uses for reading and writing.

Language and literacy learning can be infused into the classroom in many ways that make guiding children's learning in this area a continuous process. Teachers consider how to incorporate different aspects of language and literacy instruction as part of long-term studies. Work times are used to teach and practice specific reading and writing skills. "Teachable moments" also contribute to children's learning. A good place to begin is by creating a classroom environment that promotes literacy.

Creating an Environment for Literacy

Children make the connection between language and print when teachers use print strategically throughout the classroom. Children see that print serves a purpose when it is used to support and explain the organization and routines of the classroom, and when print is an integral part of everyday activities and experiences.

Using Print for Classroom Organization and Routines

A natural way to create an environment for literacy is to use print in the classroom organization and to clarify routines. Some examples of print used for these purposes include: labels for materials, attendance charts, job charts, weekly schedules, and daily messages.

Labels for Materials

In the chapter on Establishing a Structure for the Classroom, we discussed labeling children's cubbies or lockers and all the storage containers in the room. Labeled containers may be filled with pencils, scissors, books, Unifix Cubes, or writing paper. Labels assist children in locating and using materials indepedently. In this way, children see a practical purpose for print.

Labels may be a combination of pictures and words. By third grade, the label might just be a word and could be made by the children themselves.

Attendance Charts

A convenient way to record daily attendance and help children make sense of print is to have attendance charts. Teachers can record children's attendance in various ways. Some suggestions are listed below:

- Take a photograph of each child on the first day of school and have children write their names on the reverse side of the photo. Place the photographs in a clear pocket chart that is attached to the classroom door. Each morning as children arrive, they flip the signed side to show the photo. When a name shows, it indicates the child is absent. When the photo shows, it means the child is in school. At the end of each day, children flip the photograph to show their written name, indicating they have gone home for the day.

- Mount library book pockets or index cards on tag board. Write each child's name on the book pocket and also across the top of the index card. Children simply flip the index card to indicate they've arrived in the classroom. The cards could have first names early in the year; last names could be added later.

- Take attendance using a class list on a clipboard. One child checks the name of each child who is present and makes a list of children who are absent.

- Have children sign in each day on a chart. This also serves to keep track of children's handwriting development.

Taking attendance helps children learn to read the names of their classmates. Delegation of jobs and tasks to children makes teachers' lives less tedious and creates an environment where children see the importance of reading and writing in their daily lives.

Job Charts

Another way to include print in the environment is to post job charts. Children use them to keep track of their job responsibilities for the week. These charts may have pictures, pictures and words, or only words. As discussed in the chapter on Establishing a Structure for the Classroom, children can generate a list of possible jobs for the classroom such as sweeping the floor, handing out snacks, watering plants, and serving as class messenger.

Schedule and Morning Message

Children want to know what their activities are each day. They feel more secure when they know what to expect. Posting a daily schedule meets this need and lets children use text in a practical way.

In addition to the schedule, which remains fairly consistent from week to week, you can write a morning message each day as described in the chapter on Community. Reading the daily schedule and the morning message as part of the first meeting of the day can become an important classroom ritual that helps children make the transition from home to school.

There are many ways to write a morning message so that children look forward to figuring out your system. Leave out a word and have the children try to spell the missing word. Color code special words you want to talk about or use colored chalk or markers to make a pattern.

In first grade classrooms, the morning message is often simple, including sight words that children use in their reading vocabulary. Repetitive phrases allow children to read the message successfully.

```
Hello.
Today is Monday.
We will read a new big book.
We will play a new math game.
We will eat lunch at 12:00.
We will go  outside after lunch.
```

In second grade the morning message can be more complex. Using longer sentences and new vocabulary turns message reading into an interesting lesson, such as the spelling of ordinal numbers from one to ten, or a discussion about the use of descriptive phrases.

```
Good morning on a brisk, windy day.
Today is the sixth day of October.
At one o'clock we will go downstairs
to interview our principal, Ms. Smith.
Think about a question you would
like to ask her about her job.
```

Because third graders are more capable and competent readers and understand what each of these topics mean, the morning message can be written as a schedule.

> 11/7/94
>
> Greetings!
> Schedule highlights:
> Gym – 10:30 a.m.
> Projects – 1:00 - 2:30 p.m.
>
> Later today we'll be discussing frogs and toads. Let's think about some of the differences between frogs and toads.

This morning message ends with a statement relevant to a curriculum topic the teacher plans to explore with the children that day. Other examples might be: "Let's think about what makes a number odd or even." "Let's brainstorm some ideas about why December 21st is the shortest day of the year." Statements can also relate to classroom management such as, "Let's think about some reasons that we walk in a line in the hallways."

Using Print in Classroom Activities and Experiences

In addition to these organizational uses for print, teachers help children acquire language and literacy skills by using print in the environment as part of every activity. Teachers use experience charts, children's messages and signs, and children's work.

Experience Charts

Many elementary school teachers use experience charts. Preparing these charts with the children is an excellent way to document their ideas on a subject, thus clearly connecting words with print. A group discussion at the beginning of a study often focuses on two questions: "What do you know about (the topic)?" and "What do you want to find out?" Charts can be developed to list the questions children want to ask a visitor, class members' favorite read aloud books or favorite authors, or even favorite T.V. shows. In deciding whether to prepare an experience chart, ask yourself, "Will we want to read this information again?" If the answer is "yes," it's a good time for a chart. When experience charts are posted around the room, children can use them as a reference, find words needed for writing, and practice their reading.

You may want to record exactly what children say when you first begin to write experience charts each year. Later on, you can adjust for grammar and structure as children feel more comfortable in the classroom community. When children's language is written down, we show that we value what they say. They see their language recorded for future reference.

Imagine that your class is about to set up a frog environment in a glass tank. You invite the children to the meeting area where you have chart paper and colored markers. At the top of the chart is the sentence "What Do We Know About Frogs?" You pose this question to the children and as they share their ideas, you list them next to their names.

> *Marie — Frogs are green.*
> *Pavel — Frogs like lily pads.*
> *Bailey — Baby frogs are called tadpoles.*

By recording the children's names along with their statements, they can find their names and read the sentences they contributed. In second grade, you might simply write the children's initials. Such charts are also useful records for purposes of assessment.

> *K.S. — Frogs eat worms.*
> *A.T. — Frogs get oxygen through their skin.*

During such an activity a child may contribute an idea or suggestion that you know is incorrect. If this happens at the beginning of a study, record the idea as stated by the child. This is a research opportunity which may lead your children to re-evaluate and then record newly learned information. At the end of a study you might ask some extension questions before recording the children's ideas:

- Can you say more about that?
- Can you say the same thing in a different way to see if it still makes sense?
- Tell us about how you learned that.
- I'm not sure I agree. Would you like some help to figure it out?

These responses provide an opportunity for the child to self-correct and for the teacher to better understand what the child is thinking.

Two children may have conflicting information. Record both ideas and say, "You both have some good ideas. Let's read some books and do some research to see what else we can discover." In this way, both ideas are respected and the child with the incorrect information now has the opportunity to self-correct. The self-correction process is a powerful learning experience. Once children discover their errors, have them write the correction directly on the recording sheet. Children can also cross out their initial statements.

In third grade, when children have greater reading competence, names and initials are not needed to read the chart successfully. A group language experience chart may be written in paragraph form.

Charting activities naturally involve writing as well as reading. They also model handwriting and spelling at the same time. By thinking out loud as you write, you model that people think about spelling. They think about making a clear sentence. They think about what is being said. Depending on the age of the children, you can encourage them to help you sound out the words as you write them down. Older children may be encouraged to make some charts on their own as part of small group projects.

Messages and Signs

Children love to send and receive messages and make signs. When you make this part of the work of your classroom, you respond to children's interests and give them a goal for reading and writing. You can do this by:

- establishing a message board with special paper to be used for message writing and providing opportunities during the day for children to write messages;
- having a post office system with daily or weekly deliveries (mail boxes can be made from coffee cans, milk cartons, or plastic shoe pockets);
- asking children to make signs to identify their displays (art, blocks, puzzles) or to make rules (Do Not Disturb);
- providing time and materials for this kind of writing to take place.

Children's Work

When children's work—their writing, art, and constructions—is displayed with signs and labels, teachers send a message that work is valued. By placing the work where children can see and discuss it, teachers make it possible for children to observe, read, and talk about each other's work. Including print in the environment makes the point that reading and writing is a part of all aspects of our lives. In this kind of environment, language and literacy learning can be integrated into long-term studies quite naturally.

Promoting Language and Literacy Through Long-Term Studies

In the chapters on Scientific Thinking and Social Studies, we describe in detail how language and literacy activities are a natural and necessary part of all long-term studies. Finding materials for children to look at and read is one of the steps in planning a long-term study. When children want information on a topic that interests them, they have a reason to listen, speak, read, and write. Here are some examples of how language and literacy skills can be applied to several different long-term studies.

A class that is studying the nearby **river** might:

- create a chart detailing what they know and what they want to know;
- interview the parks department employee responsible for that section of the river;
- read about river life;

- write research reports about the animals that live in or near the river;
- keep charts about the salinity of the water at different times and places;
- have many group discussions about what they are learning.

The investigations of children studying **immigration** may lead them to:

- listen to or read books about people who came to this country as immigrants;
- discuss stories about moving with family members and neighbors;
- write about a time they went to an unfamiliar place;
- use a word processor to write a script for a play about the experiences of children's ancestors.

When children explore the **neighborhood** around the school, they might:

- write letters to the city department responsible for pothole repair;
- publish the recipes for school lunches;
- interview the various workers in the school;
- discuss plans for a school-wide recycling project.

As children learn about **animals** they can:

- keep a science journal of observations about the class pet;
- read about an animal of their own choosing;
- prepare an oral report about their animal;
- work with a classmate to design models of their animals;
- write a detailed description of their animal.

A study of a **construction** site near the school can lead children to:

- make lists of what they know and what they want to find out;
- read books about construction and different kinds of machines and tools;
- write about their own homes;
- keep a journal of observations about the construction site;
- write instructions for making something;
- interview the job supervisor;
- interview the family member of a classmate who works in construction;
- make up words to their own work songs;
- make a list of safety rules for their woodworking table.

While language and literacy activities will happen as part of long-term studies, planned work times for reading and writing also need to occur daily.

Planning Work Times for Reading

Work times are those scheduled times during the day when you plan particular language and literacy activities. Sometimes teachers work with the whole class, reading a chapter book aloud. At other times, children work in small groups to read or discuss a book. Sometimes children work alone on their reading. Teachers move from group to group or child to child, asking questions, or directly teaching something.

There are many different opportunities throughout the week to provide children with reading experiences and instruction. The four types of reading work times we describe can help children encounter reading from a variety of perspectives. They include:

- Reading Aloud
- Shared Reading
- Guided Reading
- Independent Reading

Following is a description of each type of reading activity. You can supplement this information by obtaining any of the excellent resources listed at the end of the chapter.

Reading Aloud

The most important way that teachers and families encourage children to become readers is to read to them. By listening to good books, children learn that reading is a worthwhile and pleasurable activity. Listening to stories is also a way to provide reading instruction because it:

- introduces children to the characteristics of various types of literature;
- extends vocabulary;
- lengthens attention spans;
- creates an atmosphere of pleasure related to language and books;
- provides children with literary models of writing that can influence their own writing;
- helps children become familiar with different story structures;
- allows children to focus on the language and story line without doing the work of reading;
- provides a "jumping off" point for science and social studies topics.

Children learn that the printed page can have many voices as they listen to various types of written material. The sound and tone of a passage depend on the type and purpose of the story, article, essay, or poem. A chapter in a non-fiction book about ducks will sound very different from a story book about ducks. Familiarity with the different voices of books is particularly important for children in the upper grades because they have to read and comprehend more complicated texts independently. This task is made easier when children have listened extensively to non-fiction read aloud. Teachers can provide the base for identifying a selection's purpose and voice by varying the materials that they read aloud to the children.

Reading aloud activities can be enhanced for children when teachers:

- select good books to use;
- allow time in the schedule to read aloud every day;
- model how a competent reader reads and reacts.

Select Good Books

You can extend your collection and include all types of books by using the school and public libraries. Some teachers make a point of reading from a fiction book, a non-fiction book, and a book of poetry each day. Many teachers keep a stack of wonderful brief books on hand to read at transitional times. When clean-up has gone particularly well and there are a few minutes before the music teacher arrives, you can read a book that is based on a song. Poems work well at transition times, too.

Read picture books as well as chapter books. Picture books can be read from beginning to end at one sitting. They can be used as examples for discussions about story development, settings, and openings, as well as for descriptive language, rhymes, and phonics. Reading chapter books aloud exposes children to more detailed story lines and introduces fluent readers to new authors.

Read Every Day

Try to set aside at least one long block of time every day to read and enjoy long stories and chapter books with the children. Some teachers read aloud following the lunch/recess period or at the end of the day. Think about additional shorter periods when a short story or poem might be read. For example, some teachers decide to make poetry a part of their morning routine. A poem is read just after everyone has been seated and prior to begin-ning the daily schedule.

Model How a Competent Reader Reads

When you come to a passage in a book that is particularly beautiful or surprising to you, take time to stop and share your reactions with children. In this way you show children that the language and vocabulary in books is something to notice and talk about. Children see how competent readers respond to books.

Because each class of children has its own unique "personality" based on the individual children in that class, often a specific type of book, author, or illustrator will emerge as a favorite of a particular group. The books selected to read aloud can reflect this. Children may begin to learn about the particular style of an author or illustrator. Such conversa-tions can form the basis for discussions about ways to communicate ideas through books, and can also inspire children to look for books by these writers on their own.

Shared Reading

Shared reading occurs when children read books or other printed material as a group. Like reading aloud, this activity builds community and allows for discussion and instruction. Shared reading differs from reading aloud in that children are verbal participants in the process of reading.

The shared reading experience sounds a bit like a reading chorus. Everyone reads together, though the teacher's (or child leader's) voice stands out. In this environment, even the most cautious reader can join in without feeling uncomfortable.

Don Holdaway, a New Zealand educator, suggested to teachers that they enlarge the books and poems that are children's favorites and read them along with the children (1979). Making the print large and displaying the material on an easel makes it possible for everyone to see the print and the illustrations as you read the words together. "Big books" are now available from many publishers.

Beginning Readers

Shared reading is an important way to teach beginning readers basic reading skills. By pointing to each word as it is read, the teacher helps children to:

- follow along as the teacher reads;
- understand that we read from left to right and from the top of the page to the bottom;
- identify exactly where a word is located on the page;
- extend sight vocabulary.

Favorite books, poems, and songs are read again and again in shared reading in response to the interests of the group. In addition to the big books that are available commercially, teachers make big books for children to illustrate, or groups of children can make their own. Poems and the lyrics for songs written on chart paper or oak tag can be used for shared reading times. The readings presented in this manner and repeated throughout a school week become part of the children's reading repertoire. Children can then read them on their own. Through the rereading of books, children extend their sight vocabularies.

Books that are particularly good for shared reading are repetitious, cumulative, predictable, contain common sight words, and use rhyme.

- **Repetitive** books repeat certain words or phrases. An example of a repetitive book is *The Gingerbread Man* where the passage, "Run, run as fast as you can, you can't catch me, I'm the Gingerbread Man," is repeated. Children listen for this part and join in when they hear it.

- **Cumulative** books add a new line on each page while repeating the previous line. *This Is The House That Jack Built* is a wonderful example. "This is the cat, that killed the rat, that ate the malt, that lay in the house, that Jack built." Children use their memory of the story and the repetition of each sentence to predict what text will be on the next page.

- **Predictable** books have stories that help emergent readers think about what they are reading by anticipating the words they may encounter on the next page. The teacher might ask, "What do you think will happen next?" modeling the question children need to ask themselves as they read. *The Three Little Pigs* and *The Three Billy Goats Gruff* are examples of predictable books.

- **Sight word** books use and repeat certain words. In addition to the familiar Dr. Seuss book, *The Cat in the Hat*, a repetitive book such as *Have You Seen My Cat?* by Eric Carle can also teach sight words. In this book, a little boy is searching for his cat. He asks the people he meets throughout the story, "Have you seen my cat?" When the cat that they direct him to is not his, he responds, "This is not my cat." These sentences are repeated again and again. A teacher might focus on a specific word, asking children to clap each time they hear it.

- *Rhyming* books or poems use rhyme to help children learn a spelling or word pattern. Teachers can write poems in large print on chart paper and highlight specific words or parts of words. For example:

Down! Down! by Eleanor Farjeon
Down, down,
Yellow and **brown,**
The leaves are falling
All over the **town.**

After reading the poem a few times to enjoy the beat, sound, and image the teacher then uses the poem to teach a skill by asking, "What do you notice in this poem?" The children may point out a number of things such as color words or that some words look the same. They may notice that some words rhyme. The teacher selects one of their observations to comment on. For example, she might say: "Look closely at the end of the rhyming words. What letters do you see? Can you think of any other rhyming words that rhyme with down?" The class generates a list of other words in the "o-w-n" family. Sometimes the teacher has a plan to teach a specific concept. In this case, she might say, "I notice that a number of words end with 'o-w-n'. Can anyone find one of those words?"

Fluent Readers

Because every class is diverse and children will always be at different levels, shared reading experiences geared to beginning readers often remain appropriate for fluent readers. Conversations about becoming a better reader do not stop with fluency. Shared reading experiences for fluent readers can serve many different purposes. Teachers might:

- enlarge a poem on an overhead projector to demonstrate how in poetry, each word is chosen carefully and unusual words are often used. Children may also begin to memorize poems, building another important skill.

- use a big book to discuss techniques authors use to depict a character or setting. Children can be encouraged to look for those techniques in their own reading and apply them to their own writing.

- use a non-fiction big book to teach children how to read for research purposes. Readers who are fluent reading fiction may need support and guidance to read more complex non-fiction material.

Shared reading is a whole-class experience designed to teach a lesson valuable to all. It is also a chance for children to respond in different ways. Some children may be ready to notice that words are separate from other words, while others may be collecting sight words they recognize. Teachers take their cues about what to teach, based on the children's observations. Shared reading times can occur daily for different lengths of time, depending on children's attention spans and needs.

Guided Reading

Guided reading occurs when the teacher meets with a small group of children to observe reading behaviors and provide specific instruction. Guided reading groups can be formed for different reasons. Sometimes a group of children is ready to learn a similar skill. At other times, a group forms around a common interest.

Guided reading is integrally linked to assessment. Observing children's reading needs and interests helps you decide what to teach. Topics for guided reading instruction can range from teaching a particular reading strategy to learning about an author's style, or investigating a literary technique. You can then select a book that will best respond to the topic, and offer multiple copies to the group.

Children learn best from reading experiences when they can respond to the text in a group discussion. The teacher is a participant, using the ideas children bring to guide the conversation and extend children's thinking. Other responses include writing, art work, skits, songs, dances, and, of course, reading related books. Sometimes responses are shared with the whole class.

> *When Ms. Hill notices that a group of children in her first grade class are not using picture clues, she plans a guided reading lesson. She chooses the book,* Our Teacher, Miss Pool *by Joy Cowley. As she introduces the book to the children, she draws their attention to the unusual transportation Miss Pool uses to get to school. She then asks the children to find those words on the page. "When I'm reading," she tells them, "and I come to a word I don't know, I look at the picture to see if it will help me. If you come to a word you don't know as you're reading this book, look at the picture to see if it helps." When the group finishes reading, they draw pictures of how they would like to come to school and, using a language experience chart, Ms. Hill writes down their ideas.*

Ms. Hill creates a lesson that places children in the role of active investigators. Guiding them through this process, she helps them to represent their learning through drawings. Later, these drawings and the language experience chart can help them reflect about what they learned.

Flexibility in Guided Reading

Flexibility is essential to guided reading. In the beginning of the school year, you choose the reading books and assign follow-up projects that support the goals you have set based on your observations of children. As the children become familiar with the routine and learn what is expected, they may choose the discussion topics and the projects they do to respond to the text. During some guided reading times you may read to the children. At other times the children may read key portions of the text aloud and then read silently. You can gradually begin to give children choices about the nature and order of reading activities. With fluent readers you may put together a collection of books that all address a specific goal. Children can select the particular book they want to read.

Groups do not have to remain static. As each strategy, interest, or reading behavior is taught and observed, the group can disband to become part of new groups. Multiple copies of books with a varying range of difficulty will permit children to form what some teachers call "book clubs" or literature groups, based on their interest in a specific book.

Personal Response in Guided Reading

Another aspect of guided reading, whether teacher-led or child-initiated, is the opportunity to talk about how books make us feel. In the following example, Ms. Bischof, a second grade teacher, plans to have children discuss their reading and relate their personal experiences to the story and characters in a book. She selects *Frog and Toad Together* by Arnold Lobel because the children are eager to read a "chapter" book. Unlike most chapter books, which are longer and more difficult for early readers, the books in the *Frog and Toad* series have short stories at a reading level appropriate to the children in the group.

> *Ms. Bischof joins a group of six readers at a table. She explains that she has six copies of a chapter book for them to read and talk about together. After giving out the book, she asks if anyone is familiar with the* Frog and Toad *books and encourages several children to comment on what they like or don't like about them. She gives the children folders to store their individual copies of the book and asks them to place the books inside. To prepare them for the story, she invites the children to talk about their friendships. Several children share stories about their friends. Ms. Bischof lets each child who wants to talk do so.*
>
> *After this introduction, the children take out their copies of the book and read the first story, "Spring," independently. As they do so, Ms. Bischof circulates from child to child, having each child read a short segment aloud to her. She listens for how they decode, how smoothly they read, and checks on strategies that have been taught previously. She notes her observations on a clipboard.*
>
> *Bringing the group back together for a discussion, Ms. Bischof asks: "What did the story make you think about?" The children don't respond. After another pause, she tries again: "We started out by talking about friends. Did anybody notice anything about friends in the story?" Ralph says, "I have a calendar in my room like the one in the story." Julie says, "The story reminds me of how my sister's alarm goes off and she wakes me up."*

Ms. Bischof feels that this was a good beginning for her and the group. She recognizes that the children's responses, though not relevant to her questions, were related to details in the story. By listening carefully to what the children tell her, she is getting to know them. Through this experience she helps children understand that they can talk about the ideas in books and that everyone can make a personal contribution to the discussion. Over the next few days, Ms. Bischof can encourage children to read the remaining chapters in *Frog and Toad Together*, use their reading strategies, and make a personal connection to the story.

Teachers often want to know how they can give this level of attention to a small group. What are other children doing during this time? Sometimes while the teacher works with a small group, other children may be doing different reading or writing related activities that don't require teacher involvement. They may be: working on drawing responses to a book, reading with partners, studying spelling words, reading or writing quietly. Or it may be a choice time when the other children are playing math or other board games, doing puzzles, working on a computer, or listening to stories on tape. Teachers generally try to schedule guided reading times with small groups two to three times a week.

Independent Reading

Independent reading time gives children an opportunity to relax and enjoy books without the direct involvement of a teacher. There are a number of interesting names for independent reading time: S.Q.U.I.R.T. (sustained quiet uninterrupted reading time), D.E.A.R. (drop everything and read), S.S.R. (sustained silent reading). The purpose of this special time is to let children choose their own reading materials and read quietly.

For independent reading to be successful, the classroom should be filled with a variety of reading materials—magazines, joke books, adventure stories, biographies, sports books, books related to long-term studies in science or social studies—at different reading levels. It doesn't matter if children choose books that you feel are too "easy" for them or books they have read before. Many adults like to take casual books to read on vacation or to reread an old favorite. This is the time to read for pleasure.

In first grade, when many children have not yet had an experience with independent reading, teachers may need to set the stage for this time of the day. Begin by explaining to your class that this is a time when everyone will spend a quiet time with books. Have children choose a handful of books. Ask them to pick a spot in the classroom where they will be comfortable. Explain that once this time starts, they will not be allowed to get up and move around the room, as this can be distracting to other readers. At first you may observe first graders flipping through the books so casually that they barely seem to be looking at the illustrations, much less the words. Once they understand your expectations for this time of day, they will relax and get into the books. During this time you might hear some children say, "I'm finished with my books. What do I do now? May I get more books?" Respond based on your knowledge of the child. You may say, "Sure." Or you may say, "Look through your books again. See if you can find or read something you didn't notice in the first reading." In this way you can help some children increase their attention span for reading.

The length of time you allocate for independent reading should be consistent with children's abilities. Early in the year, first graders may only manage ten to fifteen minutes of independent reading. By third grade, you may be able to extend the time to thirty minutes a day. Take some time yourself to read at this time of day. When teachers read with concentration, they demonstrate that they also love books, giving children a model to imitate. Many teachers use independent reading time to have individual reading conferences with children.

Planning Work Times for Writing

Work times for writing instruction and practice should be on the schedule at least three or four days a week. The following activities give children multiple opportunities to write:

- Writing Workshop
- Journal Writing
- Research Report Writing
- Spontaneous Writing

Writing Workshop

Writing workshop is an activity designed to give children ownership and control of what they write (Calkins 1994). They are encouraged to see themselves as authors who make decisions about their craft. When they write a story, they give us a glimpse of their lives away from school; when they write a "how-to" essay we learn about their interests. The form of children's writing is not as important as what children and teachers learn from the process of writing during the workshop. Children learn that writing is relevant to their lives and teachers learn about each child's perception of the world.

In writing workshop children are encouraged to write using all the information that they currently own. Their experiences and ideas are the basis for their stories. Knowing how to spell a word isn't a prerequisite to using it in a story. Children may use what is called "invented spelling." Young writers use what they have learned from reading and writing to do their best at that moment. Letting children be in charge of their writing and trusting that they already have information about the writing process encourages children to write.

The elements of the writing workshop are:

- the mini-lesson
- writing time
- conferences
- sharing
- revising
- editing and publishing

The Mini-Lesson

The first five to ten minutes of the writing period are a mini-lesson designed for the whole class. Many different topics can be discussed in mini-lessons, including: qualities of good literature, how people go about writing, concepts about print, and management issues.

A third grade teacher using a mini-lesson to focus on the qualities of good literature might initiate a discussion about how authors write the "setting" of a story.

> *Mr. Shelton reads a number of passages from different books to show how different authors describe a setting. The class talks about how one author lists the particular objects located in the setting while another uses descriptive language, setting a tone which makes the place seem scary.*

Another mini-lesson might be devoted to the different approaches people use to write. Some like to talk about their ideas with friends, others write first and then think out loud with others. Children can be encouraged to think about what helps them write, and to share their ideas with the group. Teachers can also share their observations of the children as part of a mini-lesson. "I've observed that Betsy reads through the pages that she wrote the day before so she knows just where to begin each day. See if that approach helps you."

Mini-lessons may cover basic mechanics of writing. For first graders this might mean putting spaces between words and writing from left to right. A third grade teacher might emphasize the use of quotation marks. Teachers present a concept in many different ways. This is how a second grade teacher uses mini-lessons to teach punctuation.

On Monday, Ms. Venable shows the children different ways writers end a sentence (period, question mark or exclamation point) by displaying a set of sentences on a chart. On Tuesday, the class searches for periods, question marks and exclamation points in a big book. On Wednesday, a child who has used these marks in a story she has written shares part of it on a chart. On Thursday, Ms. Venable models some personal writing in front of the children, stressing the necessary punctuation.

Management issues are also an appropriate subject for mini-lessons. When you first introduce writing workshop in your classroom, you may want to use this time to talk about how children get the materials needed for writing as well as how to brainstorm ideas. Topics that may need reinforcement are cleaning up properly at the end of writing time and not interrupting a writing conference.

Writing Time

Following the mini-lesson, the children write. Many teachers encourage children to begin by writing about things they know about: the time they fell off their bike, the first time they needed stitches, what happened when their father got a ticket from a police officer, or what it was like when their new baby sister came home from the hospital. Sometimes children write about worries or sad events: how they saw someone attacked in their neighborhood or when their gerbil died. They choose their own topics so that their writing is of interest to them—telling about something they are interested in. Children usually work on their own, but occasionally they may write with a friend. Some children will have lots of ideas for writing time. Others may need encouragement and extra time to think. You may have to reassure them that their own experiences are worth writing about.

The way that story writing begins changes as children grow and develop as writers. Young children often start by drawing a picture. As they add details to the drawing, they describe the picture in greater detail. Thus, the story is created verbally along with the drawing. The next step involves drawing the picture and writing the story. At first, just a few words may be used even though the oral story uses elaborate vocabulary. As children become accustomed to invented spelling, increase their written vocabulary, and see their invented spelling accepted, they will use more and more print. Children may plan their story by starting with a drawing, or by discussing the story plan with their peers and teacher. Gradually, children do more and more of their planning mentally.

Children talk and exchange ideas as they write. Their conversations are rehearsals for what they will write. However, some children have difficulty concentrating with discussion going on around them. To address this, teachers define a time during writing workshop for silent or quiet writing. Five or ten minutes is designated as "no walking and no talking" time. It may come at the beginning of writing time to set a tone for the period or it may come at the end to help children wrap up their work for the day.

The organizational and management systems you develop for writing are very important. You may want to consider special writing workshop folders and writing paper. Teachers often encourage children to use every other line so reading and editing is somewhat easier. The resources described at the end of this chapter offer many practical suggestions for managing children's written work.

Conferences

Two kinds of conferences take place, one between the teacher and child, one between two children. Key techniques for teacher/child conferences are:

- Begin by asking general questions: "What are you working on?" "How is it going?" "Tell me about your work."
- Keep the child's work in the hands of the child and kneel down or sit at the child's level to show respect for the writer.
- Although you may notice many things to discuss or teach the child after looking over the piece, choose just one thing to respond to, trusting that the child will learn that one thing.
- Listen to what children tell you about where they are struggling or where they would like help, and teach to that point.
- Develop a shorthand system of notetaking to keep track of the conference. This helps you keep a record of whom you conferred with so you know which children to make time for next. The notes are also useful for assessment purposes.

Conferences can be a very intense time for teachers. It involves checking in with many different children, and observing many different writing levels and styles simultaneously. It requires responding spontaneously to what each child presents. It is necessary to think on your feet and meet many needs at once. However, despite these multiple demands, it is also a special opportunity to connect positively with children and share information they care about. You may find that ideas for mini-lessons emerge as you look over your notes from conferences.

Peer conferences may be added to your writing workshop when you feel children have learned how to help each other with their writing independently of you. Children are usually better able to help each other if they are given a format to follow. Many teachers recommend that the child asking for help be encouraged to ask a specific question, such as: "Did I tell enough about the accident?" or "I don't know how to end this story," or "I'm not sure I can tell where all my sentences end." Then the helper is more likely to give the kind of specific help that is needed. Mini-lessons can be used to teach children how to have peer conferences.

Sharing

Many teachers like to end writing times by having children share their work. Sometimes a finished piece is simply read and appreciated. At other times, teachers select a child who has successfully incorporated the mini-lesson in his writing as a way to extend the lesson. Alternatively, children can come to the sharing time with a specific question for the group, "I need help with the ending" or "I need help with a title." Guide the group to respond to the question and refrain from making unrelated comments. Encourage specific comments: "I like the way the ending surprised me," is a much more helpful comment than "I liked your story" or even "I liked your ending," because it lets the author know exactly what was effective. Of course, in order for sharing time to be successful, children need to know how to comment respectfully and constructively. Teachers have to model the kinds of comments that assist in improving writing.

Opportunities to share writing build the classroom community.

Revising

Once writing workshop is an established part of the schedule in your classroom, you may want to expand its scope. As children gain confidence in their writing, they will be able to revise some of their work. Revision may include adding information, and deleting unnecessary information. As teachers confer with children, they can help them elaborate upon their ideas or try a new beginning for their story. This is the time to make sure children have conveyed their ideas clearly. The ability to reread a piece and decide if and how changes should be made shows real growth in the development of a writer.

Editing and Publishing

The editing process begins by having children look over their stories to find one or two mechanical errors. For example, children might first review their stories for periods. Children can be encouraged to underline a few misspelled words and correct those that are on their personal spelling list.

There are many ways to work on editing, particularly with older children. Some teachers of older children put an editing checklist in the back of each child's writing folder. As a child demonstrates that a skill has been learned, it is added to the checklist as something the child is now responsible for as an editor. It also gives you a record of a child's progress for assessment purposes. Before children present their writing to the class, it is expected that they will have used their checklist. The following example of an editing checklist illustrates the types of skills for which one child is now responsible:

Malcolm's Editing Checklist

9/17   My ideas are clear.
10/2   Each sentence ends with correct punctuation.
10/9   Each sentence begins with a capital letter.
10/12 The word *I* is always capitalized.
10/21 Names begin with capital letters.
11/3   I know the difference between "where" and "were."

After children have done some editing, the teacher can do a final edit. Talk with the class about how editing is done by real publishing companies and explain your editing role in that context. Children may be able to do some rewriting depending upon their age and the length of their stories. Parents are often willing to type children's edited stories for publication and to help put books together. Some children may be able to type drafts or final copies on the computer. By third grade, most children can be expected to make final drafts.

Teachers find that writing workshop is more productive when children know they have sustained writing times about four times each week for about one hour each day. This gives you time for a mini-lesson, writing, conferences, and some sharing. It takes time to build the routine so that it fits into an hour, and initially, some portions may be missed or expanded.

In the example that follows, Ms. Capalongo's second graders will begin a writing workshop time. As you read, notice how the meeting time, work time, and sharing activity all reveal opportunities for open-ended exploration and learning.

> *During the mini-lesson, Ms. Capalongo asks: "What do you think makes a good story?" Some of the children's responses are:*
>
> > *"Something exciting happens."*
> > *"It's scary."*
> > *"It makes you laugh."*
> > *"It's unpredictable and fun."*
>
> *Ms. Capalongo tells a brief story of her own in which she recalls getting a flat tire at the worst possible time. She then asks the children: "Who has a story in which something unpredictable happened to you?" Two children share anecdotes. Then she asks: "Who can remember something that happened to them that was scary?" Several children respond with memories.*
>
> *Now that she has set the stage, she says: "You all have great stories to tell. Some may be funny, exciting, or scary. Others may tell of accidents or something sad. We are ready to get started. Take a minute to make a plan for what you want to write."*
>
> *Ms. Capalongo dismisses the children a few at a time. They get their folders from milk crates they use for storage and settle in at tables.*

What you see in this example is evidence that Ms. Capalongo has established a structure for writing workshop. The children know where to get the supplies they need and where to go to pursue the task. Ms. Capalongo has built a community in the classroom and uses meetings as a forum for instruction, discussion, and sharing of ideas and experiences. Because the routines are predictable, children are relatively independent. At the same time, they work cooperatively with one another.

While children write, Ms. Capalongo is able to confer with individuals and observe how children are working. Based on what she sees, she constructs a plan for the week's mini-lessons. In addition, she uses her conference times to learn more about individual children and to suggest that the children talk with one another about their writing. Finally, she thinks about who will read their writing at the sharing meeting.

Journal Writing

Children's journals are a private place to write about anything they want to share with the teacher. Journals may be used to jot down ideas for stories, complain about friendships or homework, comment about something that happened in the class, or keep a list of things noticed. They serve as a means of communication between child and teacher when the teacher reads and reacts (orally and in writing) to the child's ideas (not the technical aspects). Sometimes children will write an entry that is so private they ask the teacher not to read it. As long as this doesn't happen too frequently, it is appropriate to respect this request.

Teachers can encourage all kinds of journal writing. Sometimes children keep separate math journals to record their thinking about new or developing concepts. Science journals may record observations. Literature journals may document reactions to books or poetry.

Research Reports

The key to making research writing a successful experience for young children is to encourage them to seek answers to questions of interest to them. Although research writing is a particular skill you want to teach, it is likely to grow out of the work children are doing in science and social studies. You will find many ideas for research opportunities as you read the chapters on these subjects. The process of doing research writing complements the methods you have established for writing workshop.

Mini-lessons are a way to introduce research writing. Teachers might present examples of several books about a topic (e.g., raccoons or bridges) and show that each book is different because each author had a different focus. One may write about the life cycle of the raccoon, another about how and where raccoons live. Someone writing about bridges might have conducted detailed investigations of different kinds of bridges, another researcher might have studied the traffic going over and under different bridges.

The next step is for both you and the children to collect resources. It is important to make sure that books are available at different reading levels. Information for research writing can also be gathered by making observations on trips, and collecting data from films, videos, and pictures. Children can also interview people who have direct experience with the subject.

Critical to the research writing process is looking for information in a focused way. Have children begin by writing the questions they want to answer so they can look for specific information. If children have their own questions to provide the framework for their report, they don't need teacher-made outlines. Research writing can and should be a collaborative process where children help one another find information and share knowledge they have acquired. Writing times can be used for children to take notes and write and revise drafts. Children can use meetings to share works in progress as a way to receive feedback from their peers.

Using Teachable Moments

All of these planned reading and writing activities and discussions ensure that children will have concentrated learning opportunities everyday to increase their language and literacy skills. In addition, you will find there are many other spontaneous things you can do to enrich their learning.

Reading and writing opportunities occur naturally throughout the day. When teachers seize these moments, children can see the varied purposes of reading and writing. Teachers can engage children in reading the morning message or daily schedule. They can engage children in using their reading and writing skills by creating an environment that encourages these activities. Here are some easy-to-implement ideas:

- Use message boards as a place for children to write notes to the teacher and to one another.
- Create graffiti boards (with rules about what is appropriate) that allow children to write spontaneously.
- Help children establish pen pal relationships between children in different classes to encourage letter writing projects.
- Provide suggestion boxes which offer a place for children to register their concerns in writing. When children notice a problem in the school (e.g., another garbage can would keep the litter from spilling all over the place), they can be encouraged to write to the custodian or the principal about the problem.
- Develop job charts that require that children read in order to know about their classroom responsibilities.

If these approaches to guiding learning in language and literacy are new to you, consider where you can begin. It's probably best to try one thing at a time. Many teachers find it helpful to begin with scheduling a read-aloud time every day as a way to link community-building with language and literacy instruction. Consider the listening, speaking, reading, and writing activities you already provide in your classroom and think about what other ideas described in this chapter you are ready to try.

Closing Thoughts

Language and literacy experiences for children are most successful when they capitalize on children's inherent motivation to communicate—to listen, speak, read, and write. Children learn these skills most naturally in the context of social interactions. Effective teachers seize the many opportunities throughout the school day to have children apply language and literacy skills in an integrated way across the curriculum.

Resources for Language and Literacy

General

Invitations. Routman, Regie. Portsmouth, NH: Heinemann, 1990.

Lasting Impressions. Harwayne, Shelley. Portsmouth, NH: Heinemann, 1992.

Teaching Reading as a Language Experience. Hall, Mary Anne. Columbus, OH: Charles E. Merrill Publishing Co., 1981.

Transitions: From Literature to Literacy. Routman, Regie. Portsmouth, NH: Heinemann, 1988.

When Writers Read. Hansen, Jane. Portsmouth, NH: Heinemann, 1987.

Whole Language: What's the Difference? Edelsky, Carole, Bess Altwerger, and Barbara Flores. Portsmouth, NH: Heinemann, 1991.

Write Me A Sign About Language Experience. Wilson, Lorraine. Crystal Lake, IL: Rigby, 1979.

Reading Aloud

For Reading Out Loud! A Guide to Sharing Books with Children. Kimmel, Margaret Mary and Elizabeth Segal. New York: Delacorte Press, 1983.

The New Read Aloud-Handbook. Trelease, Jim. New York: Penguin Books, 1985.

Shared Reading

Shared Reading Experience. Butler, Andrea. Crystal Lake, IL: Rigby, 1979.

The Foundations of Literacy. Holdaway, Don. Portsmouth, NH: Heinemann, 1979.

Reading, Writing & Language: A Practical Guide for Primary Teachers. McCracken, Marlene and Robert McCracken. Winnepeg, Canada: Peguis Publishers Ltd., 1979.

Guided Reading

Reading in Junior Classes. New Zealand Department of Education. New York: Richard C. Owen Publishers, Inc., 1985.

The Foundations of Literacy. Holdaway, Don. Portsmouth, NH: Heinemann, 1979.

Independence in Reading: A Handbook on Individualized Procedure. Holdaway, Don. Portsmouth, NH: Heinemann, 1980.

Independent Reading

Reading is Only the Tiger's Tail. McCracken, Marlene and Robert McCracken. Winnipeg, Canada: Peguis Publishers Ltd., 1987.

The New Read Aloud-Handbook. Trelease, Jim. New York: Penguin Books, 1985.

Writing

The Art of Teaching Writing, New Edition. Calkins, Lucy McCormick. Portsmouth, NH: Heinemann, 1994.

Creating Classrooms for Authors: The Reading-Writing Connection. Harste, Jerome C., Kathy G. Short, and Carolyn Burke. Portsmouth, NH: Heinemann, 1988.

Developing Readers and Writers in the Content Area. Moore, David W. and Sharon Arthur Moore. New York: Longman, 1986.

In the Middle: Writing, Reading and Learning with Adolescents. Atwell, Nancie. Portsmouth, NH: Heinemann, 1986.

Living Between the Lines. Calkins, Lucy McCormick. Portsmouth, NH: Heineman, 1991.

Toward a Reading-Writing Classroom. Butler, Andrea and Jan Turbill. Portsmouth, NH: Heineman, 1987.

Writing: Teachers and Children at Work. Graves, Donald. Portsmouth, NH: Heinemann, 1983.

Spelling

Spelling for Whole Language Classrooms. Buchanan, Ethel. Winnipeg, Canada: Whole Language Consultants, Inc., 1989.

Teaching Kids to Spell. Gentry, J. Richard and Jean Wallace Gillet. Portsmouth, NH: Heinemann, 1992.

Handwriting

D'Nealian Handwriting K-8. Glenview, IL: Scott Foresman, 1993.

Handwriting Without Tears. Olsen, Janice Z. Potomac, MD: Janice Z. Olsen, 1994.

Cursive Handwriting. Olsen, Janice Z. Potomac, MD: Janice Z. Olsen, 1991.

References

Calkins, Lucy McCormick. 1994. *The Art of Teaching Writing, New Edition.* Portsmouth, NH: Heinemann.

Clay, Marie H. 1979. *The Early Detection of Reading Difficulties, Third Edition.* Portsmouth, NH: Heinemann.

Holdaway, Don. 1979. *The Foundations of Literacy.* Portsmouth, NH: Heinemann.

Goodman, Kenneth S., Yetta M. Goodman, and Wendy J. Hood, eds. 1989. *The Whole Language Evaluation Book.* Portsmouth, NH: Heinemann.

MATHEMATICAL THINKING

We use mathematical thinking to solve problems every day. Each time we consider how many gallons of paint we need to paint the kitchen, whether fifteen dollars will pay for the groceries in the cart, or how the furniture will fit into the moving van, we use mathematical thinking skills to organize information, compare amounts, and see relationships. Learning the concepts and language of mathematics—more, less, equal, a fraction of, multiples of, and so on—helps us to plan, calculate, reason, and communicate our solutions to problems.

Children use mathematical thinking skills long before they come to school. They compare who can jump higher or ride bikes faster; they divide a pack of M&Ms among friends; they notice the patterns on the wings of a butterfly. Therefore, a logical approach to teaching mathematical thinking in school is to encourage children to continue using the skills they have and to plan experiences that promote learning new skills to solve problems like those encountered in daily life. When children are given opportunities to develop their own understanding of mathematics by applying skills to real problems, they are likely to become successful mathematical thinkers and to continue to use these skills outside the classroom.

> Teachers may need to alter the way they think about mathematics and their role in teaching it. The environment that focuses on answers must be changed to one that focuses on the thinking process itself; teaching how to solve problems is much different from teaching how to get answers (De La Cruz 1994, 1).

This approach to teaching mathematical thinking encourages educators to ask, "How can we provide mathematical experiences that will help children develop the thinking skills necessary to solve real-life problems?"

Children Becoming Mathematical Thinkers

What takes place in classrooms where children learn and use math skills purposefully? Consider the examples that follow in which children pursue investigations of mathematical problems.

*In a **first grade class**, several children make collections of "threes," while others find stories of "threes" in the class library. Around the room, an assortment of collections are assembled including three buttons, three coats, three shoes, three red cubes, etc. Using a calculator, two girls add with three and record: 3+3=6, 3+3+3=9, 3+3+3+3=12, 3+3+3+3+3=15. Several children roll dice (some with dots and some with numerals) to see how many times they get the sum three or the number three. The book collectors find* The Three Billy Goats Gruff, The Three Little Pigs, *and* The Three Bears. *Two children record themselves singing, "Three Blind Mice."*

These children explore the concept of quantity by investigating many ways to construct the number "three." They experiment with ways to use the number "three" to make larger numbers and find the number "three" in another context. The teacher recognizes that playing games is a useful way to explore numbers (and learn facts) and encourages the use of dice, card games, and board games. As the children make choices about how and what to investigate, they strengthen their understanding of how numbers are used.

*In a **second grade class**, children investigate the concept of time. One boy uses a stop watch to measure the length of time it takes to copy a ten-piece pattern block design. Using jars, tape and sand, others construct sand-clocks that measure one, two, or three minutes of time.*

These second graders explore the concept of time using a variety of materials. Rather than simply focusing on teaching children to tell time, the teacher encourages the children to investigate the passage of time and to make and use tools to track time.

***Third graders** explore estimation. First they sort acorns into two sizes, small and large. They fill two identical jars, one with small acorns and one with large acorns and estimate how many are in each jar. During the rest of the week their experiments continue, using different sized containers.*

The children discuss what happens when objects of different sizes are placed in containers of the same size. They write and explain why their estimates change if the size of the jar or the size of the objects change. As children exchange and generate new ideas about their activities, they are learning to perceive relationships, think logically, and solve real problems.

The teachers in each of these classrooms guide explorations of math concepts in order to help children become mathematical thinkers. The children apply basic skills to real situations that are appealing and appropriate for their age level. The focus of the math curriculum is not only on arithmetic, but also on measuring, sorting, classifying, problem solving, spatial relationships, probability, and number sense. The problems children think about may not be solvable in one day; they experiment, learn from their mistakes, and try again.

Children recognize changes in the math curriculum. Marilyn Burns and Bonnie Tank (1988, 1-2) asked a group of third graders what they think about when they think of mathematics. Their responses focused on numbers rather than the purpose of math:

- *"It's when you add two numbers."*
- *"It's odd and even."*
- *"Yuk!"*

These same third graders were then exposed to an approach to math in which they had opportunities to solve real problems and to think and reason mathematically. When asked again about mathematics, they responded very differently:

- *"I think about thinking because you have to think when you do math."*
- *"When I think about mathematics I think about looking at money when I go to 7-11 and adding how much there is. About subtracting a special year from 1987 to find out how long ago it was."*
- *"When I think about mathematics I think about learning and deciding if I should keep rolling the dice or if I should keep my score in the game of pig."*

To become thinkers and problem solvers, capable of understanding and making an impact on today's complex world of invention and technology, children must have experiences that spark their interest and curiosity, integrate their learning, and help structure their thinking. Teaching mathematics to achieve these goals means providing challenging activities that encourage children to think for themselves, and solve problems together.

Goals of the Mathematics Curriculum

New approaches to the teaching of mathematics have evolved from the Standards developed by the National Council of Teachers of Mathematics (NCTM). These Standards (1989) strongly encourage teachers to create a classroom environment where children can be active learners who seek answers to interesting problems. The Standards address five central goals: learning to value mathematics, acquiring self-confidence, becoming mathematical problem solvers, learning to communicate mathematically, and learning to reason mathematically. In planning the math curriculum, it is important to keep these goals in mind.

Learning to Value Mathematics

Children learn to value mathematics when they can see how mathematics relates to their own lives. Teachers can help children make this connection. On a trip to the grocery store, children might notice that products are boxed or canned in containers of many sizes and shapes. The contents of each package are weighed to determine their cost. The items are classified by their food type. The check-out computer reads each product identification code and then totals the final cost. Talking about these observations extends children's learning and encourages more observations.

Children are likely to value mathematics when they see its relationship to everyday experiences:

- as they classify a collection of rocks by attributes;
- as they use a computer to play games involving numbers, logical thinking, spatial sense, or money;
- as they compare the size of buildings in a study of the neighborhood;
- as they create and identify shapes in their artwork;
- as they recognize patterns in books (e.g., *The Very Hungry Caterpillar*, *Ten-in-a-Bed*, *The Three Little Pigs*).

In each case children learn that mathematics is a useful and important part of their lives, rather than simply a study of numbers isolated in a textbook.

Acquiring Self-Confidence

Children become confident mathematical thinkers when they create and solve problems they believe to be important. They view themselves as "measurers" when they choose what to measure and decide on the best tool and procedure to use.

*Charles and Demetrios argue about how many hours are in one week.
Deciding that adding by 24 gets confusing in his head, Charles gets two
calculators from the shelf. They decide that Demetrios will add 24 seven times*

while Charles "times 24" by 7. After comparing answers, they talk about their findings in a class meeting.

Elizabeth wants to make a life-size drawing of herself. The teacher asks, "How can we figure out how big a piece of paper you will need?" Elizabeth suggests asking her friend Sally, who is the same height, to lie on the floor. She uses a piece of string to measure Sally. Then Elizabeth and the teacher use the length of string to cut a sheet of brown paper the right size.

When we encourage children to discover their own solutions to real life problems, they begin to see themselves as capable mathematical thinkers.

Becoming Mathematical Problem-Solvers

Children's natural curiosity uncovers mathematical problems. To solve these problems, children need a repertoire of problem-solving strategies. First they must see that a problem exists. Then they have to know how to begin working towards a solution. Experiences using manipulative materials, drawing pictures, discussing, dramatizing, trying different methods, and looking for patterns, help children learn to use these strategies and discover new ones as needed. Children also have to develop the confidence and perseverance to tackle the problem again when their first attempt fails.

To acquire the strategies and the flexibility needed to solve problems, teachers create a wide range of opportunities for children to work—individually and in small groups—on open-ended problems, as illustrated in the following examples:

A pair of first graders works with Cuisenaire Rods. They have been challenged to find as many ways to "build 10" as they can. One child builds as the other records. They take turns doing these jobs. Later several pairs will talk with each other and share their recordings about how they went about solving this problem.

A bag of marbles is presented to a group of four children, and they are given these clues:

   1) There are more than 6 marbles in the bag.
   2) There are only three colors.
   3) There are 4 blue marbles.
   4) There are half as many green marbles as blue ones.
   5) There is one more red marble than blue marble.

The children are asked to figure out how many marbles are in the bag, and how many there are of each color. As they work together to solve the problem, the children come up with different solutions and learn to work cooperatively as team members. To extend this activity, the children rearrange the number of marbles and make up riddles of their own (Burns 1988).

Solving real problems enables children to learn that problem solving is a process that takes time, effort, and good communication. Several of the resources listed at the end of this chapter include riddles (such as the one just cited) to encourage mathematical problem solving.

Learning to Communicate Mathematically

To communicate mathematically, we have to know the language of mathematics. When children talk about and reflect on what they think and do in math, they (and their teachers as well) gain a better understanding of what they are learning. Language—spoken, written, and illustrated—helps children clarify their thinking and structure their ideas. Using the language of mathematics, children learn how to communicate with signs and symbols, thus translating the word problem or the math experience into a new form.

> *A third grade class decides to make a map of the school yard. They want to show the location of each piece of play equipment and the distance between each one. They measure using meter sticks and a metric trundle wheel. The children communicate their findings by plotting a map, representing distances by number, and play equipment with symbols described in a key.*

> *A second grader has chosen to study black bears as part of the class's study of forest animals. He discovers in a book that black bears are six feet tall. After measuring a length of rolled paper that is 6 feet long, he draws, cuts out, and paints a Black Bear. His sign says, "Black Bears are this big—6 Feet!"*

Children can be encouraged to communicate mathematically in a variety of ways:

- drawing their description of a problem or a solution;
- building a model to represent a solution;
- explaining how they solved a problem;
- dramatizing their understanding of a problem or a solution;
- listening to the ways other children solved a problem;
- keeping written journals about what they are learning or doing in math;
- working with a partner or in small groups to create and solve problems;
- inventing and teaching math games to each other.

For children who are not very verbal, or whose primary language is not English, communicating ideas in writing, drawings, or actions gives them additional opportunities to demonstrate their competence.

Learning to Reason Mathematically

Children love to explain things—why one object is heavier than another, why the shiny red marble speeds down the track faster than the dull blue one—and to justify their reasoning. The ability to reason mathematically begins when children make a statement and then try to explain their reasoning. To encourage this skill, teachers can ask children to explain, justify, or show how they arrived at their explanation.

> *Second graders demonstrate mathematical reasoning when they tell which of the 32 attribute block pieces is missing from the set. They say, "I know that a small, blue, diamond is missing because there are four small squares, triangles, and circles, and only three small diamonds."*

Giving children opportunities to figure out and then explain their solutions teaches them that mathematics is not just a collection of numbers and symbols, but a language that makes sense.

Keeping the NCTM five goals in mind—learning to value mathematics, acquiring self-confidence, becoming mathematical problem-solvers, learning to communicate mathematically, and learning to reason mathematically—will help you prepare a learning environment in which children pursue productive and interesting mathematical activities. As children gain confidence in their abilities as mathematicians, they will assume more responsibility for their own learning.

Components of the Mathematics Curriculum

Children need skills in specific areas to help them think mathematically. As defined in the NCTM Standards, the mathematics curriculum in the primary grades should address the following concepts:

- patterns and relationships
- number concepts and operations
- estimation
- geometry and spatial relationships
- measurement
- probability and statistics

The following chart provides an overview of the specific skills children are expected to acquire during the primary grades.

Overview of the Mathematics Curriculum

Components	Children Learn to:
Patterns and Relationships	• Recognize attributes (shape, size, color, thickness, texture) • Recognize patterns (in nature, school environment, books, as well as with numbers and shapes) • Make, copy, and extend patterns • Sort, classify, and compare objects and groups of objects • Order materials/objects • Describe relationships using language (larger, smaller, heavier, darker, etc.)
Number Concepts and Operations	• Read, write, and compare whole numbers (by building numbers with materials, counting children) • Use counting strategies (counting on, counting backwards, counting in groups) • Use whole number operations (adding, subtracting, multiplying, and dividing) • Use the calculator to perform number calculations or to check computations • Show understanding of place value (100s, 10s, 1s) • Show understanding of fractions as parts of a whole (halves, thirds, fourths)
Estimation	• Estimate quantities (measurements, weights, elapsed time, volume) • Measure with non-standard and standard units • Estimate to compute reasonable/approximate answers to problems • Recognize and name shapes according to attributes

At first glance, it may seem overwhelming to consider including so many different components in your math curriculum. As you read the definitions of each component and think about the examples, notice how often the components are interrelated. Most of the examples showing children's activities address multiple skills and span more than one component of the math curriculum.

The charts in each of the following sections illustrate examples of a continuum of learning and the progression of children's thinking in first through third grades. Based on your knowledge of the children in your class each year, you can make decisions about the kinds of experiences children need and where you should begin. It is normal for the children in any one grade to be in many different places on the continuum.

Geometry and Spatial Relations	• Classify shapes according to attributes • Compare shapes using mathematical language • Develop a sense of spatial relationships and use descriptive language (above, below, beside, to the left/right of, inside, outside, on top of) • Recognize and explore properties of two and three dimensional constructions
Measurement	• Estimate and measure using non-standard units (about 3 hands long, 6 cubes long) and standard units (inches, feet, yards, centimeters, meters) • Use words to describe and compare measurements (longer than, twice as long, area, perimeter) • Use standard instruments for measuring (scales, cups, rulers, meters, yardsticks) • Use time related words in daily vocabulary (days, hours) • Tell time and make judgments about time (relate activities to the passage of time) • Recognize and understand coins and bills
Probability and Statistics	• Collect, report, and describe data (e.g., daily temperatures, hair color, type of shoes, food preferences) • Ask questions about data • Create charts and graphs that illustrate and organize data • Read graphs and draw conclusions ("What can you tell from this graph?") • Make predictions based on data

Patterns and Relationships

Patterns are repetitions (such as stripes on a shirt or lines on a leaf), sequences (spring, summer, fall, winter) and relationships (3, 6, 9, 12 are multiples of 3). We find patterns all around us in the organization of numbers, nature, and events. By helping children notice patterns and look for the relationships between things, we help them make connections, organize information, and solve problems.

Seeing the first three pyramids made from inch cubes, Ernesto constructs a fourth pyramid based on his understanding of the relationships between pyramids 1, 2, and 3.

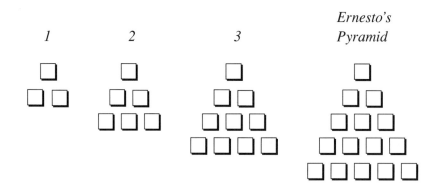

To understand patterns, children have to be able to identify or classify the specific attributes of the pattern, and describe the relationships between its parts. For example, in the number pattern, 1, 3, 5, 7, 9, 11,…, children identify that the numbers in this set are "odd" or that every other number is skipped. Children gain an understanding of patterns when they have many opportunities to identify, create, and extend patterns using many different types of materials.

Exploring Patterns and Relationships

Skills	A Primary Grade Continuum: Ways Children Might Demonstrate Skills		
Identifying patterns	• describe a pattern made with blocks: red-blue-red, or A-B-A-B • notice patterns in a shirt or in a song	• examine number patterns in a hundreds chart • see patterns in nature: stripes on a snake, lines on a spider web	• use an understanding of patterns to solve a problem: the rule is +6 for these numbers -6, 0, 6, 12, 18, ?, 30, 36
Creating patterns	• organize color tiles in a row by color: red, red, blue, red, red, blue • make circular designs connecting the beginning to the end using a pattern, such as a string of beads	• make patterns in more than one direction • make a number pattern using one rule: 12, 10, 8, —, 4, —, 0 (subtract 2)	• make line, circle, or area patterns using specific information: create an area pattern using 3 colors and 24 tiles • make a number pattern using two rules: multiply by 2, subtract 1
Extending patterns	• hear a snap, clap, click, click pattern and determine that a snap comes next • see a pattern in a Pattern Block design and be able to continue it	• say 15, 20, 25, 30, after hearing 5, 10… • plan for daily events: tell the sequence of tomorrow's events, based on a predictable pattern	• continue a pattern that repeats itself as well as grows: 1, 2, 1, 3, 1, 4…
Describing relationships	• sort and classify objects by similarities and differences and talk about their size, shape, color • order a group of objects according to size, quality, texture, or weight: describe a collection of balls organized from largest to smallest	• sort, classify, and describe objects in more than one way: first by shape, then by size • sort by given attributes: a set of large, plastic triangles, and tell how sorted	• compare two or more objects or numbers; explain that even numbers come in pairs, odds are a pair plus 1 • learn and explain tricks for multiples: 9s table increases by one in tens column, decreases by one in ones column: 9, 18, 27, 36…or the sum of the digits is 9

Number Concepts and Operations

The study of number concepts and operations, what we call "arithmetic," has traditionally been the central focus of the elementary school math curriculum. Learning number facts (3+4=7 or 7x8=56) and doing the four basic operations (+, -, x, and ÷) occupied a major portion of class time and were the basis upon which mathematical ability and achievement were evaluated. Number concepts and the use of operations are vitally important to the development of mathematical competency. However, the definition of number concepts is broader than simply performing the operations. Understanding number concepts means understanding the relationships between numbers and distinguishing the effects of operations on numbers.

Children learn arithmetic as they acquire an understanding of the meaning of numbers. Given opportunities to experience number symbols (7+4=11) linked with real-life activities (7 boys and 4 girls make 11 children), they begin to connect the mathematical symbols with real situations (who is here and who is absent). In fact, children begin constructing a sense of number in their highchairs as they finger three Cheerios, popping them into their mouths—one, two, three—their first counting lesson. And as they "ask" for more, they begin to discover the relationships between numbers: 5>3 Cheerios (five is more than three Cheerios). Throughout the primary grades, continuous real-life experiences with counting, relating, connecting, grouping, and interpreting numbers help children develop a solid understanding of number concepts.

Teachers can learn about children's number sense when they challenge them to create equations using various operations to equal 8. Some solutions might be:

8=24÷3　　　　　　　　　*8=3/4 of a dozen-1*
8=1/2 of 16　　　　　　　*2+4+2=8-0*
8=the time I go to bed　　*8=yesterday's date*
8=+15-7　　　　　　　　　*8=3+3+4-2*
8=the number of children who sit at my lunch table

Children need extensive opportunities to count, group, and manipulate numbers before they can see how the placement of a number relates to its value. When asked what the "3" means or stands for in the numeral "30," most young children seem bewildered because they only understand that "3" means three things, and that "30" means thirty things. Although children can memorize that one column is for "the tens" and the another column is for "the ones," meaning is not developed until children can see numbers both as a specific quantity and as a representation of an idea. Exploring numbers with real materials (e.g., manipulatives, classroom objects) enables children to make discoveries about numbers as symbols.

Games provide a wonderful opportunity for children to practice and reinforce number concepts independently of the teacher. Dice games, dominoes, playing cards, and board games can involve counting, finding sums, recognizing equivalent values, and figuring out number relationships.

Opportunities to explore number concepts often arise spontaneously in the classroom:

> *Ms. Whitson introduces a new painting activity to her first graders—tray painting (see the chapter on Establishing a Structure for the Classroom). She explains that there are four trays available for use. After discussing how the paint, brushes, and clean-up system will work, she asks, "How many children can work at a time?" Eager to work with their own trays, the children decide that only four children can paint at a time. She asks how many children are present in class today. When the children answer, "18," she asks how many painting groups there will be so everyone gets a chance to paint today. The children give various estimates. Then they spend a few minutes working alone or with partners, using chalk on the board, paper and markers, unifix cubes, or mental calculations to determine the solution. Each group explains how they decided on a strategy and came up with their answer. They agree that they need four groups of four and one group of two.*

Children learn about fractions as they share or trade cookies or negotiate deals: "If I eat half of my peas, may I have dessert?" The child splits the pile of peas evenly, one to eat, one to leave, etc. When teachers introduce fractions and operations with fractions in school, it helps to build upon this understanding. Teachers can talk about fractions as children build with unit blocks, as food is distributed at snack time, during cooking projects, and as materials are distributed.

> *Ms. Robinson has desks organized in groups of 4 in the classroom. When she begins a unit on fractions, the children sit at their desks and talk about each person's desk as part of their table group. Two desks in a four person grouping make up 2/4 of the group, three desks are 3/4 of the group.*

When children have many opportunities to explore and solve problems using manipulatives and real life experiences, they construct and explain their own solutions. In the process, they come to their own understandings about number concepts.

Exploring Number Concepts and Operations

Skills	A Primary Grade Continuum: Ways Children Might Demonstrate Skills		
Understanding whole numbers	• use numbers to identify quantities: count 10 plastic bears and write the number 10 • recognize the relative size of numbers: 2 is less than 6, 18 is more than 9	• recite numbers to 100 or more; keep track of how many days of school have passed and read the number on the number line • read and write numerals to 100 with a specific purpose in mind: record scores in a card game	• read and write numerals to 999: track mileage on an odometer • recognize the relative size of larger numbers: 600 is more than 500, 801 is less than 810
Using counting strategies	• count objects in a group pointing to each object as it is counted • count on: make a set of 7 cubes from a set of 4 cubes by adding on 3 to the original set rather than starting over from 1	• count backwards from numbers 100 to 1 • see multiple ways to count a group of 50 objects, by 2s, 5s, 10s	• count on or backwards mentally: add 17+9 by adding 17+10 and subtracting 1 • count in groups: by 25s, 100s, 500s
Developing an understanding of whole number operations	• use strategies (manipulatives, fingers, learning doubles, drawing a picture) to figure out 5+2=7 • solve real problems: there are 5 children who want to work at this table and only 3 chairs, how many more chairs do we need?	• use objects to show that 5 groups of 3 are 15 and 3 groups of 5 are 15 • use strategies to add and subtract: number families, 6+3=9, 9-3=6; doubles +1, 8+8=16, 8+9=17	• find differences between two numbers by subtracting or adding on • use repeated addition, number families, or understanding of multiples to solve multiplication and division problems

Developing an understanding of place value	• count quantities of objects by grouping them in tens and ones • count on from ten: 10 objects, add 3 more without beginning at 1	• use groups of objects to play trading games: chip trading with red, blue, yellow, and green chips • calculate the value of two 2-digit numbers: add 23+45 by showing 2 tens sticks and 4 tens sticks make 6 tens sticks plus 8 units (ones), or 68 altogether	• calculate the value of two 2-digit numbers using sense of tens and ones: 26+27= 40+13=53 • describe a 3-digit number in several ways: use base ten blocks to show 132 as 1 flat, 3 rods, and 2 whites, or 132 whites, or 13 rods and 2 whites, or 12 rods and 12 whites
Developing an understanding of fractions	• share a banana with a friend by splitting it into two equal parts • compare fractions: know that 1/2 of a group is more than 1/4 of the group and use the words "half" and "quarter" accurately	• identify equal parts of a whole object as 1/2, 1/3, or 1/4: see an apple sectioned into 4 equal parts, and ask for 1/4 • show and compare 1/2, 1/3, and 1/4 spatially: given three pieces of 4 inch ×4 inch paper, can fold one to show two equal parts, one to show three equal parts, and one to show four equal parts	• name equivalent fractions: in cutting a pie into 1/8s, discover that 4/8 is equal to 1/2 • label fractional parts with pattern blocks: if the yellow hexagon is one whole, then the blue diamond is 1/3, 2 blue diamonds=2/3, the red trapezoid=1/2
Using a calculator	• explore the different keys on the calculator • add 25+21+27 to find the total number of children in all the first grade classrooms	• use the +, -, ×, and ÷ keys to solve number problems • use the + key and then use the = key repeatedly to add the same number	• play number games: assign each letter a numerical value and calculate the value of names and words; collect $1.00 words

Estimation

Estimation is the ability to make a calculated guess about a problem or situation: How many people attended the party? What is the cost of a gallon of milk? How far do you live from the center of the city? How much time do you spend each week in your garden? Answers to these questions involve number, value, distance, and time—all mathematical concepts. Adults easily and correctly respond with estimated answers, responses made using number sense and experience. Knowing how to estimate is essential because quantitative and spatial problems arise continually in everyday life.

When children are given opportunities to estimate, they learn how to make decisions and take appropriate risks. They discover that walking a mile takes less than half an hour and that collecting a million soda tabs fills 8 cafeteria trash cans. Furthermore, they are exposed to another dimension of mathematics with its own vocabulary such as: *about, approximately, close to, more than*, and *in between*. Learning to estimate also helps children understand that mathematics is not always about specific answers, that reasonable estimates are often the most useful solution to a problem.

Exploring Estimation

Skills	A Primary Grade Continuum: Ways Children Might Demonstrate Skills		
Estimating quantities	• look at a group of objects and decide: the quantity is less than 50, more than 20, nearly 30 • begin to understand large numbers: guess that there are 100 M&Ms in a bag	• look at containers of objects and use estimating strategies: there are 5 objects in the first row, count by 5s to estimate the number in all • use sense of larger numbers: estimate that there are 75 children in the lunchroom	• decide to use an estimate as an appropriate solution to a problem: the principal is about 50 years old • regularly use words such as: about, near, approximately, in between, around
Using estimation with measurement	• choose a tool for measuring a certain space, object, or time: Unifix cubes to measure the width of the door • use a measurement tool to check an estimate: use a pan balance to find that 4 raisins weigh the same as a pebble	• use strategies to estimate space, objects or time: use Unifix cubes in stacks of 10 to measure the length of the classroom • predict the number of minutes it will take to complete a drawing	• begin to use standard measurement terms when estimating a measurement: the Lego® set costs about $5.00 • use specific strategies to estimate measures: one cupful holds 25 beans, the jar probably holds 6 cupfuls, therefore, the jar holds between 100 and 150 beans
Using estimation with computation	• find solutions to problems: each of three children can have 3 or 4 candies if there are 11 candies in all	• solve problems using knowledge of place value: 22+35 is about 50 because there are 5 tens	• add and subtract larger numbers mentally: 102-47 is about 50 • check calculator solutions by estimating: 584 is too large for 10×52, and therefore recalculate

Geometry and Spatial Relationships

Experiences with geometry and spatial relations are another way for children to organize and make sense of the world. Just as activities with numbers, patterns, and estimation help children see relationships and solve problems, experiences with geometric concepts and skills in the classroom lead children to develop an appreciation and understanding of our geometric world. Children begin to recognize the importance and use of a right angle in the building of houses and rooms. They laugh at the thought of a doorway built with angles of less than 90 degrees.

Geometry was once considered an enrichment unit to be explored if time permitted. The National Council of Teachers of Mathematics now considers geometry a critical component of the math curriculum because the research shows that "children who develop a strong sense of spatial relationships and who master the concepts and language of geometry are better prepared to learn number and measurement ideas, as well as other advanced mathematical ideas" (NCTM 1988, 48).

The study of geometry challenges children to solve problems using strategies of investigation, experimentation, and exploration—strategies that are necessary to mathematical thinking. There are many excellent manipulative materials—geoboards, tangrams, pattern blocks, and geometric solids—to help children develop a solid understanding of geometry.

Exploring Geometry and Spatial Relationships

Skills	A Primary Grade Continuum: Ways Children Might Demonstrate Skills		
Learning about the attributes of geometric shapes	• explore the parts of shapes and how they are constructed: build a rectangle using straws and clay • investigate geometric solids: roll cylinders and spheres, stack cubes and boxes	• use geometric language to describe shapes and spaces: a rectangle has 2 short lines, 2 long lines, and 4 angles • begin to classify shapes by attributes: squares, rectangles, and diamonds are all four-sided shapes	• match, reproduce, describe, and name shapes: all triangles have three sides, some are tall and thin, others are short and fat • classify shapes by specific attributes: some triangles, rectangles, and squares all have right angles
Comparing shapes	• build shapes using other shapes: use two small tangram triangles to build a parallelogram, a square, and larger triangle • sort and classify shapes: make three groups of shapes (one with no straight sides, one with five sides, one with two long sides)	• recognize similar and congruent shapes: match similar shapes noting the only difference is in their size • compare sizes: show difference in area by filling two squares with centimeter cubes, find that one square has an area of 9 sq cm and the other an area of 16 sq cm	• notice differences in geometric solids: one pyramid has a square base, the other has a triangular base • recognize that different shaped containers can hold the same amount of water, even though the tall thin glass looks like it holds more than a short fat one
Exploring spatial relationships	• explore ways to fill an area: use pattern blocks and put 5 diamonds or 10 triangles into an outline of a flower • experiment with containers: discover relationships between the amount of sand in a cylinder and in a cube of equal height	• construct shapes following specific rules: make a square on a geoboard that touches only 8 nails and put a triangle inside it • investigate symmetry: place a mirror on a pattern block design, showing the line of symmetry	• solve area problems: fill a space using square color tiles to find out how many will cover the area • build reflections: use the same pattern blocks to construct the other side of a 4-piece design

Measurement

Measurement activities encourage children to practice and integrate many different mathematical thinking skills. They have to make decisions about which tools to use and which strategies will work best. If they want to measure the classroom, for example, they might first decide whether to use their feet, Unifix cubes, a ruler, or a trundle wheel. When children compare their heights and figure out that Jeffrey is 2 inches taller than Scott and 1 inch shorter than Laurel, they are using computation strategies.

> *Ms. Singer's third graders go to the school yard with stacks of containers to use in the sand box. Many children crowd into the sand box and begin to work. Castles and tunnels, mazes and gardens, highways and skyscrapers appear, some made by hand, others molded from the metric containers. They add water to fill moats and swimming pools. Laughter and excitement fill the air. Later, after the children have had time to explore freely, Ms. Singer directs them to a more formal measurement task. They use a variety of tools to measure their sand constructions.*

The children in this example are using the language of measurement: castles and skyscrapers are *tall,* moats are *deep,* gardens need *area,* water is *heavy,* and mazes and highways cover a *distance.* Next they begin to compare objects that have similar measurable attributes (e.g., "Look, my skyscraper is taller than your castle.") Measuring by comparing two objects is a necessary and normal step that children take before they start to measure with standard or non-standard units because it helps them focus on what they are measuring. Children quickly learn, for example, that it doesn't make sense to say, "My highway is longer than your skyscraper." Children need many opportunities to investigate and discuss the attributes of an object that are measurable.

Once children have the concepts and language of measurement, they begin to use a variety of materials or tools when confronted by a measurement problem.

> *Some children want to know whether the maze or the block highway is longer. They quickly see that they can't lay them out beside each other to compare their lengths. Instead, they solve the problem by using string to measure each length, then comparing the length of the strings.*

Often in second grade, and usually by third, children want more information about what they are measuring. They begin to question how much water fills that cup, or how much the box of sand weighs. At this time they choose standard units of measure to determine the measurement (e.g., the cup holds 1/2 a liter of water, the box of sand weighs just under a kilogram).

Exploring Measurement

Skills	A Primary Grade Continuum: Ways Children Might Demonstrate Skills		
Measuring with standard and non-standard units	• estimate length, height, or weight using a non-standard measure: guess that a new pencil is 6 paper clips long • trace a partner's body and measure with Unifix cubes, arm lengths, or hands	• use non-standard units to determine length, weight, volume: measure tables with plastic links or the circumference of pumpkins with string • measure a specific item with a variety of tools: a chalkboard is 5 inches long and 13 white cubes long	• determine difference in weight between two objects: the piece of coal is ten blocks lighter than the piece of marble; • explore the concept of perimeter: measure perimeter of a cylinder, a house, a dog pen
Using measuring instruments	• use a balance scale to determine which of two objects is heavier or lighter • recognize the use of standard measuring tools such as ruler, scale, and thermometer and use the language that matches the tool	• begin to link measures to familiar references: 4 hamburgers weigh about a pound, a note-book is about a foot high, a fox is bigger than my dog • use common instruments for measuring: scales for weight, cups for volume, thermometers for temperature	• choose the best tool to measure: a trundle wheel to find the length of the playground instead of a meter stick • solve a problem using a measuring tool as a reference: find the distance around a canister by first using a string and then measuring its length
Developing an understanding of time and time-related skills	• read, use, and discuss the information on the calendar: notice that days, weeks, and months follow a pattern • make reasonable estimates for amounts of time: it takes a second to throw a ball, and an hour to bake a cake	• experiment with duration of time: write name 20 times in one minute • tell time on digital and analog clocks • order daily events: wake up at… go to school at… have dinner at… go to bed at…	• order events of the day, week, or year: start school in the fall, after winter holiday study mammals, science project due in two weeks • discuss a time line with understanding: order personal events on a time line

Probability and Statistics

Should a shoe store stock more velcro or more lace-up sneakers for children? If I roll two dice, what sums will occur most frequently? We answer these questions using a knowledge of probability and statistics. A probability is a number that expresses the likelihood that something will happen. For example, the weather forecaster tells us there is a 50% chance of rain tomorrow. Statistics is the area of mathematics that helps us organize, describe, and interpret information so we can solve problems or make decisions. For example, by reading a graph we can figure out that second graders this year have more brothers than sisters, and all but two brothers are older than their second grade sibling.

Children begin exploring the fields of probability and statistics when they roll dice, make predictions about which sums will occur most frequently, and record the results. They may conduct surveys to find out about favorite foods or keep records about whose turn it is to do a certain job. They frequently ask questions that can be used to explore this aspect of mathematics.

> *Ms. Chavez's class wants to plan a sledding party after the first snowfall in December. She asks the children to think about which month has the most snow. After collecting information from the almanac, the class decides to plan their party in the month of February because February had 15 snowy days last year, whereas January had only 8.*

When children have opportunities to explore statistics and probability, they learn how numbers express the likelihood that something will happen. These experiences help children understand their world and think about such things as their chances of getting chicken pox or the risk involved in bicycling. Further, the challenges presented by probability problems interest children, making numbers fun and relating them meaningfully to many aspects of their lives.

Exploring Probability and Statistics

Skills	A Primary Grade Continuum: Ways Children Might Demonstrate Skills		
Collecting, describing, and recording data	• create graphs with real objects: place shoes (e.g., velcro, tie, or buckle) on a large square grid to find out the most popular shoe type • record data: use a tally system to find out how many want bananas or how many want apples for snacks	• set up graphs in 1 to 1 correspondence with objects: line up data on a picture graph showing the colors of lunch boxes, one box to each number • conduct surveys and collect data: favorite foods, pets, siblings	• create graphs using pictures, bar, pie, or line form • graph data found in other curriculum areas: use a bar graph to show how many children in the class have read books by particular authors
Reading graphs and drawing conclusions	• notice patterns and describe relationships on a graph: guinea pigs seem to prefer apples over oranges • answer questions or solve problems using a graph's information: name 3 leaves that only have 1 point	• observe and describe data collected over time: find how many rainy days in October • compare information on a graph: talk and write about which category has more, less, the same, equal, not equal (>, <, =, ≠)	• notice and read graphs: use a weather graph from a newspaper to examine varying temperatures across America • find information on many types of graphs: pictograph, line, bar, and pie
Making predictions	• make and test predictions of simple possible outcomes or actions: if we keep this plant in the dark for more than a week, it will die • predict, then test which of 2 different colored crayons will be drawn most often from a paper bag	• make a prediction based on general knowledge: when you flip a coin, "heads" won't appear every time • predict an outcome and test it: roll 2 dice 50 times and predict which sum will occur most frequently	• invent and graph probability experiments: predict, then use a spinner with 4 colors to test which color is most likely to be selected • determine whether a prediction can be made from a sampling: the majority of first graders have one sibling; the majority of children in the whole school also have one sibling

Organizing the Math Curriculum

Teachers need a plan for addressing all the components of the math curriculum in a way that will make sense to children. Planning should be guided by the principles we outlined in the chapter on Guiding Children's Learning. Learning experiences must be purposeful for children and must be integrated with one another and with what children already know. Communication is central to all learning, and children need time to explore concepts and return to them over and over. Knowing that children construct knowledge by investigating, representing, and reflecting on their learning dictates the kind of experiences that will most effectively enable children to become mathematical thinkers. These experiences may take place as part of a long-term study, a work time, or in the context of a spontaneous "teachable moment."

Promoting Mathematical Thinking Through Long-Term Studies

When children are challenged to solve a problem that interests them, they are motivated to apply what they have learned and to learn new skills and concepts. That's why it is so effective to provide opportunities for children to work on particular math skills that arise naturally as part of long-term studies. Social studies or science projects enable teachers to integrate learning across many content areas. While a particular study is not likely to incorporate all the math skills that you want to teach at any given time, there are many components of mathematical thinking that naturally fit into the work of a long-term study.

A long-term study of a nearby **river** offers opportunities for a multi-age class to conduct first-hand investigations. In the process of studying the river, many mathematical questions arise for children to explore. Children might:

- measure the temperature of the water;
- count the different kinds of trees or plants growing along the bank;
- graph the numbers of different kinds of animals they observe living in or near the river.

Some mathematical investigations that arise when a third grade class studies **immigration** might lead children to:

- make and read historical time lines;
- use necessary dates to calculate how old people were when they came to this country;
- conduct a survey to find out where their ancestors came from and when they arrived in this country;
- figure out the size of the ships people traveled on and crowd into a space that size.

A study of the **neighborhood** around the school can be geared to all children six to eight years old. It is relevant to the children's lives and their investigations can continue after each school day. In the context of this study children can:

- count buildings, hydrants, windows, trees, etc.;
- notice patterns on buildings, in nature;
- make graphs showing different forms of transportation in use;
- estimate the number of people likely to pass a certain spot in a certain period of time;
- set up a store similar to one in the neighborhood, and "buy and sell" goods.

Animals appeal to most primary age children. Studies of local animals, whether they are squirrels and pigeons, lizards and armadillos, or bears and otters, are a good starting point. Children can:

- make life-size representations of the animals, using measuring materials to get the right size;
- compare the number of young each animal produces;
- compare the size of the males and females of the species;
- figure out how many children it would take to weigh as much as a particular animal;
- make time lines showing stages of maturation.

Long-term studies can address objectives in many subject areas while children explore interesting content. In the chapter on Guiding Children's Learning, we described a series of steps for planning a study. One of the steps described charts that a teacher might make to help focus a study and create ways to integrate learning in many content areas. The following example shows how one teacher used a chart to help him think about the components of the math curriculum and how they could relate to his social studies project.

Mr. Fuller's second graders will study the construction site across the street from the school. An eight-story college dormitory is under construction, and he has made contact with the supervisor of the project. The uncle of one of his students is a worker at the site. As part of his planning for this study, Mr. Fuller considers how he can incorporate mathematical investigations into the project.

Study of a Construction Site

Math Component	Activities
Patterns	• Examine blueprints for patterns • Observe patterns in brick design
Number Concepts	• Make time lines to indicate different stages of construction • Notice patterns in building design to explore multiplication • Count supplies and materials
Estimation	• Estimate amounts of supplies and materials • Make estimates about size: windows, doors, number of bricks needed to make different sections
Geometry	• Investigate the use of different shapes used in building design
Measurement	• Study ratio by exploring the blueprints and an actual section of the building • Measure the size of a brick and the number of bricks required for a particular wall • Design and build a model of the dormitory under construction
Probability and Statistics	• Make graphs of the number and kinds of workers • Examine the job schedule charts the supervisor uses; make a comparable job chart for the classroom • Make predictions about when different stages of the project will be completed

After he makes the chart and thinks about how much measurement work the children can do in connection with the study, Mr. Fuller decides to begin the school year exploring non-standard measurement. He hopes children will then begin to recognize the value of standard measurement in construction. With this as his starting point, he then plans math work times to teach other math concepts and skills outlined in his curriculum guide.

When children are involved in studies that hold their interest, they often generate ideas for exploration that you may not have considered. Sometimes children want to solve a problem but don't yet have the skills to do so. If children conduct surveys and want to tabulate results, but lack the math skills, what are their alternatives? They may come up with strategies of their own to do the counting; they may use calculators, or you may decide to teach a particular skill because the children want to use it as a tool. Math work times can be designed to fit into the needs of a study or they may be designed to explore what children know and what they need to learn.

Planning Math Work Times

Most teachers identify several periods during the week when they schedule time for math activities. Sometimes math work times are used to introduce new materials, a new concept, or a game to the class as a whole group. At other times children work in small groups to explore a problem using a variety of materials. A teacher may work with one group while the others work independently. There are also times when children write in journals about their math learning or share their discoveries in a meeting.

In the following example, Ms. Herman is interested in finding out about the children's knowledge and use of basic number facts, and more importantly, their understanding and use of the language of mathematics. Knowing that the children need to be active, she chooses an activity that will engage the children in spilling nine large lima beans painted red on one side, white on the other. They will record their observations.

The activity offers many possibilities for mathematical thinking and for children to practice and discuss their ideas. By asking open-ended questions that challenge children to think, analyze, and reason, Ms. Herman will pursue the goals of mathematical learning as well as help them learn their number facts.

With the whole class seated in a circle in the meeting area, Ms. Herman spills beans from the cup. This is what happens:

The children see the spilled beans and the following discussion takes place:

Teacher:	**Children:**
"What do you see?"	*"I see 9 beans, two colors, three chipped."*
"What do you see?"	*"I see 6 red ones and 3 white ones, and some beans are touching."*
"Do you see anything else?"	*"I see that they are not all the same size beans."*

Ms. Herman spills the beans a second time.

"What do you see now?"	*"I see 9 beans, 4 red and 5 white."*
	"I see one more red than last time."
	"I see the same 9 beans."
	"No, they are not the same 9 beans, they are different, there is one more red one."
"What might happen when I spill them again?"	*"I think 2 reds, 7 whites."*
	"I think 3 whites, 6 reds."
	"I think 8 white, 1 red."

Teacher:	Children:
"Why do you think this?"	*"Because the red side is heavier because it is sprayed red and the heavy side will fall down faster."*
"Let's see what happens this time."	

Ms. Herman spills the beans a third time and gets 5 red and 4 white beans.

	"If you spill them again, I think that it won't be 5 red, 4 white."
"Why?"	*"Well the last spill was 5 red, 4 white, and you don't ever get the same thing two times in a row."*
"How do you know that?"	*"It hasn't happened yet. You've NEVER spilled the same thing twice."*
	"I bet if you let ME spill the beans, I'll get all reds," says one child. "No, that's impossible," says another.
"Why is that impossible?"	*"There is always one bean that won't do what the others do. Let ME have the beans and I'll show you."*
"What other questions do you have?"	*"What happens if you spill 10 beans?"*
	"What if you spill them from way up high?"
	"What if you don't shake them in the cup?"
	"What if you use little beans?"
	"What if you spill them one at a time?"

This communication between the teacher and the children shows how children can develop mathematical knowledge when the teacher sets up an interesting problem and poses open-ended questions that encourage children to think. The children are now ready to undertake investigations of their own. They will work with partners to spill their own containers of beans and record their findings. While they work, the teacher will talk with groups of children about their explorations. She knows that sufficient time must be allowed for this activity or the children will be frustrated.

As a way of involving families in this project, Ms. Herman has the children conduct probability experiments at home using nine pennies. She sends a note home with the children asking family members to work with their children to record how many heads and tails are shown each time the children "spill" the pennies.

Dear Families:

Our class is exploring number combinations. We hope you can help us with this project by conducting penny experiments with your child at home. You will need nine pennies. Each night next week, please spill the pennies (your child knows how to do this). Together, using the attached record sheet, record the number of heads and tails you get after spilling the pennies ten times. We will compare the results in class. Make sure your child brings the record sheet to school on Friday.

Thank you for your help with this activity.

Sincerely,

In the activity with the beans the teacher can observe what children are learning as she walks about the room and talks with them. Here are some examples of the kinds of mathematical learning taking place.

- *Number sense*—finding all the number combinations for 9 beans (eg., 1+8, 8+1, 7+2, 2+7, etc.).
- *Basic number facts*—seeing and recording number combinations that add up to 9.
- *Probability*—spilling the beans 30 times and recording which combination occurs most frequently.
- *Collecting data*—having all the children spill their 9 beans 30 times, then recording all the data to observe the findings.
- *Graphing*—representing the data on charts and organizing it to show the findings visually.
- *Testing theories*—proving that 9 beans can never be 5 red, 5 white; proving that white beans do not come up more often because the red side is heavier; proving that the height from which the beans are dropped does not affect the outcome.
- *Mathematical relationships*—devising a way to use the bean spilling experiment to explore subtraction (e.g., spilling 9 beans and subtracting the red ones from nine, so the white ones will always be the answer!).

A simple activity with beans was planned by the teacher in order to focus on basic number facts and language. In the process of their investigations, children reveal their knowledge of other components of mathematical thinking. As the children work together, the teacher is able to assess their learning—writing quick anecdotal notes on a clipboard to help her remember what children know and what they can do.

Mathematical problem-solving opportunities, such as the one described above, enable children to construct their own knowledge. When children try to solve real mathematical problems, they are more likely to see a purpose to their learning and ask questions that lead to further learning. Ms. Herman's math lesson enables the children to investigate, represent, and reflect on what they are learning, as outlined below.

How Children Investigate Mathematical Problems

As they investigate math problems, children engage in several processes:

- observing
- seeing connections
- making predictions
- reasoning and using logical thinking
- hypothesizing and arguing
- questioning

The children observe as they look carefully at the spilled beans and describe what they see. They make connections as they notice that different numbers of beans are red or white, or that the second time there is one more red bean and one fewer white bean. Ms. Herman asks the children to predict what might happen the next time. They explain why they think something will happen and devise hypotheses to explain their predictions. She asks questions and the children ask questions. Knowing that all children do not engage in each element of the process all the time, Ms. Herman will build these elements of investigation into future learning experiences.

How Children Represent Their Learning in Mathematics

Writing, drawing, building, or creating charts and diagrams helps children clarify their thinking. It also gives the teacher information about what they understand and where they need additional support. Ms. Herman creates the structure for children to represent their learning in several ways. This helps her to evaluate how children's thinking changes and gives the children a record of their project. Ms. Herman provides worksheets for the children to record how many times each combination appears, as well as worksheets for them to record their homework with pennies. Some children make drawings of all the possible combinations. These are displayed around the room.

Opportunities for representation can be built into many mathematical activities by providing:

- bulletin board space for children's designs and writings about math;
- meaningful worksheets that challenge children to record findings;
- "lab" books or math journals for recording ideas and drawings that represent the process used during an activity;
- a "save and share" table that displays constructions, designs, and inventions made by the children;
- a record of the questions children want to try to answer as part of a project;
- space to showcase mathematical discoveries (e.g., the patterns in the hundreds board).

How Children Reflect on Mathematical Thinking

In the example with the beans, Ms. Herman has several meetings to discuss findings and generate some new questions. She also builds several opportunities into the work times for the children to reflect upon their learning. At the end of each day's math time, the children record their thoughts and observations in their math journals.

When children are encouraged to share the strategies they use to solve problems, they learn to value the process of finding answers. Other opportunities for reflection can be designed to have children think about what they learned. When children are asked to look at the bean recording sheet and write down one discovery they made or write about something they now understand that they didn't before, they are learning to be reflective thinkers.

Teachers can ask many kinds of questions to help children think about problem-solving strategies. However, reflecting on mathematical thinking, while valuable, can be overdone! Not every work time or lesson has to have a reflection assignment built in; think about where and when it is appropriate, useful, or interesting.

Teaching Math Through Play

Math games offer a great variety of experiences for children to practice winning strategies and number facts. By incorporating time for games in the course of the day or week, you can make sure that children get the practice they need. Dice, playing cards, and board games can be introduced to the whole class or to small groups during a math work time. (See the section on games in the chapter on Establishing a Structure for the Classroom.) New games soon become part of children's repertoire and therefore an option for choice time as well as for math periods. If oak tag, stickers, or other materials are available, children can invent their own games as well, and challenge others to play them.

Planned work times ensure that children are exposed to a certain number of math skills and concepts, and most teachers find that beginning the day with a plan is crucial. In addition, teachers can increase the opportunities for math learning by infusing math concepts into everyday activities and allowing for the unexpected, spontaneous learning that naturally emerges.

Using Teachable Moments

Sometimes the best teaching occurs when it is least expected. A question comes up, a special class is canceled, or you discover your clock is ten minutes fast and you have to "fill in time." Taking advantage of these opportunities to engage children in mathematical thinking enables teachers to demonstrate the usefulness of mathematics and to challenge children to apply what they are learning.

Taking attendance in the morning offers practice in number concepts: "How many children would be here if everyone were in school today? How many are missing?" When you write the daily schedule, plan a calendar, or organize materials, you can include patterning. Talking about the time of day or how much time you have before something else happens incorporates measurement into everyday events. Children can estimate how long it will take to do something or go somewhere. When you read a book, there are possible connections in looking for patterns of behavior, noting the ages of the characters, thinking about the time of year, and predicting outcomes. Keep these activities from becoming rote by changing them frequently.

If you have a repertoire of "math moments" to draw upon, you will find it becomes easy to infuse mathematical thinking into many parts of the day. At transition times, for example, rather than simply asking children to form a line, or wait in line until everyone is quiet, use math as a way of accomplishing the task. Here are some examples:

- Have children count off to form work groups and have signs on the tables so children can quickly form their groups (e.g., if you have 21 children and you want groups of 3, have the children count to 7 and then start over until everyone has a number between 1 and 7).

- While the children are in line say, "I'm thinking of a number between 5 and 50. Raise your hand if you want to guess what number it is." As children guess, give them hints: "10 is too low." "44 is too high."

- Have children announce their place in line using ordinal numbers: first, second, third, etc.

- Ask the children to organize themselves into various shapes: a square or a triangle; or have them form two parallel lines or two perpendicular lines.

Understanding the components of the math curriculum and the routes (long-term studies, math work times, and teachable moments) that teachers can take to guide children's learning, makes it possible to organize an approach for each year. Mapping your math curriculum on an annual basis ensures that you will address all the components at some time during the year. Even though plans invariably change, advance planning reminds you to collect and organize the materials needed, and helps you think of ways to include math learning with other subjects.

Since most skills and concepts in mathematics relate in some way to one another, the sequence of skills and concepts can be flexible. For example, should measurement or number sense be taught first? In order to explore and discover the concept of measurement, children need to have number sense, yet to have number sense children need to understand the value of numbers which can be gained through measuring. Since math skills are interrelated, you don't have to be locked into a set timetable for teaching math. You can teach math skills and concepts in a way that fits best with the rest of the curriculum and the interests of the children.

In planning the math curriculum schedule, you may want to keep these things in mind:

- Plan your long-term studies in social studies and science first and consider what math activities can be incorporated into the study.
- Start with a unit that gives children many opportunities for success, individual expression, and creativity and that gives you a chance to assess the needs of the class.
- Weave number work and problem solving throughout each topic of study.
- Focus on one area (e.g., patterns, number sense, measurement, etc.) for about a month.
- Be flexible about changing the order of skills taught if you want to use them as part of a social studies or science theme.
- Think about the components of the math curriculum as a spiral in which you return again and again to the concepts of each.

No one has to "reinvent the wheel," nor does a teacher need to feel, "I can't teach this way because I'm not creative," or "I've never understood machines." Texts, manuals, and catalogs can pave the way to expert mathematical teaching with manipulative materials. The manuals that accompany tools such as calculators discuss at length how to use them and how to teach children to use them. For the use and applications of the computer in the math curriculum, coordinate with a media specialist if one is available, or read about evaluating software in the chapters on Establishing a Structure for the Classroom and The Arts and Technology. The wealth of resources now available can augment your program and inspire your thinking about each of the components of the math curriculum. A modest collection of carefully selected resources can make for ever-changing and stimulating teaching.

Closing Thoughts

If children are to use the tools of mathematical thinking to solve problems, then the classroom environment has to encourage children to explore and question. We want to engage children in the process of solving problems to learn the value of using strategies and pursuing problems over time. Skills are learned as part of the process, not as ends in themselves. When children solve real-world problems, they engage in mathematical reasoning and thinking and construct their own knowledge of mathematical relationships. They become mathematical thinkers.

Resources for Mathematical Thinking

Teacher Resource Books

About Teaching Mathematics: A K-8 Resource. Burns, Marilyn. White Plains, NY: Cuisenaire Company of America, Inc., 1992.

"Arithmetic Teacher," monthly math magazine. Reston, VA: National Council of Teachers of Mathematics.

A Collection of Math Lessons From Grades 1 Through 3. Burns, Marilyn, and Bonnie Tank. New Rochelle, NY: Cuisenaire Company of America, Inc., 1988.

Curriculum and Evaluation STANDARDS for School Mathematics. Reston, VA: National Council of Teachers of Mathematics, 1989.

Developing Number Concepts Using Unifix Cubes. Richardson, Kathy. Menlo Park, CA: Addison-Wesley Publishing Co., 1989.

Everyday Mathematics, First, Second, and Third Grade. The University of Chicago School Mathematics Project. Evanston, IL: Everyday Learning Corporation, 1992.

I Hate Mathematics Book. Burns, Marilyn. Boston: Little, Brown, and Company, 1975.

The Good Time Math Event Books. Burns, Marilyn. Oak Lawn, IL: Creative Publications, 1977.

Learning to Think in a Math Lab. Charbonneau, Manon P. Denver: National Association of Independent Schools, 1971.

Making Numbers Make Sense. Richhart, Ron. Menlo Park, CA: Addison, Wesley, 1994.

Math for Smarty Pants. Burns, Marilyn. Boston: Little, Brown, and Company, 1978.

Math Through Children's Literature: Making the NCTM Standards Come Alive. Brandon, Hall, Taylor, Englewood, CO: Teachers Idea Press, 1990.

Mathematics… A Way of Thinking. Baratta-Lortin, Robert. Menlo Park, CA: Addison-Wesley Publishing Co., 1977.

Math in Stride, Level 1-3. Menlo Park, CA: Addison-Wesley Publishing Co., 1988.

Mathematics Their Way. Baratta-Lortin, Mary. Menlo Park, CA: Addison-Wesley Publishing Co., 1976.

Professional STANDARDS for Teaching Mathematics. Reston, VA: National Council of Teachers of Mathematics, 1991.

Wollygoggles and Other Creatures, O'Brien, Thomas C. New Rochelle, NY: Cusinenaire Company, 1980.

Young Children Continue to Reinvent Arithmetic: 2nd Grade, Implications of Piaget's Theory. Kamii, Constance, and Linda Leslie Joseph. New York: Teachers College Press, 1989.

Young Children Reinvent Arithmetic: Implications of Piaget Theory. Kamii, Constance, and Georgia DeClark. New York: Teachers College Press, 1985.

Activity Books

The following materials are most easily ordered through catalogs.

Available from Creative Publications: 5040 West 111th Street, Oak Lawn, IL 60454.

Hands On Attributes

Hands On Geoboards

Hands On Pattern Blocks

Hands On Tangrams

Hands On Unifix Cubes

Pattern Blocks for Primary People

Picturing Addition

Picturing Numeration

Problem Solver 1 & 2

Tangram Patterns

Tangramath

Available from Cuisenaire Company of America: P.O. Box 5026, White Plains, NY 10602-5026.

Cuisenaire Riddles

From Here to There with Cuisenaire

Idea Book for Cuisenaire Rods at the Primary Level

Other Catalogs

Dale Seymour Publications, P.O. Box 10888, Palo Alto, CA 94303-0878.

Didax, Inc. Educational Resources, 395 Main Street, Rowley, MA 01969.

ETA Mathematics Catalog, A Universe of Math Manipulatives, 620 Lakeview Parkway, Vernon Hills, IL 60061.

References

De La Cruz, Yolanda. 1994. Considerations in Teaching Mathematics to Young Children, *ACEI Focus on Early Childhood,* 3 (Spring).

Burns, Marilyn and Bonnie Tank. 1988. *A Collection of Math Lessons: From Grades 1 Through 3*. New Rochelle, NY: Cuisenaire Company of America.

National Council of Teachers of Mathematics. 1989. *Curriculum and Evaluation STANDARDS for School Mathematics*. Reston, VA: National Council of Teachers of Mathematics.

SOCIAL STUDIES

Social studies is the study of people—how people live, work, get along with others, solve problems, and are shaped by their surroundings. As children investigate topics related to themselves, their families, and their communities, they gain an increasing understanding of the world around them and an appreciation for the importance of culture and heritage.

Children learn about social studies before they come to school and as part of everyday life in the classroom.

> The knowledge and understanding that students already have about life come from the social and cultural communities in which they live and learn both inside and outside of school. These understandings form the platform upon which they currently stand and from which they will launch themselves into the future. The curriculum then must always be connected to as well as go forward from the students' life experiences (Short and Burke 1991, 34-35).

When the classroom functions as a community, children learn first hand about responsible citizenship: how to make choices; how to accept different points of view and different ways of thinking; how to treat others with respect and develop tolerance. They gain basic knowledge about living in a democracy where all individuals have rights and responsibilities to their community, and where all people can express and feel proud of their cultural heritage. Children also acquire social studies knowledge in the context of a long-term study. Topics that interest children lead them to ask questions, actively investigate issues, and make connections between what they are learning and their daily lives. In the process of their investigations, children learn how to be researchers and they become experts on topics related to everyday life.

Children Exploring Social Studies

How do primary grade teachers make the study of self, family, and community come alive in the classroom so that children are motivated to learn? The following examples from three classrooms provide a window on how children explore topics in social studies.

*A **first grade class** is studying the topic of "Families." The teacher, Ms. Wong, encourages the children to bring family photographs from home, engages the children in discussions about their families, and reads stories and poetry about families. The class writes letters inviting family members to be interviewed about where they grew up and the kinds of work they do. The children draw and paint family portraits, create family trees, and make maps and blueprints of rooms in their houses. Children make graphs about numbers of people living in their household, and chart on a world map where their family members were born, including themselves, their parents, and grandparents.*

To study their families, these first graders are engaged in first-hand research, collecting data by observing, interviewing, reading, and conversing. They are learning about size and configurations of families, how family members earn a living, the roles of family members today and in the past, what is eaten for meals, and how holidays are celebrated. Their constant interaction and exchange of information and ideas expands their knowledge and broadens their understanding of family structures. Ms. Wong encourages the children to think about similarities and differences among their families. The children have many opportunities to represent what they are learning and to reflect on new understandings.

*Ms. Bannon's **second grade class** is investigating bridges as part of their study of the local community. At a meeting, she asks the children what they already know about the three bridges in their town and what they want to find out. Their first trip to see one of the bridges provides them with some answers to their questions and generates new ones. Following the trip, the children reflect on what they observed: boats on the river, factories along the shore, and the elaborate construction of the bridge. Some children decide to build a model of the bridge and others to paint pictures of scenes on and around the bridge. A few children go to the library to find books about how bridges are built.*

During this study of their community, Ms. Bannon knows that the children will learn about rivers, bridges, transportation and travel, industry, history, and geography. She has created a framework for the study and lets the specific direction come from children's interests. By first providing the children with opportunities to express what they know and what they are curious about, Ms. Bannon generates interest in the study and encourages the children to take responsibility for their learning. By approaching the study of community through a topic that is in the children's immediate environment, trips can be used as primary sources of information. The children review their questions and consider new ones prior to each trip. In this way, Ms. Bannon establishes a clear purpose for the children's learning as well as a procedure for collecting new data. Follow-up activities, such as drawing, building, painting, writing, graphing, and discussions enable children to represent and reflect on what they are learning.

> *As part of their study of local history, Mr. Lucas's **third grade class** collaborates with residents at a senior citizens' home. They make regular weekly visits to the home for eight weeks. During the first two visits, children interview their senior "partners" about their childhoods. The children decide to create written and illustrated biographies of their partners. During a class discussion following one visit, Kian remarks that since he has been going to the seniors' home, he has observed that only a few places in town have ramps for wheelchairs. His distress, expressed with the passion typical of eight year olds, is shared by his classmates. Responding to their concern and interest, Mr. Lucas temporarily shifts the curriculum plan. He asks the children to think about ways they can learn more about this problem. The children decide to conduct a survey of the town for wheelchair accessibility. Based on their findings they will decide what action to take.*

Mr. Lucas has designed a study in which children interact with the elder citizens of the community. Many children in the class either have no living grandparents or their grandparents live far away from the community. By establishing relationships with senior citizens, Mr. Lucas knows children can learn first-hand about the history of their community. He also wants children to gain understanding and empathy for the older people in the community. He uses Kian's concern as the catalyst to help the children become more aware and involved in community issues.

In each of these classrooms, social studies learning is active, purposeful, and connected to real life issues and experiences. Children study topics in depth and become "experts." Rather than simply reading about families, communities, and local history in a text book, their questions about the world around them serve as the basis for exploration and research. Trips, interviews with people, artifacts, videos, films, and books are used as sources of information that allow children to acquire conceptual understandings as they develop the skills involved in conducting research.

What Children Learn

The social studies curriculum is a blend of content—self, family, and community —and process—learning how to be researchers, critical thinkers, and active members of a classroom community. Children construct knowledge of social studies by engaging in long-term studies on topics that interest them. Through their studies, they learn about themselves, about others, and about their community. They find out about how people live and work. They begin to explore culture and heritage. Actively researching topics enables children in the primary grades to develop the skills of critical thinking, reflecting, questioning, searching out information, and debating ideas and opinions. And by participating in a classroom community, children learn what it means to live in a democratic society.

Components of the Social Studies Curriculum

As children in the primary grades explore topics related to self, family, and community, they are learning broad concepts we have organized into six components:

- human similarities and differences,
- basic human needs,
- human interdependence,
- rights and responsibilities,
- people and the places they live, and
- people and the past.

The following chart outlines what children might learn in social studies by participating in a classroom community and studying topics that address each component. An understanding of each of these components and the ways in which children can investigate topics can be very helpful to teachers in planning the social studies curriculum.

Overview of the Social Studies Curriculum

Components	Children Learn to:
Human Similarities and Differences	• Demonstrate understanding of self and others as unique individuals • Recognize common and unique human characteristics • Identify similarities and differences in family structures, lifestyles, ways of communicating, customs, and habits • Recognize instances of bias • Compare and appreciate similarities and differences in cultural heritage
Basic Human Needs	• Recognize basic needs of people: food, clothing, and shelter (safety, security, sense of belonging) • Recognize that money and other forms of economic exchange may be used to obtain goods and services
Human Interdependence	• Describe roles in families and communities • Describe how people depend on one another for goods and services • Describe the kinds of work people do and the skills and tools needed to perform these jobs
Rights and Responsibilities	• Identify the need for rules at home and in school • Recognize how laws protect rights and property • Recognize reasons for leadership and cooperation, and methods of group decision-making such as elections • Use strategies for resolving conflicts peacefully
People and the Places They Live	• Identify ways the environment shapes our lives (e.g., in terms of transportation, housing, jobs) • Recognize the effects of climate on the way people live • Identify ways people get from place to place and ways they transport goods and information • Identify ways people rely on environmental resources • Identify some ways people affect the environment • Recognize that maps are symbols for actual places • Make maps • Use simple mapping symbols
People and the Past	• Demonstrate some understanding of chronological time • Identify the sequence of their own lives and that of family members • Recognize the influence of one's heritage on present day living

Human Similarities and Differences

Recognizing and respecting differences in gender, race, ethnicity, religion, ability, age, family composition and life style is an important component of the social studies curriculum. Helping children to understand human diversity includes creating opportunities for them to see events and ideas from the perspective of others.

Children learn about human similarities and differences by sharing information about themselves and listening to what others have to say. When teachers are willing to relate stories from their own lives, children feel more comfortable about telling their own stories. These sharing times often lead to interesting discussions about social issues. As children read and listen to stories about other people, study photographs, watch videos, take field trips, and work on projects, teachers can encourage them to recognize and appreciate similarities and differences. Some of these differences include how people express emotions, the size and composition of families, the types of houses people live in, what they eat, and the kinds of work they do.

Learning about similarities and differences helps children recognize and appreciate diversity in thinking, feeling, acting, and promotes understanding of the many different influences that shape people's lives. When children see that the way they and their families conduct their lives is valued, they gain confidence and self-esteem.

Basic Human Needs

Children investigate how people go about their daily lives by first examining their own actions and then gradually researching how their families and other community members live. They begin to see that basic physical and social needs—safety, security, food, clothing, and shelter—are consistent among all people, regardless of when and where they live. Children can consider the difference between people's "needs" and "wants." Questions that stimulate thinking about basic needs include:

- What do each of us need to live?
- How do we get what we need?
- What happens if we can't get what we need?

As they get older, children compare their actions and behaviors in daily living to those of people who lived long ago and those who live in other places. While basic needs are universal, the ways in which different people meet them vary. This understanding occurs gradually as children study many different topics over the course of several years.

Human Interdependence

Children in the primary grades are interested in how people work together to get what they need. The concept of human interdependence includes understanding how people depend on others to accomplish tasks, how they divide labor and share responsibility, and how they exchange goods and services.

As children explore how goods are produced and services performed, they learn about the world of work and acquire an appreciation for the different jobs people perform. Questions that children can investigate include:

- Who provides our families with the goods and services we need?
- How do people work together to produce goods and services?
- Who produces them?
- How do we pay for these goods?
- What are the services needed by our community?

Whether the study involves a food store, a construction site, immigration, or communities long ago, children can examine how people get what they need and how they accomplish goals through interdependent relationships.

Rights and Responsibilities

For children in the primary grades, fairness, individual rights, and adhering to rules are issues of great significance. As their sense of justice and fairness grows, they are ready to consider the reasons for establishing rules.

Building a sense of community in the classroom provides first-hand knowledge of rights and responsibilities in society. Children learn how respect, cooperation, and responsibility are essential to community life. When they help to establish classroom rules that ensure the safety and protection of each member of the class, they are learning why communities need rules and laws. Classroom jobs give children a chance to do tasks that maintain the community and to learn that all jobs are important. Opportunities to engage in group decision-making and conflict resolution help children become responsible citizens. Children can then begin to understand how the larger community works together to make decisions, establish rules, and elect leaders.

People and the Places They Live

How people's lives are shaped by their physical environment is an important social studies concept. Children in the primary grades can begin to understand the relationship between people and their location by exploring answers to questions such as the following:

- How do the physical features of our location affect our lives?
- How does climate affect how people live?
- In what ways do the natural resources that are available in a particular locale influence the types of houses people build or the foods they eat?

Children in first grade can explore the answers to questions such as these in the context of their own environment. By age eight, children can begin to compare their own ways of living to how people lived in the past and to how they live in other places.

As issues related to the use of the world's resources are of increasing concern, the topics explored in social studies can help children develop an appreciation for natural resources and their importance to human life. In the primary grades, children begin to learn about how people use (and abuse) the environment. For example, they might investigate how houses are built, how water is used, or how factories dispose of waste. Opportunities to raise their own questions and to express their concerns will encourage children to see how preserving the environment is important to their lives.

Another aspect of understanding people and the environment is learning how locations are recorded symbolically on maps. For young children, this means making real maps. Constructing models and block buildings of real places is one way children make maps. Drawing maps of real places—the classroom, the school, a room in their house—increases children's understanding of how to represent location using symbols. In addition, children can explore different types of maps and globes.

People and the Past

An important reason to learn about the past is that it connects us to our heritage. Who we are is in part a reflection of the history of our families. Where our parents, grandparents, and great-grandparents lived and what they experienced influences our values, ways of interacting, and how we interpret events.

Young children do not learn best about the past through stories of who came on the Mayflower. Such an approach begins too far in the past and will most likely not represent the families of children in your class. Instead, understanding the past begins with an examination of children's personal life histories. Writing personal narratives about memories of being younger, making family scrapbooks, and constructing personal time lines fosters a beginning understanding of history. Interviewing family members about their childhoods leads children to realize that they are a part of a history and helps them develop an appreciation for their heritage.

Children gain an increasing appreciation for the past by hearing and reading stories of growing up at another time period. They can relate their own experiences to those of other children and begin to appreciate how life would have been different if they had lived during another time period. How did people communicate without telephones or write without computers? What did they do for entertainment and news before television and radio existed? How did families get food without supermarkets and cook without gas or electric stoves? When children make up skits, put on costumes, and recreate scenes from long ago, they begin to acquire an appreciation and understanding of history.

Skills for Social Studies Inquiry

The skills children acquire as they investigate social studies topics teach them how to be researchers: to raise questions, seek information, and think critically about what they discover in their investigations. Researchers begin any study by identifying what they already know about a topic and what questions they want to answer. Articulating knowledge and asking questions helps them to focus their thinking. Having identified their questions, researchers determine the best approaches to obtaining answers: making on-site observations (trips), interviewing experts, reading books, watching videos, studying artifacts and maps, and so on.

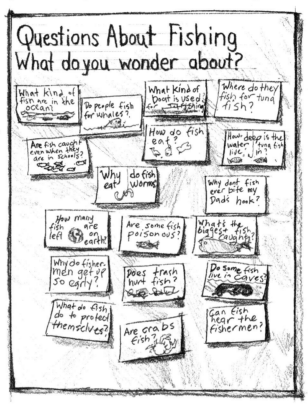

The process of conducting first-hand research involves the same "detective" skills used by anthropologists and archaeologists. Children learn how to look closely at an object or an event under study and pick up clues to help them answer their questions. Teachers continually guide children in using research skills to find answers to the questions that interest them.

Ms. Frisher's third grade class is studying the history of New York City. To find out what New Amsterdam was like, they examine old photographs and maps. They discover that the area where their school is located was originally farm land and that New Amsterdam was located in lower Manhattan. On a walking tour of this area of New York, the children note that the names of many streets are Dutch. In a class discussion on their findings, they debate whether the names of streets represent Dutch surnames or whether they are Dutch words that have specific meanings (such as the type of stores that existed at the time). "How could we find out?" asks Ms. Frisher. "We could look up the words in a Dutch/English dictionary," suggests LaShon. She and Carly go to the school library and return empty handed. "This school doesn't have a Dutch dictionary," they report. "We could call some book stores to find one," suggests Carly. Several children comb the yellow pages, discovering a listing for foreign book stores. They phone numerous stores before finding what they need to continue their research.

A central part of conducting research is comparing findings, which children do when they discuss topics under study. In daily meetings, teachers guide children to talk about aspects of a study and help children to think critically about what they are learning. Discussions also help children clarify their thinking. Because social studies involves learning about people, many questions have no single answer. Reality is a blend of multiple perspectives—each person's view of reality has merit. Sharing their own views, hearing other points of view, and getting information from many sources enable children to construct a logical understanding of a topic.

Children who have had opportunities to conduct first-hand research on social studies topics begin to internalize both research and critical-thinking skills. When the teacher introduces a new topic, these children are ready to talk about what they know and what questions they have. They begin to think in categories: workers, equipment, animal life, stores, vehicles. They have lots of ideas about ways to investigate the topic and how to show what they are learning. Children who develop these process skills in the early grades are learning "how to learn," a skill they will use throughout their lives.

How One Topic Can Address All Components

Each of the six components (broad concepts) of the social studies curriculum can be addressed in the context of a good social studies topic. Rather than focusing on a particular component, it is much more practical to focus on topics for studies that will allow children to experience these central concepts over and over within the context of many different investigation experiences (just as they do in science).

To illustrate how a topic might address several components of the social studies curriculum, let's consider a long-term study on "How People Communicate." During this several-month-long study, children could explore communication in relation to themselves, their families, and their local community. They might take trips to the telephone company, a local newspaper, a local radio station, and the post office. They might invite a sign language teacher, a computer technician, or a television producer to visit the class. Some children might write and broadcast a weekly radio show over the school's intercom system; others could publish a weekly newspaper. Depending on the age and interests of the children, the teacher could address all components of the social studies curriculum as outlined below:

To explore **human similarities and differences** children could:

- collect interview data about how different members of their families communicate with friends and relatives (e.g., visiting in person, talking on the phone, sending letters and faxes);
- explore different languages spoken in their homes and by people they know;
- learn some sign language;
- compare ways people of different ages communicate;

- compare today's methods of communication to those used in the past and in other places.

To consider issues related to **basic human needs** children could:

- discuss how people communicate their needs and feelings;
- identify ways to call for emergency help;
- investigate different ways people use communication to get food, clothing, and housing.

To relate the topic of communication to **human interdependence** children could:

- study various local work places providing communication services (e.g., telephone company, local radio station, neighborhood newspaper);
- consider how people have to work together to perform their jobs within various communications industries;
- conduct interviews with people who work at a public radio station to find out how they get money to operate (e.g., fundraising, contributions, subscriptions).

To think about **rights and responsibilities** related to communication children could:

- have a discussion about rules people might need for public and private communication;
- review classroom rules for discussions;
- discuss the concept of "freedom of speech."

To explore how communication is linked to **people and places** children could:

- compare newspapers from different cities and towns;
- consider why some people have satellite dishes;
- investigate how people in different places communicate in emergencies;
- interview people who use CB radios, car phones, or beepers to find out why and when they use them.

To examine how communication relates to **people and the past** children could:

- interview their parents and other older family members to find out what methods of communication they used as children; compare these methods with those used today;
- research inventions related to communication;
- read biographies of inventors of various methods of communication.

As children investigate these topics they gain a deeper understanding and appreciation for their world. They come to appreciate the complexities of everyday life. They ask "why" and "how" questions about their immediate, familiar environment. When children are given opportunities to think critically about their world in the primary grades, they are likely to apply these skills and understandings to future learning and living.

Organizing the Social Studies Curriculum

To address the content of social studies—self, family, and community—and support the development of critical thinking and research skills, teachers organize their curriculum in two ways. First, they make social studies a part of everyday life. Secondly, they select topics for long-term studies that will engage children and hold their interest.

Making Social Studies Part of Everyday Life in the Classroom

In the United States, a long-term goal of education is to help children see themselves as members of a democratic society in which individuals have rights, obligations, and responsibilities. Acquiring the values that underlie a democratic society—respecting oneself and others, and accepting responsibility for the community and the environment —is the foundation for learning about group membership.

Everyday life in the classroom can be a powerful "textbook" for the social studies curriculum. It is the setting in which children can acquire skills in human relationships and learn about respect and diversity. The approaches teachers take to help children know one another and to build a classroom community are part of social studies.

Knowing the Children

Learning about children in the class and helping children learn about one another is the basis for constructing curriculum and the beginning of social studies. Children learn about the individual qualities of their peers by:

- conducting interviews and surveys about one another;
- sharing personal experiences;
- exchanging greetings in many different languages;
- preparing snacks that reflect their home cultures;
- creating displays in the classroom that reflect their own interests and family life.

Building a Classroom Community

Children learn about responsible group behavior by participating in a classroom community. Group discussions about classroom concerns foster acceptance and respect for others as children recognize that different people have different opinions and different ways of thinking and expressing themselves.

Ms. Hall, a first grade teacher, is concerned about Angela who has been the target of much ridicule and rejection. After trying to deal with the problem on an individual, as-needed basis without success, Ms. Hall decides to bring up the problem at a class meeting. She talks with Angela's parents about the plan and they agree. She then discusses her idea with Angela and asks if she wants to be present at the meeting. Angela decides she would rather not participate.

Ms. Hall starts the meeting by saying, "I feel the need for all of us to work together to solve a class problem. I've noticed that Angela is treated differently than other members of our class. I wonder if other people have noticed this." Every hand in the class shoots up and the children are all eager to share their ideas. Because interest in the topic is so strong, Ms. Hall allows every child to speak. "It seems as if all of you have noticed the same problem I have," says Ms. Hall. "Let's see if we can think of some things we can do to help Angela and all of us to feel more comfortable in our class. I'll write down your ideas so we can discuss them." After the list is made, Ms. Hall says, "This is a good list of ways we can help everyone feel comfortable in our class. I'm going to post this list so we can all remember." In the weeks following the meeting, Ms. Hall notices an improvement in how children relate to one another and Angela seems happier.

A sensitive teacher can guide children to think about problems in daily life and consider solutions. In this way, children begin to see how individuals can make a difference and contribute to making the world a better place. As described in the chapter on Building a Classroom Community, teachers foster children's social studies learning by:

- encouraging participation in group decision-making;
- involving children in establishing rules and consequences;
- giving children opportunities to express opinions in a public setting;
- using meetings as a forum for children to listen to the ideas and opinions of others;
- having meetings and using role plays to discuss conflict resolution;
- comparing class rituals to those in various cultures;
- discussing differences in ways that people communicate;
- encouraging children to respect differences in general;
- teaching children how to work collaboratively with classmates and/or work with partners in a younger class;
- conducting polls and elections;
- helping children to respect public spaces by doing daily jobs to keep the classroom neat.

As valuable as a classroom community is for teaching social studies lessons, children also need opportunities to conduct first-hand research on topics that interest them. Long-term studies provide the vehicle for social studies explorations.

Selecting Topics for Long-Term Studies in Social Studies

In the process of participating in a long-term study, children become "experts" on topics that engage their interest. If the topic is appropriate, children understand the purpose of what they are learning. They are able to raise relevant questions and to go about finding answers. In the process of their investigations, children use and refine the skills they are learning in other subjects. They become researchers who know how to seek out information, think critically about what they observe, and share information with others.

The first step in planning a study is to select an appropriate topic. The six components of the social studies curriculum provide a wealth of ideas. It's not possible for a teacher to plan an in-depth study on more than two or three topics in social studies in any given year, so how do you choose?

Teachers select appropriate topics by considering children's developmental abilities, their interests and experiences, as well as the resources in the community. A teacher's interest in the topic is also essential. Your enthusiasm (or lack of it) will have a profound effect on the children and on your own level of satisfaction.

Developmental Considerations

The social studies curriculum—self, family, and community—is not a continuum of content: in first grade, children do not simply study "self" and in second grade "family" and so on. Rather, children this age continually think about how what they are learning applies to themselves, to their families, and to the larger community. Developmental considerations are a primary factor in selecting appropriate topics for studies.

We know that children's thinking and learning changes over time. First graders, for example, tend to be egocentric in their thinking; they rely on their own personal experiences as their frame of reference. What they can see, touch, and hear captures their attention. For them the idea of community is best understood in terms of the family unit, and then the school. Studying families for first graders means:

- researching what *our* families eat and trying some different kinds of food for snack;
- listing the stores where *our* families shop, visiting them, and then building models of those shops with blocks or boxes;
- recording and defining the jobs *our* family members do and visiting them at their workplaces or inviting them to the classroom to find out more.

Following these personal investigations, first graders can begin to compare their own personal experiences with what others do.

Second and third graders, gradually able to think about what is not in their immediate experience, continue to relate their learning to what is familiar. For example, if they are beginning to understand about different jobs, why people work, and the interdependence of goods and services in their own communities, they will be motivated to investigate the types of jobs that exist in a different environment or in the past. Children living in rural settings can study the city and vice versa. By third grade, a study of families might involve learning about immigration and genealogy, expanding children's thinking beyond their own experience in terms of time and place.

How children learn about human interdependence provides another example of developmental differences. First graders can study how people work together to accomplish goals in their families, in school, or in a particular industry. By second grade, children's thinking abilities have expanded so that they can investigate multiple services provided within the city, comparing how each is accomplished. By third grade, children might compare services available in the community today with what was available in the past. As children get older, the need to use the self as a point of reference becomes less pronounced. These evolving abilities are outlined in the chart below.

Learning About Self, Family, and Community in the Primary Grades

Developmental Considerations	First Grade	Second Grade	Third Grade
Degree of Egocentricity	Must have direct relation to the self	Can be vicarious, yet familiar	Can move beyond personal experience both in time and place
Area of Study	Self, family, school, neighborhood, immediate city or town	Immediate community, state, and country	Other cultures and/or other eras
Degree of Complexity	Basic concepts are applied to familiar groups	Multiple concepts can be applied to familiar groups	Multiple concepts can be applied to unfamiliar groups

Children's Interests and Experiences

Topics that inherently interest children will be more likely to engage their attention over time. Most six year olds tend to be interested in work—who does it and how. They readily focus on the particular—the workers in the apple orchard or the sanitation workers. Seven year olds' curiosity is often captured by systems—how things fit together. For example, what are the various services provided within the community, or what are all the different methods of transportation used in the city? Eight years olds begin to wonder about the past—how things that are familiar to them looked long ago.

Children's interests also grow out of their life experiences. If children live in a rural community, a study of subway systems is not relevant to their experience. However, after first learning about transportation methods where they live, they can consider what possibilities exist elsewhere and why. Children are usually interested in significant current events. For example, following a local flood or earthquake, children are likely to be curious about related topics.

A study that begins with a familiar, tangible project will be more likely to grab children's interest. For example, in a study of trash, you may begin by asking children to keep track of what goes into a particular wastebasket each day at home. After making comparisons between the contents of different household trash containers, children can then think about who picks up the trash, where it goes, and how it gets there. They may compare which rooms produce the most trash, what different households consider trash, or the difference between household, school, and industrial trash. Eventually, children may consider how different places dispose of their trash or what people did with their waste before municipal sanitation departments existed.

Relying on the Immediate Environment

Selecting social studies topics that take advantage of the resources available in your school's environment is practical and meets the criteria outlined in the preceding chart. A study of a park is meaningful if there is one close by for children to visit. A study of dairy farms is an excellent way for children to learn about food production and distribution— if children can visit one. A study of a construction site enables children to learn how buildings are built, who builds them, and what materials are used—if the children can take repeated trips to check the progress of an actual building project.

The concepts children learn in social studies can be explored through a wide range of topics. Think about places in or near your school where children can see workers on the job, goods being manufactured or distributed, or various forms of transportation. Your immediate environment can be your "textbook" for social studies.

Questions to Consider and Sample Topics

A good social studies topic is one that allows you to plan a wide range of experiences so that children can learn by investigating, representing their knowledge, and reflecting on what they have learned.

To identify opportunities for **investigation**, ask yourself these questions:

- What do children already know about the subject?
- Can the children conduct first-hand observations?
- What artifacts are available for children to observe (photographs, blue prints, site documents)? Are there collections to be gathered?
- Can the children conduct interviews?
- Can the children take trips to conduct first-hand investigations?
- Are there experts on the topic who can visit the classroom?
- Are there read-aloud books available on the topic?
- Are there books available that children can read independently?
- Do I have access to videos or filmstrips related to the study?
- Are there songs that relate to the subject?
- What open-ended questions that encourage investigations will I be able to ask as part of this study?

To identify opportunities for children to **represent** their learning, ask yourself:

- What art projects lend themselves to this study (drawings, paintings, collages)?
- Can the children build models as part of this study?
- Will children be writing interviews? What else can they write?
- Are there opportunities to make charts, graphs, or maps?
- Can children do skits or plays related to the subject?

To identify opportunities for children to **reflect** on what they are learning, ask yourself:

- Can children keep a learning log or journal as a way to record what they are learning?
- How can children return to their questions and assess whether or not they have found answers?
- When will time be allocated for children to reflect on their projects related to the study?

The following is a list of sample social studies topics that relate to self, family, and community.

Our School
Houses in the Neighborhood
Stores and Services in the Neighborhood
Buildings in the Community
Public Buildings in the Community
Roads and Bridges: Who and What Travels on Them
What's Underground in Our Community
Factories Along the River
Bridges and Tunnels
Transportation
Food: From Origin to Table
Waterworks
Garbage and Sewage
Recycling
How People Communicate
Family Histories
Recreation Places
Organizations in the Community

Use this list as a starting point and add topics that you, as well as the children, will enjoy.

Allocating Time for Social Studies

To ensure that social studies is included in the curriculum, teachers must allow time in the daily schedule. Meetings are the forum for many lively discussions on social studies topics. Time is also needed for trips, project activities, and work times.

Meetings

Discussions about issues related to community life or a social studies topic take place daily. Meetings are used to introduce a study, to plan investigation and representation activities, to bring back information following activities, and to exchange new ideas.

The initial questions that children pose in the introductory meeting for a study form the basis for their on-going investigations. Throughout the study, teachers use meetings to review the list of questions children have generated and to discuss what they have found out and what they still want to know.

Trips

Try to plan at least one or two trips related to each topic of study. If the topic relates to what is in the immediate environment, taking trips is a manageable endeavor. For example, in a study of the school building, a trip may simply be a walk to another floor of the building. If children are studying a river or the local park within walking distance of the school, several trips can be planned to conduct investigations.

When you plan a trip, it is a good idea to visit the place by yourself first. In this way, you can plan how to focus children's investigations and, at the same time, determine logistics for the trip. Then spend some time preparing children for what they will see. In a meeting, you might ask children what they think they might see. Have children reflect on the questions they have listed and consider which ones might be answered on the trip. Following the trip, children can discuss what they saw and plan how they will represent what they learned.

Using clipboards or trip boards helps children organize what they see on a trip. Trip boards are pieces of cardboard on which paper is stapled so that children can record what they find out on their trips. When children have a convenient way to record impressions and information, they can refer to their notes when they return to the classroom.

Project Time

If possible, try to schedule several large blocks of time (an hour and a half) each week for children to immerse themselves in projects related to a social studies topic. During this time, children can work in small groups on projects such as building a model, writing a report, painting a mural, making graphs, constructing maps, or preparing a play.

Large blocks of time are needed for projects because children often have to get set up, talk and negotiate with one another, complete tasks, and clean up. It is sometimes helpful to allow fifteen or twenty minutes on the day before a scheduled project time so that children can do some of their planning.

Regularly Scheduled Work Times for Social Studies

In addition to meetings and project times, you can schedule work times for social studies or integrate social studies content into work times for other subjects. Some examples are:

- using writing workshop times for research writing about a social studies topic;
- reading aloud from a chapter book related to the topic;
- conducting surveys, collecting information, and making graphs related to information about the topic during a math work time;
- reading from informational books with a partner;
- using a math time to design scale models and maps;
- using choice time for children to pursue independent interests related to the social studies topic.

Appropriate topics and time to explore concepts in depth enable children to see relationships between their own life experiences and the events, people, and places they are studying. Social studies explorations provide opportunities for teachers to help children learn to value what takes place in their own communities every day and to understand the complexity of the work people do. Without these opportunities to learn social studies content, children could easily take for granted many of the systems and people that make communities work.

A Long-Term Study in Action: Our School

In the chapter on Guiding Children's Learning, we outlined the steps for planning long-term studies. Here we show how a teacher uses these steps to think through and plan a long-term study on "Our School."

Selecting a Topic

Ms. Lourdes teaches a first and second grade multi-age class. Using the guidelines for topic selection, she decides that a study of the school is appropriate for her class for the following reasons:

- The topic is relevant to children's lives. Because the school is familiar to her students, Ms. Lourdes is certain that they will be able to offer ideas when she asks them what they already know about the school. Their interests and questions will shape the direction of the investigation experiences she devises.
- Resources and materials are readily available. Ms. Lourdes can use trips as a primary method for children to gather information. Everyone in the building is an expert; there are many opportunities for interviews.

- The topic permits children to think, question, and solve interesting problems through active investigation. Children's work will include designing research questions and seeking answers by taking trips around the building for first-hand observations, conducting interviews and surveys to collect data, and having discussions to share information with one another.

- What children learn from this study can be applied to future living and learning because it is practical and fundamental to any study of community workers. Main ideas include:

    —many different people are needed to run an institution;

    —workers need a range of skills and responsibilities to do their jobs;

    —workers use a variety of tools and machines to accomplish their jobs.

The children will also learn basic research skills which can then be used in their subsequent investigations of community workers. These skills include:

    —thinking about what is already known about a subject;

    —deciding what questions will be explored;

    —planning and conducting interviews;

    —taking notes during trips or when visitors come to the class;

    —reviewing site documents (e.g., in their school study these might include employee handbooks, time sheets, and job descriptions).

- The topic addresses curriculum objectives. The school district's curriculum guide calls for a study of community workers. The school study will be the first of several places where children can investigate the work of people in their community.

- The topic can be explored by children in different ways over an extended period of time.

Confident that her topic is a good one, Ms. Lourdes moves on to the next steps of her planning.

Getting Ready for the Study

Having selected a topic, Ms. Lourdes makes a brainstorming web. Her categories include: places, people, equipment, and activities. She has been teaching at the school for several years so she is already quite familiar with her subject. However, she takes a preliminary walk around the building, looking at it from a child's perspective.

She makes a chart of ideas about how the study can address objectives in math, language and literacy, and arts and technology. She considers having the children study how water gets into the building as part of a science study. This decision will wait until the study is well underway and she has assessed the children's interests.

Ms. Lourdes considers some open-ended questions and discussion starters that she can direct to the whole group:

- What are some of the different kinds of work that are done in this building?
- Let's think about the different kinds of machines used in our school.
- Let's brainstorm a list of all the things we could count in this building.

Materials which she collects include books, poetry, and a poster of a one-room schoolhouse. She speaks with school personnel (cafeteria and custodial workers, secretary, principal, resource teachers, librarian, audiovisual specialist) to find out if they are willing to be interviewed by the children. She also sets up a visit to another school so that the children can make comparisons. In addition, she arranges for the children to have pen pals in a school in another part of the country. Both classes will study their schools and the children will exchange information about what they are learning.

Introducing the Study to the Children

Ms. Lourdes knows that the most essential part of introducing a study is generating the children's interest. She does this by putting a few books around the room and hanging the poster of a one-room schoolhouse. On another wall is a blueprint she has found of their school building. She begins the first meeting by asking children to brainstorm a list of all the people who work in the school. Then she asks them to look around the room for clues about what they will be studying. She follows with the set of questions that begin all studies.

- What do you already know?
- What do you want to know?
- How can we find these things out?

She takes the class on the first trip for an overview of the building and uses the opportunity to teach them how she expects them to use trips to gather information. This includes both research techniques such as thinking in advance about what will be seen, or how to keep track of what is observed, and considering ways to document what is learned. Following the trip, she asks the children if they have new questions as a result of looking at the school through an "investigator's" eyes.

Inviting Families to Participate in the Study

Two of the parents in Ms. Lourdes' class attended schools in other countries where their experiences were very different from those of the children. One other parent is a junior high school principal, and another a teacher in an older grade. Ms. Lourdes decides to have the children interview members of their families about their school experiences. She will then suggest inviting family members to come and share their experiences and perspectives with the children.

Listening to and Learning with Children

Ms. Lourdes arranges for the children to take trips around the school building with a partner and in small groups with a parent volunteer so that they can conduct interviews and surveys. Their destinations are based on the questions generated by the children. For example, the children want to know the total number of classrooms, children, workers, pets, or public spaces. They take trips to observe the different types of bulletin boards, doors, and windows in the building. They visit the custodian, the librarian, and the cafeteria workers to find out about the jobs these people do, the skills they have, and the machines and tools they use. They interview the secretaries, teachers, principal, and children in different grades.

Children record and represent what they learn throughout the study. They recreate the school using blocks and make maps of different locations in the school, including the classroom, the hallway, and eventually, each floor of the school. They draw and paint scenes from the school. Based on the interviews, children document their findings in various forms. Counting and surveying experiences are used to make graphs and charts as records of the information collected. In the process of doing these activities, Ms. Lourdes talks with them about what they have learned and how they want to express it.

Ms. Lourdes begins every new investigation activity with a meeting in which the children collectively brainstorm what they want to know, what they wonder about, and what they anticipate finding out from their investigation. Afterwards, the children gather again to reflect on what they have found, comparing their predictions with their discoveries. As children work on projects, Ms. Lourdes invites them to share their work with one another. By doing this, children give one another valuable feedback, often making useful suggestions. In addition, Ms. Lourdes lets the children critique one another's work, rather than encouraging them to rely entirely on her evaluation. In this way, she finds out about the children's shifting interests. She can continually assess what they are learning.

Concluding the Study

Children are proud of becoming experts on a subject. Telling others about what they have learned serves many purposes, including clarifying thinking and recognizing accomplishments.

Based on prior experience, Ms. Lourdes anticipates that the children will be enthusiastic about all the information they collect about the school and will want to share it with other classes. She will ask the children how they want to share their knowledge. In previous years the children have suggested:

- making a presentation for another class in the form of a TV talk show;
- writing an article for the school newspaper; and
- having an open house for parents.

Ms. Lourdes has outlined a logical plan for her study of the school based on the developmental stage of the children, their interests, and local resources. She may adjust her plans depending on the interests of the children or local events.

Closing Thoughts

When social studies is presented well, it enables children to acquire the tools to become successful learners. As children pose questions, conduct research, engage in discussions, and present their findings, they learn to think critically and make connections between what they are learning and their own lives. In-depth studies of topics related to self, family, and community give vitality to the familiar, and encourage children to go beyond the superficial in their research efforts. They become experts on everyday happenings and build an increasing understanding of people, places, and events. Participating in a classroom community teaches children respect for others and the environment, as well as group living and decision making. It gives children a sense of pride in their own heritage.

Resources for Social Studies

Engaging Children's Minds: The Project Approach. Katz, Lilian G. and Sylvia C. Chard. Norwood, NJ: Ablex Publishing, 1989.

History Workshop: Reconstructing the Past with Elementary Students. Jorgensen, Karen L. Portsmouth, NH: Heinemann, 1993.

Learning and Loving It: Theme Studies in the Classroom. Gamberg, Ruth, Winniefred Kwak, Meredith Hutchings, Judy Altheim, with Gail Edwards. Portsmouth, NH: Heinemann, 1988.

Social Studies for the Preschool/Primary Child, 4th Edition. Seefeldt, Carol. New York: Merrill/Macmillan, 1993.

The Story of Ourselves: Teaching History Through Children's Literature. Tunnell, Michael O., and Richard Ammon (ed.). Portsmouth, NH: Heinemann, 1992.

Young Geographers, 4th Edition. Mitchell, Lucy. New York: Bank Street College of Education, 1991.

Reference

Short, Kathy and Carolyn Burke. 1991. *Creating Curriculum: Teachers and Students as a Community of Learners.* Portsmouth, NH: Heinemann.

SCIENTIFIC
THINKING

S cience is the search for ways to explain and understand the natural and physical world. Scientists are equipped with insatiable curiosity as well as the necessary tools for scientific investigation—the ability to observe carefully and without bias, to think logically and critically, and to reason. Conducting scientific investigations involves asking questions, gathering and analyzing information, and suggesting explanations which can be tested.

Scientific investigations can relate to straightforward questions such as why leaves change color, as well as more complex problems such as how did the universe begin or what is a cure for a mysterious disease. Regardless of the nature of the question, the core of scientific thinking is seeking explanations through systematic investigation of objects, phenomena, and living things. Critical to the scientific process is the belief that through investigation, one can begin to understand the physical and natural world.

Like adult scientists, children in the primary grades constantly seek explanations about their world. Eager to explore the phenomena they encounter every day—sound, water, light, motion, plants and animals—young children touch, manipulate, look, and listen in order to form explanations for how the world works. Science curriculum in the primary grades is most effective when it builds on children's natural inclination to seek explanations and fosters their desire and willingness to seek answers to questions through active investigations. Nurturing children's sense of wonder—their interest and excitement in finding out about the world—is at the heart of the science curriculum in the primary grades. Teaching children how to think like scientists is its focus.

Children Exploring Science

The discipline of science is so vast that it would be impossible to identify a set of theories, concepts, and facts that all children should learn during the primary grades. For this reason, learning to engage in the process of scientific thinking is a more appropriate focus for the science curriculum. Any topic that addresses scientific knowledge—living things, earth and space, matter, and energy—can be a vehicle for teaching scientific thinking.

The examples that follow show how teachers plan experiences that allow children in the primary grades to use scientific thinking as they build knowledge of the natural and physical world.

> *In Ms. Diaz's **first grade** classroom a study of small creatures is underway.
> The children have collected earthworms by searching in piles of decomposing
> leaves on the playground. They are interested in finding answers to questions
> such as, "Do earthworms have legs?" and "How do earthworms move?"
> Children work with partners using hand lenses to observe the movements of
> earthworms. They measure their worms with lengths of string. The children
> look for clues about how the worms move. They exchange discoveries about
> their observations. "My worm is a little rough. When it moves on my hand, it
> tickles," exclaims Peter. Teresa says, "I can't seem to measure mine. It gets
> small and then stretches out very long. It won't stand still." Ms. Diaz responds,
> "Peter, the tickling comes from the bristles on the worm. What do you think
> those bristles might be for?" And to Teresa she asks, "How do you think the
> worm gets bigger and smaller?" She suggests that the children make "larger
> than life" drawings of the worms so that they can document all the parts of the
> worm that might help the worm to move.*

Ms. Diaz has selected the topic of living things for children to investigate. The study, which she calls "Small Creatures," is interesting and accessible to her students. By taking children for a collecting walk and then giving them an opportunity to pose questions, she sparks their curiosity. She first guides their investigation by setting up opportunities for them to observe closely and study the creatures. She continually asks questions that encourage children to wonder, question, observe, and pose explanations. When children share their "larger than life" drawings during a class meeting, Ms. Diaz points out all the techniques children used to record their ideas on how worms move.

> *As part of their study of motion, small groups of children in Ms. Thompson's
> **second grade** construct tubes, tunnels, and runs for different sized marbles.
> She challenges the children to build a pathway for the balls that will keep them
> in motion for as long as possible and cause them to change direction at least
> once. Children talk continuously about their work as they test, observe, ques-
> tion, and pose explanations. Liz observes, "The higher we start the ball, the
> farther it goes." Ray asks, "How can we make the ball turn a corner? It keeps*

going in a straight line." Having tried several balls made of different materials, Jake concludes, "The metal ball works better than the glass marble. It bounces less." Ms. Thompson suggests that the children make drawings of their constructions so that they can share their findings at the class meeting.

In this classroom children use scientific process skills: observing, questioning, predicting, explaining, drawing conclusions, and describing findings. Their investigation is about energy and they are exploring important physics concepts: force, gravity, mass, momentum, and friction. Because they are curious to solve the problem posed by Ms. Thompson, and because they can experiment with real materials, they feel competent and purposeful about their work. They are actively engaged in solving a problem. They represent their thinking by building structures and drawing and writing about them. By sharing their ideas with each other, they clarify their thinking.

*Everyone seated in Ms. Walker's **third grade** classroom meeting area has just finished listening to* In Shadowland *by Mitsumasa Anno. Children are busily sharing personal stories about having seen their shadows at various times. Ms. Walker asks, "What do you think makes our shadows appear?" The children discuss possible explanations. Then she announces that they will take a series of shadow walks on several days. She asks, "Do you think we will see our shadows? How can we keep track of when and where we see them? What tools do we need?"*

Ms. Walker uses a story to kindle children's interest in light and shadows. She encourages them to ask questions and consider possible explanations. To prepare them for the shadow walks, she has them think about how to conduct an investigation and how to record what they see. Throughout the study, children will record, measure, chart, and graph what they observe. They will measure their own shadows at different times of the day and graph the lengths. They will do this over the course of several days and make comparative charts. In this study, the children will explore important science concepts such as the many sources of light, how shadows are produced when light is blocked, and how shadow shape and size change depending on the position of the light source and/or object.

The teachers in these classrooms have set up learning experiences that trigger children's natural sense of wonder. They give children opportunities to use the process skills of scientific inquiry to solve problems and devise explanations. Children are encouraged to ask questions, make predictions, set up experiments, test explanations, and describe and revise conclusions. They will make discoveries and gain understanding through active and purposeful investigation. While each child may take something different from these experiences, all children are engaged in scientific thinking.

What Children Learn

The American Association for the Advancement of Science (AAAS) and the National Science Teachers' Association are working to define standards for science education. In *Benchmarks for Science Literacy* (1993), the AAAS encourages an approach to teaching science that emphasizes gaining understanding and making connections, rather than simply acquiring facts. They suggest that an effective science curriculum includes three elements:

- It nurtures children's excitement and curiosity about the material world around them (attitudes).
- It familiarizes them with the process of scientific inquiry (skills).
- It helps them acquire an understanding of material and physical phenomena (knowledge).

The chart below presents an overview of each component of the science curriculum.

Overview of the Science Curriculum

Components	What Children Learn
Attitudes Underlying Scientific Thinking	• Curiosity • Openness to new ideas • Appropriate skepticism
Skills of Scientific Inquiry	• Pose relevant questions • Form hypotheses • Observe with increasing attention to details • Set up experiments • Interpret data and draw conclusions • Communicate findings
Scientific Knowledge	• Living Things • Earth and Space • Matter • Energy

Attitudes Underlying Scientific Thinking

Scientists are curious; they ask questions about the world around them, and they believe that they can find answers to these questions through systematic investigation. A central focus of the science curriculum, therefore, must be to *foster children's natural curiosity* about the world around them. Curiosity is essential for scientific investigation. It is what motivates scientists to pose questions, identify problems, use logic and reasoning to consider solutions, construct investigations, analyze evidence, and form explanations.

Having an open mind is beneficial beyond the realm of science because we live in a diverse, dynamic, and complex society. Within the field of science, however, it is especially important to be open to new ideas. Very often great scientific discoveries are the product of unexpected experimental results: for example, Alexander Fleming discovering penicillin from mold. Flexible thinkers willingly revise their thinking as they acquire new information. Therefore, an effective science curriculum will encourage children to be *open to new ideas*.

Scientists, as well as experts in other disciplines, do not accept answers without first thoroughly evaluating evidence. It is also important for children to learn not to accept ideas and events at face value, but to analyze and evaluate them. This helps children move to a higher level of thinking. A good science curriculum, therefore, promotes *appropriate skepticism*. It encourages children to search for logical explanations and to recognize that theories must be supported by evidence. Children also can learn the limits of science— that we cannot answer all questions.

Curiosity, openness to new ideas, and appropriate skepticism are attitudes that help children become scientific thinkers. Classrooms that encourage active problem solving by brainstorming, discussion, and evaluation support children's acquisition of these attitudes.

Skills of Scientific Inquiry

An essential element of being a scientific investigator is knowing how to find answers to questions. The skills used in the process of scientific inquiry include questioning, hypothesizing, observing, experimenting, interpreting data, drawing conclusions, and communicating findings.

Questioning

Children are innately curious. Teachers can build on this natural inclination to ask questions by showing children that their questions are worthwhile and helping them to see how their questions can become the basis for investigation.

> *Ms. Nolan introduces a study of the moon to her class by reading* Owl Moon
> *by Jane Yolen. After the story, she asks the children, "What do you know about
> the moon?" Hector states, "The moon is out at night." Miyoko replies, "I've*

seen the moon out in the daytime too." Other children chime in with various points of view until finally, and with some frustration, Hector asks, "Ms. Nolan, isn't the moon out only at night?" She agrees that Hector's question is a good one and asks the children to suggest ways to find an answer. The children decide to watch the moon for a month. To encourage the investigation, Ms. Nolan prepares a recording sheet so that each child can observe the moon daily. On their recording sheet they can write down the time of day they see it and draw a picture of how it looks. For several days the children bring in the data they collect. When the children are unable to observe the moon because of overcast skies, Ms. Nolan shows them another way to collect data. She brings in a newspaper to show the children that the time the moon rises and sets each day is documented.

Not every question leads to a meaningful investigation. What makes a question "scientific" is the possibility of finding an answer through careful and systematic investigation. The more opportunities children have to ask questions, the more they will learn to ask the right question at the right time. Often children ask questions that cannot be systematically investigated. For example, "Why do seasons change?" is a question that can lead to an interesting discussion and much speculation, but not directly to an investigation. Children can, however, investigate how the natural environment changes from one season to the next by observing and documenting what they see and then forming explanations for these changes, such as why trees lose their leaves.

Children's questions change as they gain experience and maturity. For example, a first grader might ask: "Why is there a filter in the aquarium?" A third grader who has had some experience with aquariums might ask, "How does this aquarium filter remove the dirt from the water?" Providing opportunities for children to answer their own questions enables them to connect previous knowledge and experience with new experiences. The increasing sophistication of children's questions comes as much with experience as with maturity. The third grader who has never had experience with an aquarium is just as likely as the first grader to ask the question, "Why is there a filter in the aquarium?"

Prior to any scientific investigation with children, it is essential to provide time for them to ask questions. Sometimes their curiosity and sense of wonder is spontaneous, as in the example of a third grader who asks, "Which weighs more: snow when it's melted or snow when it's snow?" At other times, the teacher sets the stage for questions by presenting a problem. An example of this is a teacher who challenges the children to think about what type of ramp they would have to build in order to keep a ball in motion and change directions at least once.

Finally, effective science teachers encourage children to come back to their questions and see whether they have been answered. Posting the children's questions on charts helps to create an environment for inquiry. As investigations proceed and children raise new questions, these should be added to the lists.

Predicting

Just as a weather forecast is a prediction of rain or shine based on temperature, wind, and radar readings, a prediction in science is a speculation based on information and evidence. A prediction is not a wild guess; it is based on previous experience or knowledge.

Young children generate explanations and new ideas all the time. The more experience they have with scientific investigations, the more realistic and plausible their ideas become. The science curriculum comes to life in a primary classroom when children are encouraged to make predictions and to carry out experiments to test their ideas.

> *Children in a first grade class predict that the seeds they collect from oranges and lemons will grow into plants. Using soil and cups, they test their prediction by planting the seeds, watering them regularly, and observing what happens.*

> *In a mixed-age classroom of seven and eight year olds the children are studying temperature changes. Seth predicts that an ice cube wrapped in aluminum foil and placed inside a plastic bag will stay frozen longer than an ice cube placed in the open air. He sets up a test to try to prove his theory.*

The skill of prediction is taught by encouraging this type of thinking throughout the day, particularly in the context of formal science experiences. By getting into the habit of asking "what will happen if…" questions, children learn how to make reasonable predictions. It is important to ask children to predict the outcome of situations about which they have some experience.

- What do you think will happen when we mix these two paint colors together?
- What would happen if we put this piece of clay into the water?
- Which technique do you think will be most effective for wiping the blackboards, a wet sponge or a dry cloth?

Challenging students to explain why they think something will happen helps them to make the connection between prior experiences and a new, but similar, event. When we ask children to predict about unfamiliar situations, they are likely to make wild guesses.

Observing

One of the most important ways that scientists collect data is through observation. From birth, we use our senses to learn about the world around us. Scientific investigation calls for refined observation—paying careful attention to detail and knowing when observations are relevant to the problem being explored. Learning to observe carefully also means relying on all of the senses and being able to choose and use tools for observation, such as a hand lens, microscope, or measuring device.

At first, children tend to rely on what they see. They often neglect information that their other senses can detect. Children who are developing more refined observation skills will notice details about appearance but will also use touch, smell, and hearing for more information. Teachers can promote children's observation skills by encouraging them to:

- observe by ***looking:*** discriminate size, color, shape, and position of object; count features; estimate length, volume, or weight and compare these to other known objects.
- observe by ***touching:*** determine whether objects feel rough, smooth, wet, dry, oily, scaly, heavy, light, bumpy.
- observe by ***listening:*** note the volume or the pitch of sounds and make comparisons with sounds such as falling rain or a crashing toy.
- observe by ***smelling:*** describe how something smells and compare new smells to familiar ones ("It smells like lemons." or "It smells like trash.").
- observe by ***tasting:*** identify terms such as sweet, bitter, sour, or spicy. (Tasting experiments should be carefully supervised.)

To help children observe details beyond those that are obvious, teachers can ask probing questions and offer tools such as magnifiers or simple microscopes. In order to become careful observers, children need time to study objects and events carefully. This means providing extended work times as well as encouraging children to study objects over the course of time.

Experimenting

Seeking answers to scientific questions can involve setting up a systematic test, gathering data, and then studying the results. Scientists conduct controlled experiments or "fair tests." They decide on one factor to be tested and plan the test to measure that factor alone; all other factors, or "variables," remain the same. The idea of a fair test is one that primary grade children can easily begin to grasp.

Children's understanding of the notion of "fairness" begins to develop in the preschool years. During organized games, children start to compare their own abilities with their peers. By the time they reach first grade, many children have a solid sense of what fairness means. If asked to set up a fair running race between two students, most would agree that each runner would have to start at the same point and proceed over similar terrain. All conditions would have to be the same so that the variable being tested is the speed of the runner and nothing else.

Some children studying plants in a second grade class wonder what would make plants grow faster. Several children suggest trying fertilizer. Ms. Ruiz asks them to plan an experiment that might answer this question. Diana and Inez decide to add fertilizer to a set of pea plants and then record and measure the plants' growth. Ms. Ruiz asks them to think in terms of setting up a "fair test." Inez sees that in order to test whether fertilizer makes a plant grow faster, she and Diana can't just observe a fertilized plant. Instead, they will need to compare a fertilized plant with an unfertilized plant. The children plan an experiment where both fertilized and unfertilized plants will be grown under the same conditions: the same light, temperature, humidity, soil, and pot size.

Some children will grasp the idea of a fair test more readily than others. Rather than telling children to be sure they use a fair test, teachers can pose questions so that children recognize it for themselves. For example, Ms. Ruiz might have asked Diana and Inez: "How will you know if one plant is growing faster than the other? What will you need to do so that you can compare the growth of the two plants?"

Interpreting Data and Drawing Conclusions

Analyzing information and drawing conclusions are central to problem solving and occur in many subjects, not just in science. Children use these skills as they read literature, solve math problems, or create an art project. For young children, an important part of scientific investigation is thinking critically about what is happening. In science, a believable conclusion depends on the support of evidence and logical thought. A scientist is aware that one can easily be influenced by one's preconceptions. Using evidence and logic minimizes the effect of personal bias on drawing conclusions.

Studying an object or event through observation and experimentation usually yields a great deal of information. Interpreting information means finding the significance of all the data that has been gathered. Too often, interpretation of data is left out of primary grade science activities. Instead, activities are planned more for entertainment, and children are not encouraged to think about explanations. To encourage children to interpret data and draw conclusions, teachers can ask children questions such as:

- Why is this happening?
- What does the evidence show?
- What really happened during the experiment?
- What did we find out?
- What new questions do we have now?

Careful analysis of data reveals patterns, relationships, or trends. The critical thinking skills of comparing and classifying are used to interpret these relationships. Comparing means judging the similarities and differences among observed objects or attributes. This skill is important during the process of classification. Classifying means organizing things into groups according to common characteristics. For example, to organize or group a collection of seeds into categories based on size, the seeds must be compared to see the range of sizes, then classified into categories accordingly. At first, children will use simple categories: things that float, things that are green, or things that are tiny. As they gain experience, they will be able to use more than one attribute to form groups: metal things that float, leaves that are green and don't fall to the ground in autumn.

In science, reaching a conclusion requires at least three steps:

- analyzing the collected information;
- making a generalization or conclusion;
- applying the conclusion to other situations or problems.

Typically, the processes of interpreting data and drawing conclusions happen simultaneously for young children. As children gain experience, they begin to develop the more advanced skill of making generalizations and applying these to new problems. For example, in a class discussion about why snakes shed their skin, a second grader may relate information learned the previous year about hermit crabs. Past experiences are keys to a child's ability to analyze information and draw conclusions.

Communicating Findings

Science requires the ability to communicate clearly so that ideas and discoveries can be shared. Children can be encouraged to describe their findings and ideas both verbally (in discussions) and non-verbally (drawing or making a model). Reading and writing in the context of science investigations helps children see another important use for their growing literacy skills.

Keeping records of observations (descriptions, drawings, charts) is a common and useful way to track discoveries and communicate information. Children can write descriptions, make drawings, charts, and graphs to communicate information and express ideas. Depending on the child's ability and experience, communication might include a one-word caption for first graders or a short, three-sentence description from a third grader. Record keeping serves other purposes as well. When challenged to describe their thoughts, children become aware of what they know and do not know about a subject. Questions surface and ideas can be clarified.

Scientific observations and experiments provide many opportunities for children to talk with one another. As they talk, they use increasingly detailed language to describe, clarify, and explain their ideas to one another. The importance of communication as a critical part of the learning process is discussed in the chapter on Guiding Children's Learning.

Scientific Knowledge

Every science textbook organizes content in a different way. Some suggest that there are only two broad topics for investigation: energy and matter. Others organize the discipline into the categories of life science, earth science, and physical science, or into organizational themes such as systems, models, constancy, change, and scale.

In *Constructing Curriculum*, we have organized the content of the science curriculum into four categories: living things, earth and space, matter, and energy. Within each of these categories there are many sub-topics and corresponding concepts.

Children build their understanding of science concepts slowly, based on their experiences with real materials. They need to revisit these same ideas over and over in order to refine their understanding. Rather than trying to address a definitive list of "must cover" science concepts, teachers can be more successful in teaching science by focusing on a few concepts for each study.

> Concepts are learned best when they are encountered in a variety of contexts and expressed in a variety of ways, for that ensures that there are more opportunities for them to become embedded in a student's knowledge system (Rutherford and Ahlgren 1990, 186).

An elementary school science text can help you identify the main concepts within the topic you decide to study with children. The standards referred to earlier can offer additional guidance.

To further assist you in designing your science curriculum, we have organized the four broad categories of scientific knowledge into a series of charts. Each chart identifies science concepts appropriate for the primary grades and offers ideas of topics for investigation. The four categories of scientific knowledge are:

- *Living Things:* the body of knowledge that includes big ideas such as behavior, needs of plants and animals, characteristics, habitats, and life cycles.

- *Earth and Space:* the body of knowledge related to day and night, the moon and the stars, climate and weather, and the earth's surface.

- *Matter:* the body of knowledge that includes the properties of substances and the relationship of the substance's properties to its purpose.

- *Energy:* the body of knowledge about light, sound, heat, motion, and electricity.

The ideas incorporated in the charts that follow are based on the work of Wynne Harlen in her book, *Teaching and Learning Primary Science* (1985). As you review the charts for each category, keep in mind that it would be impossible for any teacher to try to address <u>all</u> of the topics listed. These charts are offered simply to show the range of possibilities for scientific explorations. At the most, you might explore three topics in depth during a given year. It is the process of engaging in scientific thinking and acquiring a deeper understanding of the big concepts—"seasons repeat themselves" or "all living things change and go through cycles"—that are revisited year after year within the context of new studies.

Living Things

Concepts	Suggested Topics for Investigation
Organisms (plants and animals) have distinct characteristics: they grow, reproduce, need nutrients, respire (breathe), and excrete wastes in different ways.	• ourselves • birds • fish and other aquatic creatures (e.g., hermit crabs, snails, frogs) • pets • insects and other small creatures • plants • mammals • trees and leaves • terrariums • gardens
Organisms and their environments are closely connected.	• habitats (e.g., puddle, playground, field, forest, desert, pond, lake, river, ocean) • strategies for survival (e.g., the turtle's shell, creatures who lay many eggs, animals who hibernate, camouflage)
All living things change and go through life cycles.	• egg to chick • caterpillar to butterfly • mealworm to beetle • baby to adult (humans and other animals)

Earth and Space

Concepts	Suggested Topics for Investigation
The moon and the stars that are visible change in regular patterns through a month and a year. The changing position of the sun in relation to the earth is responsible for day and night and for the change of seasons.	• day and night • the moon and its changes • seasons
The water cycle causes and affects climate and weather.	• condensation and evaporation • weather (e.g., clouds, forecasting, types of storms)
The earth's surface changes over time due to the effects of water, wind, ice, and forces beneath the surface of the earth.	• volcanoes and earthquakes • weather • erosion • rocks • land forms
Soil is a mixture of living, decomposed, and non-living material; this mixture is always changing.	• recycling and garbage • compost • plants and soil • dirt

Matter

Concepts	Suggested Topics for Investigation
All substances take up space and have weight.	• balancing (e.g., weighing things, constructing block buildings, making mobiles) • solid objects (e.g., properties and uses) • liquids (e.g., flow, properties of liquids) • gases (e.g., air, steam)
Some objects float in water and some objects float in the air. Whether or not something floats depends on how heavy it is for its size.	• boats • kites, balloons, planes • sinking and floating in water
All matter has distinct properties and has different purposes because of these properties.	• structures (e.g., houses, skyscrapers) • building materials (e.g., clay, bricks, woods, steel, cement) • construction • inventions • materials and their uses (e.g., rubber for tires, metals for cars, plastic for containers)

Energy

Concepts	Suggested Topics for Investigation
Light is a form of energy that can travel. Light can be reflected and absorbed.	• light and shadows • mirrors • rainbows • color • solar energy
Sound is a form of energy that can travel when objects move rapidly back and forth, or vibrate.	• sound • hearing • musical instruments
Gaining and losing heat can change things (e.g., melt, freeze, evaporate, condense).	• water • ice • snow • inventions
Forces can start and stop motion. Speed is a measure of how fast something moves (how far it goes in a certain time—a second, minute or hour).	• balls and ramps • spinning things • machines • inventions • magnets
Energy cannot be created or destroyed; it can be changed from one form to another. There are many sources of energy.	• uses of solar energy • electrical devices
Some materials allow an electric current to pass through them (conductors). Others effectively prevent a current from flowing through them (insulators).	• batteries and bulbs • lights in our city • inventions

Organizing the Science Curriculum

Teachers who are alert to the everyday opportunities to teach scientific thinking and who generate enthusiasm about investigating any of the topics suggested in the charts can make science an important part of their curriculum.

The essence of science activity, and usually its starting point, is the encounter between the child and some phenomenon; some face to face interaction of children and things around from which they can learn directly through their own physical and mental activity (Harlen 1989, 6).

Many teachers do not feel comfortable teaching science. Their discomfort may come from the view that science is a set of facts and theories to be memorized or that it is a body of knowledge that is incomprehensible. Because discomfort sometimes leads to avoidance, science is often pushed to a back burner in primary classrooms. Periodically, children may read about a topic in a textbook or engage in clever science activities, but they do not undertake true scientific investigations.

You don't have to be a scientist to be an effective teacher of science in the primary grades. There are countless opportunities to guide children toward thinking scientifically by making science a part of everyday life in the classroom and by engaging children in studying a topic that interests them.

Making Science Part of Everyday Life in the Classroom

Science isn't a subject that just happens once or twice a week. Children can learn to think like scientists and recognize scientific questions in their everyday world when teachers use daily experiences to promote the skills of scientific inquiry. Daily experiences with objects, plants, animals, and weather provide children with opportunities to observe, think scientifically, and draw conclusions about the physical and natural world (Doris 1991). By making materials available, modeling scientific thinking, and responding to events that occur in the environment, teachers can make science part of everyday life.

Provide Space and Materials to Encourage Science Exploration

The classroom can be a laboratory for questioning, observing, predicting, and explaining on a daily basis apart from any particular study. By including materials that are interesting to explore as a part of the physical environment, you can create a setting in which children spontaneously ask questions and conduct informal investigations.

Identify an Area for Scientific Investigation

Allocating space in the classroom for science gives children the message that it is important. The area will be inviting if it includes interesting materials. Hanging maps, posters, and pictures will spark children's thinking. Calendars are a great source of inexpensive science pictures. Displays can consist of books, newspaper articles, and magazines related to particular topics, creations made by children, and objects collected by the teacher or children. Tools for investigation and collections can be kept in a science area or displayed on a shelf or table. Materials such as colored pencils, markers, journals, and different types of paper should be accessible.

It is important to change the materials and the displays in the science area so that interest is constantly renewed. Introducing a new poster, a new book, or a new tool during a meeting is likely to encourage children to select the science area at choice time. You might also display pictures of scientists at work.

Provide Tools for Scientific Investigations

An important part of science is becoming familiar with the purposeful use of tools and beginning to recognize the ways tools relate to mathematical and scientific thinking. Some tools such as scales, measuring cups, thermometers, calculators, and rulers are for measuring. Other tools such as magnifiers, microscopes, and cameras aid observation.

Children will begin to understand the purpose of tools when materials are accessible to them. Displaying tools and materials in an organized way enables children to use them on a regular basis. Initiating interesting projects for children to work on and giving children opportunities to initiate projects gives them a reason to use tools for investigation.

Opportunities to gather data over time is an important part of scientific thinking. You can encourage children to collect data over time by providing tools for recording information such as paper and pencils, colored markers, tape recorders, calculators, and computers. Weather charts and graphs, for example, can become a focus for scientific investigation when they are used to help children think about patterns of change in the environment and changes in the seasons.

Create an Invention Center

Inventing things is part of science. An invention center to inspire investigation could be a portable box of junk with a variety of materials such as corks, film containers, sponges, spools, balloons, straws, Styrofoam, springs, bottle caps, string, and scraps of wood. These materials can be collected by sending a written request home with children and by asking neighborhood merchants for interesting recyclable materials. Pose a challenge for children such as:

- Make something that spins.
- Create something that moves.
- Invent something that can move things up and down.

Children can be encouraged to draw and write about their creations.

Provide a Variety of Interesting Collections

Children can be inspired to sort and classify objects if the science area includes collections of leaves, flowers, seeds, magnets, marbles, sea glass, stones, or fabric scraps. These activities are more likely to occur if you organize the collections in bins with trays next to them on which children can sort and classify.

Provide magnifiers to encourage children to investigate objects carefully. Placing a sign that says, "What do you notice?" or "Find an interesting way to group these objects and record your method," can motivate children to begin their explorations.

Include Living Things in the Classroom

A tank for fish, hermit crabs, turtles, or a frog can be a catalyst for ongoing science discussions and observations. Class pets such as a guinea pig, rabbit, or bird, also provide opportunities for children to conduct investigations while learning how to care for living creatures. Including plants in the classroom often sparks discussions about what they need to grow, when they bloom, and how to keep track of growth over time.

Model Scientific Thinking

Children are more likely to think like scientists when they interact with adults and peers who model this way of thinking. Your own enthusiasm and curiosity can be a catalyst for children: "I just can't wait to find out how this caterpillar is going to change and how long it's going to take." If you can't wait, the children will often feel the same way!

Share Your Observations

Teachers model scientific thinking by being observant and pointing out scientific events when they happen. For example, when water forms droplets on the classroom window, you might ask, "What do you think is happening here? What's causing the water to form beads?"

Teachers also share their interest in science by bringing objects from home. For example, a piece of bread with blue and white fuzzy mold is something we all have found in our homes at one time or another. Bringing it into the classroom might lead to interesting discussions and possible investigations. After letting children know where the bread was and how long it had been there, some questions to ask might be:

- How can we find out what is growing on the bread?
- What might we use to see what is growing more clearly?
- What would happen if we left the bread out even longer?

Whether the discussion and possible investigations are initiated by the children or by you, the goal is to encourage children to be curious and consider cause and effect.

Encourage Children to Share

The way you respond to child-initiated topics can model scientific thinking. Many times children arrive on Monday morning with something they have found during the weekend or with a story of an event they witnessed. They might bring in shells, a nest, a small creature, or an independent project that they have created. By inviting children to talk about their experience or discovery and encouraging the others to ask questions, teachers help children think like investigators.

> *First grader Josie raises her hand during the meeting Monday morning and says, "Over the weekend I saw a rainbow." Ms. Douglas responds, "Mmm. Let's think about this like scientists. Tell us about what was happening when you saw it." Josie replies, "I was playing with my sister in the park." Ms. Douglas asks other questions including, "What colors did you notice in the rainbow?" and "What was the weather like? Was it raining? Was the sun shining?" After Josie shares some of her observations, Ms. Douglas says to the class, "Let's think about what causes rainbows."*

By using Josie's story about the rainbow as a focus for discussion and asking specific questions, Ms. Douglas conveys the message that paying attention to what is happening in the environment and sharing it with others is important. She uses this experience to extend children's thinking on the topic by asking questions and encouraging discussions.

Often something that a child brings in from home sparks others to try something out during choice time. Opportunities to link children's interests outside school with activities in the classroom helps children to make connections between home and school.

Respond Scientifically to Problems

The way you respond to problems that come up in daily classroom life is another way to model scientific thinking. If the water or power is suddenly shut off, you can demonstrate to children that such events require investigation. Simply posing the question, "I wonder why this is happening. How can we get to the bottom of this?" will most likely lead to an interesting discussion. When equipment fails to work, another opportunity for scientific thinking is available.

> *Ms. Arnold is about to show her class a videotape but the machine won't work. She says to the class, "Let's think about what we know. Is it plugged in? Is the power on? Do we have it on the right channel? Do we have the tape in?" The children help her check out answers to each question and add some of their own.*

By thinking aloud, Ms. Arnold models how to reason through a problem. She demonstrates that electronic devices are not objects to be afraid of, but rather objects that can be figured out if examined in a systematic way.

Responding to Events in the Environment

The location of a school automatically suggests a broad range of possible scientific investigations. Right outside your classroom window you might find material for ongoing observations such as the following:

- tracking various types of birds that land on a bird feeder outside the classroom window to learn something about migratory patterns;
- recording monthly observations of one particular tree near the school, noting changes over time;
- maintaining a graph of temperature recorded at the same time each day over a period of several months.

Environmental events that can suggest scientific inquiry might be:

- the construction or demolition of a local building,
- the change of seasons,
- a space shuttle flight, or
- a classroom pet getting sick.

A violent storm, drought, snowfall, fire, or earthquake can become the basis for a lively questioning and discussion period. Taking a walk after the snow to observe how it fell, its texture, and the effects of the wind can encourage children to note details and use descriptive language in discussion.

Like the social studies curriculum, science content will vary from classroom to classroom, depending on the age of the children and their prior experiences, the immediate environment of the school, and the interests of children and their teachers.

Selecting Topics for Long-Term Studies in Science

The topics you select for long-term studies in science engage children in the scientific process and lead them to an increasing understanding of important science concepts. Because the focus of the science curriculum is on process skills, any of the sample topics suggested in the charts can become the focus for a long-term study. By studying a variety of topics in depth over the course of the primary grades, children return again and again to central concepts in science. The concept "organisms have distinct characteristics," for example, might be studied in first grade by growing lima bean plants, in second grade in a study of insects, and in third grade during a study of mammals.

Strive to balance your science curriculum by choosing at least one topic which includes a study of living things (e.g., insects, birds, plants), one from matter (e.g., sinking and floating, things that fly), one from energy (e.g., water, air, sound), and one from earth and space (e.g., day and night, soil). This will provide children with a variety of materials to investigate and allow them to broaden their skills and knowledge of the world.

In selecting the topics you want to pursue during the year, think about what you would enjoy and what would interest the children you teach. Ask yourself what resources are available in your immediate area, and which topics will allow the children to conduct first-hand research and use scientific thinking skills. Because you can do only so much, you will also want to consider which topics provide natural linkages to other subjects you will be teaching. In this way you can alternate or integrate topics you plan to study.

Children's Interests

Without interest, motivation is likely to be absent. In first and second grades, children are often interested in topics related to their own experiences and environments. Studying living things or rocks gathered locally, their own bodies, and their pets is generally of greatest interest. By third grade, children typically have increased eye-hand coordination and like to design and create inventions, machines, structures, gardens, and musical instruments.

Make sure to leave some time during the year for child-initiated topics. A flexible curriculum makes the science program more interesting primarily because it results in changes from one year to the next. One year the curriculum might be paper airplanes, another year forest animals or recycling. When you proceed with a topic initiated by the children, you send strong messages to children: your ideas are important and together we can explore this topic to learn more. In addition, you show children that their curiosity has an important place at school and they can determine the direction of their own learning.

When children raise their own questions about a topic, they are likely to be motivated to search for answers. As you consider the timing of a particular topic, think about occasions or situations when related questions are likely to arise in the course of typical classroom discussion. For example, are there months when rain or lack of it are noticeable to children? A water study would be very effective at this point. Children are likely to raise questions about many seasonal changes. For example, the presence of seeds and fruit in early fall, and the formation of ice, snow, and frost in the winter are good starting points for studies of plants, water and weather. Children's observations of shorter daylight hours might lead to a study of darkness, light, and shadow.

Availability of Resources

A subject comes to life for children when they can experience it in many different ways. Talking with a naturalist, looking at pictures, and reading through many books provide children with ideas for questions and discussions. Videos and filmstrips are other valuable resources. When resources such as books, experts, photographs, and charts and diagrams are readily available, planning science experiences becomes easier for teachers.

Some topics can be readily explored only during a particular season. Whether you plan to study ice and snow or grow plants, you'll want to consider conditions inside and outside the classroom. For example, if you plan to grow plants, warmer temperatures and more light in your classroom will help. Outside the classroom, there may be opportunities for children to observe the life or phenomena they are studying. Children will be more involved and motivated when they can, for example, see and collect insects from the outdoor environment of the school or neighborhood.

Opportunities for First-Hand Research

An important consideration in selecting a topic is whether it can be experienced directly and therefore offers opportunities for first-hand research. Young children learn best when they can actually touch, see, hear, and manipulate the objects or events being studied. Water, sound, insects, and plants are all topics which require simple and readily available materials. Materials for the study of rain forests, underwater sea life, or dinosaurs are less accessible for scientific investigation.

Use of Scientific Thinking Skills

To help children acquire scientific thinking skills, the topic should allow them to question, predict, observe, experiment, explain, and communicate. While many topics will require the use of all of these skills, you may decide to focus on one or two (e.g., observing and communicating) during a particular study, and then on others during the next one.

Not all topics lend themselves to the same kinds of investigation. Studying life cycles relies on direct observations over time to gather data. Other topics enable children to handle and manipulate the materials being studied (e.g., sound, motion, water). Still other topics require systematic experimentation where objects studied are compared: for example, product testing (determining which paper towels pick up the most water) or growing plants (testing to see the effects of different types of soil or environment). Consider the possibilities in the topics selected and strive for a variety of experiences through the year.

Linkages to Other Subjects

Coordinating plans for long-term studies in social studies and science helps children make connections. Integrating curriculum also makes addressing all subjects more feasible. Science and social studies may be integrated, for example, by studying transportation. Boats and harbors relate easily to a study of the properties of water, including buoyancy. An investigation of tools and simple machines can be integrated with topics such as the school, a supermarket, a construction site, or a study of a city long ago. A study of plants might be integrated with a study of early America. Some teachers alternate science topics with social studies topics, rather than trying to integrate them.

Some examples of ways in which science might be integrated with other subjects include the following:

- While studying seeds and plants, organize math experiences around sorting, classifying, charting and graphing.
- While studying the neighborhood in social studies, children can interview the people who work in the school, and link their work to machines that depend on electricity.
- While studying transportation in social studies, children can investigate tunnels and bridges in science.

Children learn best by having time for extensive exploration of a few topics during the year. Therefore, it is a good idea to resist the temptation to touch briefly on many topics. Two or three topics studied indepth will allow enough time for children to delve into a subject and to learn more than superficial facts.

Questions to Consider

In selecting a topic for science, an important consideration is whether or not it will enable children to learn by actively investigating, representing, and reflecting on their learning.

To identify possibilities for ***investigation***, ask yourself these questions:

- Can the children observe first-hand the phenomena or objects for study (shadows, snow, living things, rays of light)?
- Are materials available for experimentation (soil, seeds, water, cups, hand lenses)?
- Are any measuring tools necessary for the investigation (thermometers, clocks, stop watches, rulers, balance scales)?
- Are print materials available for children to read independently to find answers to questions (field guides, biographies of inventors or other scientists, informational books, charts, captioned photographs)?
- Are videos or filmstrips available that can provide additional information?
- Is there computer software that can be effectively integrated with the study?
- Is there space and are the facilities adequate for the type of investigation being planned (sun or grow-lights for plants, sink, space to store ongoing experiments)?
- Can the children take field trips to observe or collect?
- Can household materials be used?
- Can families be involved in the study?
- Who are the "local experts" that can be consulted on the subject?
- What connections can be made between the investigation and everyday life (water study is related to water use and pollution, freezing and melting, lunch box and thermos design)?
- What open-ended questions can be asked to encourage further thinking?

To identify opportunities for children to *represent* their learning, ask yourself these questions:

- Are there opportunities to make charts, graphs, or maps?
- Can children sketch and record observations?
- How will children's observations be systematically gathered (recording sheets, in folders, in journals)?
- Can children design and build models as part of this study?
- Can art projects (painting, drawing, collage, paper maché) or dramatic skits be incorporated into the study?
- Can children record their observations and discussions on video or audiotape?

To ensure that there are provisions for *reflecting* on learning, consider the following questions:

- At what points in the study could I have children make notations in their journals?
- Can I use meetings to encourage group reflection?
- What questions will I pose to encourage children to reflect on their learning?

A Long-Term Study in Action: Insects and Small Creatures

In this section we will show how Ms. Henry, a second grade teacher, thinks through the steps for planning a study on Insects and Small Creatures.

Selecting a Topic

Ms. Henry wants to begin her science curriculum with a topic that will engage children in becoming researchers. Using the guidelines for selecting an appropriate topic, she decides on a study of Insects and Small Creatures for the following reasons:

- The topic addresses children's interests. Ms. Henry knows that many children are fascinated by and inquisitive about nature. Several children have brought insects and small creatures into the classroom to share or have pointed them out on the playground. She also appreciates the fact that some children are squeamish about bugs and will want to view them from a safe distance, at least at first.
- Resources are available in and around the school. Ms. Henry will begin this study in the fall when insects can be collected and observed outdoors. The school library has a number of resource books with detailed illustrations of insects and small creatures and a number of excellent story books. She has been collecting posters and pictures from magazines which she can display in the classroom and she has a collection of nature magazines the children can comb through.

- Children can conduct first-hand research, first by collecting insects and creatures outside the building, then by observing them closely. To continue the study, the children can set up environments for the insects in the classroom where the insects can be observed under magnifiers and microscopes.

- The study will foster scientific thinking skills. Children already know something about the topic and they will be able to generate questions to explore. They can compare different creatures and classify them. Creature habits can be studied over time, allowing children to predict, observe, and interpret data.

- The study provides natural linkages to other aspects of the curriculum. The children will make detailed drawings of the insects they are studying and label body parts. They will count body parts, categorize and graph types of insects, and note patterns in development. They will write about their findings in science journals, read stories and poems on small creatures, and pantomine or dramatize how insects move and communicate.

- The topic can be explored by children over time. Ms. Henry is alternating between science and social studies topics for long-term studies. Depending on the interests of the group, the study may resume in the spring.

The process of selecting the topic helps Ms. Henry begin planning what she needs.

Getting Ready for the Study

Ms. Henry begins by making a web on the topic of insects and small creatures. She identifies the following categories: body parts, ways of moving, environments, use of body parts, stages of development. This brainstorming activity gives her many ideas for planning. She looks through old calendars and nature magazines to find pictures. She collects books for the library and identifies poems she can teach to children. In preparation for the first collecting walk, Ms. Henry takes some preliminary field trips to see where the children will be able to find good specimens. She pulls out her box of "beautiful junk" to see what can be used to make insect cages and locates an empty fish tank that can be made into a terrarium.

Introducing the Study to Children

To generate interest in the study, Ms. Henry sets the stage by displaying some materials in the classroom. These include:

- photographs of spiders, butterflies, beetles, and bees taken from *Ranger Rick* and *Nature* magazine;

- books and magazines about insects and non-insects from the school and community library.

Prior to the first class meeting about insects, Ms. Henry uses a choice time to work with a few children to set up a terrarium in the science area. In the terrarium, they place a few hardy local creatures including crickets, beetles, and a grasshopper. Next to it she displays large pictures of worms, beetles, butterflies, bees, and spiders. She puts several books related to the topic on the table with the terrarium.

At a class meeting Ms. Henry asks the children to look at the picture of small creatures on the bulletin board. She has them close their eyes and think about a time when they have seen these or other creatures. They discuss their thoughts and she records what they say on a chart. The children list many small creatures including some that are not insects, such as salamanders, worms, and slugs.

The next day during meeting, Ms. Henry records what the children already know about insects and other small creatures. She asks them what questions they have. Ms. Henry is careful to allow everyone's questions to be recorded and reminds the class that during a "brainstorming" session, questions are only asked, not answered. The process of charting what the children know and want to find out goes on for several days. For homework, children think about some additional questions. In this way Ms. Henry assesses children's prior knowledge of the subject and makes decisions about the pace and sequence of the activities of the study.

During a subsequent meeting, the children review their list of questions. They consider which of their questions can be answered by conducting observations and experiments. Ms. Henry places a star next to those that can be the focus of future investigations and asks the class to begin thinking of ways an experiment or observation could be organized. The children work in pairs to plan some possible experiments to answer the questions.

Listen to and Learn with Children

During the course of the study, Ms. Henry takes the children on many walks. Prior to the first one, she says, "Let's think about which questions on our list we could answer if we had a collection of small creatures to observe for a few days." In this way, she assigns a purpose for the walk outside. Ms. Henry talks with the children about ways to collect insects and other creatures without harming them.

During the first walk, children collect several ladybugs, a cricket, two worms, and a large beetle. Back in the classroom, Ms. Henry encourages them to think about whether the creature they found is an insect. She adds to the list of questions, "What is an insect?"

Children use the skills of inquiry—questioning, predicting, observing, experimenting, interpreting data and drawing conclusions, and explaining and communicating their findings—as they create environments for their creatures and observe their behaviors over time. Ms. Henry encourages the children to make sense of the information they gather by analyzing it and drawing simple conclusions.

When children ask her, "Why is it that…?" Ms. Henry responds with, "Why do you think it is that…?" When children are working in pairs or groups on tasks, she circulates and asks questions to stimulate more careful observations such as:

- How many legs did you count?
- Does this creature have any eyes or ears? If not, what other structures do you notice that might help it sense what is happening around it?
- Is the outside of the body hard or soft?

As children investigate, Ms. Henry provides information about the characteristics of insects. She reads books explaining how insects are different from other small creatures. Ms. Henry invites a naturalist to come to the classroom to talk with the children about insects. She sends a letter home to parents asking if anyone has something related to the study to share with the class. She plans other activities which help provide facts and other information as children need them.

Throughout the study Ms. Henry has the children record their predictions, observations, and explanations of their investigations. They make labeled diagrams, charts, and graphs and they write in their science journals. As children make paintings, collages, and drawings of what they study, they continue to think about new information. Some children construct models of creatures; others build magnification boxes to study the insects more closely. Some children write stories using the knowledge they are acquiring about insects; others make a recording of insect sounds.

The children have numerous opportunities to reflect on their learning. They use their science journals to write about investigations and to reflect on what they have learned. Ms. Henry schedules two or three science meetings each week so that children can share their journal notes or show what they have made or drawn. Throughout the study, meetings are used for discussions of children's observations and discoveries. Meetings are also a time to record new questions.

Concluding the Study

Giving children a chance to apply the knowledge they have gained during their study by building a model, making a presentation, or building an exhibit helps them synthesize what they have learned and feel proud of the work they have done. A culminating activity provides closure for a study. Ms. Henry asks herself:

- How will children share their various representations with others outside our class?
- What are some culminating activities for this project that will enable the children to share what they have learned with children in another class or with families (an exhibition, a book, a photo album, a 'TV talk show')?
- In what ways can the class share their knowledge about this topic with family members and members of the larger community?

The children decide they want to set up a Creature Zoo. They plan the exhibits, categorize the insects and small creatures they have been studying, and write up summaries about each creature to be featured in the display. Children from other classes and families are invited to visit the exhibit over a two-day period. Ms. Henry asks a parent volunteer to take photographs of the Creature Zoo. The photographs are organized by the children into a book about the project.

Ms. Henry intends to extend what the children learned during this investigation by introducing a study of life cycles. The children will observe the transformation of a caterpillar into a butterfly, letting it go when the weather is warm. They will also apply their knowledge of small creatures to a pond, as there is one located nearby the school. In this way, Ms. Henry can encourage her students never to view a study as really ended. As scientists, they will continue to observe insects and will question and wonder. They will be likely to share their interest with others. It's often this spontaneous sharing that students do months after a study that provides a teacher with the best source of assessment of children's learning, and with a way to measure the success of a study.

Closing Thoughts

Science in the primary grades can be an exciting and integrated part of classroom life. As teachers guide children in learning to think scientifically, they have many opportunities to make brainstorming, communication, math skills, and critical thinking relevant in the context of an investigation. Children who are used to brainstorming solutions to classroom problems will readily apply this skill to suggesting hypotheses for scientific problems. Working in groups and keeping science journals enables children to apply their communication skills. As children identify patterns, measure, estimate, and use logical reasoning in the context of a scientific investigation, they begin to see the connection between math and science, and they build a deeper understanding of the world around them.

Resources for Scientific Thinking

General Resources

An Early Start to Science. Richard, Roy. London: Macdonald Co., 1988.

Developing Science in the Primary Classroom. Harlen, Wynne. Portsmouth, NH: Heinemann Press, 1989.

Doing What Scientists Do: Children Learn to Investigate Their World. Doris, Ellen. Portsmouth, NH: Heinemann Press, 1991.

Science for Children: Resources for Teachers. National Science Resource Center. Washington, DC: National Academy Press, 1988.

State of the Art, Transforming Ideas for Teaching and Learning Science, A Guide for Elementary Science Education. Sivertsen, Mary Lewis. Washington, DC: U.S. Department of Education, 1993.

Teaching Science with Everyday Things. Schmidt, Velma, Verne Rockcastle. New York: McGraw-Hill, 1982.

The Wonder of It: Exploring How the World Works. Neugebauer, Bonnie. Redmond, WA: Exchange Press, Inc., 1989.

What Will Happen If... Young Children and the Scientific Method. Aprung, Barbara, Merle Froschl and Patricia B. Campbell. New York: Educational Equity Concepts, Inc., 1985.

Activity Guides for Primary Teachers

Nature Scope Series
National Wildlife Federation
1400 16th St. N.W.
Washington, DC 20036
800-432-6564

AIMS (Activities for Integrating Math and Science)
AIMS Education Foundation
P.O. Box 8120
Fresno, CA 93747
209-255-6393

GEMS series (Great Explorations in Math and Science)
Lawrence Hall of Science
University of California
Berkeley, CA 94720

Science Programs for Primary Grades

Full Option Science System: (FOSS-K-5)
Encyclopedia Brittanica
310 South Michigan Ave.
Chicago, IL 60604

Insights: Hands-On Inquiry Science Curriculum (K-6)
Science Kits, Inc.
Tonawanda, NY
1-800-621-3900

Life Lab Science Program (K-6 garden based curriculum)
1156 High Street
Santa Cruz, CA 95064
408-459-2001

Science and Technology for Children (K-5)
Carolina Biological Supply
2700 York Road
Burlington, NC 27215
919-584-0381

Science for Life and Living (K-6)
Kendall Hunt Publishing Company
2460 Kerper Boulevard
Dubuque, IA 52001
800-258-5622

References

American Association for the Advancement of Science. 1993. *Benchmarks for Science Literacy, Project 2061.* New York: Oxford University Press.
Doris, Ellen. 1991. *Doing What Scientists Do: Children Learn to Investigate Their World.* Portsmouth, NH: Heinemann Press.
Harlen, Wynne. 1985. *Teaching and Learning Primary Science.* London: Harper and Row.
Rutherford, James F. and Andrew Ahlgren. 1990. *Science for All Americans.* New York: Oxford University Press.

THE ARTS AND TECHNOLOGY

11

The arts and technology are a natural part of children's experience. Children love to design, make, and do things with materials and tools. They mix paints, pound clay, and build structures with blocks or discarded materials. They solve problems when they plan a dance sequence, use computers, or create inventions. They experience the joy of rhythm and music, and the satisfaction of using tools effectively. Not only are these activities natural but they also allow children to relax and be playful.

Including materials for arts and technology in the classroom and providing time for children to use them on a daily basis enriches the curriculum. The arts give children opportunities to express and reflect on their ideas and feelings in another language, one that does not rely on words and numbers. As children paint, design, construct, mold, sketch, weave, sing, dance, and act, they discover and integrate what they are learning about their world. When children use the tools of technology to design structures and conduct investigations, they experience the power of creating something for a purpose, and they see the connections between learning and doing.

Some adults readily engage in creative activities, others are natural "fixers." They make all the gifts they give, repair things that break around their house, play an instrument, or dance with a community group. If you are interested or talented in these ways, you are likely to be comfortable with your ability to incorporate the arts and technology in your classroom. Many of us, however, are not dancers or portrait artists or computer wizards. We may feel uncomfortable about areas we think require special talents, and worry about not being "good enough" to teach these subjects. We say, "I can't draw a straight line," or "I can't carry a tune," or "I don't know how to work the computer." If you feel that you do not have enough time or talent to include the arts and technology in your program, we hope that this chapter will help you to see how they can become a natural part of your curriculum.

Children Using the Arts and Technology

I n each of the other subject chapters, we presented classroom examples to illustrate how and what children can learn in language and literacy, math, social studies, and science. The activities and projects that we will now label as "arts and technology" are the means through which children construct knowledge, investigate, and represent what they are learning. Previous chapters illustrated how art and technology experiences are central to the processes by which children learn. In this chapter, we will show how such experiences also give children knowledge and skills related to the arts and technology as disciplines in their own right.

The following scenes will seem familiar and could have appeared in other chapters. Read them here and see them through a new lens, a lens which views the arts and technology as a crucial part of the curriculum.

> *A small group in Ms. Peters' second grade paints a mural depicting their trip to the apple orchard. Through this activity they relive the trip and recall many details. They experiment with the blue and yellow paint, mixing two primary colors to get just the right shade of green for the leaves. "Add just a* dot *more yellow, not a* glob," *says Jason excitedly. "Cool," says Monica. Ms. Peters suggests that they can make the leaves look shiny by adding liquid detergent to the paint.*

Mural making extends children's learning about apple orchards. They also learn to use painting as a way to represent an idea. As they go about recreating a scene from their earlier observations, children develop understanding about color, line, texture, and perspective.

> *Four children are at work on the rug in the meeting area. They construct long ramps using boards and unit blocks. They want to construct a ramp that will allow a marble to make a 90 degree turn without falling off. The children manipulate the incline of the ramp and the sharpness of the curve.*

This project might be related to a science study of force and speed. Or it might have begun because the materials were available at choice time and the children set their own challenge. Whatever the context, children learn about force, speed, and direction as they exchange ideas and refine their vocabulary. They try to create a product to solve a problem. In the process, they learn about having a plan, about multiple approaches to problem solving, and about the need to be flexible and make adjustments when the initial plan does not work.

> *Several children work at the computers in the classroom. Sarah and Latitia record a collection of favorite class jokes. When they finish, Jerome and Carlos work on the script for a skit. LaVon and Michael use a software program that requires them to find the missing attributes in a pattern and create a creature that fits the pattern. Children talk continually as they collaborate on these projects.*

The children have discovered that one tool, the computer, serves a variety of purposes. They use different programs to write, store data, and work on mathematical problems.

Two children work at the construction/inventions table. Markita builds a structure with straws that will support weight. She uses tape, staples, and cardboard to hold it together. Colin designs a sculpture he plans to make with a variety of materials: paper towel rolls, wallpaper samples, wire, tape, glue, and Styrofoam chips.

When children explore with materials, they can learn about their properties and make decisions about suitability. They learn to recognize the different uses of tools and the ways that tools make tasks easier to accomplish.

Mr. Cantor just finished reading aloud Justin and the Best Biscuits in the World *by Mildred Pitts Walter. He asks, "What could we do that would give everyone a chance to show what they liked about this book?" The children brainstorm the following ideas: do a skit, create a mural of scenes, prepare biscuits, make dioramas. They talk about the kinds of ideas they want to present. After agreeing on three projects, they divide into groups to plan how they will begin.*

This teacher uses a group experience to provide children with opportunities to demonstrate their ideas in a variety of ways. In the process, they explore different forms of expression and gain a deeper understanding of content. A lesson conceived as a way to discuss the ideas and language in a book is extended when children can express their ideas creatively through arts and technology related projects.

The great advantage of making a place in your curriculum for the arts and technology is that it will expand the repertoire of experiences you offer children. If previously you allowed children simply to explore with paint, you may now think about having children create a mural depicting neighborhood stores. Drawing pictures in a journal to record science observations might now become part of a long-term project to collect data over time and analyze the results. Cooking projects can be viewed as an opportunity to talk about the use of tools. Thinking about the arts and technology as content, as well as process, will lead you to become more familiar with different forms of creative expression.

The Role of Arts and Technology in the Curriculum

Interest in making arts education an integral part of the curriculum has prompted a consortium of groups to define a new way of thinking about education in the arts. The monograph *National Standards for Arts Education* (Consortium of National Arts Education Associations 1994) describes the knowledge and skills in this arena that are important for children to acquire. The *Standards* also describes how the arts can integrate all subjects and extend learning across the curriculum.

New approaches to the teaching of technology in the classroom have been advocated by the American Association for the Advancement of Science (AAAS) in two publications: *Science for All Americans* (Rutherford and Ahlgren 1990) and *Benchmarks for Science Literacy* (AAAS 1993). These documents emphasize the importance of creative expression and problem solving.

In this section we define the arts and technology as subjects in their own right and outline what children can learn when these subjects are included in the primary curriculum. We show how the arts and technology are also a means of extending and enriching learning in all other subjects.

Defining the Arts

The arts include the visual arts—painting, drawing, molding, weaving, designing, and constructing—as well as the performing arts—music, dance, and drama. Children learn when they use materials and participate in music, dance, and drama activities.

The classroom arts, as we might call them—from painting to poetry, from dancing to singing, from computer graphics to drawing, from playing pianos and drums to composing on synthesizers, from writing dialogue to acting in plays, from architecture to sculpture, from photography to pottery—should not be seen as merely pleasant diversions from the core academic basics of schools. Nor should the arts simply serve as programmatic add-ons to fill out the shank of the school day. Those are the traditional ways of viewing arts education, and they limit the purpose of the classroom arts and diminish their potency to develop the thinking and imaginative abilities of students as they explore and learn about their world (Sautter 1994, 433).

During the course of the school year children can become familiar with a variety of art media including:

- painting and drawing (with crayons, markers, pencils, scratch-art panels, chalk, pens, watercolors, and acrylics);
- printmaking processes (stamping, etching, block printing, monoprinting, rubbing);
- modeling (using firing and non-firing clays, plasticene);
- assemblage and collage (connecting varied materials in two and three dimensional arrangements using glue, paste, tape, staplers);
- puppetry (using newspaper, paper maché, stick and felt finger and hand puppets);
- fiber arts and sewing (loom and off-loom weaving, stitching).

Other activities included in the arts are singing, dancing, creating skits and plays, and storytelling. Word-processing programs, video and audio equipment, computer drawing programs, block building, and other design and construction projects also enhance the arts program.

Defining Technology

Technology "involves the purposeful application of knowledge, experience, and resources to create products and processes that meet human needs" (Curriculum Corporation 1993, 3). Because most of us use technology on a daily basis, we often take it for granted. When design and technology activities are incorporated into the curriculum, children are more likely to become familiar and comfortable with tools. Children can learn how to use multi-purpose tools such as calculators and computers, as well as specialized tools, such as measuring devices or needles for sewing.

Activities related to technology enable children to use their creative impulses to express ideas and find solutions to problems. Tools such as computers, calculators, hammers, and measuring devices help children learn. They explore how things work and how tools shape our lives. When children learn by designing, making, and using tools and materials, as well as expressing ideas and emotions in ways other than speaking or writing, they grow emotionally, socially, physically, and cognitively.

> Young children are veteran technology users by the time they enter school. They ride in automobiles, use household utilities, operate wagons and bikes, use garden tools, help with the cooking, operate the television set, and so on. Children are also natural explorers and inventors, and they like to make things. School should give students many opportunities to examine the properties of materials, to use tools, and to design and build things.

The task in these grades is to begin to channel the students' inventive energy and to increase their purposeful use of tools and—in the process—broaden their understanding of what constitutes a tool (a container, paper and pencil, camera, magnifier, etc.) (AAAS 1993, 44).

Awareness of the need for technology education encourages teachers to think about tools and to heighten children's knowledge of the history of technology, and the important role of tools in our lives. Children can understand how the tools of technology are important to the scientist, mathematician, engineer, architect, builder, graphic artist, and many other workers.

During the course of the school year, children can acquire skills in using:

- simple tools such as scissors, string, paste, and tape;
- construction supplies and tools such as hammers, clamps, vises and screwdrivers;
- measurement tools including rulers, measuring tape, scales, measuring cups, spoons, and compasses;
- calculators, computers, tape recorders, and audio-visual equipment.

Because technology is constantly evolving, every few years there will undoubtedly be new tools and equipment for children to use.

What Children Learn

When the arts and technology are made an integral part of the curriculum, children gain valuable skills and knowledge. The arts and technology curriculum enables children to:

- use a variety of media for communication and expression;
- develop aesthetic knowledge and appreciation for many forms of expression;
- solve problems using a variety of media and materials;
- become familiar with what tools can do and with how tools can be used.

With these goals in mind, the arts and technology constitute both a separate subject in the curriculum and a means to integrate other subjects. We will first look at each of these goals and describe what and how children can learn in the arts and technology. Then we will discuss how experiences in the arts and technology enrich other subjects.

Using a Variety of Media for Communication and Expression

Children with varying skills and talents will be able to experience success if the curriculum offers opportunities for them to use a variety of media for communication and expression. To provide these opportunities means allocating times during the week when children can explore materials, discover different ways to express their ideas and feelings, and create their own representations. Special choice times might be scheduled during the week which allow for unstructured experimentation. Some examples of what children might do include:

- painting with different sized brushes, sponges, on different kinds of paper, wood;
- modeling with clay, plasticine, paper-maché;
- making collages using different textures;
- finding different ways to attach objects together to create three-dimensional constructions;
- creating a dance after hearing a new piece of music;
- recording sounds and talking about how they make you feel;
- creating a drawing that describes a mood.

Developing Aesthetic Knowledge and Appreciation

When children create, design, make, or perform—when they are artists—they gain an appreciation for the creative work of others as well as their own. Children can develop a deeper understanding of color, line, shape, balance, pattern, rhythm, movement, and texture as they figure out how to make things happen in a particular way.

Experiences with music give children opportunities to learn about rhythm, melody, aspects of pitch, loudness, and simultaneous sounds as well as the great variety of different kinds of music. When children dance, they learn about space, time, and dynamics; when they follow a dance routine, they evaluate how the movement expresses someone else's ideas. Children explore dramatic expression when they make up skits based on a known story, role play how a problem could be solved, or watch plays and discuss the production.

Some examples of what children might do to develop aesthetic knowledge and appreciation include:

- listening to many different kinds of music in the classroom;
- attending concerts, dance performances, and plays;
- examining the work of different artists and illustrators;
- exploring the way different structures are built;
- playing musical instruments, dancing.

Solving Problems Using a Variety of Media and Materials

When we think about problem-solving opportunities for children, we tend to focus on mathematical thinking. But when children create inventions, build structures or machines, and paint, they are also solving problems. Consider the child who is trying to draw a road and wants to show that one section is nearby and another is far away. As the child experiments, talks with friends, and looks in picture books, she solves the problem of using perspective.

> By participating in such activities, students should learn how to analyze situations and gather relevant information, define problems, generate and evaluate creative ideas, develop their ideas into tangible solutions, and assess and improve their solutions (American Association for the Advancement of Science 1993, 48).

Giving children opportunities to use many different strategies, including drawing, talking, modeling, writing, and experimenting is an effective way to promote problem-solving skills. Here are some examples of what children might do:

- design and gather the necessary materials to build and paint a bench for the classroom;
- draw a picture of the invention to be built before beginning to build it;
- create scenery and props for a play;
- create a computer program that makes stars appear randomly in different colors on the screen;
- combine dance steps across the floor while changing level, direction, or tempo.

Learning About and Using Tools

Using technology in today's classrooms, whether computers, video and audio equipment, calculators, hammers, or rulers, means letting children engage with the materials, use them again and again, and make choices. For technology to enrich the classroom experience, teachers must identify real purposes for the work or interesting problems to solve. Children can learn to recognize what tools are, how tools are used to make things, and that different tools have different purposes when they:

- use a needle and thread to sew a puppet together;
- use hammers and nails to construct bird feeders;
- take apart an old radio using screw drivers and pliers;
- churn milk into butter;
- make a dance of their bodies' shadows in front of an overhead projector;
- use a lever to lift a heavy object;
- design shapes of different sizes on the computer.

How the Arts and Technology Enhance Other Subjects

As noted earlier, experiences with artistic expression and technology have appeared throughout this book as a means to express and enrich children's learning in all subjects. Highlighted below are some examples of how children might use the arts and technology to support their learning in each subject.

In *math,* children:

- measure using an arm length and discuss why the results are different with different people and how measuring tools may have evolved;
- explore calculators and work with a partner to figure out what they do;
- use pattern blocks to make patterns and reproduce them onto paper, using templates or stickers;
- build sand timers to measure one, two, and three minutes;
- illustrate word problems;
- use refrains of songs to explore other kinds of patterns;
- dance through the room covering as much space as they can and still return to their spot in 12 counts, 8 counts, 10 counts, and so on.

As part of ***language and literacy*** activities, children might:

- act out scenes from a story read aloud;
- make a tape recording of jump rope chants and rhymes and write the words on chart paper;
- create sound effects that go along with a poem or story;
- act out the story of a familiar song;
- discuss the tools used by characters in a story;
- choreograph a dance that illustrates the traits of a specific character in a story they have read. Other children can guess who it is.

In ***science,*** children might:

- create skits about how animals communicate;
- dramatize a science observation: a butterfly emerging from a cocoon, a chick from an egg;
- make tape recordings of sounds in every day life: dripping water, a door closing, paper tearing, scraping nails;
- illustrate their observations in a science journal;
- investigate how tension affects range of movement by trying out different body movements in a tense and relaxed state.

In ***social studies,*** children might:

- sketch observations on a neighborhood walk;
- invent a tool they think would help them do something;
- list all the tools used by workers in the school;
- share dances or music they enjoy at home with their families.

These examples illustrate just a few of the many ways you can use the arts and technology to enhance children's learning in all subjects. Consider what is most comfortable for you and where you think both you and the children can experience success.

Arts and Technology Activities

█ n this section, we describe a range of arts and technology activities to help you get started. We highlight skits and plays, murals, block building, singing, inventions, and computers. It's important to keep in mind that you can't offer everything at once or you and the children will feel overwhelmed. Think about the time of day that best lends itself to something new. Some teachers like to try new ideas at a choice time when they are free to circulate, observe, and assist as necessary. You may want to arrange to have a parent or family volunteer in the classroom the first time you try something new, if it will enable you to be more involved.

Skits and Plays

Dramatic activities such as skits, role-playing, and class plays bring out different talents in children. Some children are natural actors and love center stage; others like to stage manage or get involved in choosing props or creating scenery; some write scripts. In drama, children learn to think creatively, take risks, and use their imagination.

Preparing skits and plays also allows children to practice social skills such as collaboration and problem-solving. New friendships develop when children work together. They share ideas and refine their acting and producing skills. Drama can also be a legitimate extension of learning to resolve conflicts (through role-plays) or explore specific content in the curriculum.

Some drama activities are easy to promote in the primary classroom because children like to act. Even if this is not an artistic arena you approach easily, you may feel comfortable trying these ideas:

- Ask children who have read the same book to choose a scene to dramatize for the class.
- Divide the class into groups of four to six children. Give each group a bag full of unrelated items (e.g., a toy telephone, a funny hat, a basket, two books, a pad) and have them create a short skit involving everyone in the group.
- Play "Charades" using book titles that the children know well.
- Ask groups to role play different ways to solve problems that occur at recess.
- Make time to share skits, plays, and puppet shows children have created during choice time, recess, or after school.

If you demonstrate that you value these endeavors, children will take them seriously and spend time on their productions, thus furthering their learning while they increase their skills.

Class Plays

Preparing and presenting a class play can be a wonderful culminating project related to a long-term study in social studies or science. Plays allow children to put their learning to use and share it. If they have had many experiences during the year in inventing skits, singing together, and perhaps even writing their own words to songs, you will have a good idea of how each child can contribute.

There are many different sources for class plays. Sometimes the play is based on a picture book that has been a success in the classroom. If a book has been read over and over again, the children may know it by heart.

> *Ms. Taylor observes that her first graders love the book* May I Bring A Friend? *by Beatrice Schenk, which she chose to read because it complements their study of animals. Their enthusiasm about the story leads to dramatizations; children act out the parts of different animals in the story. They talk about how a giraffe might walk and why the queen would frown about where the guests could sit down. The children are eager to perform these skits for their families and the other first grade classes at their school. Ms. Taylor talks with the children about what they would need to do and they generate a list: choose parts, make costumes, rehearse, make scenery, make programs. Rather than writing the script, Ms. Taylor encourages the children to continually practice their scenes. She helps them decide what changes they want to make until they are pleased with their play, and feel ready to perform it for an audience.*

The following example shows how plays can come from long-term studies, too. Don't forget that putting together a class play takes time. If you try to do a play and also try to keep up with everything else you usually do, you and the children will be exhausted rather than fulfilled. Instead, let the usual schedule go. Be reassured by all the learning that can take place when children work on a play: reading and writing activities (the script, the program, advertisements), problem-solving, and collaboration on making scenery and costumes.

> *A second grade class is studying birds. The children go on bird walks, keep records of the numbers and kinds of birds they see, draw pictures and make models of birds, learn about the size and shape of feathers and feet, learn where birds live and about their nesting habits, and so on. The teacher, Mr. Diamond, reads many stories about birds. One day he reads a modern folktale,* The Bird-Feather Rainbow, *by Marc Gellman, that has many different kinds of birds in it (1989). The children love the story, which involves quarreling birds who won't help each other. Noting their interest, he proposes they turn the story into a play.*

Mr. Diamond realizes that the children can use their extensive knowledge of birds to become the characters they choose to represent in the play. Each child makes a list of the special characteristics of one of the birds. Mr. Diamond adapts the story using the children's list of birds. Making costumes consumes a great deal of class time. The children decide to make feathered wings to go over colorful sweats or pajamas. First they design the wings, then brainstorm about materials they can use. Several children make samples using coat hangers for the shape and tissue paper for the feathers. Another child makes a design with cardboard and aluminum foil. A parent volunteers to cut simple felt hoods in a variety of colors. Several children work with the parent to sew the hoods together and decorate them with tissue paper feathers.

As the play begins to take shape, the children decide to add songs to the script. Because the class has spent time every week learning songs together, they have a repertoire of songs to think about using in their play. When the birds quarrel, they sing, "I'm Gonna Tell." When the Dove goes off after the Raven, they sing their own version of "I'm On My Way." At the end of the play, when all the birds learn to work together to make the rainbow, they change the words of "This Little Light of Mine" to "This Little Rainbow of Mine."

Don't be afraid to ask for help when your class puts on a play. It's a wonderful way to involve family members who can assist with making costumes, constructing scenery, or videotaping the play. Children love to watch themselves and you will learn from their comments as they watch. And, of course, all family members can participate as the audience for a play and join in the cast party to celebrate.

Murals

Making murals fosters collaborative work, allows teachers to guide and assess children's learning about particular content, and encourages aesthetic knowledge and appreciation. The process of creating a mural requires that children plan and work together. They engage in research and express their understandings about a subject as they plan the mural. During the process, teachers have many opportunities to observe children and notice how they interpret what has been learned, see problem-solving and conflict resolution at work, and observe how children talk to and learn from one another. They explore concepts about light, color, pattern, size, shape, and variation— concepts that may also be explored in language and literacy, mathematics, social studies, and science.

Each mural project will be different, as you involve children in planning, designing, creating, and sharing the project. If you have not done much painting in the classroom before, you may be concerned about how to start. Before beginning such a project, give children time to use paints during a choice time and make sure you have procedures for set-up and clean-up as described in the chapter on Establishing a Structure for the Classroom.

Planning the Mural

Once you and the children have decided upon a mural project—based on something you are studying in social studies or science or as a response to a book the class read—plan on using several meeting times to talk about the scope of the mural, its size, and the materials needed. Murals can be painted, made from fabric and cut-outs pasted on paper, or designed with grasses, shredded paper, sticks, or other collage materials. By planning together, children can make decisions about whether they want to use paint for an underwater scene, collage and cut-out materials for a desert landscape or river scene, or milk cartons and sticks for a three dimensional city scene. Then the class can plan a system for collecting and organizing the materials.

Designing and Making the Mural

Having agreed upon the subject and materials, children can brainstorm how the mural should look. Younger children's plans will change as they work; older children are more likely to stick to an agreed-upon design. Several problem-solving design sessions may be needed to address scale, perspective, and specific content. As with other projects, the mural may be divided into sections, with different groups at work on different scenes (e.g., animals, fish, plant life, buildings, roads). As children work you will see them reveal what they learned from their research. In the process they share this knowledge with one another.

> *A class of second and third graders studying the Sonoran Desert in the Southwest wants to produce a mural. The children research topics such as gila monsters, rattlesnakes, roadrunners, saguaro cacti, weather, and plant life. As they design and create the mural, each child contributes by drawing animals or plants, landscape, or land formations, depending upon the topic the child researched. The children talk to one another about the relative sizes of their cactus or kangaroo rat and make concessions based on new knowledge. Kim, who is an "expert" on the saguaro cactus, wants the season to be spring so her cactus can be in bloom. Hannah and Badr agree because they want to show the nesting areas where their animals lay their eggs in the spring.*

As children share ideas and information, they may also share misgivings about their contributions. You may hear complaints ranging from: "I hate my animal," to "I can't draw that!" If the mural is big enough, children will have several parts to design and make, and will become more competent. Children will discover what they are "good" at and classmates will ask one another for help: "Let's get Eric to draw the flowers— he really knows how to make them look real." Because the children have a stake in the outcome, they are willing to work hard to make their sections go together. They will mix their paint carefully to make sure the brown backgrounds blend together; they will find ways to accommodate the different perspectives and adapt as the need arises.

Sharing the Mural

A mural is a record of the learning that has taken place in the classroom—an aesthetic expression of specific knowledge. Children who are not yet experienced writers can demonstrate their understanding in a way that does not involve writing reports. In the process of exchanging information, children learn a great deal from each other. The child who is an expert on lizards works next to the child who knows all about plants. Although no individual child has researched all about the desert, the children as a group "own" the mural and absorb information from one another.

A mural can be shared with the larger community by inviting family members and other classes to view it and having children take turns explaining the various parts. Another option is to hang the mural in the hallway of the school with an appropriate title and written explanations.

Block Building

When primary age children have access to unit blocks, they can build elaborate structures that require joint planning and execution. As they talk about their designs, they form pictures in their minds which they then try to communicate through language and with blocks. In the process of building, children negotiate, share, and role-play, practicing the social skills needed to initiate and maintain friendships. Moreover, because blocks are designed in mathematical units, children acquire an understanding of concepts essential to logical thinking: they learn about size, shape, weight, length, order, area, and number as they create structures.

If you have never had blocks available in your primary classroom before, you may feel that blocks are for younger children. Or, you may feel you don't have the space for blocks. Try to visit a classroom where blocks are being used effectively. Reread the section on blocks in Establishing a Structure for the Classroom. The space in the block area, the way the blocks are arranged for use, the pictures or challenges you place there, and the procedures for their care all send messages to children about the importance and value you place on blocks.

Involve the children in the organization and rules for the area. Try out the area during choice time using any of the following suggestions:

- Hang pictures of various structures and bridges in the block area to inspire building.
- Keep measuring tapes and recording sheets in the area for children to measure the dimensions of their buildings.
- Place a scale in the area that could be used to compare the weights of different unit blocks.
- Teach a fraction lesson in the block area and then have children work on fraction problems using blocks.
- Use blocks to begin a study of mapping. Have the children work in small groups to create the shape of the room and the furniture in the classroom with blocks.
- Post a written challenge in the block area (e.g., How long an extension bridge can you build? or What kind of structure can you build using only triangles?).

After children have had experiences like these in the block area, you may feel ready to use block building as part of a larger study.

A group of second graders is studying the community around their school. They go on several neighborhood trips, first to focus on the businesses and stores in the area, and then on the community services available. Pictures, discussions, and graphing projects follow each trip. Some children use the block area to build the various places they visit.

Ms. Simpson has a meeting to plan a project connected to the study. The children decide to build a model of the neighborhood including some offices, stores, and community service buildings. They agree that blocks can be used to create certain structures and that milk cartons will be used for others. The children make decisions: they will work with partners because there isn't enough room for every student to have his or her own building; they will write letters to families asking for donations of milk cartons in different sizes; they agree on which buildings will be built by whom.

During the next week, the children work on their block community at different times of the day. In addition to the groups responsible for the structures, other groups form to build roads, stick figure people, and trees. Signs appear, designating various spaces and buildings. As they work in the block area, Ms. Simpson is able to assess their understandings to date and plan ways to extend the study.

Ms. Simpson has allowed the time needed to make this project a valuable learning experience for the children. She understands that the children will build their structures over the course of a week, modifying as they recall details and using additional information gained from discussions. The opportunity to save block buildings is critically important for children in the primary grades.

Think about what you need in order for block building to be successful. Consider the following suggestions:

- Think about the space available and find a way to protect the structures children build.
- Introduce blocks and block building to the class and develop rules together.
- Allow the necessary time for clean-up.
- If there is a problem, brainstorm some ways to solve it with the children.
- Value the children's work and have discussions about it. Allow the children to share their work with the others in the class.

Singing

When children and teachers sing together, they develop a special camaraderie. Singing becomes a ritual that the class does together in distinct ways and at special times. It can lighten up the dreariest day. Singing can also extend children's learning—when the songs you sing relate to particular subject matter—and promote music appreciation.

Even if you are one of those people who "can't sing one note on key," you can still bring singing into your classroom. Figure out what you are comfortable doing. If this is an area in which you might need some support, here's what you can do:

- Borrow tapes or records of folk songs from friends and the library.
- Bring in a tape recorder and music tapes that inspire everyone to sing along.
- Brainstorm with the children and list the songs you all know.
- Make charts with the lyrics of favorite songs. Children can take turns pointing to the words.
- Team up with a teacher who is especially skilled in this area.
- Encourage children to lead the class in song.

During their study of a nearby river, one class learned river songs such as: "Roll On Columbia," "River of Dreams," "Way Down Upon the Swanee River," "Down By the Riverside," "Peace I Ask of Thee Oh River," "Old Man River," "Erie Canal." Another class studying the harbor and ocean vessels learned some different songs: "Blow Ye Winds in the Morning," "'Twas Friday Morn," "The Sinking of the Reuben James," "Puff the Magic Dragon," "The John B. Sails." A group involved in a clean-up project around their school took to chanting the Pete Seeger song "Garbage" as they advertised the recycling campaign for the school.

You can find songbooks in libraries or ask a music teacher to guide you to source material. There are songs to be found on every subject from friendship to garbage. Family members who come from different parts of the world and other cultures can often be excellent resources for new songs.

Inventions

Invention activities offer children opportunities to represent learning in ways that invite creative thinking and novel approaches to solving problems. Children see the need for tools and may notice how inventions can improve on existing tools. When children have access to an assortment of materials and are challenged to combine them to create new products, teachers often observe aspects of children's thinking that may not appear through other means of representation.

> *Six-year-old Gisela struggles to describe objects and events in clear verbal or written language. Given an assortment of cardboard, corks, wires, and bottle caps, however, Gisela creates a moving, jointed, detailed model of a robot, which quickly becomes the center of classroom attention. Gisela experiences a feeling of belonging and acceptance that she rarely has during other types of classroom activities.*

Invention activities engage children in planning products, selecting and organizing materials, experimenting with properties of materials, using tools, and displaying and sharing finished products.

> *First graders in Ms. Carter's class are learning about simple machines as part of their science studies. Ms. Carter puts pulleys and gears at the invention table and wonders aloud one day whether or not someone might figure out a way to build an invention using these tools. Melanie works on her invention during three different choice times. On the third day, she proudly shares her invention—a windmill-like model with moving arms, complete with gears and a crank made out of self-hardening clay she found among the art supplies. Shantelle creates a make-shift crane using the pulley and discovers that it can lift a rock that weighs as much as a unit block.*

To encourage the learning processes associated with inventions, children need ample space to work and a wide variety of well-labeled, well-displayed materials. You can ask the children and families for contributions of objects and supplies, such as the following:

cardboard of various sizes and weights	rocks
boxes and containers	glitter
Styrofoam-packing, trays, egg cartons	corks, bottle caps
paper tubes, plates, and cups	clear plastic sheets
aluminum foil and pie plates	fabric, string, ribbon
lids and caps	batteries, bulbs, and wire
dowels, popsicle sticks, toothpicks	scissors, wire cutters, stapler
wood scraps	glue, masking tape

twist 'ems, pipe cleaners	ruler, tape measure
rubber bands, bread tags	hammer, hand drill
clothespins, paper clips, paper fasteners	screwdriver, clamps
film cans and old photo slides or negatives	nails, drill bits, screws
paper, pens, pencils	pulleys

When children invent, they learn about the processes and materials associated with invention. Invention activities can also reinforce children's learning in other areas of the curriculum.

A class of third graders is exploring biography as a literary genre. After reading a biography of Benjamin Franklin, the teacher challenges the students to take on the role of an inventor, like Ben Franklin. Those who accept the challenge think of a desirable invention, create a plan for the product on paper, collect the tools and materials necessary, construct the invention, and write a "news release" about the invention for the class newspaper.

The above example demonstrates one way a teacher might incorporate language and literacy into an invention project. Invention activities can relate to many areas of the curriculum:

- Children use language and literacy skills when they write and speak about their plans and products.

- Children use mathematical thinking during the invention process when they consider the dimensions and shapes of objects.

- Children's scientific thinking is promoted though the observation and experimentation that comes with inventing. As children construct and attach materials together, they have to consider how different materials react to each other (e.g., glue on plastic, paint on Styrofoam, tape on foil).

- Children enhance social studies understanding when they research inventions and try to make various improvements on them.

Invention activities engage children in active, creative, and personal learning. In the process of inventing, children take risks, experiment, produce, record, and share. You may see children taking initiative, showing persistence, sharing ideas with others, using problem-solving strategies, using tools, understanding how inventions of many kinds help people, experimenting with materials, and developing fine motor strength and control.

Computers

Computers can be valuable additions to the primary classroom when they are an integral part of learning activities. When computers are set up so that children can work in pairs, their use promotes collaborative learning and peer tutoring. Appropriate software allows children to work at their own pace on challenging and interesting activities. In the process, they develop creative and critical thinking skills. The kinds of learning experiences children have on computers should enable them to:

- question, explore, create, and solve problems, and
- record information and stories on their own, with a partner, in a small group, or with the entire class.

In the chapter on Establishing a Structure for the Classroom, we described a process for introducing new materials in the classroom. Each computer software program needs its own introduction. When you introduce a program to the whole class, you may find it helpful to bring the computer table to the meeting area and walk through a program. Alternatively, you can introduce a new program to a series of small groups, or to one group, then have the members of that group teach other pairs of children at the computers.

> *Ms. Vernon introduces the software* Thinkin' Things *by Edmark to her class. She teaches a different program to each of six groups in the class, knowing that this is the fastest way for the whole class to be exposed to the six activities. Later that day she observes Amy and Lizzy using the "Feathered Friends" program. As they try to create the missing bird, they talk about what hats have already been used, what color is left, what shirt patterns have been used, and which shoes are needed. Kenny and Robert are using "Oranga Banga," and trying to mimic the rhythm and instruments they just heard.*

These children are working together to share observations, consider their choices, and think through problems. The tasks are sufficiently challenging to hold their interest.

How to Review Software

Computers in the classroom are only as good as the software children use. To select good software, think about your goals and whether each package meets them. Try them out yourself to become familiar with the format. Some software helps children construct the correct answer following a mistake; some provides reinforcement if a child has difficulty. Other software lets children work together to solve open-ended problems and make discoveries. While drill work with paper and pencil can be tedious, some children make good progress practicing math facts or other repetitive tasks in interesting ways on the computer. Make sure that you have a variety of software in the classroom and that children have experience with many different kinds of programs. Primary grade children can also benefit from word-processing programs; some children are more comfortable writing with word-processing programs than with paper and pencil. All children can be exposed to word-processing software.

The publications we suggest in the Resources section at the end of the chapter will help you to select software. However, in order to know whether the programs will work well in your classroom with your current group of children, you will want to preview each program yourself. The following questions and guidelines can help you conduct your own review of software packages.

- *Is the software age appropriate?* The software should match children's skill levels. Is the material presented using pictorial representation or does it rely on abstract ability? Do picture "icons" represent ideas or directions so that children are likely to figure out what to do on their own?

- *Can children work independently?* Look for software that children can use independently while still making choices. You don't want children to be "trapped" in a program they can't do and be unable to change or stop. Recognize that children will experiment with all the options. Make sure that the program will not "lose" anything.

- *Is the pace right?* Children, like adults, become impatient with programs that take too long to do things. If the program takes a long time to load or too long for graphics to appear, children may lose interest. If the program moves too fast, children may get frustrated and give up.

- *Is the content open-ended?* This is the heart of any review. If the computer is to be used as a tool for investigation, there has to be something to investigate. This means the process should hold children's interest and be worth exploring. There should be different ways to do things and several ways to go about solving the problem.

- *Can children use the program in different ways?* Because children are at different developmental levels, the better software products will allow you and the children to set varying levels of difficulty and to control features such as the speed of the program and the sound level. Children should be able to learn different things from the content as well.

- *Can children work together?* Some programs encourage children to work with others to consider alternatives, make decisions, and alter the course. Children can make their own creations or design and build a project.

- *Does the program offer rewards for winning?* Be wary of software programs that offer too many rewards, bells, or whistles. These types of programs usually focus on getting the right answer and are less concerned with the process.

- ***Can children succeed without elaborate instruction?*** Good software enables children to figure out what to do on their own, without excessive (or maybe any) instruction. Appropriate software helps children become less dependent on the teacher.
- ***Will the software run on your computer?*** Hardware and software have to be compatible for programs to work properly. Check the requirements carefully before you purchase software.

In addition to the appropriateness of the software, there are some other considerations that will influence your choices. Find out what teacher-support materials are available and whether there are record-keeping functions for keeping track of children's work. There are some new programs that enable you to create a separate "desktop" for each child using the software. While this allows you to custom design programs for each child and control access, it discourages children from working together because each child has his or her own set of programs.

Children love to save their computer work and, when possible, take it to their next year's classroom. If your school is not on a network, you may want to consider putting individual work on a disk to be transferred to the computer in the next year's classroom.

If you have little experience with computers or are unfamiliar with the software you have been given, you may feel uncomfortable about having computers in your classroom. Talk to other teachers in your school; find out who knows about computers and software. Ask for a lesson. The children in your class are often the best resources.

Linking the Six Strategies to the Arts and Technology

The six strategies presented in Part One of *Constructing Curriculum* allow you to create the kind of classroom in which projects in the arts and technology are exciting as well as manageable. In turn, each of the strategies is supported by the arts and technology.

Knowing the Children You Teach

All good teaching begins with knowing about child development and the unique qualities of each child. Teachers look for the strengths that will help each child experience success. Providing a range of activities and projects allows every child to excel. One child might compose a song for a skit, while someone else writes the words. Another child may design the scenery for a class play. These may be the children who have not been the most eager mathematicians or readers. When they can show their talents in other ways, they develop self-confidence and often begin to improve their skills in other areas as a result.

Because the group of children in your class is different each year, the focus of activities is likely to be different as well. Some years you have singers who learn all the words to the songs you teach and want to sing them over and over again; other years the computer experts take over and invent new ways to use the computer for projects.

When children have time to make, design, and build things, and to work with tools, you can learn about their needs and promote their emotional, social, physical, and cognitive development.

- *Emotional development* addresses children's mental health and well-being. Many children today live with fear and anxiety because of such stresses as a difficult family situation or neighborhood violence. Emotional release and comfort can come from using drawing tools, paint, clay, and building materials. Self-worth is fostered when children create objects that are appreciated by others and proudly displayed in the classroom.

- *Social skills* are essential for children to become competent learners. When children plan a puppet show, work on a mural or at the computer together, they learn to share their ideas and opinions, listen to others, take turns, and work together to achieve results.

- *Physical development* is enhanced when children have various opportunities to use both small and large muscles. Children build their fine motor skills when they guide a pair of scissors with increasing control, staple and bolt construction materials together, or use a keyboard with increasing skill. Eye-hand coordination is refined as children use the mouse on the computer, thread a needle, or hammer nails to create a three dimensional structure.

- **Cognitive development** is encouraged when teachers provide multiple ways for children to learn. Children create music, work with the visual spatial world, use their bodies, understand and work with other people, and use their knowledge productively. Arts and technology activities give teachers and children the ways to "*represent* these other intelligences" (Oddleifson 1994, 447). Projects provide children with various ways of communicating. When teachers emphasize only verbal skills, they ignore how powerfully messages are delivered in other ways.

As you come to know the children better by observing their work in arts and technology projects, you can make decisions about how to enhance each child's growth and development. Curriculum decisions about how and when to guide learning can then be based on what you know about a particular group of children.

Building a Classroom Community

By having daily meetings, helping children to relate positively and work collaboratively, and teaching children to resolve conflicts peacefully, you have worked to build a classroom community that makes it possible for children to create, design, and make things. By the same token, these kinds of activities are natural community builders. As children work together, they talk about what they are doing and share ideas. Children gain the benefits of working in a group and the knowledge of how to make a contribution. They learn to appreciate one another's talents and seek out the class experts for help.

Meetings are a natural focus for discussions about projects—planning them as well as sharing the results. With practice, children can generate the ideas that are needed. When they have been involved in exploring and creating with art supplies and building materials and tools as part of their natural work in the classroom, children enjoy brainstorming about what kinds of project they would like to do. At meeting times, you can say:

- Let's think about what we can make or do connected with our study of the neighborhood.
- How can we design something to show all this information?
- Now that we know so much about_____, let's consider ways to show it.
- Are there several different ways to show our ideas about_____?

When children work together on projects they are engaged in community building. The community becomes a safe place to take risks.

Establishing a Structure in the Classroom

Without a clear structure in the classroom, the kinds of activities we describe could easily be overwhelming. If the physical environment of the classroom has a clear organization with places for painting supplies, for creating structures or inventions, for using blocks or other building materials, for rehearsing skits or songs, then children know where to find what they need and how to use them. As you think about resources you want to make available, consider that the way you display materials reflects their importance.

How materials are introduced to children helps to ensure their appropriate use. The message to be conveyed is that materials are used for important purposes. Children also need clear expectations for behavior. That's why teachers develop routines for setting up painting trays, for identifying the number of children who can work in a particular area, and, of course, for clean-up. It is worth taking the time in the beginning of the year to create and practice these routines so that the children can work more independently later.

The work children generate as they use materials can be displayed prominently. When teachers take care to arrange children's creations beautifully, the message is clear—this is important and valued work. You can talk with the children about design principles and plan together how to use classroom space for displays. In addition to displaying the children's work, you might include in the classroom: Newbury and Caldecott award-winning children's books, reproductions of art from a variety of cultures, books on famous architects, musicians, dancers, and other artists, and examples of a variety of music—jazz, folk, concert, opera, popular, ethnic, show tunes.

Guiding Children's Learning

Young children learn best when they are actively involved rather than listening to someone talk. They develop understanding and competence when they have experiences that enable them to figure things out for themselves. The four principles discussed in the chapter on Guiding Children's Learning apply to planning activities in the arts and technology.

Teachers *make learning purposeful* by encouraging children to answer questions of interest to them and helping them make connections between what they are learning and what they already know. Artistic experiences, materials, and tools can help children to:

- think for themselves,
- express original ideas,
- explore and discover new information, and
- explore and discover new relationships.

When teachers offer open-ended experiences with raw materials—rather than with adult-made samples, patterns for tracing or "coloring-in," or commercial activity sheets—children are able to explore, create, and make their own products. They learn that it is appropriate to have their own feelings and views about a book. With this growing confidence in their own abilities, children approach the arts and technology in purposeful ways.

The second principle is that ***meaningful learning is integrated.*** When children engage in projects using the materials and tools of the arts and technology they are experiencing an integrated approach to curriculum.

> *Cameron wants to build a model of the type of longhouse lived in by the Piscataway Indians of Maryland. Having researched the topic, he knows what a longhouse looked like and the materials they used to build their homes. He asks Ms. Swann what he should use. Together they go to the building table and the supply closet where leftover scraps and other materials are stored in buckets and bags. As they examine the items, ideas begin to form: "This rough piece of wallpaper would work as the dirt floor," says Cameron. "I've got some leftover grass from my Easter basket at home that looks like grass. I'm going to bring it in to use for a grassmat." "Could you use real sticks and dirt for the roof, or would these popsicle sticks work better?" asks Ms. Swann.*

This example shows that you don't have to plan all details in advance. What you can do is demonstrate your readiness to approach a problem and your conviction that it can be solved.

The third principle is that ***communication is central to learning.*** As children participate in creating and making things in the classroom, you can influence their growth and development by responding to their work and engaging them in conversations about what they are doing. How teachers use language and how they respond to children's efforts conveys important messages:

- I am interested in what you are doing.
- I want to hear your ideas.
- I respect your way of saying and making things.

Children need approval, permission, assurance, support, and encouragement from adults to inspire them to create and express their ideas and feelings. Here are some suggestions:

- ***Describe what you see:*** "I see so many different shapes in your painting." "You made your picture symmetrical. How interesting to see the same things on both sides of the paper." "I notice a lot of spaces to look through on all sides of your sculpture." "There are so many moving parts in what you built."

- *Talk about the process:* "It looks as if it was really hard to make all those boxes stay together." "How did you create so many new colors when you only started with three?" "How did you decide which scene to act out for the class?" "Did you think of the melody first or did you write the words first?"

- *Ask open-ended questions* to get children to think and respond. "What do you notice about the shapes in your painting?" "What were you thinking about as you built that tower?" "What do you think you could use to keep that tower from tipping over?" "Is there a different sized brush you can use to get to all those little places inside your sculpture?" "What can you do to show that the character is only pretending to be angry?"

- *Encourage and support continuing efforts:* "You solved that balance problem in your building!" "You just discovered a new way to make a stitch with needle and yarn. Would you add it to our stitch frame so that other people can learn something from you?" "That's a great discovery you just made about our new computer program. How can we record it so others can use it also?"

Social interaction fosters learning. When children are engaged in arts and technology projects you can model very important interactions by helping children ask for feedback on their products and take pride in their accomplishments.

- *Encourage children to evaluate their own work:* "Which drawing do you think best shows how the rabbit ate the carrot?" "Which did you enjoy the most—acting in the play or designing the scenery?" "How would you do this project differently next time?" "Would you describe how you figured out how to get the bridge to hold more weight?"

- *Help children articulate the feedback they want:* "Do you want the class to comment on the story as a whole, or do you want the group to give you advice about the ending?" "Would you like us to tell you what we liked the most in your dance?" "Do you want to tell us how your invention works?"

Finally, *learning takes time.* Activities that involve children in designing and making things require lots of time because the process is as important as the product. For significant learning to take place, children need to come back to their work and be able to make changes based on new discoveries. For these reasons, it is helpful to schedule several large blocks of time each week (one to two hours at a time) when children can invest themselves in project work. Additional time for children to return to projects can be found during choice times.

Assessing Children's Learning

Assessment involves observing children regularly and collecting samples of their work in order to plan instruction and evaluate children's progress. When children paint or draw, make up skits, or create a structure to show what they have learned, you have the opportunity to observe and question them as they go about their work. The physical products they create can become part of a portfolio. If arts and technology experiences are a regular part of classroom life, you are likely to have many examples of children's thinking over time. The special talents of individual children are likely to be expressed as well.

You may have to train yourself to look for things you might not have noticed before. For example, try to look for increased detail in children's art work, and how they use space and color to express ideas. Note which children are willing to try an art form they are not yet "good" at. When children feel safe taking risks and experimenting with materials, they may later be willing to try different approaches to solving other problems in reading, writing, or mathematical thinking.

Arts and technology projects give you many opportunities to assess the process of learning. In creating scenery and props for a play, children have to think about multiple solutions to problems, make a plan, change their ideas or build consensus within a group, and stay with a task until it is completed. Many of the life skills that we want children to learn can be practiced as part of projects. Children also learn that they can't always do what they want when they want to do it. Teacher guidance helps children to consider what is reasonable and possible to make at school. The discussions necessary to make these decisions are part of the design process and teach children about the *"constraints"* involved whenever a project is to be undertaken (American Association for the Advancement of Science 1993, 49).

As children work on making objects that serve a particular purpose (e.g., bird feeders for different kinds of birds, mailboxes for messages, a map for visitors, a rabbit hutch) you will notice that primary age children begin to recognize that:

- tools and materials can be used for different purposes;
- some materials can be used many times;
- they can test, revise, and redesign what they build rather than rushing into production with the first design proposal.

Your knowledge about children and what they are learning will be richer and more comprehensive with these kinds of observations.

Building a Partnership with Families

Family members can help you extend your comfort level with certain projects. The grandparent who likes to cook, the costume designer, or the computer expert may add to the experiences you are able to offer.

When children create in the classroom through the visual arts, music, dance, drama, or by building things and using tools, you have many things to share with families to further the school-home partnership. In these activities, children demonstrate directly what they are learning. Family members may be more interested in joining the class for special culminating activities because they are aware of the scope of the studies.

The teacher's role is crucial in establishing both the classroom environment and the process of learning that will take place. The strategies in Part One provide the scaffolding for constructing curriculum in the arts and technology, as well as in all subjects.

Closing Thoughts

The arts and technology are the means through which children construct knowledge, investigate, and represent what they are learning. They are also subjects in their own right, with content, materials, and tools that children must understand in order to be knowledgeable and productive adults. The arts and technology are integrally linked to each of the six strategies for constructing curriculum.

Resources for the Arts and Technology

The Art of the Young Child. Bland, Jane C. New York: Museum of Modern Art, 1958.

Art, Mind, and Brain, A Cognitive Approach to Creativity. Gardner, Howard. New York: Basic Books, 1982.

The Block Book, 2nd Edition. Hirsch, Elizabeth (ed.). Washington, D.C.: NAEYC, 1984.

Children's Play and Learning. Klugman, Edgar and Sara Smilansky. New York: Teachers College Press, 1990.

Collage and Construction in Elementary and Junior High School. Lord, Lois. Worcester, MA: Davis Publications, 1958.

Resources for Selecting Computer Software

Children's Software Revue
Warren Buckleitner, Editor
520 N. Adams Street
Ypsilanti, Michigan 48197

Edmark Parent's Guide to the Computer as a Reading Enrichment Tool
Edmark, Inc.
P.O. Box 3218
Redmond, Washington 98073-3218

The Elementary Teacher's Sourcebook on Children's Software
Children's Software Revue
520 North Adams Street
Ypsilanti, Michigan 48197

High/Scope Buyer's Guide to Children's Software
High Scope Press
600 N. River Street
Ypsilanti, Michigan 48198

Software Publishers Association
1730 M St. N.W., Suite 700
Washington, DC 20036-4510

Resources for Materials

Creative Publications
788 Palomar Avenue
Sunnyvale, California 94086

Learning Materials Workshop Blocks
274 North Winooski Avenue
Burlington,Vermont 05401

References

American Association for the Advancement of Science. 1993. *Benchmarks for Science Literacy: Project 2061.* New York: Oxford University Press.

Consortium of National Arts Education Associations. 1994. *National Standards for Arts Education.* Reston, VA: Music Educators National Conference.

Gellman, Marc. 1989. The Bird-Feather Rainbow. In *Does God Have a Big Toe?* New York: Harper Collins.

Curriculum Corporation. June 1993. *A National Statement on Technology for Australian Schools.* Final unedited manuscript.

Oddleifson, Eric. 1994. What Do We Want Our Schools to Do? *Phi Delta Kappan,* Volume 75 (6).

Rutherford, F. James and Andrew Ahlgren. 1990. *Science for All Americans.* New York: American Association for the Advancement of Science. Oxford University Press.

Sautter, Craig R. 1994. An Arts Education School Reform Strategy. *Phi Delta Kappan,* Volume 75 (6).

W

Constructing

Curriculum

for the

Primary Grades

Notes

Constructing

Curriculum

for the

Primary Grades